Famous Racing Cars

Famous Racing Cars

Fifty of the greatest, from
Panhard to Williams-Honda

Doug Nye

GUILD PUBLISHING LONDON

This edition published 1989 by Guild
Publishing by arrangement with Patrick
Stephens Limited.

CN 9247

Contents

Author's introduction

These 50 famous racing cars are very much a personal choice and I must emphasize before we begin that some readers will no doubt howl at my omissions in this selection. Here you will not find the Sunbeam GP cars of the early '20s, nor ERA, the Austin OHC Racers, nor Talbot-Lago nor the Jackie Stewart Matra-Fords. I can only explain that when it came to making my selection I found it surprisingly hard to narrow down the field to 50 without omitting several famous racing cars which are perhaps too well-known *not* to be included. However, I suppose I can always claim that we have to leave some meat for a second volume . . .

In all honesty I can find no better way of justifying my selection than merely saying, 'Well, it's my book and I have written about cars whose stories have kept me interested and impressed – and in one or two cases amused'.

Having said that, I hope that what follows perhaps describes in a reasonably digestible manner cars whose detailed history has previously been obscure to you. I have tried to flesh out some of the legends, explode a few myths and hopefully present in a more objective light some famous racing cars which I regard as having been too often over-praised and over-hyped.

Let me emphasize, all that follows is a very personal appraisal of my selection of 50 famous racing cars — I do hope you enjoy it.

Doug Nye
Farnham, Surrey

Star Ratings

Just as a bit of hopefully thought-provoking fun, I thought I would 'star rate' the cars covered in the following pages to compare their relative merits on grounds of the following:

Success level

In the face of what opposition?

Technical merit

Longevity

Innovation establishing a major advance

Do they turn me on?

You will find I have awarded only one bottom-level ★ which goes to the 1896 Panhard 'Old No 5', largely because it was not truly 'a racing car' since at that time such a genre did not yet really exist. That car did, however, establish one of motor racing's greatest maxims, pure and simple — 'To finish first, you must first finish' — and of course survival was what those pioneer races were all about.

You will further find that I have awarded only eight maximum five stars, but there are a quartet of four and a halfs for designs which to my mind border on the verge of true greatness but whose characters or careers contain some flaw just narrowly too significant to be overlooked. I must also say that if I am asked my subjective opinion rather than the hopefully objective historical attitude, there would be a couple of six stars — for the Miller speedway cars, and the Lotus 25s — both of which so far as I am concerned really *sizzle*!

But above all, just consider before we begin that fame does not necessarily indicate success, and remember that by definition the vast majority of all racing cars ever built never won a race . . .

Panhard et Levassor, the heroic years

The earliest significant motoring competitions highlighted the names of two great marques. One was Panhard et Levassor, the other was Peugeot. It is merely the difference between finishing first and finishing second which gives Panhard et Levassor priority in our story.

René Panhard was born in Paris on 27 May 1841. He began work with a wheelwright company in Longeuil after graduating from the *Ecole Centrale* in 1864, and happily secured his future by marrying his boss's daughter ... He matched his practical ability with a good business brain, and while helping to expand the Longeuil business he developed a high regard for a supplier of woodworking equipment named Paul Perin.

Perin had co-founded his company, Perin & Pauwels, at 97 Rue du Faubourg Saint Antoine, Paris, in 1845. His was the inventive brain, his partner Pauwels ran the business side. They had made a lot money since Perin had patented a band-saw in 1853, but in 1866 Pauwels died, leaving Perin in need of a new administrative partner. Rene Panhard joined him in 1867, and the company expanded rapidly through the next four years. Panhard designed saws to cut metal as efficiently as Perin's had cut wood. He became principal director, located a larger new factory and looked for a dynamic and astute recruit to run it.

An old friend from his *Ecole Centrale* days was Emile Levassor, born on 21 January, 1843, at Marolles-en-Hurepoix near Paris. After graduating with Panhard in 1864 he entered the John Cockerill machine shops at Seraing, near Liege in Belgium. There he got to know Edouard Sarazin, who subsequently became a prominent Belgian patent lawyer ... Levassor worked for Cockerill's until 1869, before returning to Paris –Courbevoie

---

Emile Levassor — the driving force behind Panhard's early interest in motor racing, originator of the *'Système Levassor'* to which most motor cars have been built ever since, and single-handed victor of the first great motor race.

in fact – as workshop manager for the Ateliers Durenne. Two years later, his old college friend René Panhard invited him to take charge of the new woodworking machinery plant at Ivry.

In 1876, Paul Perin died and Levassor became a full partner with Panhard, and the company was reformed as 'Panhard et Levassor'.

Soon afterwards, Levassor's Belgian friend, the patent lawyer Sarazin, was instrumental in introducing Panhard et Levassor to the internal-combustion engine, and through it to the horseless carriage . . .

The German engineer Nicholas August Otto, of the Deutz company, had taken exception to Frenchman Gabriel Delhaynin's rival engine which he believed infringed his Deutz patents, so he consulted Sarazin on how best to defend them. The affair evaporated, but Sarazin later represented Deutz when they were sued by Lenoir, the gas engine company. Sarazin fought Deutz's corner so well they made him their agent for France.

By this time, Deutz's chief engineer was Gottlieb Daimler who got on very well with Sarazin. When Daimler founded his own Motoren Gesellschaft company in the Stuttgart suburb of Canstatt in 1882, he granted all future French rights for Daimler engines to Sarazin. They had no written contract; it was a gentleman's agreement between friends, and Sarazin subsequently took out the first French patent for the Daimler 'high speed' petrol engine on 26 October 1886.

Now he needed a French company he could trust to manufacture under licence. Naturally he thought of Emile at Panhard et Levassor, and commissioned the company to build two Daimler-design engines for testing and demonstration. Tragically, in December 1887 Sarazin fell ill and died that Christmas Eve, with a grieving Emile Levassor by his side . . .

Gottlieb Daimler then granted continued French rights to Sarazin's widow, Louise, who had visited him in Canstatt. On her next visit in October 1888, she was accompanied by Emile Levassor who was fascinated by all that Daimler showed him – his motorized carriage, a motor boat, and an omnibus.

Daimler seems to have thought as highly of Levassor as he had earlier of Sarazin. In the summer of 1889 they drove a Daimler car to Valentigney near the Swiss border to demonstrate it to Armand Peugeot, the bicycle manufacturer. They urged Peugeot to begin building petrol-engined cars, and he agreed to research the idea, dropping his previous steam-engined experiments in favour of Panhard-built Daimler petrol engines.

Daimler exhibited his primitive quadricycle at the Paris Exhibition that year, and also patented a new design of engine, a twin-cylinder with its barrels aligned side-by-side in a 15° vee. Levassor loved the engine; shame about the quadricycle!

On 1 November 1889, Mme Sarazin formally became exclusive French distributor for Daimler engines, by which time Levassor was actively courting her. She assigned to his company rights to manufacture Daimler-patent engines, in return for a 20 per cent royalty, 12 per cent of which passed on to Daimler. Everybody was happy.

The first Panhard et Levassor car subsequently emerged from their machine-tool works at 19 Avenue d'Ivry, Paris, on 17 February, 1890. It had been built there by a team of eight tool-makers under Levassor's direction, with Panhard footing the bill. Exactly three months later – on 17 May – Emile Levassor married Louise Sarazin. As the priest blessed their union, control of Daimler's French engine rights joined that of their only French licensee in the person of Emile Levassor . . .

But it needed intensive testing through early 1891 before his reinforced wooden-chassised car could run non-stop six miles to Point-du-Jour. Levassor's enthusiastic passenger on some of these early runs was 10-year old Paul Panhard, René's younger son who later became company president from 1916 until the Citroën takeover as late as 1965.

Two weeks after the first successful run to Point-du-Jour, the target became Versailles. Levassor then ordered construction of a second car, supervised by his devoted workshop foreman, Mayade. On 31 July, 1891, Levassor completed a round trip in it to l'Etretat, averaging 6 mph (10 km/h). The first customer deposits were taken, but already Levassor was redesigning the car . . .

Where his prototypes had used a mid-mounted engine, he now moved it to the front to diminish the vibration it transmitted to the soft road springs and to help load-up the tiller-steered front wheels. Bollée had already mounted an engine at the front of his horseless carriages, but where he used the flexibility of steam, Levassor had the problem of transmitting power from a

Gottlieb Daimler — with Wilhelm Maybach, and more so than Karl Benz, the father of the modern motor car, and its racing sisters.

constant speed petrol engine up front, to the wheels he wished to drive at the rear.

By March 1893, the company was sufficiently confident to despatch René Panhard's elder son Hippolyte – and his uncle Georges Meric – on a drive across France to Nice on the Côte d'Azur. Their mount used a V-twin 72 mm x 140 mm 2 hp engine.

At Hyères, Meric's place was taken by mechanic Belhomme, and along the coastal roads to Nice Hippolyte Panhard demonstrated the machine to many prospective customers. The trip took eight days, average speeds having risen as high as 12.5 mph (20.8 km/h) at times, while the Col de la Republique south of St Etienne had been climbed at a steady 4.5 mph (7.5 km/h).

Levassor's special bond with Gottlieb Daimler was strong. They corresponded weekly, sharing ideas, views and lessons learned in development of their respective motor cars. They shared advances freely one to another – by no means was the technology traffic all one way ...

Levassor's first automotive patent is dated 24 August 1891, covering ignition improvements.

He used 'hot-tubes' – platinum tubes screwed into the cylinder heads and heated by petrol burners. As the piston ascended on its compression stroke, it forced fuel mixture into the glowing white-hot tube, where it was ignited. Six of these earliest production Daimler-engined Panhards were delivered that year. The original carburettors, even Levassor's improved float-feed type, had no proper throttle device.

Levassor disliked Daimler's preferred but primitive belt drive, adopting instead a clutch and sliding-pinion 'clash-type' gearbox and chains. Without belts he lost their progressive friction take-up, so had to substitute some alternative means of breaking the drive between engine and gearbox. After early experiments with a brush-type clutch had failed, he settled on a friction conical clutch. He fitted an override intended to disengage drive when the foot-operated band-brake – acting on the chain-drive cross-shaft – was applied. An additional hand-brake clamped brake blocks tight against the solid rear wheel tyres.

The *Système Levassor* set down what would become the classical configuration of front-mounted engine driving through a multiple indirect-ratio gearbox to the rear wheels.

What were these early cars like? How did they run, how did they behave? What were they like to drive?

Primitive is the best-matched adjective; one might add — in the extreme.

Those early internal-combustion engines were very much constant-speed units which revved at about 600-800 rpm regardless of whether the vehicle was in motion or not. The driver simply juggled his noisy gears to adjust road speed. The 'clash-type' gearbox was noisy and crude, but effective. Levassor said it all in his immortal quote *'C'est brutal mais ça marche'* – 'It's brutal, but it goes'.

All these early engines used automatic or atmospheric inlet valves, in which the suction created within the cylinder during its induction stroke drew the valve open against a spring of pre-set tension. One drawback compared to the soon-to-be-developed, mechanically-opened inlet was that it inherently limited the engine's speed range. With electric ignition, engine speed could be affected to some degree by advancing or retarding the spark. With hot-tube ignition this was only possible, within even more restricted limits, by moving the burners which heated the tubes either closer or further away from the heads, so altering the distance that the mixture had to travel before it was ignited.

The engine's speed was regulated simply by a centrifugal governor which acted upon the camshaft to prevent the exhaust valves opening above certain rpm. At rest off-load the engine would whirr away until the governor abruptly cut in; the engine would cough and die away, then pick up and whirr again until the governor re-engaged. Its behaviour was *most* unrefined.

The engine was also an unbalanced twin-cylinder so in action it communicated quite intense vibration to the chassis. This effect was exacerbated by the very soft carriage springing necessary to absorb the rugged road surfaces of the period, so vibration from the unbalanced engine when running light would set the whole machine wobbling and rocking like a jelly.

This was damped considerably once the clutch was engaged and load applied, but these early clutches commonly dragged, and silent gear-changing — at least the up-change — was virtually impossible. Changes down were usually cleaner and easier to engage as the engine's near-constant speed synchronized more closely the down-changed gears.

At this stage there seems to have been no castor angle in the front-wheel kingpins, so these early Panhards seemed utterly devoid of directional stability and needed constant attention at the tiller. But perhaps – just like steering a boat – this seemed acceptable.

By 1894 the Daimler V-twin engine produced by Panhard et Levassor developed about four horsepower at 800 rpm. The car it powered could achieve all of 3 mph (5 km/h) in bottom gear, 7 mph (11.7 km/h) in second, 11 mph (18.3 km/h) in third and 15.5 mph (25.8 km/h) in top. Its front wheels were steered by vertical shaft and tiller, its wheelbase was longer than the prototypes' but still very short at just 60 in (152.4 cm); its front track was 32 in (81.3 cm), rear track 40 in (101.6 cm) and its open bodywork was built high – and much less than handsome.

Levassor himself had gained considerable engineering confidence. In 1895 he had introduced his own design vertical-twin engine with tandem cylinders in line, one behind the other. Now he had the entire length of the car to fill with as many twin-cylinder duplications as

practical ... but initially this in-line engine was offered in two versions as the 'Phénix' 3CV and 4CV. The 3CV (3 hp) variant had 75 mm bore and 140 mm stroke, the 4CV 80 mm x 120 mm (1,206 cc). Both used a new Levassor-designed float-chamber carburettor in place of the V-twin cars' surface-type and in 1896 a further enlarged 6CV version appeared, 90 mm x 130 mm, 1,654 cc.

More significantly, because in common with the basic *Système Levassor* it anticipated future common practice, an 8CV engine was then added to the range; a four-cylinder in-line simply doubling-up the 4CV. This in-line four was christened the 'Centaur'.

It was with equipment such as this that the age of motoring competition dawned ... with Panhard et Levassor leading the winning way.

Pierre Giffard, proprietor of the news magazine *Le Petit Journal*, announced on 19 December, 1893, that his paper's great sporting competition for the coming year would not be merely for bicycles – as previously – but for horseless carriages to be '... *without danger, easily controlled by the travellers, and not too expensive to run on the road ...'*.

Following preliminary trials, the 79-mile Paris-Rouen Trial took place on 22 July 1894. Amongst a varied entry, 13 petrol cars took the start, 12 of them Daimler-engined. Every one of them finished successfully, including four Panhards and five Peugeots, but although the Comte de Dion's steam tractor made the fastest time, the judges rejected it largely on the grounds it required two men to drive it. Instead the first prize was split between Panhard et Levassor of Ivry, Seine, and Les Fils de Peugeot Frères of Valentigney, Doubs. Although the jury judiciously declared that the two companies' cars *'conformed so well to the requirements of the competition, without as yet completely realizing the dreams of the tourist or the business man ...'*, the petrol-engined motor car's pre-eminence over steam and other rivals was well appreciated.

The *Automobile Club de France* was set up, and for 1895 proposed their first-ever proper motor race, choosing a course to test human grit as much as emergent technology. The plot was to race from Paris to Bordeaux, and back — no less than 732 miles (1,220 km).

Levassor used his new Phénix vertical-twin 1206 cc engine in 'No 5', the works car which he would drive himself. The great race started at the

22 July, 1894 — Paris-Rouen Trial — Peugeot and Panhard shared the premier award, both making use of Daimler-patent engines licensed from the Canstatt manufacturer in Germany. This is Rigoulot's 3½ hp Peugeot, proudly posed and showing off 'piano wire' wheels decades in advance of Bugatti's celebrated innovation on the Grand Prix Type 59. M Rigoulot and his trusty mechanician completed the Paris-Rouen course in the eleventh-fastest time, at an average of 9.1 mph.

Place d'Armes in Versailles just after noon on 11 June. Though there were check-points *en route* no stop-overs or neutral sections were provided. If a driver had the stamina to keep going all the way from Paris to Bordeaux and back again, at his mount's downhill maximum of around 20-25 mph (33 - 42 km/h), he was free to do so.

Emile and Louise Levassor rode 'No 5' to the first check-point, where Louise dismounted and a factory mechanic took her place. By Vouvray the faster steamers were in trouble and Levassor led. By 8.45 pm he was approaching Tours in the gathering dusk, lighting his candle-lamps and clattering on into the night . . .

A relief driver was stationed at Ruffec but Levassor arrived there so far ahead of schedule at 3.30 am his hapless replacement was still fast asleep. Rather than lose hard-won time, the impatient Levassor simply drove on.

In the dawn at 5.30 am he reached Angoulême – five hours later, Bordeaux. The turning point was the Café Anglais, where the judges verified the identity of Levassor and his car. He downed a glass of champagne without leaving his seat, and at 10.40 he crunched in first gear, and set off towards Paris . . .

At Ruffec his relief driver was ready, but having driven this far in the lead the boss pressed on. He stopped every 100 km or so for water, fuel and refreshment, but his longest stop lasted no more than 22 minutes.

Two days after leaving Paris, just before 1.00 pm on 13 June, Panhard 'No 5' came wobbling across the finishing line at the Porte Maillot. Emile Levassor had won the first-ever great motor race after an heroic single-handed effort. His elapsed time was 48 hr 48 mins, an average speed of 15.15 mph (25.25 km/h). Overall he was reported to have been 'on the machine' for about 53 hours, nearly 49 of those 'on the run'. Yet he remained sufficiently alert to sign his name after the finish 'with a firm hand', and at luncheon with the Marquis de Chasseloup-Laubat at Gillet's, Porte Maillot, '. . . he took with great relish a cup of bouillon, a couple of poached eggs, and two glasses of champagne, but he said that racing at night was dangerous, adding that having won he had the right to say such a race was not to be run another time at night . . .'.

In fact the rules of the race demanded four-seat

Levassor's Paris-Bordeaux-Paris winning Panhard 'Old Number 5' was sold subsequently to the fraudulently-inclined Harry J. Lawson's British Motor Syndicate and in their ownership starred in the original London-to-Brighton Emancipation Run — another Lawson-organized function which proved to be a typical shambles.

bodies, so the two-seat 'No 5' was denied first prize which went instead to Koechlin's Peugeot, second on the road.

Both Panhard and Peugeot used similar Daimler-derived engines, the main difference being simply that Levassor mounted his engine at the front, while Armand Peugeot preferred his at the back.

For 1896, the ACF announced a great new race from Paris to Marseilles and back, starting on 24 September. Mindful of Levassor's crib about the dangers of racing in the dark, it was divided into 10 daily stages – five southerly, five return – totalling 1,062.5 miles (1,770.8 km). The race was swept by the equinoctial gales. Amedée Bollée hit a falling tree, another car was blown over, roads flooded. The storm repeatedly blew-out the Panhards' hot tube ignition burners … the unprotected crews were soaked and battered.

Levassor – allegedly driving his famous 'Old number 5' again – also allegedly swerved to avoid a dog while leading near La Palude – between Avignon and Orange in the Rhône valley. The inherently unstable car capsized, hurling him on to the road. Badly concussed and winded he was taken away for treatment while D'Hostingue drove on in the recovered car.

His faithful lieutenant, Mayade, won for Panhard using an 8CV four-cylinder engine, from the sister 6CV twins of Merkel and D'Hostingue. Peugeot's star – now using their own engines – had faded badly. Panhard et Levassor now dominated the racing world, and would continue to do so into the age of giants. But at 52 Emile Levassor never recovered fully from his crash near La Palude. He had immediately returned to his desk and drawing board at Ivry, working all the hours God gave him. He complained increasingly of headaches, blurred vision and nausea but refused to rest. Seven months after the accident he was found collapsed over his drawing board, and he died on 14 April, 1897...

The way forward

Despite the death of their inspirational director, Panhard cars maintained competition pre-eminence to the turn of the century. Their new chief engineer was a military man, Commandant Arthur Krebs. In 1897, driver Hourgieres relied upon the twin-cylinder Phénix rather than 4-cylinder Centaur engine to win the two-seat class in the Paris-Dieppe in July and Paris-Trouville in August.

International racing then began in 1898 with the Paris-Amsterdam-Paris race, 889.5 miles (1,482.5 km) in six daily stages. Many manufacturers invested heavily in building cars capable of winning to promote their name . . .

Panhard abandoned their faithful twin-cylinder engines in favour of the 8CV 2,413 cc Centaur 4-cylinder, and now had wheel steering replacing the dubious and dangerous tiller. Peugeot responded desperately with a 3,324 cc twin, Bollée a similar 3,041 cc but Panhard dominated again, Fernand Charron winning at 26.9 mph (44.8 km/h).

For 1899, Peugeot pumped up their twin-cylinder racing engine to a literally thumping 5,850 cc, Bollée at last developed a 4-cylinder but laid its barrels flat beneath the nose of his cars. Panhard built a 12CV 4-cylinder version of the old 6CV twin, making 3,308 cc. Then Mors read the Panhard message by adopting a vertical 4-cylinder in-line front-mounted engine almost identical to Ivry's. It displaced 4,220 cc and sufficiently alarmed Panhard to trigger a 10 mm increase in the 12CV's stroke to form a 16CV of 4,398 cc.

That May saw five 12CV Panhards head the Paris-Bordeaux results. A Panhard-style 16CV Mors led the rest . . .

In July's 1,350-mile (2,250 km) Tour de France, the *Chevalier* René de Knyff's 16CV Panhard won from three sister 12CVs. Mors won the Paris-St Malo, but Panhard's top men and cars were absent. Incredibly, September's Paris-Ostend saw Leonce Girardot's 12CV Panhard and 'Levegh's' 16CV Mors *tie* on time over the 201 miles (335 km). In the Paris-Boulogne, Girardot just beat 'Levegh'. Krebs' Panhards remained supreme, but they were having to fight.

For 1900 a 110 mm bore increased 4-cylinder Panhard capacity to 5,322 cc to form the 24CV. Mors reached 7,345 cc, and they, like Peugeot, favoured electric ignition by coil and accumulator; a lead Panhard was forced to follow from 1900, at last abandoning the hot-tube.

Even this late, the engines were essentially constant-speed devices, road speed being determined more by the gear the driver had selected than by fine control over his engine speed. However, the 1900 Paris-Toulouse-Paris race saw 'Levegh's' Mors at last outgunning the Panhards, winning by over an hour from Pinson's 24CV. This was Panhard's first-ever defeat in the biggest race of the year, and the supremacy of *La Marque Doyenne* had at last been wrested away, never to be retrieved. . .

Meanwhile, far-reaching developments were on the boil across the German border, where Gottlieb Daimler's son Paul and his collaborator Wilhelm Maybach were fast approaching design of the definitive 'conventional' motor car. Levassor's vertical-twin Phénix engine had initially impressed Gottlieb Daimler and Maybach as much as they remained unmoved by his *Système*. Their products' engines remained firmly rear-mounted until 1898, but they followed the Frenchman's lead in mounting their two cylinders vertically, instead of in-vee, although in this case side-by-side, not in tandem. They also placed the exhaust valves in the cylinder head, operated by push-rod and rocker.

Once the German engine moved forward, its cylinders were in tandem, the crankshaft lining up longitudinally instead of transversely as before. Maybach had perfected a new change-speed mechanism, in which he replaced the early single quadrant with two or even three shorter quadrants with an open 'gate' provided between them to allow the gear lever to be moved sideways between the various planes, inventing the practice which survives to this day.

The next step was to produce a racing version of this chain-driven design for 1899. The engine grew to 4-cylinder in-line — 106 mm x 156 mm, 5,515 cc. It was front-mounted and cowled beneath a neat bonnet *à la* Panhard, but there was another innovation – a radiator formed not from the conventional coil of thin-gilled tubing, but using a honeycomb core claimed to be so efficient that much less water than normal could be carried.

Here were the basics for all mainstream motor cars to follow, but the 1898 Canstatt-Daimler racer remained too short, too high and too front-heavy to have great impact, other than on the scenery. When the cars made their début in the Nice meeting of March 1900 – a date unfortunately coinciding with Gottlieb Daimler's death – they proved horrors to control. One crashed at the first corner of La Turbie hill climb, and its driver Wilhelm Bauer was killed.

Nonetheless, the Austro-Hungarian consul in Nice became highly enthusiastic. His name was Emil Jellinek and he virtually appointed himself as Daimler agent and promoter for the South of France, selling to the wealthy set who holidayed there. He drove a 24 hp Daimler in the 1900 Nice-Marseilles, adopting his favourite daughter's name 'Mercédès' as a pseudonym for both himself and the car. He pushed himself upon Paul Daimler and Wilhelm Maybach, who were then running the show in Canstatt.

They agreed to build a new Daimler model for Jellinek to sell under his favoured 'Mercedes' name. Paul Daimler had a lighter version of the 1899-1900 model part-schemed, and Jellinek eventually found himself with a car which would set such high new technical standards that the bulk of the automotive world would have to follow . . .

Maybach carried over the successful gate-gear-change and honeycomb radiator from Gottlieb's last car, but crucially now designed an engine with mechanically-operated inlet valves to replace the old atmospheric type, which had been efficient only over a narrow rev range. Now mechanically-closed inlet valves could accept a wider range of engine revs and, with a throttle-valve on the carburettor plus electric magneto ignition whose spark could be advanced or retarded to some degree, the driver was able to adjust his engine revs virtually at will. The old days of the constant-speed engine had passed, at last.

This ability to rev from around 500 rpm up to 1,200 or more brought the gate-type gear-change into its own. Whereas the old straight-line quadrant changes had meant passing sequentially through each gear in turn, now 'round the corner' down-changes enabled the driver to skip direct from fourth to second, or even fourth to first, whenever he wanted. The car's road speed, crucially, was now controlled by the throttle foremost, the gearbox second. It was a revolution which introduced motoring as we now know it.

However, this new 35 hp Mercedes was not an instant success in 1901. But for 1902 the original 116 mm x 140 mm engines were enlarged to 120 mm x 150 mm, 6,785 cc, and Count Zborowski promptly frightened the French racing establishment with a very fast run in the Paris-Vienna.

By 1903 the French had taken the lesson to heart, also adopting mechanical inlet valves. Mercedes, however, introduced a new 60 hp model with 140

mm bore for 9,236 cc, and its inlet valves were not only mechanically operated, but were situated more efficiently in the cylinder head. In this form it was very potent, but Zborowski suffered a near identical fate to Bauer's, crashing fatally at the same place on La Turbie.

For the Paris-Madrid that year a new 90 hp version was prepared with 170 mm x 140 mm engine, 12,711 cc, and Camille Jenatzy went well in the race intil his car's carburettor choked upon a carelessly inquisitive fly.

A squad of six 90 hp racers were prepared for the Gordon Bennett Trophy race at Athy in Ireland, but all were destroyed in a catastrophic fire at the Canstatt factory. The 'Sixty' was now a catalogue model and the company was determined to make the race, so sent three stripped production cars instead. Jenatzy promptly won in one of them, beating all the specialized racing designs representing Great Britain, France and America.

At a stroke, in the words of Laurence Pomeroy '. . . *any car which was not fitted with a honeycomb radiator, mechanically-operated inlet valves and a gate-change was soon dubbed old-fashioned'*. Between them, Panhard et Levassor and the Daimler Motoren Gesellschaft had defined the form of what would be – for over half a century – the conventional modern racing car. . .

Racing reaches maturity

Motor racing – as a grand technical and promotional forcing-house – grew so rapidly in its early years thanks mainly to the enthusiastic ambitions of the French establishment and industry. France's motor industry was by far the strongest of any nation's prior to the First World War. They had set the pace in early development of the horseless carriage following its introduction in practical form by the Germans, Benz and Daimler. Germany recouped some credit as the standard-bearers of new technology in Maybach's Mercedes of 1901-1903. Thereafter the baton returned – for the next five years or so – to the French.

Because their industry comprised so many different marques, they developed an intense dislike for the international Gordon Bennett Trophy competition, which had been introduced in 1900. Its rules restricted all national teams to three cars only, which meant the French, despite their industry being many times larger, could run no more cars than America, Great Britain, Germany, whoever. They wanted a form of international racing virtually open to all.

2 July, 1903 — Gordon Bennett Trophy race, Ballyshannon, Ireland — Only the British really took this American-inspired truly International motor race anywhere near as seriously as the donor intended. Here Henri Farman's very powerful 80 hp Panhard shows how on one of the long but narrow descents, en route to finishing third at an average speed of 47.8 mph over more than 327 miles. This season saw the Panhard and Mors cars using pressed-steel chassis frames in place of wood for the first time. Farman's actual Bennett race number was 10, the '51' visible faintly here on the Panhard's radiator was a relic of the ill-fated Paris-Madrid, in which it failed to feature.

Initially they campaigned for a proportional system of Gordon Bennett selection in which France – as possessor of the largest and most diverse industry – should naturally have the largest entry.

During the 1904 *Salon de l'Automobile* in Paris, the leading French manufacturers requested that in 1905 the Gordon Bennett should be run concurrently with a new event, to be called the *Grand Prix de l'Automobile Club de France*. All competing companies would run on equal terms, and from 1906 the ACF should only run races of this type, abandoning the Gordon Bennett Cup altogether unless its rules were revised to match.

The ACF accepted. They declared that the first 15 cars in their 1905 Gordon Bennett Eliminating Trial would automatically qualify to represent France in the new 'Grand Prix'. As before, the first three finishers in the trial would furthermore represent France in the Gordon Bennett. They then set proportionate entry levels at six cars each for Germany and Great Britain, and only three each from Austria, Italy, Switzerland, Belgium and the USA. These numbers were described as 'approximate and to be revised each year . . .'.

The magazine *L'Auto* lodged a prize of 100,000 francs – £4,000 at that time – but while the French industry applauded loudly, foreign interests howled. Every nation which had formerly contested the Gordon Bennett protested formally to the ACF, who folded under pressure. An International Commission was convened in Paris in February 1905, and it was agreed that the two events should run separately on condition that the Commission should meet again afterwards to revise the rules. Soon after, the ACF cancelled its new 'Grand Prix' race for that season, but declared firmly that whatever the outcome of the Gordon Bennett, France would abstain from both defending or challenging for the Trophy again. In future they would only support the 'Grand Prix', which would now be inaugurated in mid-summer 1906.

By common consent the Gordon Bennett was allowed to lapse. No nation challenged for it, and effort was concentrated instead upon making the new 'Grand Prix' the kind of internationally mass-supported roaring success which the restrictive Gordon Bennett could never be . . .

1906
Grand Prix Renault

★ ★ ★

One of the most prominent companies to enter the inaugural *Grand Prix de l'Automobile Club de France* in 1906 was Renault Frères, of Boulogne-Billancourt, Seine, in the outskirts of Paris.

Back in the 1890s, while Panhard et Levassor essentially reserved their Daimler-inspired engines to themselves, the rival company of De Dion Bouton had supplied their single-cylinder engines to anyone who asked. One purchaser of their early tricycle model had been a serious, hollow-cheeked and hawkish looking 20-year-old, named Louis Renault.

Born in 1877, he was the fourth son in a family of six children, following Georges, Fernand and Marcel. Their father ran a button factory and a large drapery business. He had despaired of young Louis, who was an habitual truant from school, stowing away on railway trains, and spending hours hanging around the Serpollet steam car factory. He became such a fixture there that Leon Serpollet himself took him under his wing.

This persuaded his father to relent and buy his 'difficult' 14-year-old son a very early Daimler-Panhard engine. Louis spent hours tinkering with it in a shed at the foot of their Billancourt garden. Both shed and engine still exist, and it was in that shed in 1898 that he uprated his ¾ hp De Dion tricycle into a direct-drive quadricycle to produce the diminutive first Renault car. He took drive direct from an extended gearbox main shaft via bevel-gears to the rear wheels. No unpredictable and noisy drive-belts or chains for him; the shaft-drive system he was to develop would be light, flexible, and quiet.

Though that first quadricycle was tiny, it was also very light and performed well. On Christmas Eve 1898, Louis Renault demonstrated it to a friend of his father's, Maitre Viot, who was so impressed he handed over 40 *louis* as a deposit and bought it. Eleven other friends ordered replicas.

Louis' brothers Marcel and Fernand financed plant and a staff to build the cars, and on 25 February, 1899, 'Renault Frères' was founded at 10 Avenue du Cours, Billancourt with a capital of 60,000 gold francs. Louis protected his drive system with French patent No 285,743, dated 9 February, 1899. As production accelerated, he and Marcel set out to publicize their cars by racing.

According to the company today, they tied for first place in the Paris-Trouville, on 28 August. Just three days later they set off on the Paris-Ostend, and finished first and second.* On 21 October, Louis beat Marcel in the Paris-Rambouillet. Before the old century had died, everyone in French motoring knew the name Renault . . .

By the end of 1900 the brothers employed a staff of 110 at Billancourt, and had built 179 cars. Louis – according to Rose, or Marcel according to

(*This is not supported by Gerald Rose's *A Record of Motor Racing 1894-1908* which has Louis winning the *Voiturette* – less than 400 kg – class, fair enough, but no mention of Marcel, who was third in class [*La France Automobile* 10/9/1899]. In the Paris-Trouville, Louis won both o/a and *voiturette*, with Marcel second in class, 67 min slower. Beware corporate history!)

24 May, 1903 — Paris-Madrid — Just under 5½ hours after leaving Paris, Louis Renault and Ferenç Szisz reach Bordeaux, seemingly unaware as yet of brother Marcel's accident. Their light car's in-line radiators have three cores of 20 vertical gilled tubes each; note the narrow slick tyres and zero wind-screening. They have averaged over 62 mph (103 km/h), exceeding 90 mph (150 km/h) flat-out. That shaped nose must have deflected the airstream over their heads; otherwise breathing would surely have been near impossible at such speeds.

the Renault company – had won the 837-mile (1,395 km) Paris-Toulouse-Paris class. That alone is claimed to have attracted 350 new orders.

In 1901 Louis' improved 8 hp Renault *Voiturette* won its class at Pau, and the brothers were first and second in the Paris-Bordeaux. Louis won his class in the Paris-Berlin, covering the distance 51 minutes quicker than the Panhard winner of the light car class 'above' him ...

In 1902, Renault progressed from *Voiturettes* to the heavier and more powerful *Voitures Légères* – light cars. Marcel brilliantly won the Paris-Vienna outright in a new 16CV 4-cylinder car, shaft-driven of course. He averaged 38.9 mph (64.8 km/h), despite all stops and delays, and allegedly beat the Arlberg Express by seven hours.

The ACF's major city-to-city event for 1903 was to be from Paris to Madrid. Both brothers drove their sophisticated, light and powerful 30CV *Voitures Légères*; Louis accompanied by his Hungarian-born mechanic Ferenc Szisz, Marcel

by Vauthier. Louis started third, determined to take an early lead to avoid the murderous dust thrown up by those ahead. His engine revved to 2,500 rpm, a road speed of nearly 90 mph (150 km/h), and having overtaken Jarrott's 45CV de Dietrich and de Knyff's 80CV Panhard he led the rest of the way.

The field spread out along 135 miles (225 km) of road, and an estimated three million spectators flocked to see them. At those speeds in such blinding dust accidents were inevitable. Marcel Renault fell victim.

Having started sixty-third he was hacking his way through the pack. Just beyond Poitiers he overtook Henri Farman and lined up to attack Théry on the approach to a village named Couhé Verac. There was a tight left-hand corner. Théry saw it, braked and swayed through. Marcel Renault, running blind in Théry's dust, was unsighted and unprepared. He crashed off the road and was fatally injured beneath his 650 kg

(1,430 lb) car. Mechanic Vauthier, gravely hurt, would survive. Louis was told the news at the last check-point before the stage finish at Bordeaux. Continuing, there he heard how bad it was. He fainted, subsequently withdrawing all his cars. He would never race again . . .

The overall accident toll was so bad the authorities banned the scheduled stages to Madrid. All competing cars – immobilized – were towed behind draught horses to the railway station, and returned to Paris by rail. It was only eight years since Levassor's 15 mph (25 km/h) race win over these same roads. Now victory was awarded to Fernand Gabriel's 70CV Mors at an average speed 50 mph (83 km/h) faster . . . such was progress.

But the Paris-Madrid disasters spelled the end of the great era of city-to-city racing, and circuit races now took their place . . .

Where Renault was concerned, Louis still greatly valued racing as a sales promotional tool. He abstained from the Gordon Bennett race of 1904 but then built a special racing car to the order of an American, W. Gould Brokaw. Its design was advanced, with a brazed-tube chassis like the earlier Renaults, a midships-mounted radiator behind the engine, and a streamlined engine cowl reminiscent of a mediaeval knight's armoured helm.

Its engine was a 160 mm x 150 mm 4-cylinder side-valve, effectively one of the 1903 engines enlarged and rated at 60CV. It was shipped to Brokaw in America accompanied by factory mechanic and chauffeur Maurice Bernin who drove it in the Vanderbilt Cup on Long Island that October. He retired there, but subsequently won the Eagle Rock hillclimb outside Boston, Mass., then raced the car extensively for Brokaw for two more years.

By 1905, Renault had to protect its home-market prestige with a racing come-back. Louis entered a three-car team in the final Gordon Bennett Eliminating Trials run on a demanding Auvergne circuit. Their engines were enlarged versions of the Brokaw 60CV, 166 mm x 150 mm for 12,970 cc — 90CV rating and said to develop 95 bhp at 1,200 rpm.

But it was not the side-valve engines which drew comment. These red-painted Gordon Bennett Renaults were remarkable for their deep-section steel chassis frames which were not only tapered to match the *coupe vente* — 'wind-cutting',

sharp-nosed — body shape, but also stiffened to some degree by having the upper body panels rivetted to them — semi-monocoque style. An inverted horse-shoe radiator packed the scuttle just behind the engine bay, and the semi-elliptic suspension springs underslung the axles, providing low ground clearance and centre of gravity. Pump water cooling replaced Renault's former thermo-syphon system. Brakes operated on the rear wheels and the shaft-drive transmission only, following conventional practice at that time in leaving the steerable front wheels unbraked.

Maurice Bernin drove one car, Ferenç Szisz, Louis's former riding mechanic and now chief of the Billancourt test department, another, and an ex-Darracq driver named Edmond the third, but their chances were ruined by overheating and tyre troubles. Only Szisz's remarkable mechanical sensitivity nursed one car home fifth. He won 5,000 francs and an entry in the Vanderbilt Cup. He finished fifth again in the American race, delayed by ignition and tyre troubles plus a chronic radiator leak.

But notably, his drive in the Auvergne was acclaimed as 'one of the revelations of the eliminating trials' and Leonce Théry – Gordon Bennett winner for Brasier in both 1904 and 1905 and the greatest driver of his day – praised the sophisticated cars' 'astonishing speed and flexibility'. Thus encouraged, Renault prepared a design for the inaugural Grand Prix in 1906.

The ACF Committee had decided to spread the event over two days, 26-27 June with one six-lap, 384-mile (640-km) race each day. Where most scheduled service work had previously been handled by back-up crews, outside help was now banned. The driver and riding mechanic had to change tyres, refuel and generally keep their car together quite unaided. The circuit chosen lay to the east of the industrial city of Le Mans, comprising a wobbly triangle between La Ferté Bernard, St Calais and St Mars-la-Brière.

At Billancourt, Louis Renault's design staff decided to retain the 12.9 litre Gordon Bennett 90CV 4-cylinder side-valve engine, but ditched its troublesome water pump and restored the faithful thermo-syphon. Conservatism also governed the new chassis. The 1905 layout was abandoned in favour of a conventional channel-frame, a rectangular scuttle radiator replaced the horseshoe-type, and the *coupe vente* nose cowl was replaced by a normal 'coal-scuttle' like a

Possibly Monday 25 June, 1906 — Eve of the first day's six-lap section of the inaugural *GP de l'ACF*, Le Mans. Here the boss's former riding mechanic, now number one driver, Ferenç Szisz, has his GP Renault rigged in race form with fixed-rim front artillery wheels, detachable-rim rears replacing the wire-spoked type used during practice. Significantly, perhaps, the spare rims and tyres carried in the race have yet to be loaded on the tail. The Michelin pneumatic tyres have steel studded treads for longevity.

production Renault's; only its sides were cut away and webbed with wire mesh.

The '05 cars' braking, high-tension magneto ignition, and also their three-speed shaft-drive transmission systems were retained. But studying the course, and appreciating there were only three tight turns per lap, they deleted the differential and ran 'solid' final-drives instead. The course was liable to cut up during the two-day 770-mile (1,283-km) event, so double-acting hydraulic dampers were fitted front and rear, inside the chassis rails – possibly the first-ever racing car application of such devices.

The three works cars were finished in Renault red with polished brass and bright steel. Seven of the 11 teams entered used shaft-drive like Renault, six had similar three-speed gearboxes, five had similar high-tension magneto ignition but only one other used the archaic thermo-syphon cooling.

Renault used flimsy-looking 34 in diameter wire wheels in practice. But the Michelin tyre company offered its newly-developed *jante amovible* detachable-rim wheel system to those who would listen, which is what Louis Renault did . . .

Until that time, tyre changing in a race was a frenzied business, involving slashing away the old casing with sharp knives, then forcing a stiff new cover and inner tube back on to the wheel-rim, and locking the cover in place with security bolts. Now Michelin's *jante amovible* offered instead a completely separate detachable rim, which was attached to an inner artillery-wheel by eight retaining nuts and lugs. By releasing the nuts, the used detachable rim, complete with its worn-out or damaged tyre, could be removed and speedily replaced by a fresh rim with an inflated tyre ready-mounted. Replace and tighten the eight bolts, and away you went!

The Le Mans roads were littered with sharp stones, and a fierce mid-summer sun beat down. This long race would entail many tyre changes and the time saved by the *jante amovible* could dictate the outcome. On the debit side, these *jantes amovible* artillery wheels were each 9-10 kg (19-22 lb) heavier than the wire-spoked type, which could by itself increase tyre wear. For cars already close to the ACF's maximum weight limit of 1,000 kg (2,205 lb) the new fangled wheels were out of the question. Renault became one of only three teams to adopt them, running artillery wheels all round, but *jantes amovible* at the rear only.

Renault's drivers were Szisz, Edmond and Pierre Richez, and on day one Szisz took the lead

Tuesday 26 June, 1906 — The unlucky Edmond's second-string GP Renault — complete with its race-cargo of spare rims and tyres — rumbles eastbound on the N23 towards Le Mans through the *GP de l'ACF* pit area outside Pont-de-Gennes during the first day's racing. These 12.9 litre 4-cylinder cars easily approached 100 mph (166 km/h) on the long, dusty straights.

on the third 65-mile (108.5-km) lap after changing all four tyres in only 3 min 47 sec. He paced himself and his car thereafter and never lost his advantage, nursing the car and conserving his own considerable stamina despite appalling heat, dust and flying stones. Ending the first day's race he led Albert Clément's Clément-Bayard by 26 min.

Melting tar had spattered the crews, acid-burning exposed skin. A flying stone smashed Edmond's goggles, a splinter penetrating his eye. He also sustained particularly bad tar burns, but relief drivers were not permitted until day two, so

in the pits his burns were smeared with petroleum jelly, he was given a shot of cocaine and he fumbled on, half-blind, only for the soothing jelly to melt and run mixed with tar into his injured eyes. In terrible pain, after five heroic laps, he was forced to retire.

After spending the night secure in a locked *parc fermé*, the cars began the second day's race not only in the order they finished the first, but also at an hour matching their elapsed time on day one. Thus Szisz was flagged away in the lead at 5:45.30 am, but a tyre was flat so he rumbled straight into his service depot, changed two wheels, added fuel, oil and water, fine-set the lubricators and set off again after 11.5 min, still 14.5 min before Clément was allowed to start.

Richez crashed after three laps when lying fourth and having set a wheel-change record of 1 min 15 sec. Nazzaro of Fiat – also enjoying the advantage of the *jantes amovible* – challenged Clément for second place, but neither could touch the reliable Szisz who rumbled round with monotonous regularity – and speed – until the end of lap four when he stopped with a broken rear spring. Having gauged the problem he drove off again gently, slowing the great red car for the three hairpins on the transmission brake alone to limit back-axle reaction against the broken spring. Nazzaro established his Fiat in second place but Szisz was able to win this first-ever Grand Prix race at an average of 62.97 mph (104.95 km/h) for the 769.9 miles (1,283.7 km). The margin between them was a yawning 32 min.

The big Renaults had touched a genuine 100 mph on the long Le Mans straights, and on the timed kilometre past the tribunes where Szisz was still accelerating, he had been clocked at 92.43 mph (154 km/h). Renault publicized their great victory for all they were worth; Billancourt production totalled 1,619 cars in 1906, soared to 3,066 in 1907, and reached 4,600 in 1908.

Of course, they defended their Grand Prix title at Dieppe in 1907, when the ACF devised a fuel-consumption Formula. Each car was allowed only 231 litres (51 gal) for the ten laps, 768.1 km (477.4 miles), which means a fuel consumption no worse than some 29.8 l/100 km (9.4 mpg).

Two of the '06 cars had been sold and new cars were built for Dieppe, similar but now mounting *jantes amovible* front and rear. Rear axle torque arms reduced road-spring loadings and by regulation the team cars were now painted French blue.

Szisz again drove excellently but lost ten minutes in a stop on lap three. Nazzaro led for Fiat. It was Szisz's turn to follow, but in the closing stages he believed his fuel was marginal and bubble-footed over the last two laps to accept second place, by less than six minutes. Nazzaro's victorious Fiat proved to have 11.26 l (2.48 gal) of fuel remaining, but to Renault's disgust Szisz's tank contained 30.25 l (6.66 gal). With some reliable means of knowing how much fuel remained he *might* have pressed Nazzaro harder, and perhaps have pressured him into running dry.

While Renault had come close to a famous double, Pierre Richez crashed again. He righted and repaired his car to finish thirteenth. Henri Farman retired his car after seven laps.

Renault returned to Dieppe for the 1908 Grand Prix, but their racing technology had stagnated. The Formula now imposed a maximum cylinder bore of 155 mm on 4-cylinder cars, so Billancourt's new racers used long-stroke blocks, 155 mm x 160 mm, displacing 12,076 cc. Revving to nearly 2,000 rpm they developed a claimed 105 bhp.

The '06 GP-winning Renault had been bought by an Englishman and rigged with mudguards and lamps for high-speed touring. He drove it to Dieppe for this Grand Prix, but took it on to the circuit with defective front dampers, lost control at high speed and was killed when it hit a tree.

Renault had no luck in the race itself. Michelin had introduced a new type of single-bolt fixing *jante amovible*. On lap two of the Grand Prix, Szisz limped into the pits having lost one rear rim and tyre complete and with the other wobbling madly. He could not continue. New team driver Dimitri finished eighth, only the second French car home amidst 'a horde of Huns'. His teammate Caillois was placed fifteenth.

By this time the old cars were outdated but in October 1908 Lewis Strang – nephew of inventor, racer and front-drive pioneer Walter Christie – drove one in the Vanderbilt Cup on Long Island, New York. Its clutch broke early and the gearbox succumbed to his clutchless gear-changing. One month later in the American Grand Prize at Savannah, Georgia, Strang was joined by Szisz in a works '08 model. Strang was the first American home, finishing sixth overall at 59.8 mph (99.67 km/h), but 23 min behind the winning Fiat. The Renaults had been overwhelmed by more modern and powerful cars (albeit chain-drives) but Strang's was still clocked at 101.7 mph (169.5 km/h) – fastest of all through Savannah's measured mile. Szisz had run second before retiring when a front wheel bearing broke up.

Renaults continued to race in the USA, and established quite a reputation for themselves in the 24-hour 'grinds' popular at the time at tracks like New York's Brighton Beach; but as a factory team they would not touch Grand Prix racing again for 69 long, long years . . .

1910-12
The chain-drive Fiats
★ ★ ★

While the all-too-brief series of early Renault racing cars signalled the way forward with shaft-drive transmission, some of the most powerful racing cars of the pre-Great War period retained chain drive. The longest-lived and greatest of them all were the Italian Fiats*, from Turin. They provided the last redoubt for chain drive in Grand Prix racing, not because their designers were especially backward, not ultra-conservative, but simply because chain-drive had many good points upon which their immensely large and heavy-engined cars could capitalize.

As opposed to most state-of-the-art shaft drives, a chain-drive rear end reduced unsprung weight to what was, by the standards of the time, a minimum, since there was no heavy live axle complete with final drive bounding about on the road springs. The springs themselves were relieved of driving torque. The frame contained torque reaction which was not communicated to the rear axle as in a shaft-drive system, thus diminishing the tendency to lift and therefore to unload one rear wheel under acceleration.

FIAT — *Fabbrica Italiana Automobili Torino* — had been founded on 1 July, 1899, by a consortium of well-heeled young Piedmontese. A 33-year-old amateur engineer and former cavalry officer, Giovanni Agnelli, was the dominant personality. The new company's technical brain was Giovanni Battista Ceirano, son of a watchmaker from Cuneo. He was an agent for Rudge bicycles and founded his own Turin

factory in October 1898, planning to produce bicycles, and also light cars – although his first prototype was 'built out' by a company named Martina. Curiously, he chose what he seems to have regarded as an 'English-sounding' name for his products — 'Welleyes'. They were designed largely by Aristide Faccioli, and at FIAT's foundation the new company acquired Ceirano's patents, his prototype Welleyes car and Faccioli's full attention. The mid-engined Welleyes was developed into the original FIAT *Tipo* A, and founded the new marque.

Agnelli also inherited around 50 former Ceirano employees, including men named Felice Nazzaro and Vincenzo Lancia. The company began racing very early to promote its name, and test drivers Nazzaro and Lancia both competed successfully. When Agnelli urged Faccioli to adopt the latest front-engined configuration *à la* Panhard from France, the engineer resisted. He left quietly in 1901, and was replaced by Giovanni Enrico who enthusiastically adopted the 4-cylinder engine, honeycomb radiators and gated gear-changes. By 1903 FIAT headed the emergent Italian motor industry and by 1906 they were producing over 1,000 cars a year. Agnelli vigorously diversified, adding ship-building and marine engine interests to the car company — and supporting motor racing.

In 1905, Enrico's experimental department produced a stark 100HP *Corsa* competition car with overhead-valve 4-cylinder, 180 mm x 160 mm, 16,286 cc engine, with which Alessandro Cagno set a new record for the Mont Ventoux mountain climb in France. An improved but

(*The initial form 'F.I.A.T.' was used until 1906, 'Fiat' thereafter)

dimensionally similar 110HP was developed for the last Gordon Bennett race in the Auvergne that year, and three ran there, driven by Nazzaro, Lancia and Cagno. They led for some time and finished second and third. The world took note.

In the 1906 Grand Prix, Nazzaro finished second behind the winning Renault. In 1907 a production-based 125 mm x 150 mm, 7,363 cc, model finished first and second in the Targa Florio, the nominally 28-40HP engine actually delivering around 60 bhp at 1,200 rpm. For the Kaiserpreis race in the Taunus that same season a 140 mm x 130 mm, 8,004 cc, 4-cylinder racer was developed, in which the great Nazzaro won again, with sister cars driven by Louis Wagner and Lancia 5-6. A team of monster 130HP racers developed from the 100/110 series engines then tackled the Grand Prix at Dieppe, where Nazzaro notched the emergent Italian marque's third great victory of the year. His winning chain-drive car developed its 130 bhp from 16.2 litres, barely

8 bhp per litre which can be explained by its low crankshaft speed, only 1,600 rpm. One could certainly hear the big FIAT's approach, and no doubt *feel* it, too ...

Giovanni Enrico had retired early in 1906, and was replaced by a grim and austere 36-year-old bachelor, *Ingegnere* Guido Fornaca. He had trained as a railway engineer in Romania, and gained experience on hydroelectric plant with Savigliano before joining Agnelli's FIAT. He was a brilliant technical organizer, and began building a strong design team headed by his right-hand man, Carlo Cavalli.

The Agadir Crisis of 1907 triggered a massive trade recession, and after 1908 the ACF agreed with major manufacturers to allow its annual Grand Prix to lapse until the trading climate could improve – racing at this level was expensive. The Grand Prix would not be revived until 1912.

Still the ever larger-engined chain-drive Fiat *Corsa* models emerged; like Fornaca's 1908 *Tipo*

Imposing sight — 14,137 cc of Grand Prix Fiat S74, immaculately prepared in Turin for the Italo-American driver Ralph de Palma in the *GP de l'ACF* at Dieppe on 25-26 June, 1912. These hitherto highly-successful cars were very much the last of the big-engined chain-drive dinosaurs at that time. Note the fine-mesh radiator stoneguard, deep barrel-chested undertray, shiny leather 'side tonneau' to fare the cockpit, and bolster fuel tank. There's still no attempt at wind screening, and even the hefty detachable-rim artillery wheels were then far outdated.

Tuesday 25 June, 1912 — The GP-leading Fiat S74s of American society darling David Bruce-Brown (left – lying first) and Louis Wagner (right – in second place) at the Dieppe circuit pits for fresh tyres after the fourth of that day's ten 77 km (47.8 mile) laps. Bruce-Brown drove blindingly fast — his eighth lap at 36:32 remaining the fastest of the race. But constant tyre troubles (Wagner had to change 19), a broken fuel feed and slow churn refuelling —while Peugeot used a pressure system — lost Fiat the race.

SB4, a 190 mm x 160 mm 4-cylinder, displacing 18,146 cc for 175 bhp at 1,200 rpm.

Eventually the *Tipo* S61 – 130 mm x 190 mm, 10,087 cc – emerged in 1908 virtually as a super sports road/racing model. Fiat themselves describe it as *'una gran turismo'* which seems most apt and one of these cars won the 1911 Grand Prix de France at Le Mans. This was the first revival of interest in GP-style racing, although it was not actually the ACF's great race, and it was dubbed derisively the *Grand Prix des Vieux Tacots* ('The Old Crocks Grand Prix') – due to its lack of new-built works entries. The victorious S61 driven by Victor Hemery was a privately-entered catalogue model.

It reputedly began life as a complete running chassis delivered to a Parisian coachbuilder for a closed touring body to be fitted for a wealthy customer. He subsequently refused delivery and after a long delay it was eventually sold stark and simple, and was raced as it stood. It was nonetheless very fast, and achieved at least 95 mph (158 km/h) on the long Le Mans straights.

Its massive engine anticipated several later common features. Its cylinder block comprised two integral-head 2-cylinder iron castings, each with four vertical valves per cylinder retained in detachable cages and actuated by a single overhead camshaft. The engine developed a claimed 115 bhp at 1,800 rpm, and was mounted in a limber channel-section chassis frame with beam axles on semi-elliptic leafsprings.

This 'semi-stock' racing car was tall and square-rigged, and is claimed to have achieved 30 mph (50 km/h) in first gear, 45 mph (75 km/h) in second, 65 mph (108 km/h) in third, and clearly close on 100 mph (150 km/h) on the level in top.

Notable S61 performances include FTD at Modena on 8 May, 1910, when Nazzaro was clocked at 87.77 mph (146.28 km/h). On 30 May, 1911, the wealthy young American David Bruce-Brown finished third in his S61 in the

Wednesday 26 June, 1912 — *Bbllbbddggg-bbllbbddgg* or words to that effect. Imagine the song of that gigantic 4-cylinder engine in Louis Wagner's Fiat S74 here as it gallops flat-out along one of the Dieppe circuit's awesomely narrow tree-lined straights. During the GP team mate Bruce-Brown's sister car was timed at 101.8 mph (169.7 km/ h) at such a point. The road surface, basically hard-rolled chippings, had been sealed with 'akonia' — a calcium chloride preparation — to retain moisture and keep down the dust.

Indianapolis 500-Miles, then on 23 July came Hemery's win at Le Mans, averaging 56.64 mph (94.4 km/h).

Meanwhile back home in Fiat's Turin experimental 'shop, a much enlarged S61 development to be known as the S74 was being prepared, with 150 mm bore and 200 mm stroke, a beefy 14,137 cc. It developed around 190 bhp at 1,600 rpm — fractionally less than 13½ horsepower per litre — sufficient to propel its 3,306 lb at up to 105 mph (175 km/h). David Bruce-Brown won the American Grand Prize race at Savannah in an S74, averaging 74.41 mph (124 km/h), for more than 5½ hours . . .

The 1912 season saw more American success for Fiat — sporty millionaires like 'Terrible Teddy' Tetzlaff and Caleb Bragg finished first and second in their S61s at Santa Monica, California, on 6 May, and the former second at Indy on 30 May.

Then in Europe on 24-25 June the works entered S74s in the French GP at Dieppe to fight their celebrated rearguard action for the giant-engined, chain-driven monster racing car against the new-wave of smaller-engined, more sophisticated shaft-drives from ambitious former *Voiturette* manufacturers, like Peugeot.

Bruce-Brown actually won the first day's section in 6 hr 36 min 37 sec, at 72.38 mph (120.63 km/h) but on the second day he was disqualified for receiving outside assistance and Louis Wagner could only finish second behind the victorious Boillot's Peugeot *pour la France*.

In America, Tetzlaff won again at Tacoma, but in practice for the Grand Prize at Milwaukee Bruce-Brown crashed his S74 in practice and was killed, together with his riding mechanic Tony Scudelari. Bragg won with Tetzlaff fourth in their S61s. Chavez set second quickest time in an S74 at Gaillon hill-climb that October, but at major level the era of the giant-engined chain-driven monster had now passed . . . the big Fiat S61s and S74s becoming the last significant examples of that particular breed of dinosaur . . .

The epochal Peugeots

★ ★ ★ ★ ★

Into the final quarter of the nineteenth century, the *Société Peugeot Frères* was a large and comfortable family business based at Valentigney, Doubs, not far from Belfort in eastern France, where they made household goods and corsetry.

While working in England, Armand Peugeot, born in 1849, recognized the potential of the bicycle market and in 1885 he talked his fellow directors into launching large-scale manufacture of pedal-powered bi, tri and quadricycles. He also foresaw the appeal of effective motorization and built some experimental Serpollet steam-engined tricycles. He exhibited one at the great Paris *Exposition* of 1889, and, as described in Chapter One, was soon approached by Levassor and Daimler, who persuaded him to adopt their petrol engines instead. The first Peugeot-Daimler quadricycles then emerged in 1891.

During the following year, Armand and his three cousins Pierre, Robert and Jules assumed control of the family company, and changed its name to the *Société des Fils de Peugeot Frères*.

In 1894, two of their 'cars' finished second and third in the pioneering Paris-Rouen Trial, and shared the joint petrol-engined top award with Panhard et Levassor. They promptly sold 40 cars that year, but Armand's cousins did not share his full enthusiasm. The family split, and Armand founded his own *Société des Automobiles Peugeot* to do what he liked best. Independently, Pierre, Robert and Jules came to appreciate the growing motor market, and by 1899 their Valentigney works had introduced motorcycles. In 1906 they began building single-cylinder *Voiturettes*, which

they marketed under the 'Lion' name derived from the heraldic symbol of Belfort already used on their hand-tool and bicycle badges since as early as 1858.

Armand's cousins began to see the future as clearly as he himself, and in 1910 he returned, the merged empire then becoming the *Société Anonymé des Automobiles et Cycles Peugeot*. They continued to market cars under the Lion name until the Great War. Meanwhile they were very active in *Voiturette* racing, and often locked horns with the Spanish-domiciled Swiss engineer Marc Birkigt's Hispano-Suiza team. The annual 'Grand Prix' of the *Voiturette* racing world was the Coupe de *l'Auto*, which saw the culmination of Peugeot/Hispano rivalry when run at Boulogne in September 1910. There Paul Zuccarelli's T-head 4-cylinder Hispano became the first-ever multi-cylinder *Voiturette* to win a race of such magnitude, beating the V4 works Lions by Peugeot.*

This victory presaged future *Voiturette* design, but having won the Coupe, *Ingenieur* Birkigt now withdrew Hispano from racing, leaving Italian-born driver/engineer Zuccarelli and his colleague Louis Pilleverdier at a loose end. Thereupon, Zuccarelli was invited by works Lion drivers Georges Boillot and Jules Goux to join their team in place of Giosué Giuppone, who had died in a crash during practice at Boulogne, and Pilleverdier came too, to assume the role of Peugeot team administrator.

(*These cars were and are often referred to as 'Lion-Peugeots'. In fact it seems Peugeot presented and promoted them purely as 'Lion' cars, omitting their true family name.)

18 September, 1910, *Coupe de l'Auto*, Boulogne — Jules Goux's factory Lion *Type* VX5 by Peugeot, just before the annual *Voiturette* race in which it would finish second. The organizing committee had applied a maximum bore limit of 80 mm for twin-cylinder engines, to which Peugeot's engineer Michaux responded with a 280 mm stroke, for 2,803 cc and one of the tallest-ever racing cars. A massive 62 mm diameter inlet valve occupied the top of each cylinder, exhaust valves being horizontal, to the side. The VX5 achieved 95 mph (158 km/h), but was beaten by Zucarelli's much better handling 4-cylinder Hispano-Suiza . . . the trigger for a Peugeot revolution.

Boillot and Goux persuaded their employers to take on these new men from Hispano, and after listening to what Zuccarelli had to tell, the ambitious, engaging Boillot — a born huckster — further proposed an entirely new type of high-performance engine to company President Robert Peugeot. Until that time, the Lion racing *Voiturettes* had been co-designed by two graduate engineers, Peugeot veteran Gratien Michaux and Louis Verdet.

Backed by Goux, whose family had faithfully served Peugeot for decades, the technician/sportsman Boillot, brandished Zuccarelli's inside knowledge of how to improve upon Marc Birkigt's advanced Hispano-Suiza technology. Hard-nosed Robert Peugeot was interested and offered support on a virtual no-cure, no-pay basis. What the upstart Boillot/Zuccarelli/Goux triumvirate needed was a competent design draughtsman to interpret their project. What they found, and what made the project the stunning,

trend-setting success it became, was a clever design practician with valuable prior experience to contribute, whose only problem in attaining stardom on his own account was an unaccountably weak, in some ways twisted, certainly stunted personality. He was Swiss, and his name was Ernest Henry.

Perhaps significantly, he was yet another former associate of Birkigt's — and now he joined the triumvirate to set down on paper what were primarily (it seems) Zuccarelli's technical aims; Boillot presumably offering little more than entrepreneurial cover, and Goux the inestimable proven guarantee of his family's long service to the Peugeot family. Michaux and Verdet abruptly found themselves bundled out of design pre-eminence, and replaced by a group they seem to have christened, with the contempt reserved by properly-qualified engineers for a bunch of amateurs, *Les Charlatans*.

But Pilleverdier, in conversation with the great

American historian Griffith Borgeson, recalled Henry as being '... truly creative. The peculiarities of (the new engine's) combustion chamber and valve train belonged exclusively to him ...'.

Borgeson's terrier-like researches into the truth of the *Charlatans'* story concluded that Henry had previously been involved with Lucien Picker of Geneva, a graduate engineer who developed a special interest in combustion chamber shape and valve disposition. With his brother Charles he built power boat engines for use on Lac Leman, and then in 1903 produced a Lucia car in partnership with Charles Moccand, using a head very close to what would become known 20 years later as the Ricardo head. They took a stand at the first Geneva *Salon de l'Automobile* in 1905, organized by C. Jules Megevet, who went into partnership with Charles Picker in a boat-yard, and that year entered three Lucia-engined power boats in the big *motonautique* races at Monte Carlo. By 1912 Picker won the major Monaco race, and Megevet's boatyard was regarded as the best in central Europe.

Meanwhile, power boat driver Maurice de Cleves and his partner Chevalier had adopted Picker's Lucia engine for their new Labor cars. But Picker, Moccand et Cie went bankrupt in 1908 and Picker set up a consultancy bureau in Paris, designing for Labor. It seems Ernest Henry moved to Paris to assist on these projects. Labor-Picker engines performed well in racing power boats, and Picker's office then devised the Labor-Aviation 4-cylinder twin-cam (low-mounted, pushrod-operating side valves in a T-head layout) engine of 1910-11 which significantly had too many features suggestive of Henry's future Peugeot racing engine for the similarities to be pure coincidence ...

Despite – or perhaps because of – the 1910 Coupe de *l'Auto* defeat, Robert Peugeot raised his sights to Grand Prix level, undoubtedly fired and encouraged by the image the *Charlatans* created of an advanced new design capable of beating all rivals. He offered them a contract to build a prototype, plus team cars if successful, for £4,000 per car; no argument, no extras. They could sink or swim. This was a similar deal to one made with Ettore Bugatti to produce the *Bébé* Peugeot production model. Once a prototype had proved itself, what now became known loosely as *L'Equipe* Boillot would build and operate a full

team under the Peugeot name. A more modern equivalent would be John Wyer's Ford Advanced Vehicles/JW Automotive outfit, which created and raced the Ford GT40s under contract to Ford Detroit ...

The ACF revived the Grand Prix race for 1912, and ran it concurrently with the *Voiturette* Coupe de *l'Auto* at Dieppe. Henry and Zuccarelli prepared designs for both events, sharing a common engine configuration.

Zuccarelli had probably specified increased engine revs to attain greater power, which necessitated vastly improved breathing. Henry achieved this by combining several features already used by others in isolation, but very probably — it now appears, thanks to Borgeson's researches —prompted by the Labor-Aviation experience. He combined twin overhead camshafts with four inclined valves per cylinder and hemispherical combustion chambers to form an engine capable of revving faster and breathing more freely relative to its displacement than any predecessor.

Its camshafts were housed within a barrel-shaped aluminium casing retained by long studs atop a fixed-head 4-cylinder block casting. Initially they were driven by vertical shaft and bevel from the crankshaft. The four valves per cylinder were set at an included angle of 90°, the two exhausts seating direct in the head while the inlets resided in detachable cages. Plain bearings were used throughout, with carefully devised pressure lubrication, and the block centreline was offset slightly from that of the crankshaft in what was then a popular *désaxe* form in an attempt to decrease side-thrust upon the crank during the power stroke.

This engine, with its epochal head and valvegear layout, borrowed its bore and stroke of 110 mm x 200 mm from the Michaux-designed 1910 Lion V4 *Voiturette*. It displaced 7,600 cc and with the new head delivered around 130 bhp at a hectic 2,200 rpm. In comparison the Mercedes which had won the last previous Grand Prix, in 1908, had developed only 135 bhp from an engine nearly 5 litres larger, running at only 1,400 rpm. The contemporary chain-driven Fiat S74, which the new Peugeot would face at Dieppe, produced 190 bhp, but from 14.1 litres, thumping round at 1,600 rpm. In other words, the *Charlatans'* new Peugeot L76 engine delivered 17.1 bhp per litre, against only 13.5 from the Fiat, and 10.8 from the '08 Mercedes.

This engine was mounted in a U-shaped subframe, with its gearbox remote amidships along the chassis. A foot-brake operated on the shaft-drive transmission and a hand-brake on very large rear drums. There were no front-wheel brakes, as conventional at that time. The entire frame was made as light and limber as was deemed prudent, and because detachable Rudge Whitworth wire wheels were now permitted by the regulations they were fitted as standard.

The 1912 Grand Prix was another two-day affair, the giant chain-drive Fiats clear favourites to win. Zuccarelli's new Peugeot L76 failed on lap 7 of the first day's 10-lap race; Goux lay third before a long delay to repair a broken fuel line; Boillot accompanied by riding mechanic Prévost had his troubles but stuck to his task, desperate perhaps to prove 'his' project to his demanding boss.

He succeeded in finishing the second day as overall winner, having completed the total 956 miles (1,593 km) at 68.45 mph (114 km/h). One corresponding 3 litre Peugeot L3 built for the concurrent Coupe de *l'Auto* meanwhile failed entirely, René Thomas's car running a bearing on day one. He later observed grimly, 'If Boillot hadn't won it would have been the finish with Peugeot for him, Goux, Zuccarelli and me ...'. Nonetheless, Boillot had won, and the twin overhead camshaft, inclined overhead valve, hemi-head racing engine theme had been established, as had the ability of lighter, smaller shaft-driven cars to topple the long domination of the chain-drive monsters.

Later that year an L76 won the *Coupe de la Sarthe* at Le Mans – driven by Goux against meagre opposition – and in 1913, with engines linered-down to meet the US Formula ceiling of 7.4 litres, Goux won the Indianapolis '500' in *La Glorieuse 'vingt-deux'* (GP race number '22') – the Dieppe GP winner – while the luckless Zuccarelli again retired.

Prior to that trip, on 10 March, Goux drove a well-streamlined L76 *monoplace* at Brooklands and raised the flying-start half-mile world's record to 109.987 mph (178.312 km/h), raising the old figure by over 7 mph (11.6 km/h). Since at that time the outright human speed record stood to the aviator Jules Vedrines's Deperdussin monoplane at only 104.27 mph (173.78 km/h) – and since Goux drove on to complete 150 miles

Wednesday 26 June, 1912 — Georges Boillot's fabulous Peugeot L76 smoking its way towards its rather fortunate but nonetheless historic home win in the *GP de l'ACF* at Dieppe. Here it is accelerating eastbound on to the N320 away from the *fourche* at Neuville on the circuit's closest approach to Dieppe, which lies down the road in the background. The pits area and the finish line lay 1 km (0.6 mile) ahead of Boillot and mechanic Prévost in their twin-cam 16-valve Peugeot — in gearbox trouble and really quite fortunate to finish at all.

(250 km) at 106.003 mph (176.672 km/h) – the GP Peugeot's achievement made shattering news ...

The latest Grand Prix regulations specified a

weight limit of 800 kg (1,763.7 lb) – and maximum fuel consumption of 20 l/100 km (about 14 mpg). Boillot's 1912 Peugeot L76 had averaged 28 l/100km so obviously a more economical Grand Prix engine was now required. Although the L3 was still acceptable for the concurrent Coupe de *L'Auto* race, its other shortcomings persuaded Robert Peugeot to finance two teams of new cars, Grand Prix and *Voiturette*.

The new Grand Prix Peugeot introduced dry-sump lubrication, which prevented losses by surge under acceleration and cornering, improved oil cooling and enabled more oil to be carried without recourse to a massive sump forcing the engine too high. A new two-piece crankshaft was introduced, running in ball-bearing mains supported in a one-piece crankcase, and a gear-train now replaced the original vertical bevel-shaft to drive the twin overhead camshafts. The angle between the valves was decreased to 60°, cone clutches replaced the L76s' multi-plate type, the cylinders ceased to be *désaxé*, and bore and stroke became 100 mm x 180 mm, 5,654 cc. This new L56 engine delivered around 115 bhp at 2,500 rpm – a marked improvement to over 20.5 bhp per litre – while the corresponding 3 litre L3 *bis Voiturette* measured 78 mm x 156 mm, 2,980 cc, and produced around 90 bhp at a dizzy 2,900 rpm – which represented 30 bhp per litre.

The Coupe de *L'Auto* was run separate from the Grand Prix that season, and this new *Voiturette* in fact won its maiden race in Boillot's hands at the Circuit de Provence on 15 June, 1913. Then in preparation for the Grand Prix at Amiens on 12 July he invented the knock-off hub nut to make the most of the L56's Rudge-Whitworth wire wheels. But in pre-race testing, the now habitually luckless Zuccarelli encountered a laden haywain drawing across his path near Nonancourt. He was flat-out in his new car at the time, he had nowhere to go, crashed violently, and was killed.

Delpierre took his place in the Grand Prix, and drove furiously, only to crash in an ill-advised attempt to overtake Boillot! The Delages were faster, but unlucky, so the Peugeot L56s finished first and second, driven by Boillot and Goux, their cars respectively consuming 17 and 18 litres per 100 km, and – despite Delage's performance – boosting Peugeot prestige to the skies as the first ever to win two *Grands Prix de l'ACF*.

At Mont Ventoux on 24 August, Boillot broke his own 1912 climb record by 8 secs – the new mark surviving unbroken until 1925.

On 21 September the Coupe de *l'Auto* at Boulogne saw Goux repeatedly shatter the lap record. But he was delayed so Boillot beat him again, their L3*bis* cars finishing first and second, with Victor Rigal's fifth. In three years the Henry design had enabled Boillet to lower his Boulogne race time by fully 57 minutes!

Thereafter the proprietors of *L'Auto* announced that the 1914 limitations for their *Voiturette* classic would be lowered to 2.5 litres, requiring an all-new design should Peugeot wish to defend their title, for the L3*bis* could not sensibly be reduced so far. One existing 3 litre car was streamlined in L76-style and sent to Brooklands where Goux averaged 106.91 mph (178.17 km/h) over the flying-start half-mile, and the old L76 streamliner managed only 108.56 mph (180.93 km/h) . . . true testament to the L3*bis*' ferocity.

For 1914 the Grand Prix was to be run at Lyons-Givors, and a new capacity ceiling of 4.5 litres was introduced by the ACF. The new L45 Peugeot's bore and stroke were chosen as close as possible to the L76/L56 proportion.

Goux returned to Indy, this time accompanied by Boillet with a pair of Amiens L56s, while Arthur Duray took out a private L3*bis* which had been purchased by chocolate heir Jacques Meunier for everyday sporting transport. *L'Equipe* Boillot refused this interloper any factory assistance, and Boillot himself set a new Indy record of 99.85 mph (166.42 km/h) during his great qualifying run, Goux right there at 98.13. Duray made the field at 90 mph (150 km/h) precisely.

The factory Peugeots were then beaten in the race by René Thomas's Delage . . . with Duray's 3-litre Peugeot second! Boillot blew a tyre after 140 laps, Goux finishing fourth after race-long tyre troubles.

The last pre-Great War Grand Prix followed, Boillot took the lead in the new L45, hounded by the implacably regimented Mercedes team. The Peugeots sported four-wheel brakes but the longitudinal twin-spare tyre mounting in their long pointed tails may have adversely affected roadholding and handling, and tyre troubles were many. Again as at Indy, Peugeot made a dubious tyre choice before the start, and it bit them. When

2 July, 1914 — The magnificent Peugeot factory team of three new L45 cars plus one spare lines up for the photographer, ready to tackle the *GP de l'ACF* at Lyons-Givors. Left to right the race cars' drivers are twice-GP winner Georges Boillot (5), Jules Goux (19) and Victor Rigal (32). The in-line spare wheel housing beneath the hump in those long tulip tails possibly exaggerated rear tyre wear and adversely affected the cars' handling. They lost to Mercedes after a memorable struggle.

Max Sailer's Mercedes broke after six laps, Boillot led and he stayed ahead of the surviving Huns for 12 spectacular laps, driving as hard as only he could, the outstanding driver of his era. On the penultimate lap, his Peugeot faltered and a Mercedes appeared in the lead. The L45's rear axle failed on the final lap, so Mercedes finished first, second and third. Peugeot, and France, had been defeated. Both took it badly.

A 2.5 litre Peugeot L25 – 75 mm x 140 mm –had been built for the 1914 Coupe de *L'Auto* on 23 August, but the event was cancelled as war broke out. Two, perhaps three of the cars were kept at the Peugeot works and at least one was reputedly used throughout the war years as high-speed executive transport. Though the larger cars were sold it was allegedly this very car which eventually went to Indianapolis in 1919, entered by Jules Goux for the late Georges Boillot's younger brother, André. Georges had been killed flying near Verdun on the Western Front. Now at Indy 1919, the new Boillot nearly won. With only 20 miles to go the car blew a tyre, overturned and burned. Immediately the Speedway clamped a

183 cubic inch (3 litre) ceiling on engine size.

Two L25s ran in the Targa Florio on 23 November, 1919, driven by Reville and the younger Boillot who won outright in his repaired Indy mount.

The two remaining Peugeot L45s were purchased by Carl Fisher of the Indianapolis Motor Speedway, and arrived there in September 1915. Fisher promptly despatched them to the Premier Motor Corporation in that city and commissioned them to manufacture three exact replicas, plus a stock of common spares. When Goux broke his engine in 1919, a complete Premier unit was offered up and fitted the genuine Peugeot frame exactly. The Peugeots dominated the American scene through much of the Great War period, and their technology was adopted by the best American racing marques to found the Golden Age of the American racing car through the 1920s.

L'Equipe Boillot's initiative, backed by Robert Peugeot's money, had provided what Laurence Pomeroy described as '*the very foundation of the modern high-speed engine . . .*'.

1914
Grand Prix Mercedes
★ ★ ★ ★

The Daimler Motoren-Gesellschaft won the 1908 *Grand Prix de l'ACF* at Dieppe with a disciplined team of three chain-driven 4-cylinder cars. But save for the 19 tyre failures which afflicted the unfortunate Victor Rigal's Clément-Bayard, he would surely have won for the home country. He eventually finished fourth behind Christian Lautenschlager's winning Mercedes and two similar chain-driven Benz cars, his average of 63.6 mph (10.6 km/h) astonishing in view of the delays endured. The Mercedes and Benz* cars were not so destructive of their tyres but even the winning Mercedes had completely exhausted its replacement stock in the pits for the last two laps.

Three German cars filling the first three places in their national Grand Prix – a year after it had been won by an Italian Fiat – was a grave blow to French pride. It added impetus for an already depressed industry to forego the expense of Grand Prix racing until 1912. Upon its revival, the DMG stayed away through 1912-13, but when the ACF proposed a 4.5 litre maximum capacity Formula for 1914, Paul Daimler was interested in having another tilt at French racing pride.

Back in 1902, while Wilhelm Maybach — Gottlieb Daimler's close collaborator — had still been in technical charge of the DMG at Bad Canstatt, they had been approached by a Russian named Boris Loutzky brandishing an Imperial

Russian Navy contract for a large marine engine. Loutzky was an engineer who had studied in Germany and had worked on internal combustion engines since 1888. In Nürnberg in 1896 he had helped develop a single-cylinder engine with an overhead camshaft driven by vertical shaft from the crank down below.

Loutzky's naval brief was to produce a 300 hp engine, which was five times more than anything in DMG's previous experience, but they had a go and incorporated a truncated cone combustion chamber form housing a vertical inlet valve, and an exhaust at 70° on the left side – features which Loutzky recommended. Maybach inserted a single camshaft between the valves, driven by vertical shafts and worm gears. This one-off developed a successful 272 bhp at 550 rpm on test.

Maybach followed up with a single overhead-camshaft straight-six engine of 11,080 cc which produced 106 bhp at 1,400 rpm. It had wide flat combustion chambers, with very large overhead valves at each side. The single ohc was itself driven by vertical shaft and bevel gears. Late in 1906 two such engines were mounted in racing chassis with exceptionally low and rakish bodies. Hermann Braun won the Semmering hill-climb in one.

Meanwhile the DMG had broken into aero engine manufacture. One Daimler engine had been used in an airship as early as 1888, but it was 20 years later when a 60 bhp 4-cylinder aero engine series was laid down, accompanied by an in-line 6-cylinder with shaft-driven single ohc. In May 1912 the *Kaiserpreis* competition was

*These two great German marques, the DMG's Mercedes line from Stuttgart Unterturkheim and Benz & Cie from Mannheim did not merge to form the Daimler-Benz Aktiengesellschaft until 1926).

announced to select the manufacturer of the best German aero engine on the basis of fuel economy and high power-to-weight ratio. Benz won, with a pushrod ohv 4-cylinder, but DMG designs were rated second and fourth. The first of them was the *Typ* DF80 6-cylinder of 105 mm x 140 mm, displacing 7,250 cc, which produced 90.5 bhp at 1,400 rpm and weighed only 388 lb; that's 12.48 bhp per litre, or 0.23 bhp per lb. Not bad by 1913 standards. Its light weight was achieved by abandoning heavy cylinder block castings in favour of lathe-turned steel cylinder barrels clad in welded-up fabricated sheet steel water-jackets.

Now, the requirements for aero engines and motor racing engines are very similar, and high power-to-weight ratio is one factor which is common to both. While the DF80 was being perfected, Mercedes's Belgian agent Theodore Pilette commissioned a team of Grand Prix cars for the ACF's 1913 race at Amiens. But they refused his entry on the grounds that he was not the manufacturer, as required. The regulations for the Sarthe GP at Le Mans were more accommodating, and his entry of four white Mercedes was accepted. One car used a 1908 GP-type chassis with tuned 37/90 production engine, but the other three were entirely new. Fitted with vee radiators, sleek bodies and high cockpit sides they looked modern and aggressive. They were chain-drive as preferred by Pilette, but rode on detachable wire-spoked wheels. Two were powered by the new 6-cylinder DF80 aero engines, while the third – for Pilette himself – had a G4F aero engine developed from the 1908-originated 4-cylinder series, now with shaft-driven sohc. Measuring 140 mm x 150 mm, 9,230 cc, it developed 100 bhp at 1,350 rpm.

In the race, Pilette ran second but finished third after tyre trouble, behind two Delages. Otto Salzer and Christian Lautenschlager finished fourth and sixth in the 6-cylinder cars. One of the cars was then shipped to Indianapolis for the 1914 '500', but under Speedway conditions it vibrated too severely to be a contender.

Meantime, in Stuttgart, Paul Daimler put the knowledge gained into a new design for the *Grand Prix de l'ACF* at Lyons-Givors on 4 July, and entered the maximum five cars. The regulations had not been confirmed until early-September 1913, when weight was limited to 2,420 lb (1,098 kg) and engine size to 4,500 cc.

This was in fact the first time a capacity limit had been applied by Grand Prix regulations. It would emphasize higher revs to retrieve adequate horsepower previously achieved by simple cubic inches. It clearly favoured experienced *Voiturette* manufacturers like Peugeot, Delage, Sunbeam and Vauxhall. In the DMG's case, they now had to develop racing engines a whole litre smaller than anything they had yet tried in that area – and in less than nine months they had nearly to double their racing engines' normal reliable rev range.

Paul Daimler's engineers chose a 4-cylinder layout, designed by the automotive office but tested by the aero engine section. A vertical shaft drive for a single overhead camshaft was placed at the output end of the engine, leaving the crankshaft nose to drive only the water pump in a configuration which would remain typical of DMG racing engines for years to follow. The vertical shaft was bevel-geared to run faster than crankshaft speed, to reduce the torque it had to endure. The bottom end had five main bearings, with high-pressure lubrication. Aluminium pistons were produced and looked promising, but the choice of whether to race them or conventional iron pistons was left to the team drivers – three of whom were DMG master mechanics – and they opted for reliable old iron. Individual, rather than paired, steel cylinders were adopted for ease of manufacture, and each was a machined steel sleeve with welded-up water-jacketing and fixed head. Four inclined valves resided in each pent-roof combustion chamber. Two spark plugs were introduced on the inlet side and another on the exhaust, plus space for a fourth if necessary! Induction was via a single updraught carburettor with barrel throttle.

The engine emerged as the DMG's *Typ* M93654, the serial being derived from its 93 mm x 165 mm 4-cylinder form. It burned petrol/benzol fuel mixture, and developed around 105.5 bhp at a hearty 3,100 rpm — 23.44 bhp per litre. It drove through a double-cone clutch which replaced the DMG's famous scroll-type and, to please Pilette, Paul Daimler came close to insisting they should retain the lightweight chain-drive rear end.

Max Sailer — a board member as well as chosen driver — talked him out of it. He argued that a Peugeot-style shaft-drive system was also light and effective, after all they had won the GP

Saturday 4 July 1914, just before 8:09.30 am — Two of the 4.5 litre shaft-driven Mercedes prepare to set off in the *GP de l'ACF* at Lyons-Givors, '39' on the left being that driven by Otto Salzer into third place while '40' is Louis Wagner's sister car which finished second behind Lautenschlager's victorious number '28'. The cars were flagged away in pairs at 30-second intervals.

two years running ... Daimler was still wary of lateral torque in a live axle unloading one wheel under power, so the cars emerged with a sophisticated final-drive mechanism in which the pinion shaft carried two driving pinions with the differential between them; each pinion meshed with a separate crown-wheel, one to each half-shaft, thus cancelling out the torques.

A four-speed gearbox was fitted, and chassis frame kick-ups to clear the rear axle appeared for the first time on a racing Mercedes. There were no front brakes, only a single transmission brake and large rear drum brakes. Knock-off wire wheels carried white-rubber Continental 815 mm x 105 mm front tyres and 820 mm x 135 mm rears.

Paul Daimer signed-off the chassis drawings on 24 February, 1914, the body lines on 3 March. At least two cars were ready for exhaustive testing at Lyons-Givors in early-April before racing cars were barred there. They had long 113 in wheelbases, shortened one inch for the race by moving the rear axle forward. The original long tapered tail was amputated to save weight and provide better spare wheel access. Louis Wagner's car eventually ran with no rear body at all, and an abbreviated scuttle. Christian Lautenschlager's bonnet sides were louvred along their full length.

The other three cars had small access hatches at the front of the right-hand panel, two with six louvres behind it, and five on Salzer's car.

DMG's entire Grand Prix operation was planned and organized to an unprecedented degree, setting the peerless standards which the Daimler-Benz *Rennabteilung* would perpetuate in later decades. Each car was individually tailored to its driver's preference. Time was arranged during practising to enable each of six alternative final-drive ratios to be tested on each car. Maximum claimed speed was 112 mph (187 km/h), which with a 2.5:1 final-drive meant 2,900 rpm. Absolute control of the drivers from the pits by signal was introduced, all but Director Sailer – and maybe Louis Wagner – having to take notice. Containers in the pits were painted red for fuel, yellow for oil and white for water. One scheduled pit stop was to be made, all cars to change tyres whether necessary or not. Only the veteran Wagner objected.

Peugeot provided Mercedes' main rival in the race itself, the L45 car driven by Georges Boillot. It had four-wheel brakes and at one stage pre-race at least one of the Mercedes was rigged in similar manner, though rear-wheel only were used in the race. Max Sailer took upon himself the task of hare, trying to break Boillot's Peugeot if he could. He gained a lead of 2¾ minutes in the first five laps, but ran a big-end bearing and threw a rod on lap six.

By that time the Peugeots were already in tyre trouble, but even so, Boillot led laps 5 to 15. On lap 11 Lautenschlager lost two minutes through slow pit work. But on orders from the pits, Lautenschlager, Wagner and Otto Salzer closed inexorably. On lap 18 Lautenschlager circulated at 68.7 mph (114.5 km/h) and took a 23 sec lead over Boillot whose Peugeot broke on the final lap. He had had to change eight tyres against Lautenschlager's four. Peugeot and France had been beaten on home soil by Mercedes and Germany . . .

The Mercedes finished first, second and third, Lautenschlager winning at 65.83 mph from Wagner – 65.3 mph – and Salzer – 64.8. Their three victorious cars were then rigged with mudguards and lights for the long drive home. Another car, perhaps a spare, was sent to England for display.

But on 28 June 1914 the Austro-Hungarian ArchDuke Franz Ferdinand and his wife were assassinated at Sarajevo, and the Great War erupted.

One of the Lyons cars was sold to the American driver Ralph de Palma. It left Unterturkheim on 25 July, just pre-empting the British Naval blockade of German ports, for the USA. He promptly won with it first time out at Elgin, Illinois, on 21 August. In 1915 he won the Indianapolis 500-Miles – surviving the last three laps with a broken rod and two holes in the crankcase – and he went on winning with the car . . .

After the Armistice, in 1922, three of the cars featured in a massive DMG works outing to the Sicilian Targa Florio, each now modified to four-wheel brakes and with aluminium pistons freeing them to exceed 4,000 rpm. Quite possibly they had also been enlarged to 5 litres, which must have boosted them to possibly 130-135 bhp. The DMG's double-Grand Prix winning driver, Lautenschlager finished tenth in one car, Otto

---

Saturday 4 July, 1914 — Max Sailer's Mercedes, seen here at the *Virages les Sept Chemins* just before the pits where the D42 meets the RN88, led the first five laps of the GP easily, setting a pace beginning the destruction of Peugeot's home defence. The German cars had no front wheel brakes but handled quite well, were fast and most crucially reliable. Knock-off hub Rudge-Whitworth type spoked wheels for rapid tyre changing were by this time standard GP wear.

2 April, 1922 — Count Giulio Masetti leading the Targa Florio in his red-painted works-supported 1914 GP Mercedes, confusingly numbered '40' on the radiator stone-guard but '19' on the scuttle . . . Masetti had no problem in winning on the last lap as Goux's leading Ballot ran out of brakes, tyres and water.

Salzer thirteenth in another, while the Florentine Count Giulio Masetti's red-painted version won.

In 1914, in winning the race at Lyons for which they had been designed, the 4.5 litre Mercedes won the most-diversely supported Grand Prix in motor racing history; that they could also win when the challenges were as different as Indianapolis and the Targa Florio indelibly confirmed their true class.

The Duesenberg Straight-8s

★ ★ ★ ★

Duesenberg was, as it sounds, a German family name but it came to apply to one of the most glitteringly charismatic of all American automotive marques. Its founding brothers were in fact German-born, from Lippe – Frederick (Fred) Samuel born 1874 and August (Augie) Samuel born 1879. There were six children in all, but their father died when they were small, so elder brother Henry hunted for work in America. He found it in Rockford, Iowa, and called for his mother and the other children to join him.

There Fred displayed special mechanical talent, and at 17 he was paying his way by repairing agricultural machinery. He became a great cyclist, began racing, then built his own bikes. At 21 he had his own small factory. In 1898 – according to US sources – he held the world's 2 mile and 3 mile cycle records. He developed a motorcycle, and in 1902 joined the Rambler Motor Car Company in Kenosha, Wisconsin.

By 1903 he was in Des Moines, where Augie joined him, running the Iowa Automobile & Supply Company. Fred was fast becoming a fine engineer, a dynamic magnetic man who imbued both respect and affection in like-minded men. Augie was quieter, more retiring, but an able mechanic and an excellent craftsman. They designed and built a car ideal for the mid-western farmer, won backing for its production from an attorney named Mason, and set up the Mason Motor Company around 1906.

Fred began toying with racing car designs to promote the Mason image, and when washing machine manufacturer Frank Maytag bought the company and moved plant to Waterloo, Iowa,

Fred continued to develop racing machinery. He perfected his Duesenberg 'walking beam' 4-cylinder engine. It was characterized by use of two horizontal side-valves in each combustion chamber, which were actuated by foot-long vertical rocker arms – the 'walking beams' – which were pivoted well towards their lower end where the overhanging section bore direct on the camshaft lobes. It was a simple and inexpensive idea, and it worked.

After much development the brothers could claim almost 100 bhp from their 5.7 litre walking-beam racing engine and with Maytag's backing were successful at venues like Milwaukee and Brighton Beach, New York. They qualified four Masons for the 1913 Indy '500', and Willie Haupt drove one home ninth.

Then in 1914, they moved to St Paul, Minnesota, and founded their own Duesenberg Motors Corporation. There they began racing under their own name, Eddie Rickenbacker and Willie Haupt finishing 10-12 in Duesenbergs at Indy. On 4 July, Rickenbacker won the Sioux City '300' with Tom Alley fifth – and Duesenberg were on the racing map.

When power-boat racer Commodore J. A. Pugh commissioned them to build him two engines for the 1914 Harmsworth Trophy, they produced two walking-beam in-line 12-cylinders. Fred carefully cast the cylinders in pairs, thus originating patterns usable for an entire new range of 2, 4, 6 and 8-cylinder marine engines should a market exist.

It did, and it was dominated at that time by the Loew Victor Engine Company of Chicago. Despite the Harmsworth Trophy race being cancelled due to the war, Commodore Pugh's Duesenberg-engined boat *Disturber IV* became the first to exceed 60 mph (100 km/h). Loew Victor promptly persuaded Fred to sell them manufacturing rights for Duesenberg 6 and 8-cylinder marine engines and they retained him as consultant. With money in the bank, the brothers then detuned their 4-cylinder racing engine for production use, and in February 1915 offered it to the motor industry — with very poor response.

Their racing cars still won at Glendale and on Des Moines Board Speedway, and finished 5-8 at Indy. Engineer Cornelius van Ranst joined them, and in 1916 he added an extra camshaft and 'walking beam' platoon to produce a twin-cam 16-valve 4-cylinder. Loew Victor accommodated Duesenberg Motors in a corner of their Chicago plant. They built new racing cars and a stock of 16-valve engines, and in 1916 completed a monster walking-beam 300 hp V12 aero engine ... which progressed little further. They also geared-together a pair of 4-cylinder engines to produce a 'parallel-8' aero engine which flew in the Gallivet amphibian.

Having powered vehicles on land, air and water, Duesenberg enjoyed their best racing season yet, winning at Corona and Ascot and finishing second at Indy, Tacoma and Cincinatti. When the new 16-valve engines were introduced late that season, they added a crisper edge.

Industrialist J. R. Harbeck, who owned Loew Victor, talked Fred into a joint engine venture for a renewed assault on the proprietary motor and aero industry markets. They built a new plant in Elizabeth, New Jersey, and until it was ready the peripatetic brothers moved their people into Harbeck's American Can Company premises at nearby Edgwater, New Jersey. There Fred schemed a walking-beam straight-eight automotive engine, but the wartime Government really wanted aero engines. So Van Ranst drew a 16-valve 4-cylinder to match, developing 125 bhp, and it was accepted for trainer planes.

At Elizabeth, Duesenberg was selected to wrestle with the experimental Bugatti-King coupled-crankshaft 16-cylinder aero engine problems. Fred and his people designed a 16-cylinder 48-valve walking-beam aero engine of their own, with Mercedes-style machined cylinder sleeves and welded-up water-jacketing. Despite a capacity exceeding 55 litres and producing

over 800 bhp, this brute weighed only 1,250 lb, fully 1.56 bhp per lb, but its future evaporated as the war ended. However, the Duesenberg design team emerged with massive experience of what Bugatti had done wrong in his coupled-crankshaft 16-cylinder, and their plant was equipped wth a superb Government-funded dyno facility capable of testing even the largest engines.

Throughout, they had continued racing. Tommy Milton and Eddie Hearne had placed first and third at Providence in September 1917, then 1-2 in that year's last two events at Uniontown and Ascot. Then in 1918 the first customer production cars to use Duesenberg power – the Revere, Roamer and Wolverine – went on sale.

Fred had been fretting at the limitations of his simple walking-beam racing engine, and he led the design of a single overhead camshaft 5 litre straight-eight replacement. It powered a team of new Duesenberg racing cars in time for the 1919 Indy '500', but they were completed late, in a terrible rush which was apparently quite typical of the way the brothers worked. Only one made the race, driven by Tommy Milton. Its splash-lubrication was ineffective, he snapped a con-rod (or two) but the French Ballot straight-eights nearly won and their performance convinced Fred he was on the right track.

But otherwise that race was a promotional disaster for Duesenberg; five cars ran 16-valve 5 litre engines derived from the trainer plane's, amongst which Arthur Thurman's Special killed its driver, Louis LeCocq's Roamer killed both driver and riding mechanic, Kurt Hitke's Roamer ran a bearing, Eddie O'Donnell's true Duesey popped a piston, and finally Wilbur d'Alène's Duesenberg-Shannon Special snapped a half-shaft.

Now the single-ohc racing straight-eight's lubrication problems were worried out at Elizabeth. Fred, Augie and van Ranst realized how much heat was generated in the bottom-end's heavy bronze bearing shells used to support the actual bearing surface of white metal babbitt. Seeking to conduct heat away from the bearing more rapidly, they tried con-rods bored barely 40-thou over crank-journal diameter, and applied white metal direct to the rod surface. It worked – it was the dawn of modern thinwall shell-bearing technology – and it trebled Duesenberg straight-eight bearing life.

Tommy Milton won the Elgin road race and fit-

26 July, 1921 — Winners; the determined and very capable Irish-American speedway star Jimmy Murphy and his riding mechanic Ernie Olson proudly display the star-and-stripes before taking the start at Le Mans. That three-rib tread rear tyre is in for a terrible time . . .

ted a modified 16-valve trainer plane engine in a racing chassis and during a packed Duesenberg records session that November at Sheepshead Bay he smashed 19 records from one to 300 miles and one to three hours, including an astonishing 25 miles (41.6 km) at 116.2 mph (193.6 km/h). Jimmy Murphy and Eddie O'Donnell broke all records in the 161-183 cid (cubic inches displacement) class between the same limits as Milton. The session established no fewer than 52 new records, and the 4-cylinder 16 valve's stature soared.

Now Duesenberg was really famous. Soon 11 different makes used their engines, and in 1921 even a Roamer stock chassis was timed at 105.1 mph (175 km/h) on Daytona Beach.

Fred profitably sold his walking-beam 4-cylinder engine rights to J. N. Willys who took over the New Jersey plant to mass produce the Rochester-Duesenberg. In December 1920, Fred introduced his prototype Duesenberg Model A passenger car at the New York Show fitted tem-porarily with a walking-beam engine, with sales-men assuring the public the production model would feature a single overhead camshaft unit. Fred settled-up with Harbeck, and then in 1921 – fully independent – he and Augie moved their team to new premises in Indianapolis.

By this time the American Automobile Association had cut its racing Formula ceiling to 183 cid, 3 litres, for 1920-22. The 3 litre straight-eight racing Duesenberg set out as a scaled-down version of the sohc 24-valve 300 cid unit. New castings did not reach Elizabeth until a mere 21 days before the 1920 Indy '500'. The four team cars made the trip without axles which were still being machined, and they were completed barely in time for late qualifying, but Milton, Murphy and Hearne finished 3-4-6 in the Speedway classic. Milton won at Uniontown and Murphy at Fresno Board Speedway. Early valve-spring failures were cured by reprofiled cams, designed by specialist Colonel E. J. Hall, which not only solved that problem but boosted power from around 98 bhp closer to 115 bhp – 38.3 bhp per litre. But the Hall camshaft did not appear until late 1921, and without it Eddie Hearne won at Cotati, and at Indy Duesenberg 183s finished 2-4-6-8. With the Hall camshaft, Hearne won the Beverly Hills '250' ending that season.

Meanwhile, across the Atlantic in France, the ACF revived its Grand Prix race to run at Le Mans on 26 July 1921. They were desperate for entries and adopted the American 3 litre Formula. Ernest Ballot was fielding four of his splendid straight-eight cars driven by the best drivers his money could buy – Jules Goux, Louis Wagner, Jean Chassagne, and Ralph de Palma from the USA. Sunbeam entered a team, and there was a lone 1.5 litre Mathis makeweight. Fred Duesenberg cabled an entry for three 183s, later adding a fourth as Albert Champion – the Franco-American spark plug manufacturer – stumped up the entry fees. Drivers were to be Jimmy Murphy, Joe Boyer, Albert Guyot and Louis Inghibert, and the cars were shipped to Le Mans.

A most unusual feature was their hydraulic instead of mechanically-operated drum braking system. Unfortunately, the drums were the same size front and rear, which over-braked the rears as weight transference lightened the load on the cars' tails when the driver braked. The rears tend-ed to lock, and in practice the hard-driving Jimmy Murphy was caught out and flipped into a ditch, breaking a rib and injuring his passenger Inghibert so badly he would miss the race. André Dubonnet – the aperitif millionaire – took over his car.

Meanwhile, the French carburettor manufact-urer Claudel offered attractive bonuses to anyone using his instruments, and Murphy was the only Duesenberg driver to refuse, wisely sticking to the Miller carburettor. His riding mechanic, Ernie Olson, had also recognized that Ballot's front brakes were smaller than their rears and they worked well. He pointed this out to Augie and they sawed 2 in off the front brake linings; 'I got Joe Boyer to try it ... we hurtled down the straight, he hit the brakes and the car just squat-ted. It tried to bury itself in the road without a bobble. We really had it over the French after that ...'

The Americans also decided it would be better on such a short course – now 10.6-mile (17.6-km) lap – not to bother with carrying hefty spare wheels and struggling to change flat tyres out on the course. They planned instead to limp back to the pits for any wheel-change, and proved to themselves this saved time.

Jimmy Murphy took the start swathed in crêpe bandage to support his damaged ribs, Olson

July 1921 — Joe Boyer's second-string works team Duesenberg at Le Mans prior to the *GP de l'ACF* there on 26 July, the Indianapolis-bred straight-eight car showing off its Speedway-style streamlining with well-cowled cockpit and long bullet-faring tail. The large four-wheel drum brakes are the first upon a Grand Prix car to be hydraulically operated.

26 July, 1921 — The road surface of the shortened Le Mans circuit used for the 1921 GP broke up appallingly as the race progressed. Here Albert Guyot's number three Duesenberg rips over the flints and gravel on one of the still fast straights. That right-rear tyre is actually just clear of the road surface, upon a particularly large stone. The challenge in early Grand Prix races came not only from rival cars . . .

alongside in the incredibly slender Duesenberg's staggered-seat cockpit. The 13 runners set off at 30-second intervals, de Palma of Ballot and Boyer of Duesenberg both averaging 78 mph (130 km/h) for the opening lap.

On lap 7, Murphy called at the pits for a tyre check on his gum-dipped Oldfields. Chassagne's Ballot took the lead. Boyer lay second, until Murphy stormed ahead. Chassagne retired when the Ballot's fuel tank was punctured by flying stones. The road surface had completely broken up, every car showering flints, gravel and dust in its wake.

Murphy led from Boyer until the second Duesenberg threw a rod on lap 18. Guyot took second place only for his mechanic to be struck by a flying stone. He stopped and Arthur Duray took the victim's place, the car rejoining sixth. De Palma's Ballot now lay second behind Murhpy, but the Italian-American was very disenchanted with M. Ballot after a practice altercation. A case has been made for him allegedly being light on the throttle and 'bubble-footing' to give America victory.

But still Murphy's Duesenberg was simply

'going like gangbusters' until, on lap 29, the penultimate lap, its radiator was punctured by a flying stone, and almost simultaneously a tyre blew. There was 12 miles to run. At the pits water was added to the holed radiator, while Olson changed the wheel. The added water pumped away through the torn radiator, the system boiled, they drove on. With eight miles to go, another tyre deflated, but Murphy bumped the stricken, steaming car home to win, 14 mins 59 sec clear of de Palma's Ballot. A full 'safety lap' was still required, and with his winning car's engine virtually glowing, Murphy managed to limp through it at 30-40 mph (50-66 km/h). Dubonnet's sister Duesey finished fourth and Guyot's sixth.

The French and Ernest Ballot claimed a moral victory as his cars could begin the race all over again, in marked contrast to the ruined winning Duesenberg . . . but the best of contemporary American track-racers had won the Grand Prix, and the supremacy of the straight-eight engine, well set-up four-wheel brakes and naturally-talented driving had all been amply demonstrated.

The Fiat Tipo 804-805s

★ ★ ★ ★

As we saw in 'The chain-drive Fiats' (page 24), Senator Agnelli's Fiat company of Turin built a formidable racing reputation for themselves in the early years of the twentieth century, and were only narrowly beaten by Peugeot as late as 1912. They abstained from racing in 1913, and then reappeared at Lyons in 1914 with a 4.5 litre car with a promising overhead camshaft engine and four-wheel brakes. Immediately after that appearance, their engines were rebuilt with Mercedes-style welded-up steel cylinders, and after storage throughout the Great War they were revived in time for the first major race of the inter-war period, the 1919 Targa Florio. They were unsuccessful there, but one car sold to Count Masetti went on to win this Silician classic in 1921.

Agnelli's experimental department in Turin was still headed by the ascetic *Ingegnere* Guido Fornaca, whose large and talented design and development staff included names like Giulio Cesare Cappa, Carlo Cavalli, Vincenzo Bertarione, Walter Becchia, Tranquillo Zerbi, Luigi Bazzi and Vittorio Jano. Cappa headed the design team which produced two new Grand Prix types tailored to the 1921 3 litre Formula, a 4-cylinder and a straight-eight, both with twin overhead camshafts.

'Nando Minoia won the Parma-Poggio di Berceto mountain climb in one of the 4-cylinder *Tipo* 801.401 *Corsa* cars on its first time out on 8 May, 1921. Its 85 mm x 131 mm, 2,973 cc engine developed around 112 bhp at 4,000 rpm. The straight-eight *Tipo* 801.402 *Corsa* had internal dimensions of 65 mm x 112 mm, for 2,973 cc, but developed 120 bhp at 4,400 rpm in the similar

'801' chassis. It pioneered valves inclined at the wide included angle of 100° in a fixed cylinder head, plus the use of roller-bearing big-ends in concert with a one-piece crankshaft.

The very wide valve angle enabled exceptionally large valve heads to be used, while the roller-bearing big ends on a one-piece – instead of made-up –crankshaft was quite daring. Obviously it meant the roller-bearings had to be split to enable them to be fitted, but Fiat's system worked well and encouraged the low-friction bearings' wider acceptance.

Fiat missed the French race at Le Mans, but contested the Italian GP at Brescia, where they succumbed to mechanical problems even though Pietro Bordino set a new lap record.

The Turin technical team also produced a *Tipo* 803.403 *Corsa Vetturetta* model that year, which used effectively half the 3 litre straight-eight engine. The factory team of four of these cars finished 1-2-3-4 at Monza on 3 September, 1921, Bordino driving the winning car. Much valuable experience had been gained, which was then built into new 6-cylinder twin-cam 2 litre *Tipo* 804.404 *Corsa* cars for the French Grand Prix at Strasbourg in 1922.

Their *Tipo* 404 engines were based on the 1921 3 litre straight-eight *Tipo* 402, using the same 65 mm bore but destroked 12 mm for 1991 cc. Their steel cylinder blocks were now fabricated in pairs of three instead of pairs of four. The crankshaft was heavily counter-balanced and ran in eight main roller bearings whose compactness enabled this to be a notably short engine, measuring only 27½ in (69.85 cm) front to rear, but tall due to its long stroke. It used light-alloy pistons, while its valves were closed by triple valve-springs and opened by twin overhead camshafts, driven by vertical shaft, bevels and spur gears. Dry-sump lubrication was used and at Strasbourg these 6-cylinder engines developed 92-96 bhp at 4,500 rpm, a figure raised to 112 bhp at 5,000 rpm in time for the Italian GP.

A multi-plate clutch drove a four-speed gearbox in unit with the engine, as introduced to Grand Prix racing by Fiat in 1914. A torque-tube transmission was used to a live rear axle suspended on very short and stiff semi-elliptic springs. The axle itself was welded together from thin-gauge pressings. Unfortunately, one of its outboard flanges proved to be weak and in the Grand Prix at Strasbourg it broke away, causing two of the three cars to lose a wheel. A tubular front axle was used, with the springs passing through it. The four-wheel drum brakes were operated by cables and bell-cranks, and the foot-brake was servo-assisted by an oil-pump off the engine.

Director Fornaca decreed that the whole car should be kept as compact as possible, and its wheelbase was finalized at only 8 ft 2 in (2.49 m) and its track 47 in (1.19 m). Both the frame and axles had very slender proportions and the frame tapered in planform front and rear to match the body contours, which included a deeply enclosed cockpit and long tapering tail. The year's Grand Prix regulations stipulated a minimum weight of 645 kg (1,422 lb), and these factory Fiats weighed in around the 662 kg (1,456 lb) mark after being *driven* to Strasbourg from Turin! They became in fact the lightest cars to win a Grand Prix prior to 1939 ...

At Strasbourg, they were in a performance class of their own, exceeding 105 mph (175 km/h) along the narrow straights. Unfortunately, their back axle fragility caused an accident which killed Felice Nazzaro's nephew, Biagio, driving the number three car. Bordino's also broke, but on a slower part of the course where he could bring the car to rest safely. However, the veteran Nazzaro, who had last won the French classic 15 years earlier, won again in the surviving Fiat. Not only

July, 1922 — The ill-fated Biagio Nazzaro poses proudly in his factory team Fiat 803 at Strasbourg before the *GP de l'ACF* in which he was killed when the car's delicate back-axle failed at high speed near Entzheim. These lovely little 2 litre machines were otherwise quite the smallest, sleekest and fastest Grand Prix cars yet produced.

16 July, 1922 — Biagio's uncle Felice Nazzaro carefully guides his sole-surviving, mud-covered and victorious factory Fiat back into the paddock after the Strasbourg race, yet to learn the severity of his nephew's accident, while this shot emphasizes the Torinese car's small size against the surrounding crowd of officials, photographers and all-purpose hangers-on.

did Fiat's fastest lap of 87.75 mph (146.25 km/h) exceed Bugatti's best by over 7 mph (12 km/h) and Sunbeam's by over 9 mph (15 km/h), but Nazzaro's winning average speed of 79.2 mph (132 km/h) was a clear 10 mph (16.6 km/h) faster than the Bugatti which finished a very distant second. The new Fiats were uncatchable unless they broke. No serious rivals emerged for the Italian GP, where Fiat enjoyed a walk-over.

These cars established total superiority in the road racing field and made Fiat's pool of engineers vulnerable to poaching by other interested companies. Almost immediately, in fact, Louis Coatalen of Sunbeam-Talbot-Darracq engaged Bertarione who produced copy-cat GP Sunbeams for 1923-24. But Fornaca's men had not finished yet, because for 1923 they prepared what were to be the first-ever successful supercharged Grand Prix cars. Now we must digress. . .

Supercharging as a means of extracting increased horsepower from an internal-combustion engine had been known for many years. As early as 1907 Lee Chadwick in America had supercharged one of his racing engines, and Marc Birkigt of Hispano-Suiza had toyed with a system in Europe. Then, during the Great War, the need to maintain sea-level standards of power

output in aero engines operating at high altitude gave enormous impetus to supercharging and turbocharging technology. In Germany, Mercedes had developed a keen interest.

Immediately after the war French and British factions had agreed to stay away from major racing in 1919-20, and from 1921 to 1924 the revived French Grand Prix in common with other major international sporting events specifically barred German and Austrian entries.

During the war, the Mercedes experimental department under Wolfgang Schwerdtfeger had first experimented with supercharging in 1915, trying both vane and piston-type compressors. Paul Daimler had been disappointed by the performance of his Knight sleeve-valve engines for which he had high hopes, and in 1919 he tested one boosted by a tiny Roots-type supercharger. The idea proved disappointingly unreliable. The Mercedes-Knight programme quietly died, and in its place a range of small new single overhead camshaft 4-cylinder engines was introduced from 1921.

The first of these was the '10/40' unit, 80 mm x 130 mm, 2,600 cc, and in 1922 this became the '10/40/65' with a supercharger added. Later that year the DMG built their first engine designed from the ground up to be supercharged. It was called the '6/25/40' – or in-house the 'M68084' unit – 68 mm x 108 mm, 1,568 cc. It used a small Roots blower mounted vertically at the front and driven by bevel gears from a multi-plate clutch on the crankshaft nose. This device enabled the blower to be engaged only when the throttle was depressed to the floor. Otherwise it was at rest, relieving the engine of power drain which would diminish fuel economy. The supercharger blew pressurized air into an otherwise sealed carburettor. This would remain Mercedes' favoured order for many years.

In Sicily, Count Vincenzo Florio had no qualms about admitting German entries to his races, and in May 1921, Max Sailer drove a production-based Mercedes 28/25 in the Targa Florio and was only very narrowly beaten by Masetti's 1914 GP Fiat. Mercedes then returned to Sicily in 1922, with a massive and diverse team of cars. A 1,500 cc *Vetturetta* class was included which also held promise of races elsewhere, even in otherwise forbidden France.

Consequently, work began at Unterturkheim to develop the 1,568 cc M68084 supercharged engine into a 65 mm x 113 mm, 1,499 cc supercharged racing engine; the 'M65134'. This became the first Mercedes engine to use twin

overhead camshafts (driven by rear-mounted vertical shaft and worm gears) actuating four narrow-angled valves per cylinder. A 2.2-to-1 bevel gear step-up drive was provided for the supercharger, via a cone clutch for engagement. Power unblown was around 54 bhp at 4,000 rpm, rising to 72 bhp at 4,500 with the blower engaged. Up to 5,000 rpm was considered safe.

Two Targa cars were prepared with these engines amongst a massive works team of seven assorted machines for the 1922 race. The operation was planned in thorough 1914 style, 20 drivers and mechanics being posted in Sicily with test cars a month before. The new supercharged *Vetturetti* were to be driven by 'Nando Minoia and Unterturkheim employee Paul Scheef, but only in support of the uprated 1914 GP cars for Lautenschlager, Salzer and Masetti who won. A similar car to Sailer's 1921 production-based model was entrusted to Christian Werner, while Max Sailer had a basically similar 28/95, but supercharged with a gear train up the back of its block powering a vertical-mounted Roots blower. Credited with 140 bhp, this car was faster than all other Mercedes except Masetti's winner, and Sailer finished sixth in it. Minoia retired his supercharged *Vetturetta* and Scheef, slowed by

---

3 September, 1922 — Italian GP, Monza — Pietro Bordino's factory Fiat is hastily refuelled in the Autodrome's pit lane en route to winning the company's national Grand Prix race against feeble opposition. After the albeit marred demonstration at Strasbourg, no rival relished the thought of making the unprofitable trip to Italy to tackle the Italian marque on their home soil.

hitting a stray dog, finished twentieth overall, third in class.

The new 2 litre Grand Prix Formula for 1922-25 was also adopted for Indianapolis. The Americans had no objection to German entries so Mercedes built a team of blown 2 litre racers for the 1923 500-miles. They used a production-based 10/40/65 engine, with 10 mm narrower bore and 1 mm shorter stroke for 70 mm x 129 mm, 1,989 cc. Small-bore, long-stroke, was still fashionable at that time.

These 'M7294' Indy engines had twin overhead camshafts and four valves per cylinder like the Targa cars, plus roller-bearings, and for some reason their ports were reversed, exhausts moving to the right side, inlets on the left. Paul Daimler had just left to join Horch, so they were finalized at the last moment under Dr Ferdinand Porsche's direction who officially replaced him at Unterturkheim on 30 April 1923.

Four cars were shipped to Indy for drivers Max Sailer, Lautenschlager and Werner. They soon found the cars notoriously tricky in the wet and Sailer crashed when a brief shower interrupted qualifying. In the race, Lautenschlager engaged the blower too early in the South Turn and spun into the wall, hurting himself and his passenger, engine specialist Jakob Krauss. Werner, driving alone, finished eleventh, Max Sailer with his nephew Karl eighth. The two damaged cars were sold in the USA, one reappearing at Indy in 1924 as the Schmidt Special, and later with different engines . . .

Thus, Mercedes were already racing supercharged engines when Fiat adopted the new technology for their 1923 French Grand Prix cars. Their new *Tipo* 805.405 *Corsa* straight-eights – 60 mm x 87.5 mm, 1,979 cc – featured the usual twin overhead camshafts, gear-driven this time, actuating two valves per cylinder set now at 96°. Welded-steel cylinder construction was retained, in two sets of four this time, and the engine used roller bearings throughout.

Fornaca's engineers selected a Wittig vane-type compressor driven off the crankshaft nose. It was permanently engaged, delivering compressed air through a conduit cast into the engine base chamber and passing to the intake side of a sealed carburettor. A hinged flap or dump-valve was provided, operated by the riding mechanic, and it was intended to run the engine unblown in this manner 'at moderate speeds' or presumably

when the opposition was so far behind the crew could concentrate purely upon reliability rather than dicing. The Wittig supercharger was not very efficient and its boost was low, but Fiat claimed 130 bhp at 5,500 rpm – a stunning 65 bhp per litre. The engine was installed in a lengthened 8 ft 11 in (2.72 m) wheelbase chassis.

Fiat's engineers, however, disregarded a fatal flaw in their design. The Wittig blower's low-mounted intake was entirely unguarded and unfiltered, and at Tours for the 1923 Grand Prix the compressors ingested dust, stones and grit, wore, seized and disintegrated, and retired all three cars. They had, however, lapped 5 mph (8 km/h) faster than the 6-cylinder Fiat copy unsupercharged Sunbeams designed for Coatalen by Bertarione –which eventually inherited victory – and the significance of supercharging as the next great leap forward in Grand Prix technology had been rammed home.

Fiat had also had the point rammed home that the Wittig supercharger, even suitably guarded, had distinct limitations. They therefore adopted a permanently-engaged Roots-type compressor – *à la* Mercedes and still blowing into the carburettor – in time for the Italian GP, and in this form the *Tipo* 405 2 litre straight-eight gave around 140 bhp – 70 bhp per litre – and 136 mph (227 km/h) which gave Fiat a second consecutive home victory at Monza, quite untroubled. It was the first Formula victory with a supercharged engine.

By that time, however, Luigi Bazzi and Vittorio Jano had both been lured away to Alfa Romeo, and although Fiat ran their supercharged Grand Prix cars in the French Grand Prix of 1924 at Lyons-Givors they were soundly beaten by Jano's new supercharged Alfa Romeo P2 – another 'Fiat copy' . . .

The Lyons Fiats' power output had been raised to 146 bhp at 5,500 rpm, the Roots supercharger now drawing its air from a large cooler mounted between the dumb-irons. Mechanical brake servos replaced the hydraulic type and although they led at one stage, mechanical problems eliminated the entire team. Agnelli was not merely disappointed. He was enraged: 'With others stealing our best brains, we have become merely a training school . . .' Apart from one last brief but brilliant project in 1927, Fiat withdrew from Grand Prix racing – and have never yet returned under their own name.

The Alfa Romeo P2s

★ ★ ★ ★

The Alfa Romeo 'P2' Grand Prix car of 1924 was the vehicle which catapulted not only its designer, Vittorio Jano, to international prominence but also the fresh young Milan-based marque which it represented and which he had so recently joined from Fiat.

A.L.F.A. was taken from the initials of the *Societa Anonima Lombarda Fabbrica Automobili*, Milan being the capital of Lombardy. This enterprise had developed as the Italian wing of Frenchman Alexandre Darracq's motor business. He had been born in Bordeaux in 1855 and developed more as money man than engineer. He foresaw the profit potential in the infant bicycle trade as early as 1891, experimented with motor cycles and then in 1899 bought the rights to Léon Bollée's belt-drive quadricycles, such as inspired Louis Renault, whose shaft-drive in fact torpedoed Darracq's hopes for the Bollée system.

He lost a reputed £10,000 in the venture, but bounced back – with a degree of British financial backing – to sell a new shaft-drive car under his own name and aimed at the inexpensive end of the market. He built up quite a market in Italy, thanks to some good and energetic local agents, and the *Soc Anon Italiana Darracq* was founded in Naples in 1906, moving to Portello, on what was then the north-eastern fringe of Milan, at the end of that year.

Portello was to assemble kits supplied from Darracq's French factory at Suresnes, but the scheme flopped in the Agadir Crisis recession from 1907. In 1909 an enthusiastic Italian consortium raised a loan of 500,000 lire from the Milanese Banca Agricola, *Italiana Darracq* was liquidated and reformed as the company usually referred to as ALFA. Their products were designed by *Cavaliere* Giuseppe Merosi and proved superior to the cheap Darracqs, and sold well. Each one carried a *quadrifoglio* – four-leafed clover – badge for good luck.

The uncharacteristically cheerful-looking master engineer — Vittorio Jano, of Alfa Romeo.

In 1911 two ALFAs ran in the Targa Florio, and in 1914 Merosi produced a 4.5 litre Grand Prix car. Then came the Romeo take-over.

The Italian industrialist Nicola Romeo was born at San Antimo outside Naples on 28 April 1876. He graduated from Naples Polytechnic in 1900 with a degree in civil engineering, then added a degree in electrical engineering at Liège in Belgium. In 1902, he founded a Milanese agency associated with Ingersoll-Rand, and this became *Accomandita Ingegner Nicola Romeo e Cie*, manufacturing mining plant. He drove a tunnel through the Appenines for the Bologna-Florence railway, and when war broke out he made a fortune producing portable compressors for the Italian Army. He had over 1,000 employees, and in December 1915 he more than doubled his empire by buying a majority of shares in the ALFA car plant from the Banca di Sconto. Other businesses were acquired, and in February 1918 the group's name became *Societa Anonima Italiana Ing Nicola Romeo e Cie*. It had quickly absorbed an aircraft company (RO) in Naples, and added extensive railway rolling-stock plant.

Total manufacturing capacity at Portello had been turned over to wartime utility, but Romeo now encouraged Merosi to revive car production, under the name 'Alfa-Romeo', according to the badge; or popularly 'Alfa Romeo' without the hyphen.

Through the early 1920s, Fiat ruled the Grand Prix racing world. Their *Tipo* 804 2 litre design had set new standards in 1922, as did their supercharged *Tipo* 805 of 1923. At that time they had the most experienced and best technical brains in the Italian motor racing world, and Enzo Ferrari became instrumental in luring two of their best brains to Portello. The first was his friend Luigi Bazzi, a skilled fitter and development-tester; the other was *Ingegnere* Vittorio Jano – a hatchet-faced, stern young lion of Guido Fornaca's racing design section.

Nicola Romeo had been anxious to promote Alfa internationally, and had authorized *Ing* Merosi's attempt to produce a competitive GP car, the 'GPR' or 'P1', in 1923. It used a 6-cylinder unsupercharged twin overhead camshaft engine, but by the time it appeared it had already been outmoded by the latest supercharged straight-eight Fiat. Bazzi was involved, but the project ended in tragedy at Monza where popular chief tester Ugo Sivocci was killed in a crash during

practice, and Romeo withdrew the rest of the team in respect and grief.

Not only had Sivocci been chief tester at CMN, he had also been instrumental in arranging a job there for that enthusiastic young Emilian from Modena, Enzo Ferrari. Ferrari joined Alfa Romeo, having driven CMN – *Costruzione Meccaniche Nazionali* – cars in competition. Now he became an energetic 'Mr Fixit' in the racing world, and a pillar of Portello's racing activities.

Within the month, at Bazzi's urging, Ferrari called on Vittorio Jano at his modest third-floor flat in Turin's Via San Massimo, and offered him a more senior post with Alfa Romeo than anything he could expect short-term from Fiat. Jano was attracted by Ferrari's promise of becoming a bigger fish in a smaller pond, and after moving to Portello late in 1923, he combined all his personal genius plus his Fiat experience to produce the 'P2' Grand Prix car design which emerged in the metal in 1924.

He was son of the chief of the Torinese Arsenal, born in Turin on 2 April 1891. He had begun work in 1909 as a draughtsman with STAR (Giovanni Battista Ceirano's *Societa Torinese Automobili Rapid)*, but left them to join Fiat in 1911. There he worked under Guido Fornaca on both road and racing cars, and assumed major racing responsibility in 1923. Now through Ferrari, Nicola Romeo was grooming him to replace Merosi as Portello chief designer, which he would do in 1926.

Obviously, Jano's new 2 litre supercharged straight-eight Alfa Romeo 'P2' with twin-overhead camshafts was deeply influenced by Fiat practice. Its engine was made in a similar style with welded-steel cylinder blocks. Jano had experimentally supercharged an old 'P1', achieving 118 bhp against Merosi's original 80 bhp, and on the 'P2' his new supercharger conventionally – for the period – blew pressure-air into the carburettor, at around 10.5 psi. Like the Fiat both Alfa 'P1' and 'P2' engines used roller bearings, and the 'P2' even resembled the GP Fiats in its bodystyle and appearance, though its bullnose radiator was distinctive. Its gearbox was in unit with the engine.

Jano had the first 'P2' engine bench-testing in March 1924, and at 6 pm on 2 June the prototype car was completed at Portello. Drivers Giuseppe Campari and Antonio Ascari tested it at Monza, then on the Parma-Poggio di Berceto hill-climb.

3 August, 1924 — French GP, Lyons-Givors — Giuseppe Campari at speed in the Alfa Romeo P2 on his way to winning the great classic race, albeit by default when his team-mate Ascari's leading car broke down while leading. The well-fared bull-nosed P2 was a compact, balanced design with its major masses visibly well within the wheelbase, and a neat aerodynamic form by the standards of the time.

On 9 June, Ascari – with Bazzi as riding mechanic – won the 200 mile Circuit of Cremona race in it, averaging a remarkable 98.31 mph (163.85 km/h), and being timed at 121 mph-plus (202 km/h) along the 10 km straight. Campari drove at the inaugural Pescara meeting, but struck trouble, leaving Enzo Ferrari to win in an old Merosi-designed RL model.

Romeo despatched a works team of four new 'P2s' to Lyons-Givors for the French GP on 3 August. Drivers should have been Campari, Ascari, Louis Wagner and Enzo Ferrari but according to the latter he suffered a nervous breakdown before the race and his entry was withdrawn. At Lyons only the Campari and Wagner cars retained their Fiat-like long tapering tails, that on Ascari's car being cut short to house a single spare wheel.

The cars shone in Alfa's Grand Prix debut, Ascari trailing the leader Segrave's supercharged Fiat 805-copy Sunbeam until it struck trouble and Bordino's Fiat took over, still with Ascari and the 'P2' running second. But after 12 laps the Fiat's brakes failed, leaving Ascari leading for five laps until he stopped to change wheels. Lee Guinness's Sunbeam moved to the fore until his transmission broke, so Ascari and Campari were left in first and second places for the new marque from Milan. Wagner lay fifth, behind two V12 Delages.

Only three laps remained when Ascari stopped at his pits but his car's engine refused to restart, despite heroic efforts at push-starting by Giulio Ramponi – his riding mechanic. The car's block had cracked, and the leader was out. Campari thus inherited maiden victory for the 'P2', ahead of two Delages and Wagner, fourth.

The following month Mercedes withdrew their cars from the Italian GP at Monza, leaving Alfa a walk-over in which Ascari won by 16 min from Wagner and Campari in a 'P2' 1-2-3 triumph. By this time the 'P2s' used two Memini carburettors instead of just one, raising output from 134 bhp at 5,200 rpm, to 145 bhp at 5,500 rpm – 72.5 bhp per litre. The oil tank was resited under the passenger seat instead of mounting in the scuttle, where a reserve 5.5 gal (25 l) fuel tank was now adopted to cope with the twin-carb spec's increased fuel consumption. This lay out remained standard for the 5-600 mile (833-1,000 km) GP races contested through 1925, but for the remainder of the 'P2's factory racing career from 1926-29 none of its races exceeded 300 mile (500 km) in distance so this reserve tank was deleted and the scuttle-mounted oil tank reinstated.

For 1925, riding mechanics no longer had to be carried, although two-seat width bodies were retained with the single driver's seat off-set to one side. Alfa's programme did not recommence until 28 June when three team cars ran in the European GP at Spa-Francorchamps in Belgium. All carried spare-wheels in place of the original streamlined tail cowls. Wagner had moved to Delage so Count Gastone Brilli-Peri took his place in the third-string 'P2', only to break a spring and retire. But the Delages faltered too,

June 1925 — Belgian GP, Spa-Francorchamps — Antonio Ascari's winning Alfa Romeo P2 is replenished in the pits probably during practice judging from the pristine highly-polished appearance of the factory team car. The sister P2 driven home in second place by Campari stands beyond with Luigi Bazzi, Giulio Ramponi and Vittorio Jano looking on from left. From this season, GP team mechanics stayed in the pits and were no longer required to ride in the cars.

leaving Ascari and Campari to finish first and second – Alfa Romeo still dominating the Grand Prix field. The Belgian crowds gave the Italians' easy victory the bird, and Jano responded by calling in all his cars merely to be cleaned and brightly polished at the pits. He had a table laid there with great flourish, and entertained his drivers to a leisurely five-minute 'meal'. They knew how to rub-in supremacy, these Italians . . .

In July, the French GP was run at Montlhéry where the 'P2s' wore long tails, by this time relieved with three air-exit louvres to release pressure build-up within. But while leading the race, the exuberant Ascari pressed too hard, tangled with a paling fence lining the apex of a very fast left-hand curve, and crashed violently, rolling the 'P2' and sustaining fatal injuries. Campari inherited a four-minute lead from Delage and

Sunbeam, but as at Monza two years before, the tragedy persuaded the Italian team immediately to withdraw their surviving cars.

They reappeared in the Italian GP at Monza on 6 September, wearing 15 cm (6 in) shorter louvred tails, and against very thin opposition Brilli-Peri won from Costantini with American guest driver Pete de Paolo fifth in a single-carburettor 'P2'. Reserve driver was a racing motor cyclist named Tazio Nuvolari, but during practice his car's transmission seized, he crashed heavily and was injured. He would return . . .

The Italian GP win clinched that year's AIACR World Championship title for Alfa Romeo and to celebrate the fact a laurel wreath was added to the company's badge; it's still there today, over 60 years on.

The replacement 1.5 litre Grand Prix Formula for 1926 held no interest for Nicola Romeo, but his 'P2s' continued to contest the many *Formule Libre* events still being organized.

What may have been Ascari's 1924 Lyons-winning car was sold to Campari who had it modified with a spare wheel mounting added to the tail's left-side, where the exhaust pipe was swept down to accommodate it. He won the important Coppa Acerbo race at Pescara in both 1927 and 1928 with this car, before selling it to 26-year-old Achille Varzi for the European GP at Monza, in which Campari shared the driving and they finished second behind Chiron's Bugatti. Another 'P2' had been sold to the Materassi team, whose patron Emilio Materassi was killed – together with 23 hapless spectators – when he crashed his Talbot opposite the pits at Monza. The 'P2' went to Brilli-Peri, and he ran it for the first time with an enlarged 2,006 cc engine at Cremona on 28 September, being timed at 138.4 mph (230.7 km/h) along the straight on which Ascari's prototype 1,987 cc car had clocked 121 mph (202 km/h) five years earlier . . . such is progress, and Brilli-Peri won handsomely.

The 2,006 cc capacity was achieved by a tiny increase in bore, from 61 mm to 61.5 mm, matching the unchanged 85 mm stroke. Varzi retained a 2 litre engine in his car and during 1929 he won the Monza GP and at Rome, Alessandria and Montenero (Leghorn), placed second at Cremona and became the year's *Campione Assoluta d'Italia*.

Through the following winter into 1930, Alfa Romeo reconsidered the continuing potential of the 'P2' in view of such success. Jano schemed modifications to give the ancient cars another season at or near the top, and the company bought back both Varzi's and Brilli-Peri's cars, and also retrieved one which had been used in the Argentine by Vittorio Rosa. It would be assigned to the newly-formed independent Scuderia Ferrari organization in Modena.

Jano ordered all engines enlarged to 2,006 cc, and paid great attention to refining the induction system and experimenting with newly- formulated Shell fuels to replace the original 'Elcosina' mix. The supercharger now drew mixture from the carburettor instead of blowing pressurized air into it, and these 1930 'P2' engines developed around 175 bhp at 5,500 rpm – 87.5 bhp per litre.

While the chassis wheelbase was left unaltered, new 6C-1750 production axles were adopted front and rear to increase track, the whole suspension was updated and the 6C braking and steering fitted. Rear springs became parallel to the centreline instead of following the tapering chassis rails, and all road-springs were now outside the rails, as close to the wheels as possible to improve control. A spare wheel was housed longitudinally to add rearward weight bias, in a central slot sunk into the tip of the tail. The original bullnose radiator was also replaced by a raked, modern flat matrix, and the bonnet was remade to match, adopting a slightly less round-shouldered form. The oil tank returned to beneath the passenger seat for the first time since 1925. Cockpit space was also improved simply by enlarging the cut-out.

Standard capacity became 2,006 cc, and output rose to 175 bhp. The cars were referred to at the time simply as the *Alfa Corsa* - presumably because they were the only proper racing models Alfa had at the time. One penalty of Jano's modifications, however, was a hefty increase in weight from something like 750 kg (1,653.45 lb) to nearer 780 kg (1,719.59 lb), including the spare wheel. However, the lighter figure with the former 145 bhp provided 0.08 bhp per lb – while in comparison the 1930 figure corresponds to 0.1 bhp per lb — a distinct improvement.

Varzi drove his former car to win handsomely first time out at Alessandria, and Portello then entered him in the Targa Florio, where he demolished Bugatti's long record of consecutive victories and won again. This was received in Italy as a sensational coup.

Thereafter, the incredibly fast new Maserati 8C-2500 generally ate the modified 'P2s' for breakfast. At the Monza GP the three powerful '30-spec 'P2s' gobbled their tyres, but Nuvolari – who had set three major FTDs in important mountain climbs in a Scuderia Ferrari-entered car – and Campari finished 1-2 in the Consolation race, and Borzacchini finished second in the 3 litre heat.

The Czechoslovakian GP at Brno on 28 September saw the swansong of the elderly 'P2s', Nuvolari leading towards the finish in Borzacchini's original car after his own had retired, only for the engine to overheat badly – leaving him to limp home, the car crippled and steaming, in third place behind private Bugattis.

The long career of the cars which Vittorio Jano loved most had reached its end.

The Miller Straight-8s

★ ★ ★ ★ ★

Once Jimmy Murphy had won the French GP for Duesenberg in 1921, he stunned many of his admirers back home in the USA by mounting a new 3 litre straight-eight engine in his Duesey, an engine made not by Duesenberg, but out in Los Angeles, Calfornia, by the carburettor specialist, Harry Armenius Miller. Murphy was scolded for 'wasting his time with those cowboys out West . . .', but he came back with the perfect answer — he won the Indianapolis '500' in his Miller-engined Duesenberg. This launched Miller on a course which established his cars and engines as the ultimate jewels in what has rightly been called 'The Golden Age of American Racing '.

Harry Miller was a first-generation American, born in Menomonie, Wisconsin on 9 December 1875, the son of a German father, Jakob Müller, and a Canadian mother. His father had studied in a seminary before emigrating to the USA, where he became a teacher. He was a creative man, a skilled linguist, a capable musician and a painter. He had five children, and Harry showed natural mechanical aptitude. He left school at 13 and settled in Los Angeles in 1895 where he worked in a bicycle shop, building racing 'bikes on the side. He became engaged to Edna Inez 'Nezzie' Lewis, from Azusa, and they settled briefly in Menomonie where Harry became foundry fore-man at the Globe Iron Works, and in his spare time built motor cycles. By 1899 he had established his own bicycle shop in Santa Monica, but then he moved to San Francisco, joining Leavitt & Bill cycles. From 1902-05 he worked in the Pawling & Olive machine shop back in Los Angeles.

While there he patented a spark plug design, sold the rights to Peerless and around 1905 built a primitive prototype car. For a few brief months that year Miller worked at Kirk Manufacturing in Toledo, Ohio, building the Yale car, then for much of 1906 the wandering technician earned his keep at the Olds Motor Works in Lansing, Michigan. There he had his first taste of motor racing, preparing a stripped 4-cylinder production Oldsmobile for the 1907 Vanderbilt Cup Eliminating Trials. Miller rode as mechanic to driver Ernie Keeler, but the car was hopeless.

Soon after this episode, Miller returned to Los Angeles, developed a range of carburettors and fuel pumps and founded what became the Miller Carburettor Co to manufacture them. His car-burettors soon won a fine reputation in racing, and Harry Miller's modest factory became a West Coast Mecca for the racing fraternity. Miller as a man was extraordinarily popular amongst both his workforce and his customers. He was very much an intuitive engineer, an aesthetic 'feel' emerged in all his designs. In generally 'shooting the breeze' with some of the most capable and talented racers of his day he absorbed perhaps more of their knowledge than they of his . . .

In 1915 contemporary superstar driver Bob Burman came to Miller with his wrecked 1913 Peugeot L56 engine. He asked Miller to replace it with new, and if possible to improve its original *Charlatan* design. Working with his practical-minded but similarly perfectionist shop foreman Fred Offenhauser, Miller drew up a slightly improved version of this Peugeot 4-cylinder which promptly out-performed the French original on track.

Through 1916 he then experimented with original engine designs of his own. He produced a 5 litre 16-valve 4-cylinder unit powering an impossibly claustrophobic Coupe named '*The Yellow Submarine*' which was supplied to Barney Oldfield. He set new US dirt-track records from one lap at 45 sec to 50 miles (83 km), and on Chicago Board Speedway exceeded 107 mph (178 km/h) with this car.

In 1917 the US Government commissioned Miller carburettors and fuel pumps for the Bugatti-King 'U16' aero engines which Duesenberg were helping develop in the east. Experience of these engines taught Miller and Offenhauser much, especially about what not to do ...

Postwar, Duesenberg built a 5 litre racing straight-eight, two of which Tommy Milton used in his 155 mph (258 km/h) LSR car in 1920.

That year, Miller and Offenhauser took on a brilliant young design draughtsman named Leo Goossen, and when Milton split from Duesenberg, he approached Miller for a speedway racing engine to put Duesey in their place ... and one was already on the stocks. All Miller had been waiting for was a client to fund its building. On Milton's behalf, mutual friend Barney Oldfield borrowed $5,000 deposit from Henry Ford to finance the Miller job.

The Duesenberg straight-eight, with three-main bearing crankshaft, dry-sump lubrication etc, was Miller's starting point. His experience with the Burman Peugeot came into play, as he instructed Goossen to detail a twin overhead camshaft, 32-valve top end for the new Milton engine. The valves were inclined at an included angle of 60° in pent-roof combustion chambers, actuated by piston-type cam followers – an improvement on Peugeot plunger-type practice and one already made by Ernest Henry's new Ballot straight-eight.

Driver Ira Vail ordered a second engine, but early tests revealed problems with detachable head sealing and fragile crankshafts. Miller recast the blocks with fixed heads to eliminate the head-seal problem. The three-bearing crankshaft was continuously developed, eventually to carry careful counterweighting. A wider plain bearing replaced the Duesenberg-style ballbearing at the rear main, and Bosch magneto ignition replaced the original battery type. Eventually a cam-form derived from Duesenberg's Hall-Scott modification set the new Miller engines singing. Using four twin-choke Miller carburettors, these 3 litre straight-eight racing engines delivered around 125 bhp at 3,500 rpm – 41 bhp per litre – and ultimately Milton's own approached 185 bhp at 4,400 rpm – 61.6 bhp per litre.

Original Leo Goossen drawings for the Miller 183 Straight-8.

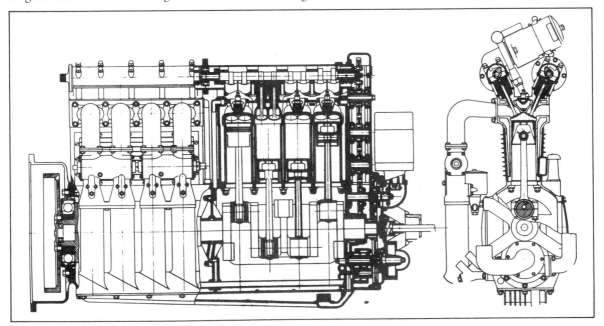

Razor-blade—The AAA Formula's deletion of the riding mechanic from 1923 enabled Miller to adopt purebred single-seater body forms for his new series of 122-in³ cars, as demonstrated here on the Indianapolis bricks by Cliff Durant — son of the founder of General Motors — who entered a team of five. Eddie Hearne won the 1923 National Championship in one of these Durant Millers and in 1924 Jimmy Murphy secured the title in his own ex-Durant team car, only to die in it at Syracuse in the last event of the series.

At least eight of these 183 cid cars were built, but the 183 cid Formula expired at the end of 1922. The third Miller 183 engine was the one fitted by Jimmy Murphy into his French GP-winning Duesenberg, to win the 1922 Indy '500', and the AAA National Championship.

Miller had begun building his own super-light chassis once he was satisfied that the new engine was debugged, and the true age of the Miller racing car had dawned. As Miller authority Griffith Borgeson has noted, 'Practically every part of every Miller car was made in Miller's own plant. All non-ferrous castings were made in the factory's own foundry and only the cast-iron cylinder blocks were cast elsewhere. All machine work and sheet metal work was done on the premises and even the flawless frames were hammered out of flat sheet stock by hand. Miller purchased the rims for his wheels but, profiting from the failures of others, machined his own Rudge-type hubs

from forged billets. He made his own axles, steering linkages, steering gearboxes, clutches, transmissions, gears, crankshafts and even shock absorbers. And there was an engineering drawing for every part. Only such obvious items as magnetos and instruments were purchased from the outside . . .'

Light weight was a Miller obsession, as well as finish and detail aesthetics. He insisted upon the removal of machining and file marks from finished parts, and castings were hand-scraped and polished to a satin sheen; through the 1920s every Miller car embodied some 6,000-6,500 man hours work. According to Fred Offenhauser, '. . . betwen 700 and 1,000 hours went into beautifying, just putting the finish on each machine . . .'

At the behest of Indianapolis Motor Speedway owner Carl Fisher, the AAA introduced a new 122 cid – 2 litre – Formula from the Indy '500' on 30 May 1923. This was a sharp rebuff for wealthy Cliff Durant of General Motors fame, who had just had an entire team of *six* brand-new 183s built for him by Miller! His cars still notched considerable success until Indy '23, where three of them ran in linered-down 122 cid form.

Riding mechanics were dispensed with and true narrow-bodied, central single-seat racing car configuration was established. Miller and Goossen's new 122 cid straight-eight corrected the 183s' weak bottom end with five main bearings instead of three, and the superb result assumes special historic significance as the first pure-bred racing car ever to enter series customer production . . .

These Miller 122s produced around 120 bhp at 5,000 rpm – 60 bhp per litre – and the engines weighed just 303 lb (138 kg). Three two-seat-bodied Grand Prix versions were also built, possibly based on the 'other three' Durant team 183s. European rules still demanded a riding mechanic. Bought by the Argentinian playboy Martin de Alzaga (two) and Count Louis Zborowski of Brooklands 'Chitty-Bang-Bang' fame they really proved unsuitable for road racing.

The Miller 122s utterly dominated board speedway racing through much of 1923 and on through 1924, Eddie Hearne and Jimmy Murphy winning the Championship titles, although the Le Mans and Indy victor crashed fatally at Syracuse in September '24.

At Indianapolis that year a centrifugally-supercharged Duesenberg narrowly won the '500'. Fred and Augie had kept their experiments in this area top secret until the race. Now Harry Miller and Leo Goossen reacted swiftly, and although a supercharged Duesenberg won Indy again in 1925, thereafter it was Miller's centrifugally-supercharged straight-eights which reigned supreme. Miller mounted his exquisitely sculptured blower laterally at the rear of his 122 engines, stepped up to 5.65 times the crankshaft speed via gears off the camshaft tails. Retro kits were sold for $1,100 to owners of existing unblown cars. At Indy in 1925, 16 Millers ran, 11 of them blown. As the 122 cid Formula ran into the early months of 1926, Bennett Hill raised the Atlantic City board speedway record to a mind-boggling 146.7 mph (244.5 km/h) in a blown Miller 122, and Harry Hartz's sister car completed a full 300 miles (500 km) there at 134 mph (223 km/h) . . . The cars also established 12 world records between five and 500 miles.

Miller chewed on ways to lower his cars' centres of gravity, reduce unsprung weight and improve handling. Front-wheel drive was a possibility, and he considered a transverse engine, but rejected it as a better alternative occurred. His drivers were sitting above the prop-shaft in the rear-drive cars, a front-drive would delete the prop-shaft, which would enable the driver's seat to drop down between the chassis rails. With a longitudinal engine mounting up front he could capitalize upon the absolute minimum package size, a car whose frontal aspect was hardly greater than that of its engine cross-section, axles and wheels.

Jimmy Murphy eventually listened to Miller's arguments and during 1924 ordered a 122 front-drive – Miller historian Mark Dees reporting it as 'Job 6117' – but he was killed two months before its completion that November.

Miller had turned around a straight-eight engine, putting the clutch end in the car's nose, and with Goossen devised a jewel-like front-drive

Articulate, respected, highly-skilled; Tommy Milton in his new blue and red Miller '183 convertible' at Indy in 1924. This was the last of the 3 litre Millers to be built, and the first 183 to use single-seater bodywork from new. With the 183 in³ engine it was intended for record-breaking and non-Formula match races, but a 122 in³ — 2 litre — engine would go in for AAA Formula events. At Muroc Dry Lake in April 1924 Milton achieved 151.26 mph (252.1 km/h) in it — over 17 mph (28 km/h) beyond Europe's fastest at that time. The truss rods below the frame were a Milton tweak intended to stiffen the notoriously whippy Miller chassis. The wheel discs clipped over the spokes were claimed to be worth a second a lap on board speedways.

transaxle. Its output shafts on each side support-ed inboard-mounted front drum brakes, acting through the half-shafts to the front wheels which were carried on each end of a de Dion axle, a layout inspired by the cars already laid out this way by front-drive pioneer Ben F. Gregory from Kansas City, Missouri. Miller, however, patented his system, and the famous 'coffin-nosed' Cord L29 sedans subsequently adopted it in product-ion. Miller racing cars became available in either front-drive or rear-drive form. At least 12 Miller front-drives seem to have been built between 1924 and 1929.

When the Formùla was again down-rated to only 91 cid – 1,500 cc – from Indy 1926, the new Miller '91' engines differed mainly from their 183 cid – 2 litre – predecessors by driving the supercharger via gear-train from the flywheel-end of the crankshaft instead of using gears from the camshaft tails where torsional problems had arisen.

The original centrifugally-supercharged 1926 Miller '91' delivered no less than 154 bhp –102 bhp per litre. Development through the next four seasons raised this figure to an astonishing 252 bhp at 8,000 rpm – 168 bhp per litre! Europe's outstanding Grand Prix car during that period was the Delage straight-eight, also a supercharged 1.5 litre straight-eight; it produced at best 170 bhp – 113 bhp per litre. In its defence, this is the mark of differing characteristics between the Roots-type supercharging beneficial for road racing, and the Americans' centrifugal supercharger, ideal for their high-rpm steady-state racing round the speedways.

Nonetheless, Miller power outputs were way in advance of contemporary European technology, and most astonishing of all was the engine super-tuned by young genius driver Frank Lockhart, which achieved 280 bhp at 8,500 rpm – a magnifi-cent 186 bhp per litre . . .

In 1927, burning normal petrol/benzol fuel, Lockhart's Miller '91' clocked 171 mph (285 km/h) one-way on Muroc Dry Lake, California, and averaged 164.009 mph (273.348 km/h) two-way. Since the contemporary Land Speed Record stood to Malcolm Campbell's monstrous *Bluebird* at only 174 mph (290 km/h), Lockhart was inspired to set-up a serious LSR project. He conceived a V, coupled-crankshaft 3 litre engine by combining two 1,500 cc Miller straight-eight blocks on a common crankcase. The exquisitely-

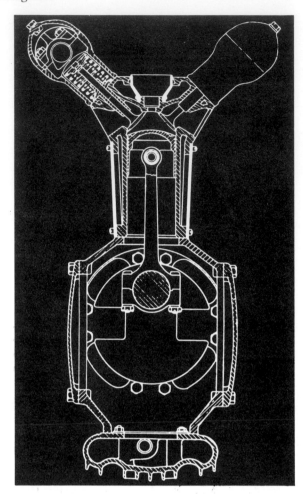

Sculptured simplicity: engine section of the American Speedway Miller 91.

detailed and streamlined car to carry this engine was backed by Stutz, and the result was a gorgeous stiletto compared to the blunt-instrument LSR cars common until then. Lock-hart was driving this *Black Hawk Stutz* at well over 200 mph (333 km/h) along Ormonde Beach at Daytona when a tyre deflated and he was killed in the ensuing disaster.

Meanwhile, regular track-racing Miller '91s' were effectively available to all. The '91' engine cost a round $5,000, a complete, ready to go rear-drive car $10,000, a front-drive car $15,000. Millers finished 1-2-3-4 in the 1926 Indy '500' and dominated the Formula until it ended in' 1929.

In 1926 Ernest Eldridge had broken many world records at Montlhéry in a 2 litre Miller, including the flying-mile at 136.26 mph (227 km/h). In

1927 Pete Kreis and Earl Cooper took their Miller '91s' to the European GP at Monza, and Kreis finished third. In 1929 Leon Duray fielded two '91' front-drives in Europe, breaking Class F records at Montlhéry, including the flying-start five-miles at 139.22 mph (232 km/h). He then broke the lap record, both his cars and his bank balance in the Monza GP. Ettore Bugatti bought the damaged cars, faithfully copied the Miller twin-cam hemi-head layout for his own engines and profited greatly from it in succeeding years.

While in America the Depression brought about the all-time low of the Indianapolis 'Junk Formula' and Miller's gorgeous little jewels were hacked about or forgotten, Miller engines still reigned supreme in 8-cylinder and 4-cylinder form, the four-cylinder 4.2 litre marketed under Offenhauser's name winning every Indy '500' save three until the Lotus-Ford V8 invasion in 1965.

Through the 1930s, the fearless lady driver Gwenda Stewart set new world records at up to 139.41 mph (232.35 km/h) at Montlhéry in her Miller. With this car then modified as a Derby-Miller in 1934, she set an all-time class record of

---

Showman — George Stewart, alias 'Leon Duray', showing off his brilliant purple and yellow '*Packard Cable Spl*' front-drive Miller 91 in Europe, in the autumn of 1929. This was the only front-drive to be produced by the Californian factory that year. After breaking the transmission during the Italian GP by trying to change-down on the Monza Autodrome's road section when in hot pursuit of local opposition, Stewart sold two of these cars to Ettore Bugatti who faithfully copied Miller's twin-cam head design from them for his Bugatti Type 51.

147.79 mph (246.32 km/h) for the flying mile.

Throughout a period when Europeans were too often blinded by what they saw as the brilliance evident in Grand Prix race engineering, Harry Armenius Miller and his Californian-based team were setting truly new standards on the other side of the Atlantic . . . but in a very different kind of racing. All their cars were exquisitely engineered, and delightfully well-finished. Their creator has been described as an American Ettore Bugatti – but this writer will readily accept that H. A. Miller was the greater genius . . . Mr Bugatti never quite made it as a European Harry Armenius Miller. . .

There can be no doubt that the mainstream American motor industry's total lack of support for racing opened the door to Harry Miller's cars. If you wanted to race and win in America between 1922 and 1930, in effect you bought a Miller. Big industry's total disregard for racing deprived the sport of promotion, general public interest and big money – save for Indianapolis which always protected its primacy by amassing the biggest purse from sponsors.

Even the sanctioning body, the American Automobile Club, seemed to regard racing as an onerous activity to which it was wedded merely by tradition and necessity rather than interest and enthusiasm. No other body would have it.

The AAA's National Championship series was wedded securely to the board tracks, which from 1920 to 1927 hosted all but a very few of the Championship rounds. But the board tracks dried, splintered, rotted and died. Even before the Wall Street Crash in October 1929, of the big board tracks, only Altoona – at Tipton, Pennsylvania – survived, and it was closed down and demolished after 1931.

In January 1929 the AAA Contest Board announced their new rules to take effect from the Indy '500' of 1930. They were going to abandon the form of racing which had brought Miller to prominence, and which had projected US racing car technology so far ahead of Europe's. They were going to ban supercharging, to admit large-capacity production-based 'stock-block' engines and insist upon two-seat bodies again carrying (and risking) riding mechanics. The new class was derisively dubbed 'The Junk Formula' and it would run at Indy, and elsewhere largely upon the one-mile oval dirt racks mostly originated for horse-racing at the annual State Fairgrounds

Bob McDonough at Indianapolis in 1929 with M.R. Dodds' ex-Pete de Paolo Miller 91 front-drive. In 1927 this car had carried de Paolo to the National Championship. Note its forward de Dion tube, inboard drum brakes, bulbous front-drive unit and exceptionally low build — only thigh-high to the bystanders. With the advent of the 'Junk Formula' for 1930 — which cost so many lives by reinstituting the riding mechanic — this front-drive frame was sold to Harry Hartz. Converted into his two-seat Miller-Hartz front-drive it gave Billy Arnold dominant victory in the 1930 Indy '500', using a Miller 122 engine somehow enlarged to 151.5 in³.

Lou Meyer at Indy, 1929, in the most famous rear-drive Miller 91 of them all — the original 1926 car taken over from Pete Kreis by Frank Lockhart for that year's '500'. The Kid promptly won, and finished that season Championship runner-up, grossing nearly $67,000. He and the Weisel brothers then perfected their supercharge intercooler on this car in 1927, and Lockhart clocked 171.02 mph (285.03 km/h) at Muroc, 147.7 mph (246 km/h) for the Atlantic City lap and took the first 120 mph-plus (200 km/h) Indy pole in it. After Lockhart's death on Ormond Beach in 1928, Tony Gulotta drove the 91 at Indy then Lockhart's widow sold it to Alden Sampson II for Champion Meyer's use. As late as 1932, with an unblown 230 in³ engine, the old car contributed to Meyer's protégé Bob Carey's National Championship.

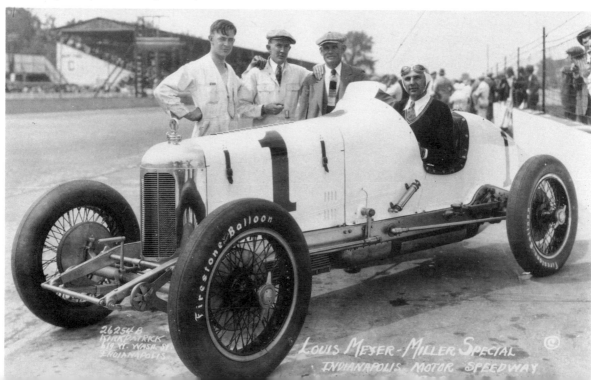

around the nation. By 1932 only Indy offered National Championship racing on a hard-surfaced (brick) oval; the other five races in a pathetic shadow series each being run on dirt.

Still Miller engines, and the occasional Miller chassis, featured strongly, but the glory days were long gone. Few appear to have researched this era more thoroughly – nor done more to separate race-result fact from myth – than American enthusiasts John Printz and Ken McMacken. Their findings show that Miller cars won 87 significant AAA races in the 17 seasons from 1921 to 1937 – including every event run at this level in 1923, 1928 and 1929. From 1922-29 they were beaten only 16 times in National Championship level races. Their winning record included astonishing average speeds on all the board speedways (which were always much faster than Indianapolis); over distances up to 300 miles, the track-racing Millers always averaged 100 mph-plus and all of this 60 or more years ago ...*

On 19 April 1925, Harry Hartz's Miller won a 50-Mile race at Culver City at an average speed of 135.23 mph (225.5 km/h).

On 1 May 1926, Hartz and his Miller won a 300-Mile race at Atlantic City at an average speed of 134.091 mph (223.485 km/h).

Ultimately, during qualifying at Atlantic City on 5 May, 1927, Frank Lockhart's Miller '91' lapped at an average speed of 147.729 mph (246.215 km/h)!

Relative to Hartz's April 1925, 135 mph (225 km/h) average over 50 miles at Culver City, in England that year J. G. Parry Thomas raised his own Brooklands Outer Circuit lap record to only 129.36 mph (216 km/h), then unofficially to 129.7 mph (216.17 km/h), which was more than 5 mph *slower* over nearly 48 miles *less distance* than the American mark.

In 1929 the Brooklands Outer Circuit record was raised by John Cobb and Kaye Don in V12 Delage and Sunbeam respectively, each lapping at 132.11 mph (220.18 km/h) ...

This was two years *after* Frank Lockhart had circulated Atlantic City's high-banked boards more than 15 mph *faster* with an engine just 37.5 per cent the size of the Sunbeam's 4 litre V12 and a measly 14.3 per cent the size of the Delage's 10.5 litre V12. Regarding the relative merits of these opposing kinds of closed-track racing, there's clearly a moral in there somewhere ...

Perhaps this says as much about the venues as about the cars which used them, but such flat-out speed and reliability was something which the perhaps more celebrated European *grands marques* had no way of matching. This was truly the golden age of the American racing car and Miller's single-seaters were its apotheosis.

* The fastest of the Board Speedways were the 1¼-mile Culver City track, at Los Angeles, California, and the 1½-mile Atlantic City track, at Hammonton, New Jersey.

AMERICAN TRACK-RACING MILLER VICTORIES 1921-37
Key: B introduces a wooden Board Speedway; FrWD = Front-Wheel Drive Miller car; (dirt) = dirt track.

	Miles		mph
1921			
Tacoma B	250	Tommy Milton	98.3
1922			
Beverly Hills B	250	Tommy Milton	110.8
Beverly Hills	25	Tommy Milton	115.17
Beverly Hills	25	Frank Elliott	114.52
Beverly Hills	50	Tommy Milton	115.24
Cotati B	50	Frank Elliott	116.15
Cotati	100	Frank Elliott	113.7
Kansas City B	300	Tommy Milton	107.86
Fresno B	150	Bennett Hill	103.8
Beverly Hills	250	Jimmy Murphy	114.6

(During this season, Jimmy Murphy also won the Indianapolis '500', Cotati 100, Uniontown 225 and Tacoma 250 with his Miller-engined GP Duesenberg.)

1923				
Beverly Hills	250		Jimmy Murphy	115.65
Fresno	150		Jimmy Murphy	103.55
Indianapolis	500		Tommy Milton/Howdy Wilcox	90.95
Kansas City	250		Eddie Hearne	105.76
Altoona B	200		Eddie Hearne	111.51
Fresno	150		Harry Hartz	103.20
Kansas City	250		Harlan Fengler	113.20
Beverly Hills	250		Bennett Hill	116.6
1924				
Beverly Hills	250		Harlan Fengler	116.6
Altoona (June)	250		Jimmy Murphy	114.7
Kansas City	150		Jimmy Murphy	114.43
Altoona (Sept)	250		Jimmy Murphy	113.95
Fresno	150		Earl Cooper	105.68
Charlotte B	250		Tommy Milton	118.17
Culver City B	250		Bennett Hill	126.78
1925				
Culver City	250		Tommy Milton	126.88
Charlotte	250		Earl Cooper	121.6
Altoona	250		Bob McDonough	118.4
Laurel B	250		Bob McDonough	126.3
Culver City	250		Frank Elliott	127.87
1926				
Culver City	250		Bennett Hill	131.29
Atlantic City B	300		Harry Hartz	134.09
Charlotte	250		Earl DeVore	120.08
Indianapolis	500		Frank Lockhart	95.88
Altoona	250	FrWD	Dave Lewis	112.43
Salem B	200	FrWD	Earl Cooper	116.37
Atlantic City	60		Harry Hartz	128.66
Atlantic City	60		Norm Batten	120.75
Atlantic City	60		Fred Comer	124.74
Atlantic City	120		Harry Hartz	123.41
Charlotte	25	FrWD	Earl Cooper	128.93
Charlotte	25	FrWD	Dave Lewis	125.32
Charlotte	50		Frank Lockhart	122.54
Charlotte	150		Frank Lockhart	120.88
Altoona	250		Frank Lockhart	116.38
Salem	25		Bennett Hill	130.05
Salem	25	FrWD	'Leon Duray'*	130.39
Salem	200		Harry Hartz	123.26
Charlotte	25		Frank Lockhart	132.40
Charlotte	25	FrWD	Dave Lewis	127.02
Charlotte	50		Harry Hartz	129.35
Charlotte	100	FrWD	'Leon Duray'	122.04
1927				
Culver City	250	FrWD	'Leon Duray'	124.71
Atlantic City	200	FrWD	Dave Lewis	130.06
Altoona	200	FrWD	Pete de Paolo	116.57

*Racing pseudonym of George Stewart

Salem	200	FrWD	Pete de Paolo	124.35
Altoona	200		Frank Lockhart	116.70
Charlotte	25		Frank Lockhart	127.66
Charlotte	50		Frank Lockhart	125.99
Charlotte	100		Babe Stapp	119.91
Salem	65		Frank Lockhart	125.70
Salem	75		Frank Lockhart	126.67

1928

Indianapolis	500		Louis Meyer	99.48
Detroit (dirt)	100		Ray Keech	77.87
Salem	15	FrWD	'Leon Duray'	130.59
Salem	185		Ray Keech	122.73
Altoona	200		Louis Meyer	116.62
Syracuse (dirt)	100		Ray Keech	75.30
Salem	62.5		Cliff Woodbury	117.00

1929

Indianapolis	500		Ray Keech	97.58
Detroit (dirt)	100		Cliff Woodbury	76.22
Altoona	148.75		Louis Meyer	119.00
Syracuse (dirt)	100		Wilbur Shaw	81.06
Altoona	200		Louis Meyer	112.55

1930

Langhorne (dirt)	100		Bill Cummings	77.30

(Six more major events were won with Miller engines powering chassis of other manufacture.)

1931

Altoona	100		Lou Moore	108.70
Syracuse (dirt)	100		Lou Moore	75.00

(Four more major events were won by Miller-engined cars.)

1932

Oakland (dirt)	150		Bill Cummings	90.45

(Five other major events were won by Miller-engined cars.)

1933

Indianapolis	500		Louis Meyer	104.16
Detroit (dirt)	100		Bill Cummings	73.90
Syracuse (dirt)	100		Bill Cummings	81.86

1934

Indianapolis	500		Bill Cummings	104.86
Springfield (dirt)	100		Billy Winn	77.76

(One other major event was won by a Miller-engined car.)

1935

Springfield (dirt)	100		Billy Winn	80.38
Syracuse (dirt)	100		Billy Winn	83.54

(One other major event was won by a Miller-engined car.)

1936

Syracuse (dirt)	100		Mauri Rose	82.37

(One other major event was won by a Miller-engined car.)

1937

Syracuse (dirt)	100		Billy Winn	87.49

The Delage Straight-8s

★ ★ ★ ★ ★

Louis Delage was one of the last great French manufacturers to have found his feet in racing around the turn of the century, yet be still actively involved come the late 1920s. His straight-eight engined 1.5 litre Grand Prix cars of 1926-27 were his last grand gesture before this flamboyant, big-spending extrovert's money finally ran out. In building his team of four new Grand Prix cars, he is reputed to have spent £36,000 – a staggering sum by the standards of the time.

Heart of these low-slung, offset single-seat GP Delages was an engine design by *Ingenieur* Albert Lory which won universal acclaim for its complex architectural beauty. Louis Delage's cousin, *Ingenieur* Planchon, had produced an even more complex 2 litre V12-cylinder Grand Prix engine for the marque in 1923. Development of this 2LCV model had continued successfully to the end of 1925, and it had won the French and Spanish GPs. But now the Grand Prix Formula had changed, cutting engine capacity from 2 to 1.5 litres, and Delage had fallen out with Planchon.

In his place he commissioned Albert Lory, who had joined the Courbevoie company from Salmson along with the man who would became Delage's leading driver, Robert Benoist. Lory examined the problems posed by the new GP Formula and decided that rather than develop a smaller-capacity version of Planchon's fiendish but exquisitely effective V12, he would opt for the simpler straight-eight layout.

His new engine emerged with an iron fixed-head cylinder block mounted above an alloy crankcase. Twin overhead camshafts driven from the nose of the crankshaft by a complex train of spur-gears actuated 16 overhead valves. Two Roots-type superchargers were fitted, and what really captured the motoring world's attention was Lory's implacable vendetta with internal friction, which he fought by using ball and roller-race bearings throughout.

No less than 62 were used – the 10 built-up main bearings for the one-piece crankshaft, the big ends, camshaft bearings, and within a cascade of 21 timing and auxiliary gears powering water pump, oil pumps, camshafts and magneto; all were ball or roller-bearings. The two superchargers were slung on the engine's left-hand side driven by internal shaft from the forward gear-train, providing some 7.5 psi boost. The ignition magneto was driven off a similar shaft on the right-side of the engine. Both shafts ran, of course, in ball-race bearings. Fuel mixture was petrol/alcohol/benzol/ether and when introduced in 1926 the new GP Delage developed around 165 bhp – 110 bhp per litre.

Lory adopted dry-sump lubrication, with powerful scavenge and pressure pumps clearing the engine base chamber and feeding the main-bearings via jets, the big-ends by centrifugal flow. His engine revved to a staggering 8,000 rpm. Its dashboard rev counter had a green segment ranging from 6,000-7,500 rpm, orange from 7,500-8,000 rpm and red from 8,000-9,000 rpm where things became even more expensive . . . It drove via a multi-plate clutch and five-speed gearbox – fourth direct and fifth an overdrive. A mechanical brake servo was driven off the gearbox, and an open prop-shaft drove to a bevel back axle.

These mechanicals were housed in a sketchy, rather uninspired channel-steel chassis which was quite light but rather flimsy. The right-side driver's seat was buried low beside the central prop-shaft, with the exhaust manifolding sweeping alarmingly down that same side, close against the scuttle bulkhead and his foot pedals ...

The new Delages missed the 1926 French GP at Miramas which became a farcical Bugatti walk-over with only three cars starting and two finishers.

A month later the *GP d'Europe* was held on San Sebastian's Lasarte circuit in Spain. In 110° heat Bugatti won after the Delages had proved very fast, but their badly-arranged cockpits were just too hot to endure, the drivers being roasted by radiant and conducted heat from that exhaust manifolding. Holes were hacked into the bodywork in a frantic effort to cool relief drivers. André Morel was taken to hospital with burnt feet, and his face was blistered by the sun. Benoist and his reserve driver Louis Wagner both needed medical help, Edmond Bourlier was sprawled out semi-conscious behind the pits, huge water blisters bulging on his bare feet and ankles, while anxious colleagues splashed him with cold water.

The cars stood silent, cooling before their pits while the more habitable Bugattis ripped round and round in an ever-increasing lead.

Later, as temperatures fell under an onshore breeze, volunteer driver Robert Sénéchal took out Bourlier's car; he drove well and eventually inherited second place, his team-mates fourth and sixth. Fastest lap fell to Wagner. There was no mistaking the Delages' superior performance.

In August they entered the inaugural English GP at Brooklands, but again the driver-side exhaust manifolding roasted the drivers. The body of Wagner's car caught fire, and he took over Sénéchal's to share Delage's first victory with the new cars. Another was third.

Now Delage set about redesign, missing the Italian GP as Lory reversed the engine ports, moving the induction to the right-side and the exhausts to the left. He then followed the rival Talbot team's lead in offsetting the entire power train centreline some 4 in (10 cm) to the left, which gave the driver more room as the prop-shaft moved across. But it left no room for the two originally left-side blowers, which had to move in any case to match conveniently the altered induction.

---

3 July, 1927 — French GP, Montlhéry — The extrovert Louis Delage has no need yet to go cap in hand as his number one driver Robert Benoist celebrates victory after a Delage first, second and third place demonstration of peerless mastery; the sister cars of Edmond Bourlier and André Morel followed Benoist home after four and three-quarter hours of racing.

September 1927 — Factory Grand Prix cars — The wonderful 1927 Delage team lined up and ready for business at Brooklands in preparation for the 2 October *GP de l'Angleterre*; the cars are for Edmond Bourlier (left), Robert Benoist (centre) and the rotund Albert Divo (right). Note the raked radiators, offset starter-handle holes and exhaust systems removed from the driver-side this season.

Complex excellence — The exquisitely-finished straight-eight supercharged engine of the 1.5 litre Grand Prix Delage has gone into legend as a no-expense-spared mechanical marvel. By the standards of its time that is no exaggeration. Thirty-four studs retain the cam-cover, note the steering box with side drag-link, ignition advance/retard linkage beside the crankcase, large blower feeding that neat manifold, external brake cable and primitively airfoil-sectioned splash-guard behind the front wheel.

In their place, Lory adopted one long single compressor of the same capacity, which he mounted high ahead of the engine, driven from the timing gears. Where the 1926 cars used a slabby upright radiator with central starter-handle hole matching the centreline engine, the new '27 Delages carried a much neater raked-back radiator with offset starter handle hole matching the resited engine.

As developed for the new season, the straight-eight engine gave 170 bhp – 113 bhp per litre – and Robert Benoist dominated. He won the wet *GP de l'Ouverture* at Montlhéry in an upright-radiator interim car before the definitive '27-spec works team returned there in force for the French GP. Benoist, Bourlier and Morel finished comfortably 1-2-3, leaving the troubled Talbots for dead. At San Sebastian, Benoist had to fight off Emilio Materassi's works Bugatti until the Italian crashed while leading with nine laps to run. Benoist spun in the dust raised by the crashing Bugatti, became disorientated and initially rejoined in the wrong direction. He quickly recovered, and won handsomely from Conelli's Bugatti with Bourlier's Delage third.

Bourlier then lost the minor La Baule GP sand-race to George Eyston's Bugatti after spinning away the lead and fouling the plugs.

Delage then entered Benoist alone for the Italian GP at Monza, in which he spreadeagled meagre opposition (no Bugattis, no Talbots). Back at Brooklands for the second British GP, Louis Delage watched his magnificent cars wail home 1-2-3, the European Championship for Drivers falling resoundingly to Benoist.

The works cars were then sold into private hands as Delage renounced racing. Malcolm

Campbell bought one, which he raced successfully in 1928, and in 1929 Louis Chiron ran another in the Indianapolis 500-Miles, finishing seventh. Raoul de Rovin bought a third which he drove in the inaugural Monaco GP of 1929. He then sold this car to Sénéchal who drove it in the French GP in both 1930 and '31. Brooklands character W. B. Scott bought the Campbell car while Earl Howe bought one from Courbevoie which he raced widely before totally destroying its chassis frame against a stout Monza tree in 1932. Its power-train was salvaged, and the irrepressible Earl promptly bought the ex-Chiron, ex-Sénéchal sister car to continue racing until 1935.

When he finished third with this car in the Albi and Berne *Voiturette* races of 1935, and placed an ERA order for 1936, Giulio Ramponi – who was a former Alfa Romeo mechanic and engineer now resident in England – persuaded Dick Seaman to buy the Earl's old Delage. He did so rather reluctantly, but it came complete with a spare engine, and under Ramponi's direction the nine-year-old machine was modernized to tackle 1936 *Voiturette* racing.

New dural wheels saved 7 lb (3.2 kg) each, a remade radiator saved 20 lb (9 kg), new exposed fuel tank (doing away with the original tail bodywork) saved 95 lb (43.2 kg), and Howe's preferred British pre-selector gearbox was replaced by a 70 lb (31.2 kg) lighter five-speed Delage unit from one of the 2LCV V12 cars. Ramponi added Lockheed hydraulic brakes, higher-compression pistons, and raised supercharge pressure to 12 psi.

The revamped engine now delivered over 185 bhp, and chassis modifications included outrigged front springs, a rebuilt front axle and the packing of the front dumbirons to resist chassis twist. Resprayed black with silver wheels, 'the Seaman Delage' promptly won its first two short races at Donington Park in May, then non-stop at Douglas, Isle of Man, and he led the Eifelrennen at the Nürburgring before crashing. He won his heat at Picardie before crashing again, and then won the Pescara and Berne 1,500 cc races. The team then returned to Donington Park for the JCC 200-Miles in which Seaman not only won his 1,500 cc class, but also won overall ... These results secured Seaman a works Mercedes-Benz drive in 1937.

15 March, 1929 — Indianapolis-bound — The Monegasque Champion Louis Chiron poses in his newly-acquired GP Delage probably in the factory yard at Courbevoie before shipping it across the Atlantic to compete in the 500-Miles Sweepstake classic. The Delage's road racing front-wheel brakes were removed before the Speedway event, in which Chiron finished seventh after qualifying at 107.351 mph (178.9 km/h) — 13 mph (21.6 km/h) off Cliff Woodbury's pole position pace in a better-suited indigenous Miller. Europe's day would return at Indy: all it needed was 32 more years ...

The much modernized 'Dick Seaman Delage' was owned for many years after the war by the great British enthusiast and team patron Rob Walker. It tragically sustained very severe damage in a fire which destroyed his racing workshop at Dorking in 1968, but was painstakingly rebuilt to running order by Rob's veteran mechanic, John Chisman. By 1988 it had returned to France, being acquired by another great enthusiast — Serge Pozzoli.

With ambitions to match Seaman's success, the British-based Siamese racing cousins Prince Chula and 'Bira', then acquired both his much-modified black car and its unmodified sister owned by Captain Davis, ex-W. B. Scott, ex-Campbell, plus all available Delage spares. They contacted the company at Courbevoie to redesign the chassis frame and adopt independent front suspension but this move was ill-advised.

Two new Delage IFS frames were delivered but the resultant 'Chula-Delage' special which appeared in 1938 never felt right to 'Bira' and the project was shelved. When war began in 1939, Reg Parnell from Derby bought all Chula-Delage material, including the new car, and three spare chassis, one an IFS 'special', one the Ramponi-modified ex-Seaman frame and the third the

standard '27-spec ex-Davis/Scott/Campbell frame, plus all engines, drive-trains etc.

After the war Parnell assembled three cars from all these bits, two in '37/'38 IFS form, the other 'The Seaman car'. One IFS frame became the ERA-Delage familiar for many years now in British VSCC racing, the other going to America where De Rovin's car also ended-up – as the most original of them all – in the Cunningham (now Collier Historics) Collection. Rob Walker owned 'The Seaman car' for many years during which it was burned out in a workshop fire and then comprehensively rebuilt before recently selling back to France to veteran collector Serge Pozzoli. The '27-spec ex-Parnell/'Chula'/Davis/Scott/Campbell frame meanwhile went to Alan Burnard, a VSCC member who has spent years rebuilding it towards original factory trim.

The Bugatti Type 35s

★ ★ ★

Rightly or wrongly, the Bugatti Type 35 series of cars built during the 1920s has attained a sparklingly charismatic reputation as one of the most brilliant of all racing car designs. Why should I now infer that this reputation is perhaps misplaced? Let me explain. It's purely a matter of applying the simple criterion – who did they beat? Where the Bugatti Type 35 is concerned the answer very often has to be nobody of much much stature, driving cars of much merit.

Having said that, it must be emphasized that this state of affairs was hardly Bugatti's fault. Nor did it demonstrate any mediocrity in the Type 35s' design, for there was precious little of that. But particularly through the latter part of the 1920s, few other high-quality factories or teams remained involved in racing.

In his factory at Molsheim, Alsace, not far from Strasbourg in the north-eastern corner of France, Italian-born Ettore Bugatti had effectively put a lightweight, well-handling high-performance competition car into quantity production for sale to anyone who could afford it. A great number of professional and near-professional drivers campaigned Type 35s as works, works-backed or valued private-entrant competitors, and a great many more enthusiastic or fashionably daring young souls followed their lead. Eventually Bugatti Type 35s in myriad guises provided the virtual backbone of motor race, sprint and hill-climb entries certainly throughout Continental Europe ...

Hardly surprising then that they accumulated such an extensive tally of victories at such levels of the sport. Even so, the fact that they achieved such acceptance, and became so popular, was not merely a question of availability. It was also very much a question of aesthetic charm, technical quality, good power, excellent handling and – by the standards of the time – high performance capability which persuaded so many to part with their deposits ... and become part of the Bugatti legend.

The Type 35's engine was a straight-eight 24-valve, based on that introduced in the tiny 'tank'-bodied Type 30s built for the 1923 French Grand Prix at Tours. The unit's three main-bearing bottom end and indifferent lubrication were corrected when the Type 35 was introduced in time for the French Grand Prix at Lyons on 3 August 1924. It comprised a far more refined and improved chassis, a beautifully simple and integrated body design, and its much-superior brakes introduced the integrated road wheel-cum-drum spoked castings which became such a Bugatti trademark from that moment.

The Type 35 series developed into quite a wide-ranging family of variants and special sub-types. They may be summarized – after the style of Bugatti authority Hugh Conway – like this:

The original **Type 35 Grand Prix** cars (Lyons 1924 model) was an unsupercharged 60 mm x 88 mm, 1,991 cc straight-eight, using magneto ignition and the newly-cast alloy wheels which at that time incorporated eight simple flat-plane spokes and detachable rims.

Subsequent **Type 35A** detuned production model used a Type 38 three-ball-bearing crankshaft with plain big-end bearings and battery ignition, fitted in the latest Type 35 chassis and body, but fitted with wire wheels. This most humble of the Type 35 family became known as the '*Tecla*'.

The 1925-26 **Type 35 Grand Prix**, still unsupercharged until the 1926 French GP with small-bore 52 mm x 88 mm, 1,500 cc engine.

The Alsace GP **1,100 cc *Voiturette* Type 35**, supercharged with very narrow-bore 51.3 mm x 66 mm engines, tailor-made for one event in 1926, the first successful blown Bugattis.

The **Type 35T** – 'T' for 'Targa Florio' – still unsupercharged used a longer-stroke 64 mm x 100 mm 2.3 litre – actually 2,267 cc – engine.

The **Type 35B** – a Roots-supercharged improvement to the enlarged 2.3 litre 35T-spec, radiator enlarged to cope with the additional cooling demand and moved further forward in the chassis frame to accommodate blower drive. Larger brake drums and wider wheel rims to mount more beefy tyres also progressively introduced.

The **Type 35C** was a supercharged 2 litre version of the Type 35B as above, produced in parallel from 1926.

The **Type 39** – (Type 39 in a listing of Type 35s? Yes, it does make sense) a further direct variation of the Type 35 design, built in very small quantity in 1926 with a short-stroke 60 mm x 66 mm 1,493 cc unsupercharged engine.

The **Type 39A** – the supercharged version of the basic Type 39, produced essentially as a works car, winner of the 1926 French GP, of which it has been said 'So what?' because three Bugattis were the only starters.

Ettore Bugatti and his virtually anonymous design draughtsmen at Molsheim based their Type 35 upon a 2,400 mm (7 ft 10.5 in) wheelbase chassis, fashioned in channel-section steel with typical Bugatti grace, its main longerons varying from ¾ in deep at the front dumb-irons to 6¾ in amidships. The frame also tapered towards its extremities in planform, widest at the scuttle and cockpit, then tapering into the nose and tail. The engine stiffened the forward part of this frame, the separate gearbox adding rigidity at the cockpit. Tubular cross-members braced nose and tail.

Semi-elliptic front leafsprings actually passed through an exquisitely forged and polished hollow front axle, which dipped low in the centre then swept upwards towards the wheels each side. Reversed quarter-elliptic leafsprings were used at the rear, in other words half a conventional semi-elliptic 'cart-spring', anchored rigidly at its 'thick end'. Two external radius rods ran forward to the frame to anchor the axle against driving and braking torque. These stubby rear springs were angled in line with the tail body sides and so were neatly hidden, another touch of Bugatti's aestheticism.

Brakes were cable-operated with chain and bevel-gear compensators, handbrake outboard on the right of the body, operating the rear brakes only. The gearchange was on a cross-shaft, protruding through a neat slot in the right-hand body side, offering gate selection of four forward speeds and reverse. The rear axle was in two cast-aluminium sections, enclosing the bevel gears, offering a choice of 15/54, 14/54 and 13/54 final-drives. The tapering tail housed a 20 gal (91 l) fuel tank.

The straight-eight engine had two 4-cylinder cast alloy blocks in tandem, united by a common camshaft housing up top and the crankcase down below. The single camshaft operated three valves per cylinder, two small inlets and one large exhaust. The crankcase was split in half horizontally, the lower portion forming into four mounting legs. The crankshaft was built-up by interlocking pins and tapers, each section having a roller or ball-bearing race slipped over it during assembly to emerge as a complete assembly with five main bearings – outer bearings being ball-races, the three inner bearings roller, as were the big-ends. The sump was deeply finned and also pierced front to rear by 13 copper tubes through which the airstream was free to flow. This proved a most effective oil cooler.

When supercharged, the Type 35s used a three-lobe Roots compressor beside the engine, gear-driven at crankshaft speed from the front. Fuel mixture was drawn from a vertical – usually Zenith – carburettor, while the unblown cars normally used two Solexes.

Drive passed via a typically Bugatti wet multiplate clutch which offered virtually zero flywheel effect since Bugatti believed the massive crankshaft was sufficient rotating mass. Throughout manufacture and assembly of the Bugatti engines, sheer craftsmanship was the keynote, every major joint was hand-lapped metal to metal without gaskets.

Motor men — Prof Dr Ferdinand Porsche with Count 'Sascha' Kolowrat and Ettore Bugatti at Lyon for the 1924 French GP.

Where the earliest Type 35 cast road wheels carried detachable rims, attached by 24 set screws, they were later cast on. The idea of casting the wheels in unit with the brake drums was to improve heat dissipation from the drum itself, and also to enable instant access for adjustment during tyre change stops. There was also an

unsprung weight-saving of some 30 lb (18.6 kg) per wheel which contributed to the faithful manner in which the Bugatti's wheels would follow the uneven road surfaces of the time, finding grip where others had none and enhancing the lightweight cars' superb agility. A spare-wheel mounting was provided on the left-side of the cars, which were all right-hand drive.

The original works team of six Bugatti type 35s made its début at Lyons in the 1924 French Grand Prix. They were of course driven down to Lyons from Molsheim, but despite proving extremely nimble and faster in some places than the supercharged Alfa Romeos and Fiats, their race was ruined by rear tread failures due to faulty vulcanisation. Two finished, seventh and eighth.

They reappeared at San Sebastian on 25 September for the Spanish GP. The Lasarte circuit was in very dangerous state. Segrave won for Sunbeam from Meo Costantini's Type 35 which set fastest lap.

The 2 litre Formula ran its last through 1925, but many manufacturers anticipated the 1.5 litre rules planned for 1926. While Ascari's 2 litre Alfa 'P2' led the French GP at Montlhéry until his fatal

25 July, 1925 — French GP, Montlhéry — Faithful Bugatti employee, the engineer/driver Bartolomeo Costantini, in his Type 35 the day before the great 1,000 km race which Delage would win after Ascari's fatal crash. Costantini led the five-car Bugatti team home, as it filled fourth to eighth places. In an event lasting nearly nine hours, much was made of this being the first occasion in such a gruelling event that one make's complete team had survived intact, Bugatti making the most of another defeat by *proper* Grand Prix teams. . .

Typical of Bugatti's real role in motor racing history — The Type 35 family proved itself a fine-handling, vivid-performing and affordable sporting car for any enthusiast with the wherewithal to buy one. Here on Southport Sounds, Lancashire, Raymond Mays and his RAF-trained engineering friend Peter Berthon prepare for a sand-race. Their shared experience and knowledge would surface in the ERA production racing car series from 1934 and culminate in the postwar BRM.

accident, Costantini, Goux, Foresti and the banker brothers Pierre and Fernand de Vizcaya drove 1.5 litre Bugattis to finish fourth to eighth.

In the Italian GP at Monza, Costantini finished third overall amongst the 2 litre Italian cars and won the *Voiturette* class. Bugattis also won the Rome, La Baule and Alessandria races that season.

In 1926 Grand Prix racing was virtually non-existent until Delage weighed in with his great factory team. To approach their performance Mr Bugatti had to swallow his reservations about supercharging and adopt it in the Type 39A and 35B. Three 39As ran unopposed in the farcical French GP at Miramas, near Marseilles, Jules Goux winning. For the Spanish and European GPs only Delage and Bugatti fielded full teams, Goux at last scoring the Type 35's first major Grand Prix victory, with Costantini second – thanks largely to the Delages' overheating-cockpit design fault as described on page 65. In the inaugural RAC GP at Brooklands, Malcolm Campbell finished second in his Bugatti, but a Delage won.

The cars still won at least a dozen secondary races, including Louis Charavel, racing under the pseudonym 'Sabipa' taking the demoted Italian GP.

From 1927 Grand Prix racing was opened to virtual *Formule Libre* just to attract worthwhile entries and make a spectacle which the public might pay to watch. Delage's works team dominated, and persuaded Bugatti to non-start the French and Italian GPs but run at Brooklands, where they were destroyed by the Delages. However, at a secondary level, their successes continued, with at least ten more second-division events falling to them.

When Delage and Talbot both withdrew from Formula racing in 1928, and Fiat opted out of their brief return with a twin 6-cylinder car, the way was laid open at last to the popular Bugatti hordes. The Monegasque driver Louis Chiron made his name in his private Type 35s, winning at Reims, Rome, Monza and San Sebastian. By 1929 the Type 35 was long in the tooth, but 'Williams' (William Grover) still won the inaugural Monaco GP, and three other events.

Meanwhile, the Type had found its true *métier* in the Sicilian Targa Florio, racing around the rugged Madonie mountains east of Palermo. The 35's matchless agility compensated for its relatively modest power, its drivers had no heavy steering nor unruly handling to endure, they remained fresh and must have had *enormous* fun ... riding a perfect horse for that particular course.

In 1925 Costantini won in a works 2 litre Type 35. In 1926 using the 2.3 litre Type 35T Costantini and Minoia finished first and second, beating a good quality field which included 2 litre V12 Delages, a new Peugeot and Ernesto Maserati's straight-eight 1,500. Even so, the Delages were withdrawn after previous Targa winner Masetti rolled his and was killed.

In 1927, Costantini retired from regular driving to manage Bugatti's racing affairs, and Emilio Materassi's 2 litre blown car won the Targa from Count Conelli's 1.5. Amongst only eight finishers, five were Bugattis. In 1928 Mme Junek in a Bugatti ran strongly second behind Divo who won, but Bugatti filled the next four places. In 1929 after a torrid duel, Alfa Romeo at last broke Bugatti's stranglehold on the Targa Florio, but the classic Sicilian race had proved the true *métier* – and class – of the greatest all-rounder from Molsheim.

The Alfa Romeo Tipo B Monoposti

★ ★ ★ ★ ★

Alfa Romeo produced their first true *Monoposto* racing car – which means literally 'single-seater', in the motor racing sense a normally open-wheeled Formula car with driving seat upon the longitudinal centreline – in Vittorio Jano's twin-6-cylinder *Formule Libre* experiment, the hefty *Tipo A*. Although these two large, heavy and rather fearsome cars had some success in 1931, Jano was fully aware of their limitations as a practical GP car. That September, the Alfa Romeo board authorized him to proceed with design of an altogether lighter, more nimble and far more practical GP design, which was to become immortal.

Grand Prix racing in 1932 was virtually *Formule Libre*, rather more liberal in fact than in 1931 because the governing body, the AIACR*, now reduced the duration of previously 10 hour *Grande Epreuve* races to a minimum five hours and a maximum seven. The old two-seat body width requirements had been tacitly ignored by the Italians in 1931, and was now officially discarded, so Jano was free to perfect his new *Tipo B* design as a true *Monoposto* built as narrow as he could make it within the restraints of accommodating a grown man and all the normal mechanical assemblies within its chassis and bodyshell.

To power this new car, Jano decided to develop a full-house GP version of his already very successful straight-eight 8C-2300 engine. He retained the basic structure of two separate 4-

(*Association International des Automobiles Clubs Reconnus)

cylinder fixed-head – *testa fissa* – blocks in tandem upon a common crankcase, with a cam-drive gear train between the blocks powering two overhead camshafts and such ancillaries as the oil pumps and superchargers. The 2300 bore of 65 mm was retained but the stroke was now stretched from 88 mm to 100 mm for 2,654 cc. The crankcase was recast in elektron instead of aluminium. Two superchargers were used, mounted upon a common drive spinning at nominally 1.448 times crankshaft speed. Boost was 0.75 kg/cm² (about 10.6 lb psi – and Alfa Romeo claimed 215 bhp at 5,600 rpm – 81 bhp per litre).

A four-speed gearbox was mounted in unit with the engine and the rear of the gearbox carried a differential mechanism from which a vee drive comprised of two individual prop-shafts splayed outwards to power each rear wheel via bevel-drives just inboard of the wheel hubs. Some writers have concluded that this vee-drive was to enable Jano to lower the driver's seat between the two shafts, and so minimize overall height and frontal area. This is nonsense. In reality the driver's seat is every bit as high above this vee-drive as it would need to be above a conventional centreline prop-shaft.

One of Jano's true aims seems surely to have been to minimize unsprung weight, in that he could now dispense with a heavy conventional live rear axle. The vee-drive prop-shafts and individual bevel final-drives were each relatively light, as was the dead axle tube linking the hubs laterally. This lighter weight enabled the wheels and tyres to follow undulations much more faithfully, improving traction and cornering

As Mercedes-Benz officially desisted from racing in 1932, German driver Rudolf Caracciola signed for Alfa Romeo while promising Neubauer of Mercedes that he would return to them whenever they resumed competition. Caracciola quickly found his feet in Jano's new slimline, lightweight *Tipo B Monoposto* cars and is shown here on test at Monza, tended by his assigned mechanic Bonini. That ribbed radiator grille was soon replaced by the definitive mesh design with a slotted surround.

power through the elimination of 'hop'. The method was undoubtedly rather complex and it would find no imitators, but Jano had done the job of all serious racing car designers in deciding what important parameters he would tackle, and choosing the best possible compromises to achieve his aims. He clearly considered that improved handling would compensate for any power disadvantage dictated by Alfa's always parlous financial state. They simply did not have the money to fund some fancy all-new racing engine. Now his concept was in the forefront of a technological area which had remained stagnant for the previous decade.

Otherwise, there was nothing very advanced about the new Alfa Romeo's channel-section, beam front-axled chassis design, but it confirmed Jano's attention to weight-saving wherever possible. With empty tail tanks the new *Monoposto* weighed only 700 kg (1,543 lb). All considered, it is extraordinary that when it made its racing début in the Italian GP at Monza on 5 June 1932, it was almost totally ignored by the specialist press, which published only the broadest details . . .

They referred to the car simply as the '*Monoposto*', or even merely by quoting its dis-

placement – 'Alfa Romeo 2600' – to differentiate it from the existing and already proven 8C-2300 *Monza* offset-single seat GP car. Although Alfa Romeo officially described the new model as the *Tipo B*, the logical successor to the *Tipo A*, the press eventually came to describe it as the 'P3', logical successor to the Grand Prix racing 'P1' and 'P2' cars of the 1920s. This nickname became used with increasing frequency –particularly in the British specialist press – but as with so much which appeared in the contemporary press, it was strictly inaccurate. It is interesting to reflect, that since the sobriquet 'P3' had not been applied to either the *Monza* or the *Tipo A* perhaps neither was regarded as a proper or worthy successor to the World Championship-winning 'P2's. In any case, I prefer the *Monoposto's* proper title, the Alfa Romeo *Tipo B*.

Initially it was good enough to enjoy a relatively easy time, very much on merit, for its advantage over contemporary competition was immense. What it couldn't outrun on the straight it could out-handle through the corners. The Portello works team's *Tipo Bs* won all their outings in 1932 apart from the Masaryk GP at Brno in Czechoslovakia. Tazio Nuvolari won the Coppa Principe di Piemonte, Coppa Acerbo, Coppa

Ciano, French and Italian GPs, while the German driver Rudi Caracciola – without a Mercedes drive since D-B* had renounced racing on cost grounds – joined the Italian works team instead and won the German and Monza GPs in *Monoposti*.

But then in 1933 Alfa Romeo was forced to abandon direct factory participation in racing by financial restraints. Still they stubbornly refused to release their *Monoposto* fleet to the Scuderia Ferrari, which was at that time doing its best to uphold Alfa Romeo's waning racing prestige with a motley collection of old *Monza* cars uprated with the 2.6 litre engine, and various sports Alfas. The *Monzas'* standard transmissions proved incapable of withstanding the 2.6's extra power and torque, and broke repeatedly. The Scuderia Ferrari's drivers bitched incessantly about the equipment available, and the team was virtually in collapse at GP level before Mr Ferrari, with political and financial backing from Pirelli, managed to twist the Portello board's collective arm, and won the *Monoposti's* release for a return to competition.

Thereafter, the board could hardly grumble, for the Scuderia Ferrari *Tipo B* entries promptly obtained victory in six out of seven races, Luigi Fagioli winning the Coppa Acerbo, the Italian GP and Comminges GP, Louis Chiron the Marseilles, Masaryk and Spanish GPs, then Count

(*Daimler-Benz AG, of Stuttgart-Unterturkheim)

Carlo Felice Trossi the Monteceneri mountain-climb.

Until this time, the *Tipo B* had raced virtually unchanged save for minor detail developments, but entering 1934 this period of stagnation abruptly ended as the new generation of German high-performance Grand Prix cars appeared and their specification and potential plainly shocked the enthusiastic and established – if perennially penurious – Italians.

The AIACR's new 750 kg (1,650 lb) maximum weight Formula excluded such over-engined monster cars such as the *Sedici Cilindri* Maserati and Alfa Romeo *Tipo A* of recent memory. One of its requirements was a minimum bodywork width at the cockpit of 85 cm (33.5 in) with which Jano's ultra-slim *Tipo B* now had to comply to compete at major level.

Alfa's board was now confident of Ferrari's ability to uphold the marque's prestige, and not only all existing *Tipo B* cars but also all available spares and such valuable technician-testers as Luigi Bazzi and Attilio Marinoni were consigned to the Scuderia's HQ in the Viale Trento Trieste, Modena. The Scuderia was now to develop and modernize the cars 'in-house' with assistance in-kind from Portello when necessary. To meet the new 750 kg Formula requirements and to meet the new German challenge, Alfa Portello/Scuderia Ferrari revised and uprated the *Tipo B*. They bored out the engines to 68 mm, raising displacement from 2,654 cc to 2,905 cc, and

11 September, 1932 — Monza GP — Tazio Nuvolari's *Monoposto* being wheeled rapidly past the pits ready to compete, showing off its twin superchargers protruding through the cut-out in that narrow engine enclosure and its very large-diameter drum brakes.

1 July, 1934 — French GP, Montlhéry — Louis Chiron's new wide-bodied 750 kg Formula *Tipo B* roars into the lead from Caracciola's new Mercedes-Benz W25, Scuderia Ferrari team-mate Achille Varzi's *Tipo B* (6), René Dreyfus's Bugatti (18), Hans Stuck's Auto Union (4) and Count Trossi's third Alfa (20). The Italian old-guard cars will win while the new German cars will fail, but the writing is on the wall . . .

supercharge pressure was raised. Bulged side panels were fitted around the cockpit on the existing narrow-chassis cars to balloon the body-width to the required 85 cm. Nicely-fashioned slotted skirts hung down outside the narrow-set chassis rails each side. The *Tipo Bs* modified in this manner were employed only – or perhaps mainly – in second-division races that season.

Meanwhile, the first of the tailor-made 750 kg Portello *Tipo B* cars made its début at Alessandria, wearing a completely different body which replaced the original shell's severe contours with a smooth but still essentially upright form, in which the bonnet flared rearwards in planform to meet the new regulation 85 cm-wide scuttle and then the tail tapered rearwards into the usual vertical knife-edge. Where the twin superchargers in the narrow cars and on the interim 750 kg hybrid had protruded through cut-outs on the left side of the bonnet, in this definitive 750 kg Formula version they required no such cut-out, because the bonnet was so much wider.

A special body form, styled by the Caproni aerodynamicist Pallavicino, then appeared on a very special *Tipo B* prepared for the AVUSRennen in Berlin, which it won, driven by the brilliant young Algerian, Guy Moll. This very special car emphasized the Scuderia's awareness of aerodynamic effects, and also the ability of the joint Portello/Scuderia programme to react quickly and effectively within their slender means when required.

But their budgetary and in some areas technological means remained quite incapable of matching those now unleashed by Nazi Germany's Mercedes-Benz and Auto Union concerns. Consequently the *Tipo B*'s success declined at major level, and the enlarged engines' enhanced performance began to expose transmission fragility just as in the *Monzas* which had preceded them. The Portello plant could not react to Scuderia pleas for more power and more modern chassis, since it was heavily committed to military contract work for the Government at that time. Its experimental department simply lacked the capacity to respond to the German racing threat. Eventually, Alfa Romeo refused to supply any more spare parts to the Scuderia beyond raw unmachined blanks or forgings. Ferrari agreed to accept them and arranged to have them fine-finished – to excellent standards – by Daldi e Matteucci in Porretta Terme.

But even then, improved reliability was no substitute for adequate horsepower, and so towards the end of 1934 the Scuderia experimented with engines enlarged to 3,165 cc and these '3.2 litre' units were then used widely during 1935. According to some sources two engines with a bore of 78 mm – for 3.8 litres – were then prepared for the French GP, although Giovann Battista Guidotti, technical head and chief tester at Portello told me in recent years that this was not so. The 3.2 litre engine was the limit of available enlargement from the basic 2.6 litre block, the 3.8 requiring new castings which were only then being prepared for the forthcoming 1935 all-independently suspended 8C-35 model. He did not recall 3.8 litre blocks being supplied to Modena before production of the definitive 8C-35 cars late in 1935.

Neither could extra power fully compensate for the outdated *Tipo Bs'* chassis and brakes. The opposing German cars featured independent suspensions all round, and the latest in hydraulic brakes.

Still the *Tipo Bs* won at least 16 events in 1934, including the French GP (Louis Chiron), the Monaco GP (Guy Moll), and the Targa Florio, Coppa Ciano and Penya Rhin (Spanish) GPs (all Achille Varzi).

On 7 February, 1935, Nuvolari and Marinoni test-drove a *Tipo B* at Monza fitted with a low-mounted transverse rear leafspring, but this idea was improved upon immediately by adoption of reversed quarter-elliptic cantilever leafsprings *à la* Bugatti, with hydraulic dampers. Two *Tipo Bs* thus modified succeeded at Pau.

Within weeks, at the La Turbie hill-climb, René Dreyfus drove a car fitted with a new Dubonnet independent front suspension system plus Ariston hydraulic brakes made by the Farina plant in Turin, and featuring driver adjustment from the cockpit. The Dubonnet IFS system had been designed in 1932. It was now well-developed and understood and was considered to be the best answer to the problem of giving the *Tipo B* life after death. Despite considerably improving their lap times round all kinds of circuit, it was only a restricted stay of execution, and they puttered into obsolescence as perhaps the first of the internationally-recognised vintage racing cars.

According to Alfa Romeo, six original form narrow-chassised *Tipo B Monoposto* cars were produced in 1932-33, plus three more intended for customer sale. No fewer than 11 750 kg formula versions were then manufactured during 1934/35, some no doubt based upon the original series narrow chassis. When sold, ex-Ferrari, into predominantly English private hands they became the most valuable of Alfa Romeo's Grand Prix cars. One 2.9 while in Scuderia Ferrari hands had also been rigged with a vestigial passenger seat for the 1935 Mille Miglia, and crewed by Carlo Pintacuda and a cramped but intrepid *Marchese* Della Stufa, it won by the embarrassing margin of over 40 minutes! This *Biposto* ran subsequently in the Targa Florio and several mountain-climbs, and its chassis is believed to survive today.

5 April, 1936 — *Mille Miglia* — Clemente Biondetti driving the two-seat *Tipo B Biposto* special which he had acquired from Scuderia Ferrari after its 1935 season in which it had been specially created for — and had won — the *Mille Miglia* round-Italy classic driven by Carlo Pintacuda. Here accompanied by Cesara, Biondetti corners in Modena town centre.

The *Tipo Bs'* fourth and final front-line season of 1935 yielded at least another 16 victories, mostly at secondary level, but Count Antonio Brivio carried off the Targa Florio in one, and Nuvolari defeated the Germans in their own Grand Prix.

Known *Tipo B* chassis numbers on surviving cars include six successive four-digit serials '5001' to '5006' – the latter being Yoshiyuki Hayashi's 750 kg car ex-Neil Corner, ex–Georges Raph, believed to be Moll's 1934 Monaco GP winner; and seven five-digit serials, '50001' to '50005', '50007' and '50009'. Of these, '50002' ex-Count Villapadierna in Spain with 3.2 litre engine, led a full life, selling to American Frank Griswold in 1939 and being driven by Lou Tomei in the Indianapolis '500' finishing twelfth. In the 1949 '500', with 2.9 litre engine Al Miller retired; Griswold won the New York World's Fair race at Flushing, and then after the war it became the *Don Lee Spl* at Indy driven by Hal Cole in 1946 and Ken Fowler in 1947.

But by far the most famous of all these glorious cars is chassis '50005', for Tazio Nuvolari used this car to defeat all that Mercedes-Benz and Auto Union could throw at him in their own German GP at the Nürburgring in 1935, and with luck on his side he scored the most emotional and sensational victory of these Alfa Romeo cars' long frontline career. For many years now, '50005' has been preserved lovingly by New Zealand enthusiast Bill Clark . . . a monument to Italian flair against all the odds in arguably the greatest era of motor racing.

1934-36
The Mercedes-Benz W25 series
★ ★ ★ ★

The years of the Great Depression bit desperately hard into Germany between the wars. By 1932 Daimler-Benz's workforce had shrunk to merely half its 1928 level. A majority espoused Adolf Hitler's National Socialist Party – the Nazis – and on 30 January 1933 elected them to power with him as Chancellor.

Meanwhile, the AIACR had announced its new Grand Prix Formula to replace *Formule Libre* for the seasons 1934-36. They wanted to exclude the 'monster' cars developed during the years of free-for-all. Consequently, they adopted a maximum-weight of only 750 kg (1,653.45 lb) believing this would reduce engines to around 3 litres and perhaps 250 bhp. The announcement was made in October 1932.

D-B's Mercedes SSKL was way over the new limit, but the central design office had toyed with some exploratory racing designs. Max Wagner worked up a front-engined sports car with swing-axle rear suspension and 2 litre, supercharged, 6-cylinder engine. Dr Porsche had floated a 3.2 litre dohc straight-eight with 260 bhp – 81 bhp per litre – also using swing-axle rear suspension and a transaxle gearbox-cum-final drive. Otto Schilling drew it, then in 1930 laid out a 70 mm x 82 mm, 5,060 cc V16 aiming at 350 bhp. D-B could not possibly finance it, but despite these restraints racing manager Alfred Neubauer maintained managing director Wilhelm Kissel's enthusiasm for racing's promotional possibilities.

Kissel had been forced to abandon racing publicly in 1930, but without necessarily informing his board he still assisted drivers like Rudolf Caracciola and Hans Stuck through the back door in 1931-32. He also declared that an adequate return to Grand Prix racing would require a million *Reichsmarks*, and where could such a sum be found?

Then came the Nazi take-over, reviving German industry almost overnight. Industrialists' fears of nationalization were swept aside. The Government instead suppressed union opposition, offered valuable armaments contracts, freed credit and introduced an upsurge of ambition and optimism.

D-B's branch manager in Munich, Jakob Werlin, was close to his leading local politician, Hitler. Werlin was a great proponent of international racing to enhance national and industrial prestige, and was instrumental in Hitler's approving Transport Minister Brandenburg's announcement of a state bounty for the manufacture of a German Grand Prix racing car.

Brandenburg offered 450,000 *Reichsmarks* per year, plus success bonuses of RM20,000, 10,000 and 5,000 for first, second and third-place finishes. D-B were attracted, but so was the new Auto Union outfit. When both declared their intention to build new 750 kg Formula cars, Brandenburg split the bounty 50/50 between them.

At Unterturkheim, D-B's ex-Benz design director Hans Nibel was to head the new GP project, Max Wagner supervising chassis, Albert Heess and Otto Schilling engines. Fritz Nallinger's experimental department would then build, test and develop the cars, his staff led by Otto Weber (engine assembly) and Jakob Krauss (chassis). The Unterturkheim works was managed by Max Sailer – the racing pedigree ran deep . . .

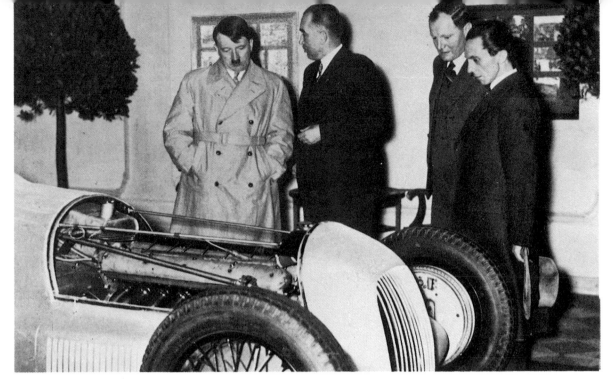

Dr Hans Nibel of Daimler-Benz describes the technicalities of their new supercharged straight-eight cylinder W25 Grand Prix car to *Reichschancellor* Adolf Hitler and propaganda chief Josef Goebbels. Racing for one's country was about to assume what was — if perhaps only in retrospect — a rather sinister new significance.

Where to start? In February 1933 the Mercedes 380 passenger car had just been launched, with supercharged straight-eight engine, and all-independent suspension. It used swing-axles at the rear and parallel wishbones up front. This was to be the basis of Nibel's new *Wagen Zwanzig-Funf* GP car, the 'W25' which simply signified the central office's twenty-fifth car design. Max Sailer had minuted as early as 1923, *'If it's possible to drive single-seated then absolutely make a single-seater car . . .'* That's exactly what Nibel did, dropping the centreline seat as low as possible by adoption of a rear-mounted transaxle gearbox. The new design's chassis comprised pressed box-section longerons, liberally drilled for lightness and united by tubular cross-members. Hydraulic drum brakes were a D-B racing car novelty, and multiple friction-disc dampers were developed for the coil-and-wishbone front suspension and to control lateral quarter-elliptic leafsprings under the rear swing axles.

Meanwhile, Heess's engine designers, listened to Caracciola's experience of the Alfa Romeo *Monoposto* in 1932. He had just bought his own for 1933 but a bad crash in practice in it at Monaco would smash his thigh. Still the German design team understood that the Italian 2.9 litre straight-eight developed around 215 bhp - and projecting such a figure towards a possible situa-

tion in 1934 they calculated a minimum 280 bhp would be vital. Their contemporary 2 litre M218 engine developed 85 bhp per litre, so 280 bhp should require 3.3 litres . . .

The preferred configuration for the new M25A GP engine was a straight-eight, so dimensions of 78 mm x 88 mm were chosen for 3,360 cc. The engineers adopted forged steel cylinders in two 4-cylinder blocks, with four valves per cylinder inclined at 60° actuated by twin overhead camshafts spur-gear driven up the rear of the block. At the front, bevels drove a vertical Roots-type supercharger at twice crankshaft speed, pumping pressure air through a heavily-finned cast manifold to two updraught sealed carburettors. This blower was permanently engaged, but a linkage vented boost to atmosphere as the driver backed-off. A massive aluminium crankcase carried a one-piece counterbalanced crankshaft in five main roller-bearings.

The finished unit weighed 448 lb (203.6 kg). It drove through a single-plate dry clutch via propshaft to the rear transaxle. The car was clothed in neat and quite pretty alloy panelling, and the first M25A engine was mounted in the white-painted prototype W25 in mid-February 1934. It was tested by Manfred von Brauchitsch at Monza but crashed, possibly due to a tyre failure.

It was returned rebuilt to Monza in March.

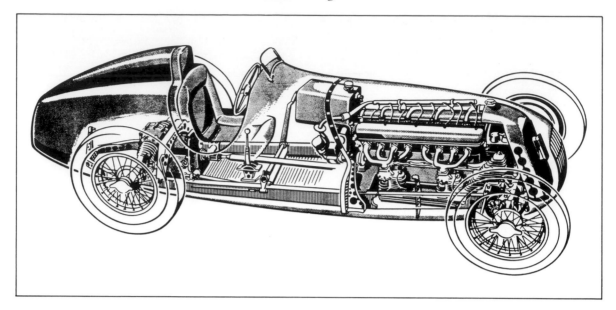

The Mercedes-Benz W25 of 1934 — the first 'modern' GP car.

From the start, the new engines had exceeded expectations. On the dyno unit 'M25A-2' registered 325 bhp at 5,500 rpm – 98.72 bhp per litre (0.72 bhp per lb). Famous motor cycle racer Ernst Henne spun off when his engine chimed in on full power during early tests at the Nürburgring. Engine 'M25A-3' was tested detuned for driveability's sake, then gave 302 bhp at 5,500 rpm. Headrest tail bodywork was perfected through April, and then on 3 June 1934 – after a last-minute D-B cancellation of entries for the AVUSRennen in late May – came Mercedes's return to Grand Prix Formula racing at the Eifelrennen, Nürburgring.

Dramatically, the W25s were 1 kg (2.2 lb) overweight at scrutineering. Neubauer ordered their paint to be stripped and in bare aluminium the new cars made their racing début, driven by von Brauchitsch – who won! – and the experienced Italian Luigi Fagioli. At the French GP the cars failed after showing terrific speed, and then Fagioli won the Coppa Acerbo at Pescara, and the Italian and Spanish GPs. Journalists wrote of '*the screaming Mercedes, the noisiest car on earth . . .*'.

But the rival Auto Unions were also very quick, and Heess's men rushed out an enlarged M25B engine, 82 mm x 94.5 mm, 3,990 cc. It weighed 455 lb (206.8 kg) and used a longer-barrel, larger-capacity supercharger. Just the new blocks and

pistons of the M25B raced first, matched to a smaller blower in an interim 88 mm stroke M25AB engine of 3,710 cc, delivering around 348 bhp at 5,800 rpm. This was burning normal fuel, but on the Standard Oil Co's volatile WW mix – 86 per cent methyl alcohol, 4.4 per cent nitro-benzol, 8.8 per cent acetone and 0.8 per cent ether – the dyno testers saw 398 bhp, 107.27 bhp per litre.

In October 1934, D-B hit the headlines after Henne suggested they attack Class C (3 to 5 litre) world records on the Gyon record-road near Budapest. They used 430 bhp M25B engines burning WW fuel, in an unlikely-looking closed coupe W25 open-wheeled car which Caracciola took through the flying km and mile marks at 197.35 and 196.78 mph (328.92 and 327.97 km/h) respectively. He also raised the standing start mile record to 117.23 mph (195.36 km/h). In December at AVUS, he then covered a flying-start 5 km at a sensational 193.86 mph (323.1 km/h)!

Just previously, on 25 November, Dr Nibel had suffered a fatal stroke. He was only 54. Max Sailer took his place early in 1935.

For the new season, the existing W25 chassis were updated in an effort to cure excessive steering kick-back, uneven braking and gearbox fragility. The ZF limited-slip differential was introduced. Four latest-spec frames were built new, enabling the experimental department to have four cars under preparation while the team were out racing a similar quartet. The two squads of cars could then alternate race by race.

In their first two 1935 outings the practice cars used M25A engines and the race cars M25Bs, but the latest 240 mm (9.4 in) long-barrel supercharger wore rapidly, so an improved AB blower 220 mm (8.7 in) long was used instead.

Meanwhile an M25C engine was being developed, using the B-type blocks with a new crankshaft and longer stroke, 82 mm x 102 mm, 4,310 cc, using 255 mm (10 in) barrel-length blowers. Four M25Cs were built, and by the end of the season D-B had six M25Bs available. According to Mercedes historian Karl Ludvigsen's researches D-B's engine production totalled 22 M25A/B/C variants combined by 1935.

The latest M25C developed 402 bhp at 5,500 rpm plus a beefy 424 lb/ft torque at 3,000 rpm on 16.1 psi boost, delivered by its 255 mm (10 in) blower although this was usually replaced by the better-trusted 240 mm (9.6 in) B-series. This 4.3 litre engine weighed 473 lb (215 kg) so while developing up to 93.4 bhp per litre, it also produced nearly 0.85 bhp per lb weight. One M25B

used a Hirth built-up crankshaft experimentally, doing away with the need for split roller bearings. In any case, it was D-B's year. Their W25/35s won five of the seven *Grandes Epreuves*, plus four lesser events – nine victories in all, including five 1-2 finishes and a 1-2-3 demonstration at San Sebastian.

Then D-B tripped up. For 1936 a lighter variant was developed which was lower and fully 10 in (25 cm) shorter in wheelbase, together with a *Typ DAB* 82 mm x 88 mm, 5,577 cc, 60° V12-cylinder racing engine to replace the two-seasons old straight-eight.

Four short-chassis 'Model 1936' cars were built, two being complete as early as October 1935. They featured lowered transaxles, and introduced a form of de Dion rear suspension, with the road wheels linked by a 'shallow Y'-shaped beam sprung on quarter-elliptic leaf-springs. It was located laterally by a guide on the rear of the chassis-mounted transaxle, from which universally-joined half-shafts drove to the wheels. As power had increased during 1935 the cars lacked the traction to transmit it to the road. This new SWB configuration added rearward weight-bias but this of itself would have emphasized the

Late June 1934 — French GP, Montlhéry — During practice for the new Mercedes-Benz W25's first really major test, Caracciola's car is posed for photography in the Parisian Autodrome's paddock, showing off its exquisitely packaged and well-streamlined form, with copious louvring to rid the engine-bay of under-bonnet heat.

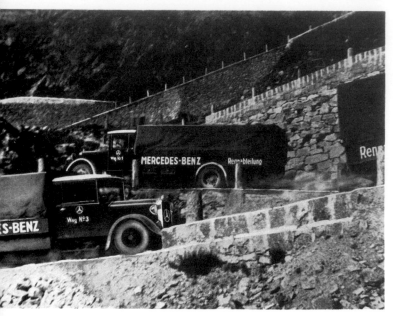

Somewhere in Europe, the Daimler-Benz *Rennabteilung's* transport section takes the Grand Prix cars over the Alps to war. The company seems to have enjoyed its ever-growing reputation for military precision — note the trucks here are climbing in numerical order, '*Wagen No 1*' leading, *No 2* presumably in the middle and that is certainly *No 3* in the foreground.

shortcomings of a swing-axle rear end, hence the de Dion idea.

Meanwhile, the completed 5.5 litre DAB V12 weighed 650 lb (295 kg) which was considered excessive. Consequently, in mid-September 1935 a straight-eight ME25 with a new designation system was laid-down, marking the limit of expansion for the M25's 95 mm bore-centre spacing. The M25C had already achieved the maximum 102 mm stroke, so an 86 mm bore now gave 4,740 cc. Larger valves lived in new cylinder forgings, while the blower rotor diameter now grew to 125 mm (5 in) with barrel-lengths of either 240 or 255 mm (9.6 or 10 in). Six ME25s were hastily prepared for 1936, but D-B had been badly wrong-footed. Eventually four more ME25 engines were built, to make 10 in all, and all these engines joined the race pool.

The ME25 produced 430 bhp on normal fuel, and one with the 255 mm blower gave 473 bhp at 5,800 rpm, with 465 lb/ft torque at 3,000 rpm, blown at 14.5 psi. This represented no less than 99.78 bhp per litre, quite something by road rac-

ing standards, but of course a joke by the established Miller Indy–car criteria . . . Irrespective, the engine weighed only 465 lb (211kg), so it was churning out 1.01 bhp per lb weight, the first time a D-B racing engine had exceeded parity in this department.

In the rain at Monaco, Caracciola won, but through the fast curves at Tripoli the 'short cars' handled queasily. The engines began to fail. Caracciola won at Tunis after the leading Auto Unions crashed, and this was to be the 'short cars' last win, the last for the W25-series. In mid-season D-B missed races to sort out the Model 1936's problems, Louis Chiron crashed his at the Nürburgring and left the team, but a new era was dawning for the company.

Realizing that the experimental department's approach to racing born pre-1908 was inadequate for the crowded calendar demands of the 1930s, D-B's management created a new racing department, the *Rennabteilung,* which would assemble, prepare and test the cars before Neubauer's sports department took them off to race. The new department was in turn to be supplied with components made in the main Unterturkheim factory, and designed and engineered by Wagner and Heess's central design office.

The man placed in charge was the 30-year old son of a German father and British mother, a brilliant young engineer and exceptionally fine analytical driver in his own right who had been with D-B only five years. His name was Rudolf Ühlenhaut.

He test-drove the troubled Model 1936 cars himself at the Nürburgring after the stars had departed, and identified inadequate suspension-travel as a major cause of their dissatisfaction. Loading the nose of the car with lead to alter its weight distribution towards a higher polar moment of inertia improved its stability. With Ühlenhaut's involvement, the cars became good enough for Caracciola to lead the Swiss GP at one stage, but Bernd Rosemeyer promptly showed him an Auto Union power advantage so great that D-B then opted out of the Italian GP, the last of the season, and the W25 family's active life had ended.

But this was by no means the last we would hear of Mercedes-Benz, nor of Rudolf Ühlenhaut's *Rennabteilung*.

Auto Union had won a battle, but they had not won the war . . .

The Auto Union Types A-C

★ ★ ★

The AIACR's announcement of 12 October 1932, setting out the requisites of their new 750 kg maximum weight Grand Prix Formula for 1934-36, fired not only Daimler-Benz but also the recently-formed Auto Union AG from Lower Saxony in eastern Germany.

Jorgen Skafte Rasmussen's Zschopauer Motorenwerke manufactured DKW cars and motor cycles, and in 1928 he took over the Audi-Werke AG of nearby Zwickau. In 1932 another Zwickau motor works, Horch, was added to the group together with the Wanderer-Werke AG of Chemnitz, another industrial town within 20 miles or so of Zwickau. These four marques gave the Auto Union its four-ringed emblem, but in the short-term at the end of that depression year they had a promotional problem of informing the public of their new strength and unity, and of the quality of their products.

Since 1930, Wanderer at Chemnitz had employed the consultancy services of the Berlin-based design *Büro* of veteran ex-Austro-Daimler and Daimler-Benz chief engineer Prof Dr Ferdinand Porsche. His imagination was running riot at news of the new GP Formula, 750 kg maximum weight but engine capacity unrestricted.

He acted at once and on 1 November 1932 formed the *Hochleistungsfahrzeugbau GmbH** to investigate, design, develop and race a 750 kg Formula GP car. His business manager Adolf Rosenberger – a one-time amateur racing driver using the Benz *Tropfenwagen* rear-engined cars – raised backing for the venture from the *Herrenklub* – a

(*High Performance Vehicle Development Co)

Berlin men's club.

Through the first two weeks of November, Porsche and his associates, Josef Kales and Karl Rabe, laid out a startlingly radical design – a kind of grown-up *Tropfenwagen* with 45° V16-cylinder engine mounted amidships behind the driver. Projected bore and stroke were 68 mm x 75 mm, 4,358 cc, to run at 4,500 rpm. Kales detailed the engine, Rabe the running gear, and by July 1933 drawings were complete.

Meanwhile Porsche and Rosenberger had been trying to raise backing to see through the project. Initial negotiations with the usual fuel and tyre companies yielded little, but driver Hans Stuck invested some money in the project and talked with Adolf Hitler about the possibilities of Porsche's 'P-Wagen'. This primed him to make state funds available as for Mercedes – see page 78.

Then through Wanderer, the project was outlined to the new Auto Union board, via sales manager von Wertzen. They were fascinated by its potential, sought Government backing to fund it and won a share in Transport Minister Brandenburg's 'racing for Germany' bounty. The 'P-Wagen' was to be built in Auto Union plants, and it would carry their new name to war ... but the contract insisted they would only accept the design if it proved capable of lapping Berlin's AVUS track at an average of 200 km/h (124 mph).

Under Porsche's consultant direction, a hand-picked team of fitters including brothers Ludwig and Wilhelm Sebastian, began manufacture and assembly in the quality-engineering Horch works at Zwickau. The team's preparation and racing 'shop would subsequently be set-up at the Wanderer-*Werke* in Chemnitz, the racing programme employing just over 100 men. Willy Walb, a former Benz *Tropfenwagen* team-member, joined AU from Daimler-Benz to direct racing affairs, and he drove the prototype Auto Union A-Type GP car on its first run around the factory site in October 1933. He then tested it seriously on the Nürburgring south-circuit on 13 November, and on 12 January 1934 at AVUS interested party Hans Stuck hammered the aeronautical-looking new car, with its rear fuselage fabric-panelled, round for an hour at 134.9 mph (224.8 km/h), hitting 165 mph (275 km/h) on the straights. The Berlin Motor Show opened within days, Germany's new-hope Grand Prix car its sensational centrepiece.

Now the name Auto Union was on everybody's lips, even before its first race ...

The A-Type's chassis was composed of twin large-diameter tube main longerons interlinked ladder-fashion by tubular cross-members. The independent trailing arm front suspension used torsion bars as on the front-drive Citroën *Traction Avant* announced that same month, to the immense irritation of both parties. The A-Type's torsion bars were set laterally within the front cross tube, connecting to trailing links supporting the hub carriers. At the rear a transverse leafspring swing-axle IRS system was used.

The driver sat far forward, with a 46 gal (209 l) fuel tank behind him to accommodate changes in fuel load well within the wheelbase and so minimize handling changes during a long race.

The V16 engine set out to achieve the greatest possible usable power and torque for the lightest possible weight. Its short one-piece crankshaft ran in lead-bronze main bearings; the big ends too were plain in original form, and a single shaft-driven camshaft in the vee drove overhead valves via long pushrods. Unusually, Porsche and Kales preferred detachable cylinder heads, and wet-type cylinder liners (in direct contact with cooling water). They added a single Roots-type supercharger gear-driven off the camdrive, mounted vertically behind the block and delivering mixture drawn from two Solex carburettors through integral manifolding cast into the heads.

Porsche knew that road racing demanded more mid-range torque than sheer top-end horsepower. Consequently the V16 was quite slow revving, only 4,500 rpm, and produced around 290-295 bhp from its 4.4 litres capacity – no more than 67 bhp per litre.

Meanwhile, the Nazi rise to power had forced Rosenberger, a Jew, to move away. He realized what lay ahead, and so would not be a part in the

1 July, 1934 — French GP, Montlhéry — Hans Stuck has his A-Type Auto Union just beginning to roll after his team's very first and quite inept 2 min 35 sec stop to load fuel, water and fresh rear tyres. His was the last of the new-wave German cars to retire, to the great joy of the crowd. This shot shows the rear-engined Auto Union's low build and Porsche trailing-link independent front suspension very well. Note from the shadows on the radiator core that it has a reverse-vee shape.

1 July 1934 — French GP, Montlhéry — Stuck leaning his A-Type Auto Union around the *Epingle du Faye* corner, this angle emphasizing the German car's rear-engined configuration. The large vent on the scuttle side exhausted hot air from the nose radiator, the external starter dog socket is visible in the extreme tail and just admire the size of that rev counter on the dash panel . . .

success of the scheme he had helped create.

The AU team's racing debut was made at AVUS on 27 May, 1934, three A-Types facing Alfa Romeo before the *Fuehrer* and 200,000 expectant Berliners. Stuck built a lead of 85 sec until clutch-slip retired his car around two-thirds distance. Prinz zu Leiningen had already retired, August Momberger was the only AU finisher, third behind two Alfas.

At the Eifelrennen the new Mercedes-Benz W25s joined the fray, where Stuck finished second. The major French Grand Prix followed at Montlhéry; only two AUs ran and both retired – but Stuck's had led for 32 long laps.

Now the German cars matched their speed with reliability and at the Nürburgring for the German GP Stuck won by over two minutes. Mercedes-Benz began winning at Pescara, while at Berne in the Swiss GP, Stuck's wet-weather driving proved unbeatable, and Momberger was second for AU's first 1-2. Stuck and Leiningen shared second place in the Italian GP, they shared fourth in Spain and then Stuck won at Brno with Leiningen fourth.

This had been an excellent début season, Stuck emerging as effective Champion as he added to

his stature by winning the Kesselberg, Freiburg and Mont Ventoux mountain climbs in the V16 cars. Back at AVUS at season's end, he broke more records; raising the 50 km average to 150.21 mph (250.35 km/h), 50 miles to 151.54 mph (252.57 km/h), 100 km to 152.18 mph (253.63 km/h), standing-start km to 101.37 mph (168.95 km/h) and the standing-start mile to 116.73 mph (194.55 km/h).

Into 1935 Auto Union's racing director, Dr Feuereissen, signed on the Italian star Achille Varzi for that year, and the A-Type cars were modified; tail pipe exhausts replacing the original stubs, fabric side panelling giving way to alloy sheet, cooling modified with external pipes instead of relying upon the chassis tubes which had cracked and leaked coolant away – and overheated the cockpits. The heavy rear leaf-spring was replaced by longitudinal torsion bars within the chassis longerons; and detachable steering wheels eased cockpit entry. During the new season the engine big-ends were changed to rollers, a Hirth-type built-up crankshaft replacing the original one-piece design. Bore and stroke became 72.5 mm x 75 mm, 4.95 litres. Blown at 11 psi this produced 375 bhp at 4,800 rpm, and

26 May, 1935 — AVUSRennen, Berlin — newboy Bernd Rosemeyer makes his Grand Prix car début in the 'Lucca' model record-breaking coupé car — actually Auto Union A-Type chassis '*Nr 76003*' (4) — lined up on the front row at the high-speed German track alongside team leader Hans Stuck's new B-Type chassis '*Nr 76012*'. This is not to be the Chemnitz team's day — Luigi Fagioli will win for Mercedes-Benz.

boosted torque from 391 lb/ft to a massive 478 lb/ft at 3,000 rpm against the A-Type's 2,700 rpm peak. Maximum speed climbed from around 170 mph (283 km/h) to 180 mph (300 km/h). This became the Auto Union B-Type spec, and its gigantic torque enabled the cars to be driven in only two gears round many circuits, and reputedly without any gear-changing at all at Monaco!

Surviving team documents mention a five-digit chassis number form, prefixed 76, and Stuck's 1935 Tripoli car was chassis '76012', his AVUS car '76013' and Varzi's '76014'. Equally, the Rosemeyer and Leiningen 1935 AVUS cars were described as '*Typ 1934*'; serials '76003' and '76004' so circumstantially AU seem to have built at least 14 chassis by that time, and '76014' remains the highest number I have seen in AU engineering records from 1936-37.

Varzi won on his AU debut at Tunis in 1935 but at Tripoli lost the lead when a tyre burst and finished second, to a Mercedes, which team now took the upper hand. At AVUS Stuck won his heat but lost the final due to tyre trouble; Varzi finished third, Leiningen crashed at 150 mph (250 km/h) – his last appearance for the team – and a new recruit from the Auto Union/DKW motor cycle team named Bernd Rosemeyer also retired.

The B-Types demanded special sensitivity to drive them quickly. Rosemeyer proved his ability quite outstanding. In the Eifelrennen at the Nürburgring he caught and passed Caracciola's Mercedes and led until the last lap, only to be pipped to the line by 1.9 sec.

Two Hirth-crank engines, retaining the 72.5 mm bore but introducing an 85 mm stroke for 5,610 cc, ran in the French Grand Prix, but succumbed to plug, lubrication and brake problems. Only one finished, fifth, and the cars were then withdrawn for modification until the German GP where Stuck finished second behind Nuvolari's amazing Alfa Romeo *Tipo B*, the rest of the Zwickau team 4-8-9. At Pescara Varzi won from Rosemeyer, and was timed at 183 mph (305 km/h) on the Montesilvano Straight. Stuck again won the Freilburg and Kesselberg mountain climbs, and the Italian GP. At Brno, Rosemeyer won for his new team.

A C-Type version of the car was then developed for the 1936 season, 75 mm x 85 mm, 6,010 cc delivering 520 bhp at 5,000 rpm – 85 bhp per litre. Its torque was a monstrous 630 lb/ft at merely 2,500 rpm at which level it yielded 300 bhp. An even wilder *Typ R* unit was produced, with 87 mm bore for 6,330 cc and 545 bhp – essentially for record breaking.

Mercedes's GP car development stumbled that season – see page 82 – which left the way clear for the modestly financed Auto Unions to do most of the winning. At Tunis Varzi survived a huge accident in which his car somersaulted at 175 mph (291.6 km/h). Ernst von Delius joined the team in Barcelona, finishing fourth from Rosemeyer who had demolished a lamp-post along the way. At the Eifelrennen in dense mist and drizzle Rosemeyer took a two minute lead and won brilliantly – the *Nebelmeister* they called him – the 'Fog Master'.

Nuvolari just beat Rosemeyer in Hungary, but Rosemeyer won the Geman GP, Coppa Acerbo (AUs 1-2-3), Swiss GP (again a team 1-2-3) and Italian GP. He won the European Championship and the Freiburg mountain climb, breaking Stuck's hill record.

The AIACR then extended the 750 kg Formula for one more season, 1937, to allow extra time for teams to prepare their new 3 litre supercharged or 4.5 litre unsupercharged cars for what now became the new 1938-40 Formula. AU ran the C-Types little changed from 1936 trim, Rosemeyer in a class of his own amongst their weakened driver team as Varzi and Stuck were both semi-retired. Two cars were shipped to South Africa for Rosemeyer and von Delius, who won the Grosvenor GP – a minor handicap race. Rosemeyer subsequently won the Eifelrennen, the US Vanderbilt Cup, Coppa Acerbo and Donington GP against the strongest-ever Mercedes-Benz opposition. Rudolf Hasse won the Belgian GP from Stuck who won the La Turbie and Freiburg climbs, but tragically tubby, balding little von Delius was killed in a collision with Dick Seaman's Mercedes W125 during the German GP at the Nürburgring. Rosemeyer's Donington GP win saw Auto Union triumph in the last 750 kg Formula race to be held – a great finale to an extraordinary era in which Auto Union had frequently shone and presaged a rear-engined future.

---

2 October, 1937 — Donington GP, Donington Park — An Auto Union mechanic gives the left-rear hub-nut of H.P. Muller's C-Type Auto Union one last precautionary clout just before the engine cowl will be clipped and strapped into place ready for the start of the pre-war 'British GP'. Note the heavy treaded Continental racing tyres, the ultra-light gauge alloy body-panelling and the V16-cylinder engine with its supercharger and carburettor under scrutiny above the final-drive.

1937
The Mercedes-Benz W125s

★ ★ ★ ★ ⸕

The vicissitudes of the Model 1936 short-wheelbase Mercedes-Benz GP car overstretched the capabilities of the Unterturkeim company's experimental department. Racing with a system proven by the relatively relaxed two or three-race schedules of 1908, 1914, and the early-to-middle '20s, was no longer viable in the mid-'30s when the calendar had become so crowded and intense. The D-B board recognized this, and in late-summer 1936 they formed a new racing department, the *Rennabteilung*.

Meanwhile the 750 kg Formula was being extended through one extra season – 1937 – before delayed introduction of a replacement for 1938-40. New Rennabteilung head, Rudolf Ühlenhaut, had joined D-B's experimental department direct from engineering college as a carburetion specialist.

D-B blooded him in competition; he twice competed in the 2,000 km Trial, sharing a Team Prize in 1933 with *Typ* 200 cars and in 1934 winning a gold medal in a *Typ* 500. Until the *Rennabteilung's* formation during the winter of 1936-37, he had been engaged in design of Mercedes's first large-volume production car, the 170V. Now he had Jakob Krauss's car construction department and Georg Scheerer's test and inspection section under his control, and reported direct to Fritz Nallinger, head of the main experimental department. His *Rennabteilung* was to assemble, prepare and test the cars, liaising closely with Alfred Neubauer's sporting department which handled entries, bookings, transport, race direction and general activities at the races.

Wagner and Heess still wielded engineering direction, and all racing components were manufactured in the Unterturkheim production plant's main workshops.

Ühlenhaut immediately made his presence felt, directing extensive track tests of the Model 1936 to analyse its handling faults. When the professional drivers were engaged elsewhere, Ühlenhaut tried driving the GP cars himself at the Nürburgring. He discovered he was capable of analysing their behaviour first-hand, and found that constant bottoming of the front suspension was one major problem so he strongly recommended long-travel front suspension for a replacement car design. The Model 1936's new de Dion rear end was much superior to the W25 swing axles, but under heavy acceleration it juddered violently, due to flexion within the de Dion tube itself.

After Ühlenhaut's labours, these 'short cars' were improved, and on 14 August 1936 Nallinger prepared a brief: 'To have as soon as possible a usable vehicle for 1937.

'Frame stiffer, most probably an oval-tube frame.

'Front suspension: Wheels with more spring travel and eventually springs with progressive effect.

'Rear suspension: Retention of the present axle, yet with guidance of the axle toward the front instead of toward the rear.

'Lengthening of the wheelbase over that of today. Since the new light alloy engine already being designed will probably not be ready, it is to be considered whether the present engine should not be increased in power through an increase in

Mercedes-Benz, 1937 — The team, including (left to right) *Ing* Rudolf Ühlenhaut, Manfred von Brauchitsch, Rudolf Caracciola, Dick Seaman, former 1914 team driver, now Director, Max Sailer, and team manager Alfred Neubauer.

speed, and with that a better gear ratio for acceleration'.

As late as December 1936, the design team hoped to perfect a new 75 mm x 85 mm 6,010 cc V16-cylinder engine with iron liners sunk into a light-alloy block, but it did not materialize satisfactorily.

Meanwhile, Georg Scheerer had been experimenting with more efficient supercharging. Late in September 1936 he tried a system on an M25B engine in which the 220 mm *Typ* AB blower drew a fuel-air mixture from the carburettor, instead of feeding pure pressurized air into an otherwise sealed carburettor. This suction type was used successfully by Auto Union and Alfa Romeo, but D-B were haunted by the decade-old failure of such a system on their slow-accelerating 2 litre GP straight-eight. Scheerer's tests, however, revealed an astonishing 17 per cent power increase with the suction system. He then rigged an ME25 engine with a suction system, and watched its output soar 32 per cent at 2,000 rpm and 11 per cent at 5,700 rpm – peaking at 488 bhp at 'five-five'.

Nallinger's chassis designers pursued his proposal for an oval-tube chassis frame, derived from that of the small 170V saloon. The W125 chassis for 1937 consequently emerged with oval-section main chassis longerons, 5.5 in (14 cm) deep, straight front to back and interlinked by four round-section cross-members of 4 in (10 cm) diameter. The rear engine bearers formed a fifth cross-brace. Fabricated from steel alloy only 59-thou thick this frame with brackets weighed 114.4 lb (52 kg). Torsionally it was almost three times stiffer than the W25 box-section affair *sans* engine, and half as stiff again with the engine installed.

The de Dion rear axle was now controlled by long radius rods trailing rearward from pick-ups by the driver's knees, but to allow the rear wheels independent vertical movement the de Dion tube itself was made in three parts, united by a bronze-bushed, rotating centre section. While the radius rods were initially in steel a Dural set was used on Caracciola's W125 for the Eifelrennen, surviving 467 miles (778 km) of Nürburgring pounding and consequently becoming standard on the W125s.

Torsion bar rear springs were used, taking a leaf – to coin a phrase – out of Dr Porsche's Auto Union book. Total rear wheel movement was now 7 in (18 cm). The parallel wishbone idea was retained up front, a coil-spring interposed between the wishbones, but arm length was now doubled in comparison to the W25-series and vertical movement became 5.75 in (14.61 cm). Improved steering and much improved drum brakes were fitted.

The prototype W125 chassis had a 1936 ME25

engine installed for Monza testing in February '37, where it was driven by Caracciola. Ühlenhaut and 27-year–old motor cycle racing works team mechanic, Hermann Lang. Rear-end chatter under power highlighted the need for improved damping now that torsion bars had replaced the self-damping effect of the earlier leafsprings. Steering kick-back remained a problem. The trim and slender 1936 'short car' body-style was elongated into the definitive W125 form, the complete shells weighing 67.1 lb (30.5 kg).

In test form, with Continental tyres mounted, car 'W125-1' weighed 1,770 lb (804.5 kg) dry, biased 53 per cent to the driving wheels with the ME25 engine. Without tyres it weighed 728 kg (1,604.95 lb). Not until late February was the latest M125 straight-eight engine mated to this chassis.

The new engine was longer than its predecessors, cylinder centres now 104 mm (4.09 in) apart to accommodate a larger bore, 94 mm x 102 mm, for 5,660 cc. Twin overhead camshafts actuated four valves per cylinder disposed at 70° included angle. The cylinder blocks still employed welded-steel fabrication but were more robust following the failures of the ME25 – see page 82.

Initially these M125 or 'F-Series' engines had five main bearings and solid crankshafts – built-up Hirth type shafts being produced but seldom fitted. A nine-main-bearing bottom end was also developed, featuring a much lighter crankshaft but inevitably heavier crankcase, which became standard M125 wear. With roller-bearing bottom end, pressure carburettors and 240 mm supercharger the M125 power unit weighed 491 lb (223 kg) complete.

In mid-February with Scheerer's latest suction carburettor supercharging, the first M125 delivered 580 bhp at 5,800 rpm – representing 102.4 bhp per litre, or 1.18 bhp per lb – but down at Monza the testers cursed the poor throttle res-

Early July 1937 — Dick Seaman in his Mercedes-Benz W125 during practice for the Vanderbilt Trophy race on Long Island's Roosevelt Raceway. Team manager Alfred Neubauer and a partially hidden mechanic seem to be checking that the fuel filler cap is locked shut or the tail mopped dry. The 5.66 litre W125 was the pinnacle of 750 kg Formula racing design. Seaman didn't miss the old-style supercharger system's whine; he wrote 'I always found it extremely tiresome when driving. . .'

2 October, 1937 — Donington GP, Donington Park — Manfred von Brauchitsch opening up his 550 bhp-plus Mercedes-Benz W125 out of Coppice Corner on the approach to the farmyard in desperate pursuit of Bernd Rosemeyer's long-gone C-Type Auto Union which beat him by over half a minute. Power-on oversteer such as this was balanced in the W125 design by its essentially stable inherently understeering long-wheelbase chassis with major mechanical masses widely separated to front and rear.

---

ponse of the suction-carburettor ME25 in their W125 hack chassis. In March a proper M125 engine was tested at Monza but behaved worse, so Nallinger decreed that pressure carburettors would be used for the start of the season and suction carburettors would be adopted only if the new system could be debugged.

A suction-carburettor eventually made its debut in the Eifelrennen at the Nürburgring on 13 June, Kautz finishing ninth. Dick Seaman, seventh at Tripoli in his first D-B race, had a suction-carburettor engine for the Vanderbilt Trophy on Long Island, USA, and placed second to Rosemeyer's Auto Union. Only suction-carburettors were then used for the German GP on 25 July in which four of the five W125s finished, two placing first and second.

By June the W125s had become 8 kg (17.6 lb) overweight, so in a slimming programme redundant chassis stiffening was excised, and lighter dampers, seat and brakes and the dural radius rods were adopted.

The W125s placed 1-2-3 at Monaco, second at Pescara, 1-2-3 at Berne, 1-2 at Monza and 1-2-4 at Brno, but only second and third at Donington Park in the 750 kg Formula's finale. Rudi Caracciola emerged as European Champion – again – and the W125 had set the style for front-engine/rear gearbox/front coil-and-wish-

bone suspension/de Dion rear suspension, which would dominate Grand Prix racing design until 1959-60.

These very powerful cars were inevitably extremely fast. The highest available gearing for the W125 – used at AVUS in streamlined body form – corresponded to 211 mph at 5,500 rpm. Using 3.43:1 Monza gearing, the W125 could achieve 88 mph in first, 137 mph in second, 159 mph in third and 199 mph in top!

Its 5.66 litre straight-eight supercharged engine set new records for outright GP car power output, averaging 550-575 bhp towards the end of 1937, or on WW fuel 580-610 bhp – power which the well-developed chassis could transmit to the road at full throttle in second gear if the ratio was high enough. Such power outputs were as much as 107.7 bhp per litre in racing tune, while on the test bed an all-time high of 646 bhp was recorded – which is 114 bhp per litre.

No Grand Prix car would produce greater total horsepower until c.1981-82 when the second generation of 1.5 litre turbocharged F1 engines from Ferrari and BMW really began to come on song.

Nine complete W125 cars were assembled and campaigned by the *Rennabteilung* – using drivers Caracciola, Lang, von Brauchitsch, Seaman, Kautz and Zehender – during 1937, as follows:

Hermann Lang enjoyed himself greatly in later years by reappearing behind the wheel of the Daimler-Benz Museum's Mercedes W125 cars, as here at Montreux, Switzerland, in 1977. This was one of the first of what became a flood of historic car '*retrospectifs*' into the 1980s — the braying 1937 Mercedes providing a magnetic attraction for many wherever it ran.

Chassis 'W125/1' – Race début 13-6-37 – Kautz Eifelrennen*; possibly Lang Freiburg mountain-climb**; Seaman Masaryk GP. Car retired from GP service.

Chassis 'W125/2' – Race début 9-5-37 – von Brauchitsch Tripoli GP, Eifelrennen, Belgian and German GPs, *lst* Monaco GP; von Brauchitsch Masaryk GP; Caracciola *lst* Swiss GP. Car withdrawn from GP service.

Chassis 'W125/3' – Race début 9-5-37 – Caracciola, Tripoli GP, Eifelrennen, Vanderbilt Cup, *1st* German GP; Caracciola, Monaco GP; von Brauchitsch Coppa Acerbo, Italian and Donington GPs. Car withdrawn from GP service.

*First use of *Saugvergasermotor* – suction carburettor engine – the other four W125s in this event each used *Druckvergasermotoren* for the last time; see text.
**Chassis 'W125/1' and 'W125/8' were possibly those used by Lang and Caracciola in the Freiburg mountain climb on 1-8-37, the intervening weekend between the German and Monaco GPs.

Tripoli GP, Lang Eifelrennen, Belgian, German, Swiss and Masaryk GPs; Zehender Monaco GP. Car withdrawn from GP service.

Chassis 'W125/5' – Race début 9-5-37 – Seaman Tripoli GP, AVUSRennen, Eifelrennen, Vanderbilt Cup, German GP (damaged in collision) – rebuilt – Kautz Italian GP; Caracciola Donington GP. Car withdrawn from GP service.

Chassis 'W125/6' – Race début 11-7-37 – Kautz Belgian, German, Monaco and Swiss GPs; Seaman Italian and Donington GPs. Car withdrawn from GP service.

Chassis 'W125/7' – Début 13-8-37 – Seaman Coppa Acerbo, car written-off in accident diving practice.

Chassis 'W125/8' – Race début 15-8-37** – Caracciola Coppa Acerbo, *lst* Italian GP and *1st* Masaryk GP; von Brauchitsch Swiss GP. Car withdrawn from GP service.

Chassis 'W125/9' – Race début 12-9-37 – Lang Italian GP and Donington GP. Car withdrawn from GP service.

The Auto Union D-Types

★ ★ ★ ✦

Having completely misjudged the potential pace of development with their unlimited-capacity 750 kg Formula (which had been intended to restrict power and speeds in 1934 but which by 1937 produced 500 bhp-plus cars capable of exceeding 200 mph/330 km/h) the AIACR introduced a better spelled-out Formula for 1938-40. They restricted supercharged engines to 3 litres, and allowed unblown engines a little extra capacity, 4.5 litres. They then applied a *minimum* weight limit of 800 kg (1,763.68 lb).

Both Mercedes-Benz and Auto Union buckled down to design and build new cars to these regulations to continue their highly successful state-assisted GP programmes for the new Germany. With the wisdom of hindsight, Prof Dr Porsche had not got it quite right in his initial series of Auto Union V16s. The combination of enormous mid-range torque, spindly wheels and tyres and their tendency to be up-edged by the use of swing-axle rear suspension proved an enormous driver challenge which few could meet. There was much discussion of the manner in which AU's far-forward drivers were only able to sense an incipient tail slide once it had already developed to uncontrollable proportions. Such debate clouded the real folly of unleashing well over 500 bhp and nearly as many ft/lb torque through 6 in wide tyres and swing-axles!

Dr Porsche was becoming increasingly involved with the KdF Volkswagen project, and prime AU design responsibility for the new Formula fell upon Dr Robert Eberan von Eberhorst, a young Viennese engineer who had been responsible for testing and engine development at Zwic-

kau. For 1938-39 a new midship weight-concentrated 3-litre V12 Auto Union D-Type was designed and developed under Eberan's direction. A rather primitive form of de Dion rear suspension had already been adopted on the production 8-cylinder Horch introduced late in 1935, and an improved version was now perfected for the GP cars by Chemnitz's Dr Siebler.

It was combined with unusually soft, though firmly-damped, long-travel springing to produce a remarkably controllable rear-engined GP car. Unfortunately for proponents of rear-engined configuration, AU's 1938 season was late in reaching full song due to the death of number one driver Bernd Rosemeyer in a record attempt that January. The 1939 season was riven by shortage of funds and, of course, culminated in the outbreak of the Second World War.

Auto Union was understandably devastated by Rosemeyer's death, but before the tragedy Eberan and his colleague Werner K. Strobel laid out a 3 litre 12-cylinder version of the big 6 litre 16-cylinder, but employing a wider 60° vee between cylinder banks. Its bore and stroke were 65 mm x 75 mm, close to the A-Type of 1934, with the conrod length of the 1936 C-Type. The new engines actually commenced 1938 using V16-stock plain main bearings. Power was subsequently increased by use of roller mains, and roller bearing big-ends also featured on the Hirth built-up crankshaft. Where the low-speed V16 shafts had been only partially counterweighted, the V12's were completely counterweighted for higher rpm. The 60° vee was too wide for the V16's single central camshaft valvegear to be used unchanged, so

The D-Type Auto Union's 3 litre V12-cylinder engine was housed well amidships in Eberan von Eberhorst's vastly improved chassis design, pannier fuel tanks on each side drawing another major mass within the wheelbase around the car's centre of gravity to minimize handling changes between full and near-empty. The blower is still at the back of the engine above the final drive. Note the painstakingly finned and drilled brake drums and the detachable steering wheel here resting on the seat.

instead a central bevel-driven camshaft was retained, actuating only the intake valves through rocker arms while bevel gears at the back of the camshaft then powered cross shafts operating cams and rockers on the exhaust valves. It was thus a three-cam V12. A new scaled-down Roots-type supercharger was designed, now cast in magnesium instead of aluminium, driven at 2.4 times crankshaft speed – up to 17,000 rpm – and displacing almost 1.4 litres of air per revolution ... With this blower the 3 litre V12 Auto Union D-Type engine developed 460 bhp at 7,000 rpm – 153 bhp per litre.

22 October, 1938 — Donington GP, Donington Park — The naturally diminutive Tazio Nuvolari is positively dwarfed by his D-Type Auto Union *en route* to victory in the last pre-war 'British GP'. Here the car shows off its smoothly-formed pannier tanks; note the shapely vent which ducts hot air away from the nose radiator above this left-side pannier, and the starter shaft protruding just above the tip of the tail. Supercharger air was drawn in through the belled-out leading-edge deflector topping the engine cowl.

But the Roots blower proved inefficient at such high speeds and pressures, so AU developed an alternative gear-driven two-stage system to compress the mixture in progressive steps. This was introduced in the 1939 French GP and featured a larger first-stage blower – in reality a shorter version of the *Typ S* V16 unit – sweeping 2.25 litres per revolution into a smaller second-stage blower which was a shorter-lobe version of the 1938 V12 type, displacing 1.2 litres per revolution. Both blowers were run at 1.63 times engine speed, producing 24 psi boost. In this form the V12 developed 485 bhp at 7,000 rpm, and 500 bhp at 7,500 rpm which was 166.6 bhp per litre, even though this was not considered prudent for racing use. More remarkably, peak torque remained enormous in the best Chemnitz tradition – 405 lb/ft at 4,000 rpm, still very slow for a GP car.

The D-Type chassis was simply a twin-tube ladder derived from the 1937 C-Type, but swing axles were replaced at last by Siebler's improved de Dion system. The axle tube dipped under the final-drive transaxle, radius arms provided further location, and a cuff-joint at the left hub where the tube entered it prevented the tube itself from acting as a giant anti-roll bar. A Panhard rod provided lateral location, placed very low to lower the rear roll-centre. This was the only practical application of a de Dion tube to a rear-

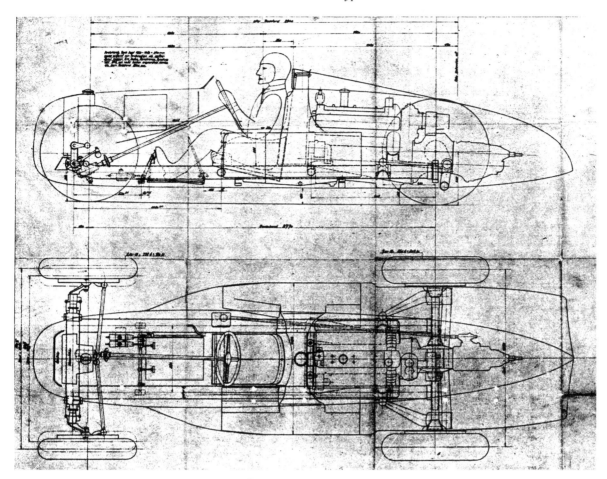

An Auto-Union works drawing based upon the V12 D-Type layout.

The 1938-39 Auto Union D-Type V12.

The 1939 3-litre Auto Union D-Type should have established the efficacy of mid-engined design into the 1940s, but its message was submerged when war intervened. When the author arranged for 1961 World Champion Phil Hill to drive Kerry Payne's newly-restored D-Type here at Donington Park in 1979, the analytical American was hugely impressed with its advanced ride and handling. The car subsequently found a loving home with English driver/collector Neil Corner.

engined racing car and it vastly improved AU's hitherto tail-happy Porsche-type handling. Gearbox and final-drive were virtually unchanged from 1934-39, and for the de Dion rear end application in '38-39, all it needed was plunging joints at the outer ends of its half-shafts.

In mid-March 1938, AU took two C-Type V16s to Monza plus the prototype V12 D-Type, which very closely resembled the 6.1 litre cars externally save for deep pannier fuel tanks each side. To fool onlookers, an additional quartet of dummy stub exhausts protruded from the rear cowl, suggesting the new 3 litre was another V16. Only the most observant spies noticed that only 12 of the stub exhausts issued smoke...

While the new 3 litre V12s were built and prepared for GP racing, two *Bergwagen* mountain-climb cars were maintained, one a 1937 C-Type V16, the other a V16-engined D-Type chassised car. Three D-Types were earmarked as *Trainingswagen*, two more as experimental and test hacks – construction of nine more team *Rennwagen* being projected.

Two D-Types appeared in definitive form with shapely beetle-backed bodies and curvaceous nose cowls in the German GP on 3 July. But without Rosemeyer they struggled. Christian Kautz and Rudi Hasse had earlier both retired in the opening laps of the French GP at Reims. Dr Feuereissen signed-on Tazio Nuvolari in time for

the German GP at the Nürburgring, but he and Hasse retired, Stuck finished third and Müller/Nuvolari fourth. Stuck's fourth place was the best AU achieved in the Swiss GP at Berne, but he won the Grossglockner mountain climb, then Nuvolari thrilled all AU supporters by victory in both the Italian and Donington GPs to close the season.

In 1939 Stuck won La Turbie, Nuvolari was second in the Eifelrennen, Müller second at the Vienna climb, Hasse second in the Belgian GP, Stuck won at Bucharest, Rumania, and H.P. Müller and 'Schorch' Meier were 1-2 in the French GP at Reims. Müller was second in the German GP, fourth in the Swiss and then in the Yugoslav GP at Belgrade on 3 September 1939, Nuvolari finished first and H. P. Müller third in the Auto Union team's final outing. The engineering report of that race reveals that Nuvolari drive *'Wagen 76010'* and Müller *'Wagen 76011'* so AU continued their A to C-Type chassis numeration, and probably used pre-existing customs paperwork as well since there were V16-cylinder cars using those same numbers. Number '11 seems to be the highest D-Type serial recorded.

However, on the day of Nuvolari's Hungarian victory, Britain was forced to declare war on Germany... and the products of Chemnitz and Zwickau were destined for oblivion ...

The Alfa Romeo Tipo 158-159s

★ ★ ★ ★ ★

The 1.5 litre supercharged straight-eight *Vetturetta* design which became known as the Alfa Romeo *Alfetta* was born out of Italian despair at Germany's total financial and technical domination of Grand Prix racing in the late-1930s. The under-financed Italian teams like Maserati and Alfa Romeo had already decided that if they could not beat the Germans at top level then they might as well concentrate their resources instead upon racing between themselves in the 1.5 litre *Voiturette* – in Italian *Vetturetta* – class.

That arch-practician Enzo Ferrari recommended this approach in the autumn of 1937, and Alfa Romeo President Ugo Gobbato approved the secondment of one of Vittorio Jano's assistants, *Ing.* Gioachino Colombo, to the Scuderia Ferrari in Modena's Viale Trento Trieste where he worked with Alberto Massimino and Angelo Nasi on design of a suitable car. Components for six cars were commissioned and during the winter of 1937-38 the first four were assembled in Modena. Meanwhile, following the failure of his 12C-37 GP car, Jano had been dismissed on 28 September – a grossly unfair decision according to every surviving member of his team – and Gobbato decided to concentrate all Alfa's racing activities in-house at Portello, as 'Alfa Corse' – 'Alfa Racing' – from 1 January 1938. Alfa completely absorbed the Ferrari team which as an independent company was placed in liquidation. Mr Ferrari moved to Portello to manage Alfa Corse.

The new straight-eight *Vetturetta* was given the type number '158' derived simply from 1.5 litres, 8-cylinder. Colombo had virtually used one half of the contemporary *Tipo* 316 V16-cylinder GP power unit. The V16's gear train drive to the twin overhead camshafts and other ancillaries was at the rear of the engine whereas in other Alfa eights it had always resided amidships, between the two tandem cylinder blocks. Now for his 158, Colombo juggled this cam-drive around to the front of the engine, enabling use of a shorter crankshaft.

The engine was based upon two aluminium block castings, 58 mm x 70 mm, 1,479 cc, initially with dry steel liners. The crankcase was cast in elektron, its crankshaft machined from a single chrome-steel billet and running in eight main bearings and a ninth subsidiary. Dry-sump lubrication was used. There were twin overhead camshafts and two valves per cylinder, and a single-stage Roots blower boosted at 17.6 psi. In first testing at Modena, this 1,500 developed 180 bhp at 6,500 rpm –120 bhp per litre. Six months later upon its racing debut, Alfa Corse had raised these figures to 195 bhp at 7,000 rpm – 130 bhp per litre.

This engine and four-speed gearbox were mounted in a twin-tube steel chassis frame with trailing-arm and transverse leafspring front suspension and swing-axle and transverse leaf at the rear. Very neat, slender bodies were fitted, with a potato chipper radiator grille steeply raked. For *Vetturetta* racing the tail tank was quite compact, only 37.5 gal (170 l) . . . it would grow as the cars' long career developed . . .

The *Vetturetta* class had hitherto been dominated by Maserati's mass production of 4C and 6C cars, since they had toppled ERA's brief superiority of 1934-5. The new *Alfettas* made their

11 September, 1938 — Milan GP 1.5 litre *Vetturetta* race supporting the Italian GP, Monza — Francesco Severi showing off the swing-axle rear suspension's camber change as he applies a touch of opposite lock to his original-form Alfa Romeo 158 *Alfetta* on the way to second place behind team-mate Emilio Villoresi's winning sister car.

début in the Coppa Ciano at Livorno on 7 August 1938, driven by Emilio Villoresi – Luigi's brother – Clemente Biondetti and Francesco Severi and they immediately finished first, second and seventh respectively. The cars then had troubles in both the Coppa Acerbo at Pescara and the Circuit of Modena but Villoresi and Severi finished 1-2 in the Milan GP. Bottom-end weakness had to be corrected in time for 1939, lubrication being improved and needle-roller big-end bearings adopted. Power reached 150 bhp per litre – 225 bhp at 7,500 rpm.

First 1939 event was the Tripoli GP, its regulations altered to *Vetturetti* only to keep the Germans away. Mercedes promptly designed two W165 1,500 cc V8 cars clandestinely, shipped them over at the last minute and ruined the Italians' party. The *Alfettas* overheated in the desert and although Dr Farina managed to hold off the second W165 for some time in second place only Villoresi finished – third – by carefully *under*-revving throughout.

Wet liners had already been adopted but coolant feed to the heads was now improved and system pressure raised, lubrication reworked for the second time and the cars rebodied into the more bulbous form which became famous. Farina won the Coppa Ciano; Biondetti, Pintacuda and Farina placed 1-2-3 in the Coppa Acerbo, Farina and Biondetti 1-2 in the Prix de Berne and in the accompanying Swiss GP – against the German

cars – Farina actually held second place for a rousing seven laps!

Two of the first batch of *Alfettas* were reputedly destroyed, Emilio Villoresi being killed testing one at Monza and motor cyclist Giordano Aldrighetti in another during practice at Pescara.

Alfa Corse returned to Tripoli in 1940, the Hun was away at war, so the 158s enjoyed a virtual-walkover 1-2-3-5 finish, Farina, Biondetti, Trossi and Pintacuda. Then Italy entered the war.

Seven complete 158s including an experimental model known as the 158D with de Dion rear axle, were hidden first in lock-ups at Monza and then in a cheese factory at Melzo, following the German take-over in 1943. Attilio Marinoni was killed testing the 158D on an open Autostrada, hitting a lorry head-on over a blind bridge.

When peace returned, Alfa Romeo instantly decided to promote post–war recovery by racing their old cars. Two were hastily prepared and competed in the June 1946 Paris GP at St Cloud, Farina and French driver Jean-Pierre Wimille both retiring with clutch troubles. One month later four *Alfettas* contested the GP des Nations at Geneva, two in 1940 Tripoli form, but the 158/46B models for Farina and Varzi having two-stage supercharging, raising power to 254 bhp at 7,500 rpm – 169 bhp per litre. This two-stage system went on to all the cars for the Turin and Milan GPs, and they were quite unbeatable.

In 1947 they contested four races and won each one easily. The two-stage normal engine now developed 275 bhp at 7,500 rpm while the 158/47 spec used a larger low-pressure compressor raising output to 310 bhp at 7,500 rpm –206.6 bhp per litre! To cope with this engine's thirst an additional fuel tank was mounted in the right of the cockpit, and externally a single exhaust pipe was fitted instead of twin pipes.

But even the smaller increase in power that year exposed crankcase weaknesses. Cracks propagated from the main bearing webs. Tie rods were therefore added between the crankshaft main bearing caps and the blocks, and this fudge sufficed for four more years.

Alfa Corse's first race of 1948 was the Swiss GP but in practice Achille Varzi rolled the 158/47 in drizzling rain and was killed. The team still raced, Trossi winning from Wimille and chief tester Consalvo Sanesi fourth, Luigi Villoresi third in his new Maserati 4CLT/48.

Wimille went on to win the French, Italian and Monza GPs, the team totally dominant. Having scored 13 consecutive victories Alfa Corse then withdrew from competition for 1949 owing mainly to financial strictures at Portello, plus the technical demand upon the *Reparto Sperimentale* to develop the 1900 production car. They had also, tragically, lost their drivers – for Varzi's death had been followed by that of Wimille in a Simca-Gordini in Buenos Aires, and of Trossi in hospital from cancer. Even so, Portello had a 158/47 engine on the dyno by the end of that year developing 350 bhp at 8,600 rpm – 233.3 bhp per litre.

With financial support from an enthusiastic Alfa distributor, the factory returned to racing for

21 July, 1946 — GP des Nations, Geneva — Dr Farina finger-tips his revived factory *Alfetta* towards Alfa Corse's maiden postwar race win. Here his car shows off the definitive 158 body-style finalized in 1939, with its characteristic sharp-pointed tail (rounded-off in 1951) and copious louvring. Note the generally slightly battered and utilitarian look — even at frontline factory level the function of the GP car was all-important, finish largely irrelevant.

The distinctive 'elephant's trunk' carburettor air intake ducting of the later *Alfetta* straight-eight supercharged engines dominated the installation. Note also here the large ribbed compressor casing, simple head casting and single-plug ignition, and the bifurcated shiny pipework between radiator header tank and the voluminous head galleries carefully arranged to cool those hard-pressed exhaust-valve seats.

18 July, 1948 — French GP, Reims-Gueux — A rare shot of a rare occasion, Alberto Ascari — Maserati-driving son of Alfa Romeo's late, great P2 Champion of the 1920s — during his one-off appearance. Here at Reims he is accelerating along the finishing straight from the Thillois Corner towards the village of Gueux in a GP Alfa, displaying its graceful profile and extensively ventilated drum brakes. He finished third in a team 1-2-3, behind Jean-Pierre Wimille and works test-driver Consalvo Sanesi.

---

2 July, 1950 — French GP, Reims-Gueux — If you've got it, flaunt it, as Alfa Corse did with their definitive 158-series cars and the formidable 'Three Fs' driver team in 1950. Here on the starting grid at Reims, Fangio (6) is in pole position with a best practice time 1.9 sec faster than Farina (2) whose best time was in turn 2.2 sec faster than Fagioli's (4). In comparison, Philippe Etancelin's next-fastest unblown 4.5 litre Talbot-Lago (16) had not come within 4.3 sec of Fagioli's time . . .

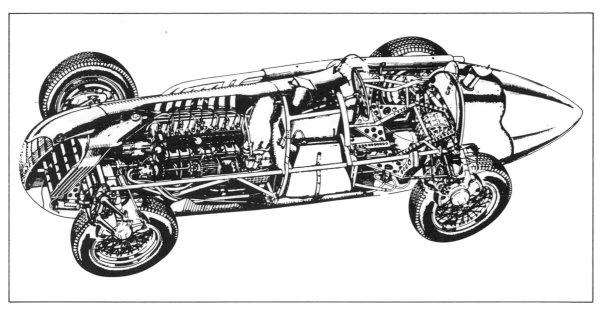

The ultimate *Alfetta* — 1951 *Tipo* 159 as used in the Italian and Spanish GPs.

The Alfa-Romeo 159's final form, from a factory drawing.

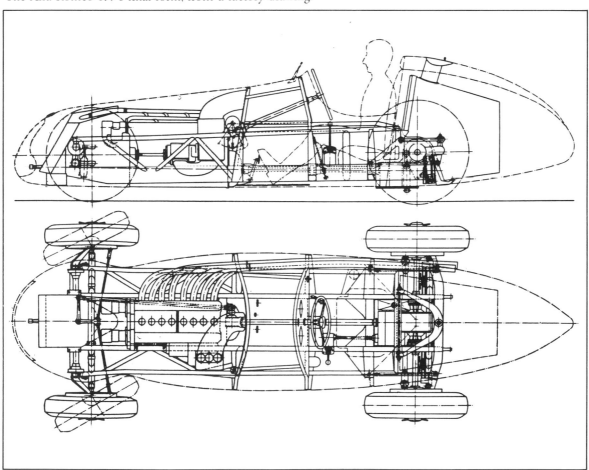

the first season of the new Drivers' World Championship in 1950, Farina, Fagioli and the new Argentinian star Juan Manuel Fangio forming their legendary 'Three Fs' team. Fangio opened his account by defeating a bevy of the new V12 Ferraris at San Remo in a lone Alfa Corse 158, and then in their first British appearance for the Championship-opening GP at Silverstone, Farina, Fagioli and guest driver Reg Parnell finished 1-2-3 after Fangio retired.

In the Belgian GP, the performance of Ascari's unblown 3.3 litre Ferrari V12 caused a stir and at Geneva his 4.1 litre Ferrari ran second led only by Fangio. Ferrari were clearly threatening Alfa Romeo's long-held supremacy but were not yet strong enough to capsize it. Fangio won the Monaco, Belgian, French, GP des Nations and Pescara races, Farina the British, Swiss, Bari, International Trophy and Italian GPs and the inaugural Drivers' World Championship title. Alfa Romeo were on top of the world . . .

But Ferrari's unblown developments had caused Alfa Corse to squeeze another 20 bhp from the 158s by raising supercharge pressure still further, and brakes were also improved. At the time, some described the cars modified in this way as the Alfa Romeo 159. Into 1951 engines screamed up to 10,500 rpm on the Portello dynos, and were run at a sustained 9,500 rpm, but in racing the red line was usually 8,500-9,000 rpm and thus power was restricted to less than 400 bhp. But the twin superchargers' drive now absorbed 135 bhp, the 98 per cent methanol fuel was cascaded through the engine to act as an additional internal coolant, and the *Alfetta's* consumption had become a grotesque 1.6 mpg. Extra fuel tanks were attached everywhere around each car, one even going alongside the engine in the warm and snug engine bay. With 66 gal (300 l) of methanol loaded they still required two refuelling stops in a 300 mile (500 km) Grand Prix. The swing-axle rear suspension reached its limit under such power and load and a de Dion rear end was adopted at last.

Alfa Romeo and Ferrari first met in 1951 at the Swiss GP, Fangio beating Taruffi in the latest 4.5 litre unblown, fuel-economical Ferrari. Farina won in Belgium, Ascari second for Ferrari. Fangio and Fagioli shared victory in the French GP at Reims, Ascari second again. This was Alfa Corse's twenty-seventh consecutive victory since 1946, discounting the 1951 International Trophy at Silverstone which had been abandoned due to torrential rain when Parnell's *Thinwall Special* Ferrari was leading.

But it was again at Silverstone, on 15 July 1951, that Alfa Corse's long run was finally broken. Froilan Gonzalez's *muletto* unblown Ferrari 375 beat them in a straight fight. At the Nürburgring in the same car, Ascari beat them again, the rugged circuit exposing chassis flexion which team manager Guidotti subsequently told me was corrected by introduction of the true 159 – with extra triangulated superstructure stiffening tubes in their chassis – for Monza. Old Alfa hands tell me these were *il vero 159* – the true 159 — while Luigi Fusi of the drawing office staff at that time described them as the 159M for *Maggiorata*, 'enhanced' or 'increased'. At Monza three *Alfettas* retired, but Farina fought Ferrari to the death, and his car died.

With three wins each, the Spanish GP at Barcelona's Pedralbes boulevard circuit would decide the Championship. Ferrari blew their hopes by choosing to run small-diameter wheels which over-speeded and ruined their tyres. Fangio won the race and the World Championship in the long-lived Alfa 158/159's swansong. Alfa Corse had also won the minor Ulster Trophy – Farina – the Bari GP – Fangio – and three minor races at Goodwood, all falling to Farina.

In its ultimate 159M form, the *Alfetta* straight-eight was boosted at 42.6 psi and produced a peak of 425 bhp at 9,300 rpm – 283 bhp per litre – a figure which would remain a pinnacle of Grand Prix racing technology for more than 25 years . . .

The Maserati 4CLTs

★ ★ ★

The Maserati brothers – Alfieri, Ernesto, Bindo and later Ettore – built their motor-manufacturing company upon early experience with Isotta-Fraschini and Diatto. The business was born in 1926, and grew slowly in poky premises at the Ponte Vecchio, Bologna. The brothers were more racing car enthusiasts than aggressively ambitious businessmen. They manufactured a long series of Grand Prix, sports and *vetturetti* cars in near penny numbers. Alfieri and Ernesto were both very capable racing drivers, but in 1932 the senior, Alfieri, died – at the age of only 44 – after allegedly botched abdominal surgery.

Ernesto led the surviving brothers in continuing the business, which by this time had diversified into producing good-quality speciality spark plugs in addition to the cars and engines. Through the early '30s, Maserati's business boomed as many wealthy amateur drivers appeared on the scene, anxious to buy competitive cars, notably the supercharged 1.5 litre *vetturetti* – for the Formula 2 of the time – which Maserati built quite effectively and offered at reasonable cost, with quite good after-sales support.

Unfortunately, Mussolini's Abyssinian adventure in 1936 triggered League of Nations sanctions which seriously depressed the Italian economy. Looking for protection against the financial draught, the brothers sold out to the Modenese industrialist Adolfo Orsi in 1937. He retained their expertise on a 10-year service contract. New GP cars were produced to the 1938 3 litre supercharged Formula, accompanied by a new range of 1.5 litre cars. In 1939-40 Orsi moved *Officine Maserati* from its cramped Bologna plant into new premises in the Viale Ciro Menotti, Modena.

Machine tools became another major sector of Maserati activity during the war, but as early as 1945 the design staff were thinking towards new racing car designs, while many pre-war *vetturetti* filled the service 'shop as well as the grids at most immediately post-war races. When their service contract expired in 1947, the Maserati brothers returned to Bologna to establish their own rival company under the name OSCA – *Officine Specializate Costruzione Automobili* – and Orsi replaced them with younger designers briefed to build GP cars around existing technology but suitable for series-production, and for use by private owners.

Ernesto Maserati's pre-war *vetturetti* had started out as 4-cylinder 1500s, powered effectively by half the 3 litre 8C GP engine of 1933-34, mounted in a suitably scaled-down centre-seat channel chassis. In 1936 an all-new 6C 6-cylinder was introduced, with torsion-bar independent front suspension. Some 6C frames were also fitted with 4C engines, and Maserati accumulated considerable success with this range of racing cars, 1936-38. Then for 1939, Ernesto introduced a much-modernized 4-cylinder engine, the 4CL, which combined twin-overhead camshafts with four valves per cylinder. Its bore and stroke became graven on the heart of every schoolboy enthusiast – 78 mm x 78 mm – and since it now breathed so freely these new '16 valve' supercharged Maseratis screamed up to 7,000

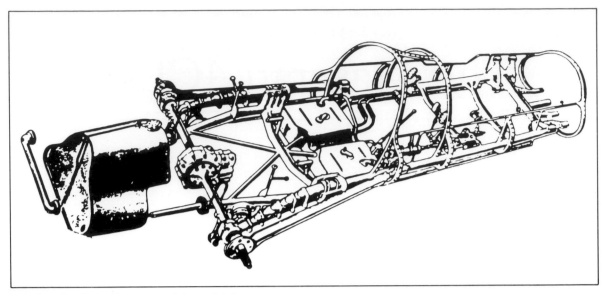

Tubular chassis — the Maserati 4CLT/48 frame.

rpm. A channel-type chassis was retained in improved form, still with torsion-bar IFS, and many of these cars returned to fight again after the war, alongside newly-built sisters, and enjoyed continuing success.

But in 1947, upon the expiry of the brothers' contract, *Ing* Alberto Massimino became chief engineer, closely assisted by *Ing* Vittorio Bellentani and Gorrini. For 1948 they produced an improved '16 valve' Formula 1 – or at that time some preferred to call it Formula 'A' – car, which they called the 4CLT/48. The additional initial letter 'T' stood for '*Tubolare*', describing a new tubular chassis frame which used twin round-tube main longerons (101.6 mm –about 4 in– in diameter) in place of the obsolescent channel-type. Independent front suspension now featured upper rocker arms bearing on inclined coil-springs tucked away inside the bodywork. The live back axle was still carried on splayed-out quarter-elliptic leafsprings as on the 4CLs but the 4-cylinder 16-valve engine was now two-stage supercharged.

According to Maserati historian Luigi Orsini, this tubular chassis frame – which reached its definitive form in the two-stage supercharged 4CLT/48 – had in fact been introduced as early as the European winter/Argentinian summer races of 1946/47. Onc tubular frame (serial '1583' – but still retaining the standard torsion-bar IFS) was prepared at that time by Ernesto Maserati and

Massimino to carry a 4CL engine. It was raced successfully in Argentina by Luigi Villoresi. Upon its return, it was then used by Alberto Ascari in the 1947 Marne GP at Reims-Gueux.

Thereafter, the Maserati brothers left, Massimino assumed sole technical directorship and another interim tubular-chassised car, chassis '1592', was built up with one of the new two-stage supercharged engines and again went well, driven by Farina.

The new supercharging system comprised two compressors, the lower one – with 160 mm bore – being driven off the crankshaft, the upper 115 mm stage driven off the camshaft-gears. The 4CLT engine redesign included a rugged new crankshaft, new H-section con-rods, new pistons, strengthened crankcase and sump. Still measuring 78 mm x 78 mm for 1,490.8 cc, the 4CLT/48 burned either Standard 'R' fuel mix or a close equivalent derived by mixing 85 per cent methyl alcohol, 10 per cent benzol and 5 per cent acetone, with 1 litre castor oil added for every 100 litres of mixture and – advised the factory – 2 litres of distilled water. Burning this 'jungle juice' developed a claimed 260 bhp at 7,000 rpm . . . 173.3 bhp per litre . . .

The definitive Maserati 4CLT/48 car combining this engine with the new rocker-and-coil-spring IFS tubular frame, made its successful début in the San Remo GP on 27 June 1948, driven by Alberto Ascari and Luigi Villoresi of the quasi-works Scuderia Ambrosiana. They immediately finished first and second, and the new model instantly became known as the 'San Remo Maserati'.

Thereafter Ascari and Villoresi completed an extremely successful season in the shapely new Fantuzzi-bodied GP cars, and when more appeared in private hands they became the highly-successful backbone of late 1940s 1.5 litre supercharged F1, mixed in with numerous older cars from the trident marque. But, in the presence of the factory *Alfettas*, and once the new V12 Ferraris came on song, they had their work cut out to win.

Most significantly, the *Automovil Club Argentino* bought two 4CLT/48s for their 'drivers-to-

Europe' teams of 1949-50 which launched Juan Fangio and Froilan Gonzalez to staggering prominence. Fangio's 4CLT season of 1949 was a *tour de force* – see the following table – winning him his place in the works Alfa Corse team for 1950-51, *en route* to the first of his five Drivers' World Championship titles.

Two uprated 4CLT/50 cars were built in 1950, as used by Fangio to win the Pau GP that year. They used a built-up crankshaft with lightweight rods, raising the power output to some 280 bhp while weight-saving reduced the car to 620 kg (1,366.8 lb) against the 630 kg (1,388.9 lb) of the earlier series. A 290 bhp 1,720 cc version of the engine was also produced for the 1950 Temporada, using a 90 mm stroke, and although it was

14 May, 1951 — Festival of Britain Trophy, Goodwood — The reigning World Champion Dr Giuseppe Farina doing his best with the then obsolescent Maserati 4CLT. This shot exemplifies two things, the rugged Farina's artistic long-armed driving style and the neat and handsome lines of Fantuzzi's Maserati coachwork. The 4-cylinder supercharged cars still looked the part but they could not really compete — here even Farina finished only third, typically after banging wheels violently with those who dared oppose him.

unsuccessful in road racing one such engine was acquired by Piero Taruffi to power his *Tarf II* twin-boom car to several World records.

The two-stage Maseratis also attracted wide interest as a basis for 'improvement' in the attempt either to extend their competitive life or to win the valuable cash bonuses offered by the organizers of each year's Italian GP for the introduction of 'a new' Italian GP car.

The Ruggeri brothers' Scuderia Milano funded Professor Giovanni Speluzzi's high-pressure boost experiments, which drew upon experience with a 4CL engine used in power-boat racing by the Leto di Priolo brothers. Speluzzi's much-modified two-stage Maserati engines allegedly exceeded 300 bhp by the end of 1948, over 200 bhp per litre.

Dr 'Nino' Farina beat Ascari's new Ferrari in the 1949 Lausanne GP driving a Milano 4CLT/48 and for the cash bonus at the Italian GP the team's cars were billed as 'Maserati-Milanos' or simply the *'Gran Premio Milano'*. By this time Speluzzi was claiming 325 bhp at 7,000 rpm – 216.6 bhp per litre – but this was more than the engines could contain for very long, and they regularly blew apart.

By 1950 the Scuderia Milano had built themselves a special whose distantly Maserati-derived engine used an enormous single supercharger, a tube frame and de Dion rear suspension in place of the 4CLT/48's live axle. A sister MM special used transverse leafspring IRS allied to torsion-bar IFS, these machines eventually passing to Egidio Arzani and Giampaolo Volpini as the basis for their ill-fated Arzani-Volpini 2.5 litre F1 car of 1955, which killed driver Mario Alborghetti upon its tragic début in that year's Pau GP.

Meanwhile Enrico Platé had campaigned two 4CLTs very effectively for Baron de Graffenried and later Prince 'Bira' and with the change to unsupercharged F2 for 1952, he modified their engines into unblown 2 litre form – first 90 mm x 78 mm, then 84 mm x 90 mm for 1,995 cc. Without the bulky superchargers ahead of the short engine, the chassis could be cut down to reduce wheelbase, but only 150 bhp at 7,000 rpm – a measly 75 bhp per litre – was insufficient to keep this descendant of what had been the classical 'San Remo' Maserati line in contention.

By 1950-51 the strain of attempting to combat high-powered opposition from the modern Ferraris and comparatively formidably-resourced

Alfa Corse, had reduced the handsome Maseratis to little more than over-stretched, oil-oozing non-entities in any front-line race, though they continued to accumulate some success at minor level.

A factory-prepared listing of the 20 4CLT-series cars built in the Modena works – with delivery dates – is as follows:

Chassis '1593' – engine '1590' – 1948 Alberto Ascari, Milan.
Chassis '1594' – engine '1591' – 1948 Luigi Villoresi, Milan.
Chassis '1595' – engine '1592' – 29-8-48 Leslie Brooke, GB.
Chassis '1596' – engine '1593' – 14-9-48 Reg Parnell, GB.
Chassis '1597' – engine '1594' – 15-9-48 Officine A. Maserati.
Chassis '1598' – engine '1595' – 23-9-48 'B.Bira', GB.
Chassis '1599' – engine '1596' – *Automovil Club Argentino.*
Chassis '1600' – engine '1597' – *Automovil Club Argentino.*
Chassis '1601' – engine '1598' – 7-3-49 Enrico Platé, Milan (For Baron E. de Graffenried)
Chassis '1602' – engine '1599' – 15-6-49 *Dott.* G.Farina, Milan.
Chassis '1603' – engine '1600' – 8-9-49 Maria Theresa de Filippis, Naples – to Clemente Biondetti, Florence.
Chassis '1604' – engine '1601' – 8-9-49 Franco Rol, Turin.
Chassis '1605' – engine '1602' – 8-9-49 Pascal Puopolo, Buenos Aires.
Chassis '1606' – engine '1603' – 21-9-49 Louis Chiron, Monte Carlo.
Chassis '1607' – engine '1604' – 14-11-49 Enrico Platé, Milan.
Chassis '1608' – engine '1605' – 9-9-49 Piero Carini, Milan – to Andrea Viannini, Buenos Aires.
Chassis '1609' – engine '1606' – 14-11-49 *Dott.* G. Farina, Milan.
Chassis '1610' – engine '1607' – 14-11-49 *Ing.* Piero Taruffi, Rome.
Chassis '1611' – engine '1608' – 7-3-50 *Officine A. Maserati* – to Scuderia Milano*
Chassis '1612' – engine '1609' – *Officine A. Maserati* – to Scuderia Milano.*

*The Maserati-Milan special cars.

The Ferrari Tipo 125s

★ ★

When Enzo Ferrari walked out of the factory Alfa Corse racing team in 1938 he severed a close relationship with the Milanese marque which had endured for over 15 years. He had risen from the test 'shop to run his own quasi-works Scuderia Ferrari for eight seasons, 1930-37, and Alfa President Ugo Gobbato's 1938 directive to centralize all competition activities in-house as Alfa Corse affected him quite badly. His now fiercely independent style was badly cramped, and when he found he detested the new organization's Spanish chief engineer, Wifredo Ricart, it became a case of 'him or me' at Il Portello, and so Mr Ferrari left.

His severance agreement prevented him racing under his own name for five years, and he returned to Modena where he set-up a new company which he named *Auto-Avio Costruzione* – note the hyphen, often forgotten – in his old Viale Trento Trieste ex-Scuderia premises. He planned short-term to undertake high-quality sub-contract work for the motor and aviation industries, long-term to build cars of his own.

He was not to stay away from racing very long. One day late in 1939, he was visited by the 21-year-old son of the deceased great Alfa Romeo champion driver, Antonio Ascari. Burly young Alberto had already raced motor cycles with some success, and he was accompanied by another young enthusiast, the aristocratic *Marchese* Lotario Rangoni Machiavelli di Modena, scion of one of the city's most prominent families – so not a gentleman the peasant in Ferrari's psyche could refuse. They asked if he would build them suitable sports cars for the 1940 Mille Miglia, to be run on an abbreviated course, Brescia-Cremona-Mantua-Brescia.

Ferrari's design engineers were Alberto Massimino and Vittorio Bellentani – later to join Mascrati as described in the previous chapter – and Enrico Nardi. According to Nardi the decision to build cars as requested by Ascari and Rangoni was taken over dinner on Christmas Eve 1939. Fiat was offering cash bonuses to Mille Miglia class winners using Fiat bits, and the 1,500 cc class was targeted so Massimino could base his design for a straight-eight sports on as many Fiat 508C Ballila components as possible.

The two Touring-bodied cars were ready in time, known simply as '815's – ie 8 cylinders, 1.5 litres – in deference to Ferrari's 'no racing under his own name' agreement. They led their class on the first 110-mile lap of the Brescia race, but Ascari retired with valve-gear failure on lap two while Rangoni, passengered by Nardi, had the timing chain break later when leading the class by 33 minutes.

Italy then entered the war, Ferrari moving what was by this time his machine tool business into new premises at Maranello in the Appennine foothills just south of Modena, and there it survived the conflict only mildly battered. As early as July 1945, Mr Ferrari set in motion his ambitions to re-enter the motor racing world.

He summoned to Modena *Ing* Gioachino Colombo, former leader of the Scuderia Ferrari's 1937-38 *Alfetta* design team, who had been laid off by Alfa Milan in the immediate post-war recession. Ferrari asked his thoughts for a new 1,500 cc racing car design. Colombo recalled his

Possibly 26 August, 1948 — Parco del Valentino circuit, Turin — Something of a mystery, this *might* be the prototype GP Ferrari, on private test at Valentino a week before official practice began for the new GP team's public début, in practice for the first postwar Italian GP there on 5 September. The three race cars had more elaborate nose cowls, but were otherwise very similar. Perhaps significantly none of the hangers-on look very happy, nor — far right — does Farina.

answer: 'Maserati has an excellent 4-cylinder, ERA a 6-cylinder, Alfa Romeo an 8-cylinder. You, in my opinion, should build a 12-cylinder . . .'

'*Caro* Colombo, you are a mind-reader: I have been dreaming of building a 12-cylinder for years . . .'

He had never forgotten the smooth flexibility of the first World War era V12 Packard US Army staff cars, as later used by the lady racing driver, Baroness Antonietta Avanzo. Now Colombo was to do his bidding, initially putting pencil to paper – by his own account – on 15 August 1945 under a tree in the garden of his sister's house at Castellanza. Back in his Milan flat at Viale Certosa he began proper drawings for 'the 125 – so-called because of its unit (each cylinder) displacement . . .' – 125 cc per cylinder x 12 cylinders = 1,500 cc. Another engineer laid-off from Alfa Romeo, Angelo Nasi, helped in this original drafting, and the first Ferrari V12 engine emerged with two cast-iron 6-cylinder blocks mounted at an included angle of 60° on a common cast-

aluminium block. He chose to install this unit in a brief oval-section tubular chassis frame, its construction to be sub-contracted to GILCO Autotelai, run by Gilberto Colombo (no relation). Gioachino Colombo's original drafts laid out both 125S sports and 125C – *Corsa*, racing – cars, and were then fine-detailed and worked-up into working drawings by Ferrari's full-time staff at Maranello, on *Auto-Avio Costruzioni*-headed drafting paper.

In November, Alfa Romeo recalled Colombo to Portello, leaving an ex-Alfa engineer named Giuseppe Busso in charge of the Maranello project as Ferrari's first full-time engineering director. His assistant from October 1946 to March 1947 was *Ing* Aurelio Lampredi. Mr. Ferrari's long time friend Luigi Bazzi, ex-Fiat, ex-Alfa, supervised development testing.

On 12 March 1947, the very first car to carry the Ferrari name ran under its own power in the cobbled factory yard at Maranello. It was completed with a full-width roadster body, and was driven in its first race by Franco Cortese at Piacenza, on 11 May. Two more V12 cars appeared with cycle-wing bodies.

There were many problems with the prototype V12 engines, primarily involving gaskets and failures of Colombo's white metal plain-bearings which couldn't resist the high rpm loadings. Lampredi found the answer with needle roller bearings, but that brought new problems as ammonia-hardening the 12-cylinder crank to bear the rollers was fraught with danger of distortion. Then to prevent the needle-rollers seizing they had to machine the crank journals microscopically convex. Suddenly Alfa Romeo and Scuderia Ferrari old boy Giulio Ramponi visited from England where he now lived, acting as a liaison man between the British and Italian motor and component industries. He introduced Ferrari to Vandervell Products' patent *Thinwall* lead-indium shell bearings. G. A. 'Tony' Vandervell himself visited Maranello and talked bearings with Mr Ferrari, and they proved the answer to reliably launching many thousands of V12 engines . . .

Towards the end of that year, Colombo and Busso effectively swopped places – Busso returning to Alfa, Colombo to Ferrari – and on 1 January 1948, Colombo formally replaced Busso as *Capo Ingegnere* to review all existing projects; and Lampredi was invited to rejoin on Bazzi's recommendation. Initially Lampredi – a tough, aggressive and brilliant man – felt he would be happy to learn at Colombo's feet. Instead he found him '. . . a very intelligent person, but also a little eccentric, who improvised a lot . . .', and his patience began to wear thin.

Still it was under Colombo's direction that the first short-wheelbase *Monoposto* 125 was introduced in 1948, its claimed power output (supercharged) of 225 bhp at 7,500 rpm comparing to the basic unblown 1,500 sport's approximate 118 bhp at 6,800 rpm – a suspiciously neat 150 bhp per litre blown against 78.6 bhp per litre unblown.

A team of three of the new F1 cars made their début – driven by Dr Giuseppe Farina, Raymond Sommer and 'B.Bira' – in the Italian GP at Turin's Valentino Park, late in 1948, where their nervously short-wheelbase design and rear swing-axles handled poorly in heavy rain. Farina then scored Ferrari's maiden F1 win at Lago di Garda.

The chassis were improved for 1949, when Alfa Corse opted out of racing for a cost-saving season. Alberto Ascari and Luigi Villoresi moved from Maserati to Ferrari, as works drivers, and won the Swiss, Italian and Dutch GPs between them.

British private entrant Peter Whitehead bought

The two-stage supercharged four-cam 1.5 litre Ferrari 125 V12.

one of the original cars, and G.A. Vandervell bought another which he christened the *'Thin-Wall Special'* to be used by BRM to gain experience while their V16 was being developed. The *'Special'* ran only in the British GP, driven by Raymond Mays and his chief mechanic, Ken Richardson, who spun into the crowd.

The latest works cars made their début in the 1949 Belgian GP, but their heavy fuel consumption handicapped Ascari and Villoresi enabling Louis Rosier's non-stop unblown Talbot-Lago to win. At Berne, Ascari, Villoresi and Whitehead finished 1-2-9, the works cars' IRS now having the transverse leafspring mounted above the axle to reduce wandering at high speed, instead of below as on Whitehead's.

At Reims for the French GP, Villoresi retired early, but Whitehead looked set for certain victory until his gearbox faltered with just three laps remaining, and he finished third. At Zandvoort, Villoresi won after Ascari broke a stub axle.

The *Daily Express* Silverstone meeting then saw Ascari and Villoresi finish 1-3, split by Dr Farina's Maserati. Farina avenged this defeat at Lausanne, Ascari second, Franco Cortese in the other works car fourth, and Whitehead ninth.

Meanwhile, Colombo had been extensively redesigning his engine. He added twin overhead camshafts to each cylinder bank in place of the sohc valve actuation used in the original-series units. Central spark plugs were fired from twin horizontal magnetos at the rear of the engine, and two-stage supercharging was provided by twin Roots-type compressors mounted one above the other at the front of the unit, the upper one feeding an intake manifold between the blocks. Vitally, the wheelbase was now lengthened, the bodies were lowered, and the cars better-balanced to match their higher power.

Ferrari completed two of these new two-stage LWB cars in time for the Italian GP at Monza, and naturally entrusted them to Ascari and Villoresi, while the two older single-stage SWB cars were entered for Sommer and Felice Bonetto. Ascari won easily, leading throughout. Villoresi, Bonetto and Whitehead retired, and Sommer finished fifth. Peter Whitehead then rounded-off the season successfully by winning the Czech GP at Brno after most of his opposition fell over each other in the opening stages.

The factory continued to race the two-stage Ferrari 125s through 1950, but Colombo's star had waned – Mr Ferrari at Bazzi's encouragement was listening more to Lampredi – and attention was shifting from supercharged 1.5 litre F1 cars towards unblown alternatives, a 2 litre F2 and a 'big-block' extending towards the full 4.5 litres for Formula 1. These unsupercharged projects were

Probably 3 June, 1950 — Swiss GP, Bremgarten, Berne — Alberto Ascari had dominated the *Alfetta*-less 1949 season in his 1.5 litre supercharged F1 Ferraris. Here he is in his four-cam Colombo-designed *Tipo* 125 V12 preparing to do battle with the revived Alfa Corse, but unable to approach within 4.7 sec of Fangio's pole time. The fabricated radius arm visible in the rear suspension identifies primitive swing-axle suspension. Ascari would have an exciting ride ...

Probably 3 June, 1950 — Swiss GP, Bremgarten, Berne — The way ahead, Raymond Sommer driving his own unsupercharged 2 litre V12 Ferrari 166, its twin radius rods visible ahead of the rear wheel locating the outboard hub-end of de Dion rear suspension — a great improvement to these cars, and especially those with the powerful 4-cam and later unblown 3.3, 4.1 and 4.5 litre 'Lampredi' engines.

to go ahead under Lampredi's direction, and Colombo rejoined Alfa Corse in January, 1951.

Meanwhile, the two-stage supercharged LWB four-cam cars introduced victoriously in that 1949 Italian GP, reappeared at San Remo early in the 1950 season. But Alfa Corse were back after their year's sabbatical, and although Villoresi finished second the Ferrari 125 even in its latest form was no match for the factory 158 *Alfetta*. Ferrari opted out of the British GP to prepare adequately for Monaco, where Ascari finished second to Fangio's *Alfetta* and it was Villoresi's turn to retire. One car was then prepared with a four-speed rear-mounted gearbox plus de Dion rear suspension configuration, this replacing the previous swing-axle IRS layout with five-speed gearbox in unit with the engine.

Villoresi drove this car upon its début in the Swiss GP, but both Ferraris retired early. In the Belgian GP, Villoresi reappeared in the 'Berne special' while Ascari sprang a real surprise with the prototype 3.3 litre unsupercharged 'Lampredi big-block' V12 in an LWB swing-axle chassis. Ascari and Villoresi finished fourth and fifth, not very quickly but reliably. At Zandvoort, Villoresi drove a single-stage LWB car while Ascari handled an unblown 2 litre F2, but by 30 July and the

Geneva GP two 3.3 litre unblown F1 cars were ready which qualified second and third fastest, right amongst Alfa Corse's entries . . .

Now the complex, costly, difficult to prepare and pernickety supercharged engines were to be dropped completely. One two-stage LWB car was loaned to Vandervell as a new *'ThinWall Special'* along with Ascari's services for the International Trophy at Silverstone. Ferrari fitted fresh cam boxes to add authority to the car's new identity but Anglo-Saxon spellings never are an Italian strong suit, and when the bonnet was removed at Silverstone the cam-box lettering proudly announced *'Thinwell Special'*. It ran very badly and spun off in the rain.

During that season, Ferrari had campaigned no fewer than *eleven* different variants of *Monoposto* Formula 1 and 2 cars; three different F2s, *six* assorted F1 combinations and finally two Argentine-bound *Formule Libre* specials, one an SWB 2 litre F2 with single-stage supercharging added, and the other an early LWB five-speed gearbox swing-axle frame with similar engine.

Ferrari had now emerged from the supercharged era, and would not return to it in earnest until 1981 . . .

1950-55
The BRM V16s
★ ★

In many ways the V16-cylinder BRM was in its day the most famous of all the 50 famous racing cars discussed within these pages. In fact the British Motor Racing Research Trust's public relations office was probably the most effective department of the entire industrial co-operative which built the British Racing Motor through 1948-51.

Seldom before and seldom since have such an inflated reputation and such great expectations been publicly promoted for a new Grand Prix car before it has even turned a wheel, never mind actually raced in anger ... But such massive publicity back-fired catastrophically upon an organization which had set its sights on becoming a British Mercedes-Benz *Rennabteilung*, and which ended up as the wettest of motor sporting damp squibs.

The budgets drawn up by its founders in 1945-46 were first absorbed and then far, far outstripped by post–war inflation. The idea had been for the best of the British motor industry's facilities to club together to manufacture parts for a sensationally high-spec new GP car which would rule the post–war racing world. But through the cheerless, grey late-1940s, against the numbing social and political background which triggered George Orwell's albeit exaggerated vision of *1984*, Government was exhorting industry to 'export or die', and toolroom capacity for work on BRM components was rarely available on time. Delays stretched ever longer, every week or month lost meant that much extra twist of the inflation rack to stretch the team's small but already controversial budget ever further. Target

dates were missed, race entries would be made and cancelled, and when the car did finally emerge in December 1949 the startling concept suffered so many problems it proved almost beyond the development abilities of its creators.

BRM began as a post–war British great white hope, and virtually foundered in 1951 with national newspaper headlines berating the entire programme as producing merely a '*Blooming Rotten Motor*'. The captains of British industry who had backed it, like Bernard Scott of Lucas, Sir John Black of Standard and G.A. 'Tony' Vandervell of Vandervell Products Ltd, the makers of *Thinwall* shell bearings, were each very big fish in their own individual ponds. When it came to co-operative efforts such as the BMRR Trust, set-up to fund and supply the BRM team based at Bourne in Lincolnshire, these great men seldom thought alike. Each was accustomed to his say directing the way, but the BRM programme emerged virtually as the thoroughbred horse designed by a committee – ie, a camel.

Only one great industrialist had real single-minded visionary faith in the project's eventual success, and he was Alfred Owen of the Darlaston-based Owen Organization, who eventually bought total interest in the concept and who, long-term, would nurse BRM to international success and widespread acclaim.

The devout Alfred Owen was a Godsend in this way to the man whose original ideas had created the entire project. His name was Raymond Mays, and he was responsible for its flair, its zest and fire – and in many ways also for the seeds of its own failure. He was an inter-war British sprint and hill-climb star driver, a talented and successful road racer, and the man who with his engineering-minded friend Peter Berthon had created the ERA project with backing from wealthy Humphrey Cook, in 1934. Those famous initials ERA stood for 'English Racing Automobiles', whose 1.5 litre *Voiturette* racing cars were effectively the first of British manufacture to enter series production. Peter Berthon oversaw their design, developed from his work on the 6-cylinder 'White Riley' sprint car which Mays had campaigned most effectively through 1933. Now Mays had developed his vision of an all-British Grand Prix car, conceived and designed essentially by Berthon and manufactured with the backing of British industry both in money and material.

Mays always maintained that had he not become a racing driver, entrepreneur and entrant he would have loved to have gone on the stage. He and his friend Berthon certainly loved the grand theatrical gesture, and perhaps their BRM Project 15 racing car design was the greatest stroke of theatre either would ever make. Its stunningly complex 135° V16-cylinder engine, with Rolls-Royce-developed centrifugal supercharging derived from wartime aero engine practice, made it perhaps the most sensational Grand Prix car ever built. It made a sensational noise, literally bursting the eardrums of those who ventured too close to its exhausts. The centrifugally blown engine could scream round at an earth-shaking 10–11,000 rpm. It produced more horsepower per litre than any other racing engine until the advent of modern turbocharged F1 in the late '70s. Long after the 1.5 litre supercharged Formula to which it had been built was set aside, at

Section through BRM's Project or Type 15 1.5 litre V16-cylinder engine.

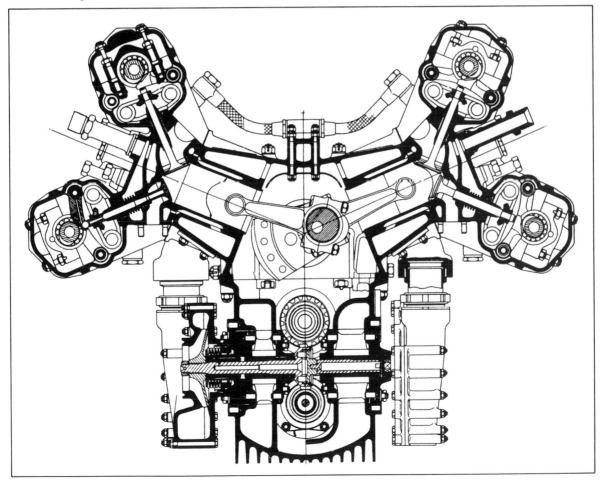

30 September, 1950 — Goodwood Trophy — Not a nice day in Sussex as the rains came pelting down, but popularly perceived as vindication for BRM's amazing V16-cylinder car as the brave Reg Parnell performed spectacularly despite such dread conditions and easily won outright. Few observers at the time harped upon the fact that this was only a twelve-lap race . . .

the end of 1951, its power output finally peaked at over 585 bhp –that's 390 bhp per litre, realized over 30 years ago.

At the time of its design, the best 1.5 litre racing engines, like the Italian *Alfetta,* were producing little more than 300 bhp. To reach 350 bhp would be a great achievement. Yet Berthon set his sights on 500 bhp, and went for the short-stroke big-bore high-revving option of a 135° V16, and then brought in Rolls-Royce to flex their aero engineering muscle with the centrifugal two-stage supercharging system to give it higher boost than had ever been applied before to a road-racing engine.

But this single-minded pursuit of peak power paid little regard to the unfortunate driver, which was remarkable considering Mays's pedigree. One can only conclude that the prospect of such enormous horsepower totally dazzled any practical sense he might have had.

Designed to boost at anything up to 70 psi the two-stage centrifugal system made the BRM V16 a real wheel-spinning terror. Where a conventional supercharger promotes a falling torque curve beyond peak revs, the centrifugal type's curve just soared on up until the mechanical limits of the engine were exceeded. If wheelspin

developed at, say, 100 mph (166 km/h) and 6,000 rpm on an indirect gear in a conventionally supercharged car, its driver had some hope of the wheelspin dying out with the rise in engine speed because blower efficiency would drop, torque would fall away and the wheelspin tendency diminish. It was then relatively simple to control the car.

But with the BRM if engine speed rose from, say, 7,000 rpm to 9,000 rpm then instead of falling away its torque actually increased by a shattering 45 per cent, and the faster the engine revved the more the boost increased, confronting the driver with runaway wheelspin, until he backed off or the engine burst itself asunder. He could only drive comfortably within a restricted rev range, and he always needed to be absolutely in the right gear at the right rpm at all times to be competitive against drivers of equal ability in more conventional but less highly-strung cars, so he was continuously stirring away at the gearbox to keep his BRM in balance. The BRM drivers like Fangio, Gonzalez, Parnell, Walker, and Wharton might have the edge in power, but they had to work overtime to make use of it all.

Tony Rudd, who today is engineering director of Group Lucas, was in charge of ultimate V16 development at Bourne and he once told me how '. . . the basic problem was that we had an engine as powerful as a modern non-turbo Formula 1 trying to put its power through to the road through a pair of tyres the same size as a Formula Ford and there was just no way it could be done . . . the tyres lived in a world of spin so the compound had to be relatively hard to cope with the high temperatures generated by the spin. This led to the engine gaining an entirely undeserved reputation for having no mid-range torque due to its centrifugal supercharger. It actually had plenty of torque . . . everywhere . . . more than you could put on the road in fact, and anything over 7,000 rpm would spin the wheels and over 10,000 rpm you could get the most monumental wheelspin . . .'. He knew what he was talking about first-hand, as he did much of the later V16 test driving at Folkingham.

The engine itself was effectively two 750 cc V8s in tandem, with drive taken from a 'midship gear on the crankshaft stepping down to a separate output shaft in the bottom of the crankcase.

Bore and stroke were a mere 49.53 mm x 48.6 mm, displacing 1,488 cc providing tiny little domed pistons like coffee cups, the R-R blower drew mixture through two of the biggest SU car-

burettors you would ever see and in ultimate form Rudd and his men could more or less rely upon 150-200 miles (250-330 km) of trouble-free running, up to 585 bhp at over 11,500 rpm and deafened adulation from the British race crowds, for – above all – these stub-piped V16s produced sheer decibels on the threshold of pain.

The engine was angled across the chassis frame, to send the prop-shaft to the left of the driver's seat into a Mercedes-Benz W165 crib transaxle. The prop-shaft drove a brake servo pump to boost the four-wheel disc brakes which BRM had pioneered in Grand Prix racing. It needed their efficiency.

Suspension springing and damping was provided by Lockheed oleo-pneumatic struts, which were much lighter than comparable coil-spring-cum-damper systems, Porsche-type trailing link location up front, the de Dion arrangement at the rear.

On 13 May 1950, a very brief public début was made – in between some catastrophic mechanical disasters during private testing – at the British GP meeting at Silverstone. The smooth-bodied car was sensationally low-built and its original pale-green unlouvred body very handsome, but Mays merely made a demonstration run, as the car was

14 July, 1951 — British GP, Silverstone — Only the BRM V16's second but also its last World Championship Grand Prix. Two hastily-prepared decidedly fingers-crossed entries had arrived on race morning. Reg Parnell and Peter Walker started from the back of the grid, but braved out the race despite burned feet and shins and the effects of exhaust and alcohol-fuel fumes in the cockpits, finishing respectively fifth and seventh. Here 'Uncle Reg' displays true grit, his still smooth-bodied car roughly modified about the nose.

not yet fit to race.

After more testing failure and under immense Trustee pressure, one car was cobbled on to the International Trophy grid at Silverstone on 26 August. Raymond Sommer managed minimum practice on race morning, then had the transmission snap at flagfall. Later in the paddock, cheated spectators tossed pennies in the cockpit. Reg Parnell then drove in two insignificant Goodwood races (5 laps and 12 laps) that September and won them both, and on 29 October two cars ran in the Spanish GP, where both ran fourth – and both retired.

Continuing test disasters saw the BRMs appear for only two races in 1951, the British and Italian GPs. Parnell and Peter Walker finished 5-7 at Silverstone, prostrated by fumes and cockpit heat, but management created a terrible muddle at Monza and after practice the cars for both Parnell and, at the last moment, Hans Stuck were withdrawn.

Cancellation of entries for the F1 Turin GP early in 1952 killed the class as Ferrari were left with no credible opposition. World Championship status was conferred upon Formula 2 instead, and suddenly the discredited BRM was no longer a Grand Prix car – now eligible only for the minor Formula 1 and *Formule Libre* racing. The team's 1952 programme – using three Mark I cars – comprised 18 starts in eight events, 10 retirements, three firsts – in laughably minor 5, 15 and 20-lap events, at Turnberry, Scotland (now better-known as a championship golf-course) and Goodwood – one second and two thirds. Drivers were Parnell, Fangio, Gonzalez, Ken Wharton and (once only) Stirling Moss.

In 1953 they started 21 times in 11 events (counting the Albi GP Heat and Final as two), retiring only four times, winning six – at Goodwood, the Albi F1 Heat, two races at Snetterton and at Castle Combe – with six seconds, three thirds, a fourth and fifth. Drivers were Fangio, Gonzalez, Parnell and Wharton who wrote-off Mark I chassis '3 after a tyre failure at Albi – and then there were two . . .

These original long-wheelbase big-tanked Mark I GP cars were really out of their natural element in the short-distance *Libre* races to which they were confined. At Goodwood on Easter Monday 1953, one was beaten by a little 2 litre Maserati. Alfred Owen who had taken over BRM asked Rudd how that could happen? Tony told

18 July, 1953 — *Formule Libre* Trophy supporting the British GP, Silverstone — Fangio took pole position in this definitive-bodied V16 Mark I but could only finish second to Farina's *'ThinWall Special'* Ferrari 375. What had been a beautiful child had by this time become a scarred and cut-about bruiser. It still sounded great, and was sufficiently reliable to win races of adequate if not full GP distance — but few who mattered could care . . .

Sole survivor — Of the three complete BRM Mark I Grand Prix cars built, only this one, chassis '1, survived; Ken Wharton had destroyed one car at Albi following a tyre failure and another at Goodwood in a collision, from which he recovered to win despite the car subsequently being judged 'beyond economic repair'! In 1984, the author was instrumental in this car being purchased on behalf of the nation, and entering the National Motor Museum collection at Beaulieu.

him the Maserati was shorter and lighter, and better suited to the wet track that day. Owen responded by ordering two lighter and shorter *Libre* Project 30 V16s, to use existing engines, transmissions and other parts. The first of these P30 or BRM V16 Mark IIs was built using Accles & Pollock tube originally purchased by Rudd to build himself an Aston Martin special. They differed from the P15 Mark Is in having a one-piece instead of built-up de Dion tube located by twin radius rods in the rear suspension, plus Morris rack-and-pinion steering, a 92 in (2.34 m) wheelbase shorter than the Mark I's by fully 6 in (15 cm), with smaller wheels and tail fuel tank.

In 1954 the Bourne team's V16s again made 21 starts – all but four with Mark II chassis – again retiring only four times in 15 races, and they won five, with three seconds, five thirds, four fourths, a sixth and an eighth. Drivers were Ken Wharton and Ron Flockhart.

The Mark I's swansong was in the Glover Trophy at Goodwood on 19 April 1954, when Wharton survived being rammed by Roy Salvadori's Maserati 250F and limped across the line to win, with chassis '2 written-off beneath him; something of a record for a written-off car to win a race . . . Thus only Mark I chassis '1 survived intact of the three Mark I 'entities' regularly deployed. I'm quite proud of having helped to arrange its purchase for Britain's National Motor Museum at Beaulieu, Hampshire, to 'save it for the nation'.

The two Mark IIs raced were driven in 1955 by Peter Collins and Ron Flockhart, making seven starts in six races, neatly retiring, winning and finishing second twice each, and adding a fifth place. The last race win for a factory BRM V16 was at Aintree on 3 September 1955, when Peter Collins beat Salvadori's 250F and Tony Brooks' Connaught over 17 laps in Mark II chassis '2.

Many, many enthusiasts deeply missed the sight and sound of these always exciting cars – the grand theatrical gesture which was intended to win Grand Prix races at the highest level, but which only ever ran in two of them . . .

And whether the surviving cars are a monument to folly or genius may be, perhaps, a moot point.

The Ferrari Tipo 375s

★ ★ ★ ★

As related earlier, Mr Ferrari dispensed with Colombo's services at Christmas 1950, and elevated *Ing* Aurelio Lampredi in his place as *capo ingegnere*. Lampredi was convinced that the supercharged engine could be beaten by a truly modern and sophisticated unblown unit, and he was right.

The supercharged Ferrari V12 despite displacing only 1.5 litres had become complex, bulky and heavy and its fuel consumption was soaring as boost increased with development. In 1950 the best 1.5 litre supercharged GP engines delivered around 220-235 bhp per litre, but a reliable unblown 4.5 litre need only deliver 70-80 bhp per litre to become competitive. Lampredi's train of thought ran further. Norton in England were building 100 bhp per litre unsupercharged air-cooled motor cycle racing engines. He now adopted that magic target for an unblown water-cooled racing car engine.

He directed production and development of unblown V12s, initially using the standard 'Colombo block' units enlarged from 2 litres first to 2,560 cc, then followed by his own newly designed 'long-block' units of initially 3,322 cc introduced in the Belgian GP of 1950, through 4,104 cc and finally that autumn achieving the full *Tipo* 375 – 375 cc per cylinder x 12-cylinders = 4,500 cc. These actually displaced a nominal 4,494 cc, ready in time for the Italian GP at Monza.

Lampredi, always ruggedly outspoken and emphatic, described the differences between his V12 long-block engine design and Colombo's original series like this; 'It had a double-wall crankcase to increase its rigidity, roller-type rocker arms to reduce wear on the cams and screw-in cylinder liners to avoid head-gasket failures...' It also had wider spacing between the bore centres – 108 mm against the Colombo units' 90 mm – to enable greater bore enlargement.

At Monza, just prior to the 1950 Italian GP, Ascari had unofficially broken the lap record during testing. The big unblown engine was installed in an LWB chassis with four-speed gearbox and de Dion rear suspension, and in the race Ascari hounded Farina's leading and hitherto uncatchable *Alfetta* in brilliant style. Onlookers suddenly realized that the highly-supercharged *Alfetta* would have to stop twice to refuel, while the new Ferrari – which was matching it for speed – could continue non-stop. Ascari seemed to have victory sewn-up for 22 laps, until the Ferrari broke.

Meanwhile, motor cyclist Dorino Serafini had been running sixth in Ferrari's second 375, which Ascari took over when Serafini stopped for fresh tyres. The burly blue-helmeted Ferrari number one driver simply tore into the deficit, powered his way into second place and finished there – the new Ferrari's threat to Alfa Romeo's supremacy was clear for all to see.

Into 1951 the *Alfettas* were at the limit of their development, straining out some 425 bhp from 1,500 cc, and with a new twin-plug cylinder head Lampredi's Ferrari 375s responded with 370 bhp at 7,500 rpm. These proved to be 370 far more usable horsepower than the *Alfettas*'.

As Lampredi recalled; 'What prevented us from reaching the power of the Alfa Romeo in-line eight-cylinder immediately was the lack of an adequate ignition, which the magnetos of the day were unable to provide. Nonetheless, had the F1 of the time continued until its scheduled expiration at the end of 1953, we would have had no difficulty improving the magnetos until the engine realised a specific power of 100 bhp per litre; we practically reached it shortly thereafter, in fact, with the model 500 . . .'

After the Italian GP, Ferrari ran three unblown cars at Barcelona, Spain; 375s for Ascari and Serafini and the interim 4.1 litre '341' for Piero Taruffi. In Alfa's absence they simply left their opposition for dead, finishing 1-2-3.

The team's 1951 début was made at Syracuse, Sicily, where Ascari and Villoresi dominated for 70 of the 80 laps until the former's 1950-spec 375 overheated, leaving Villoresi victory. The Pau GP fell to the older man in similar fashion. A new 1951-spec engine was ready in time for the San Remo GP, which was expected to mark Alfa Romeo's return to the fray. This improved 4.5 litre V12 employed twin-plug ignition, the plugs being on opposite sides of the head, fired from a single large aviation-style magneto mounted at the front of the engine, replacing the 1950-spec pair of 6-cylinder magnetos driven from the camshaft tails. Where all previous Ferrari V12s sited their spark plugs within the engine vee, this new 24-plug version carried them outside, and this necessitated re-routing both internal water passages and the external exhaust primaries to make room. Stiffened drum brakes were fitted to prevent the distortion and resultant uneven braking performance experienced in 1950.

Ascari drove the first '51 375 at San Remo, while Villoresi and Serafini had the 1950 versions. But Alfa Corse did not appear, leaving Ascari an easy win from Serafini, while Villoresi crashed mildly.

One 1950-spec 375 was sold to Vandervell in England as his third *ThinWall Special* and when the Final of the International Trophy at Silverstone was abandoned after only six laps due to torrential rain, Reg Parnell happened to be leading in this green-painted Ferrari, and was declared the winner. Alfa Corse had been beaten for the first time since the war, but nobody could take it seriously . . .

The two factory teams finally met in the Swiss GP at Berne, Ferrari running two 24-plug cars and one 12-plug, all three 375s using the latest stiffened brakes. Serafini had been injured in the

Mille Miglia, so Piero Taruffi replaced him in the second 24-plug car, Villoresi being relegated to the 12-plug *'muletto'*. Again, it rained. Again, Villoresi crashed. Ascari was off-form due to burns received in an F2 race fire at Marseilles, so Taruffi took up the cudgels for Ferrari – running third amongst the *Alfetta* team before wresting second place from Dr Farina with one lap to run. Ascari finished sixth – again Alfa Romeo had won, but only just . . .

In England the *'ThinWall Special'* began winning minor races, normally with Parnell driving, and in June the Belgian GP at Spa saw all three works Ferrari 375s using the 24-plug engine, claimed to deliver 375 bhp at 7,500 rpm – 83.3 bhp per litre. Ascari and Villoresi finished 2-3 on the same lap as the victorious *Alfetta*, but still marginally out-paced on straightline speed.

Taruffi retired in Belgium and was unable to drive in the French GP at Reims due to a prior Belgian commitment with the Gilera motor cycle team – he was their racing director. Mr Ferrari had been impressed by Fangio's pudgy compatriot, José Froilan Gonzalez, who had shone in *Temporada* races back home the preceding winter, in a 2 litre *Libre* Ferrari. He jumped at the chance to drive at Reims at Taruffi's place. All three cars were '51-spec models, with improved bodywork featuring curved Perspex windscreens matching the scuttle shape in place of the original traditional flat aero-screens. Ascari's gearbox broke after only ten laps and when Gonzalez stopped for fuel and tyres after 34 laps Ascari took over, to finish second, with Villoresi third and Parnell fourth – despite the *'ThinWall's* transmission having broken. Once again, a lone surviving *Alfetta* denied the 'Lampredi' Ferraris victory.

The British GP followed, at Silverstone on 14 July, where Ascari and Villoresi drove '51-spec cars with the curved screen bodywork and Gonzalez found himself with the 1950-spec *'muletto'* prototype car with its 12-plug engine. He seemed deliriously happy with it, and in practice lapped at 1:43.4, 100.65 mph (167.75 km/h), the first-ever 100 mph Silverstone lap! None of the *Alfetta* brigade could match this time, and in the race Gonzalez took on and defeated his friend and mentor Fangio on even terms, and Ferrari had at last ended Alfa Corse's postwar *Grande Epreuve* supremacy. Villoresi finished third and Ascari broke his gearbox again. Peter Whitehead finished ninth in the *'ThinWall'*.

14 July, 1951 — British GP, Silverstone — A day graven on the hearts of F1 Ferrari enthusiasts as the team's *muletto* 375 driven by José Froilan Gonzalez inflicted Alfa Corse's first post-war defeat at *Grande Epreuve* level. The even exhaust manifold spacing identifies the early-series 12-plug engine (the 24-plug units had uneven-spaced manifold primaries) and here the car has apparently hit a bump at high speed — note the rear radius rod angles but the nose is low as well. Perhaps Gonzalez was just very heavy: he was certainly a committed racing driver . . .

Taruffi made up the four-car Ferrari 375 works team for the German GP at the Nürburgring, where Ascari took over the 12-plug '*muletto*', found why Gonzalez loved it so much and won from the inevitable *Alfetta*, with Gonzalez, Villoresi and Taruffi 3-4-5.

Gonzalez won again at Pescara, in Alfa's absence, while Ascari retired both his 1950-spec car and his team-mate Villoresi's which he took over as replacement. But Alfa Corse had regrouped, squeezed just a little more out of their *Alfetta* and Fangio proved uncatchable at Bari, beating Gonzalez's 24-plug 375 while Ascari and Villoresi again retired.

The stage could not have been better set for a dramatic showdown in the Italian GP at Monza. Two brand-new 375s with reshaped head-faring bodies – engine numbers '05 and '06 – made their début amongst the five-car Ferrari entry, for Ascari and Villoresi, Gonzalez a '51-spec, Taruffi a '51-spec and Chico Landi the '*muletto*'. They finished 1-2-4-5, Ascari/Gonzalez/Villoresi/Taruffi while Landi broke his always rather suspect transmission on the opening lap. Only one *Alfetta* lasted the distance, placing third.

The World Championship title now depended upon the Spanish GP result at Barcelona. Alfa Corse's latest-spec 159M *Alfettas* appeared in full fuel-bloated force, facing the Ferrari 375 foursome, but a drop in rear wheel and tyre diameter proved fatal to Ferrari hopes, and Fangio won the race and the World Championship for Alfa Corse in what was to be their Formula 1 farewell until 1979 saw a half-hearted return. Gonzalez finished second and Ascari fourth, both delayed by tyre failures.

Formula 1 racing died for lack of support in 1952, and unsupercharged 2 litre F2 took its place at World Championship GP level. Ferrari, however, had been invited to supply 375s – suitably amended – to US clients for the Indianapolis 500-Miles track classic. Revised long-wheelbase chassis were built and fitted with revised-style headrest bodies. When the Turin GP was run to F1 regulations at short notice on 6 April 1952, two of these 'Indianapolis' 375s were entered for Ascari and Dr Farina, while Villoresi ran a normal '51-spec car. Ascari looked set to win, only for his car's fuel tank to split three laps from the finish, so Villoresi won while Farina

crashed – mildly by his peerless standards . . .

Vandervell Products continued to race their '*ThinWall Special*' Ferrari 375 in British events, and the two '51 Monza headrest-bodied cars had meantime been sold to private owner-drivers, Chico Landi of Brazil – who bought Ascari's Monza winner – and Louis Rosier of France –who acquired Villoresi's second-place car. At Albi when the BRM V16s failed, Rosier and Landi finished 1-2, and a week later at Dundrod, NI, for the Ulster Trophy a brand-new '*ThinWall Special*' Ferrari using an all-new chassis and body and 24-plug engine won upon its début driven by Taruffi.

At Indianapolis, four 375s attempted to qualify, Ascari succeeding in his works car, but only at 134.30 mph (approx 224 km/h) ninteenth on the grid. The sister customer cars for Johnny Parsons (the 1950 Indy winner), Johnny Mauro and Howard Keck were all too slow. Parsons opted out of his drive, Jerry Grant lapping that car instead at just 133.8 mph (223 km/h). Mauro could not better 132 and Keck's best in his car was 4 mph (6.7 km/h) slower than his alternative Offenhauser-powered roadster, which he chose instead. While the 375s were well-suited to road racing, the peaky V12 power curve necessitated changing down for the short chutes between Indy's Turns 1 and 2, and 3 and 4, while the predominantly Offy-powered opposition accomplished the whole lap virtually flat-out in 'high'. Ascari ran twelfth in the race until a rear hub failed and spun him out as the Borrani wire-wheel collapsed.

Back in Europe the works armed Villoresi with a 375 for the British GP meeting's 100-mile *Libre* race, facing Taruffi in the latest '*ThinWall*', Landi and Rosier in addition to the BRM V16s. Taruffi, Villoresi and Landi finished 1-2-3, and at Boreham amid rain showers Villoresi won, despite Mike Hawthorn's little F2 Cooper-Bristol initially outpacing him while the road was wet. Mr Ferrari took note . . .

This was actually the last appearance of a works-entered Ferrari 375, and although the '*ThinWall*', Landi and Rosier cars raced on, they achieved little of real significance. And in any case, another Lampredi-designed Ferrari was by this time on top of the world . . .

The Ferrari Tipo 500s

★ ★ ★ ★

Few name-combinations of driver and car have had a more euphonious ring than 'Ascari (Ferrari)'. During the early '50s that phrase featured in almost every news broadcast or sports bulletin deigning to mention motor racing at all.

Alberto Ascari often set the performance standards of his time. 'Who's the greater – Ascari or Fangio?' was a common enthusiast argument of the time, and many a pint must have been sunk to lubricate such debates. Although Fangio would build the greater career, he was sidelined by injury for most of 1952, and into '53 the racing world was owned by Ascari and his near-unbeatable 2 litre unsupercharged, *Tipo* '500' Ferraris. He drove them brilliantly to secure the Drivers' World Championship titles in both 1952 and '53, he was the first to win consecutive Championships, and these were also Ferrari's first World titles.

When the unsupercharged 4.5 litre Ferrari 375s at last toppled Alfa Corse's post–war supremacy in 1951, Alfa still escaped with Fangio as new World Champion, but the Portello board promptly withdrew from racing forthwith, leaving only Ferrari and the desperately untrustworthy BRM V16 as serious F1 contenders for 1952. There they would be backed by an oil-oozing mixture of blown – sometimes too literally – Maseratis and even older ERAs, plus the geriatric unsupercharged Talbot-Lagos.

Race promoters were unimpressed as they planned for 1952, and when BRM capriciously opted-out of the early-season F1 Turin GP, condemning it to become the Ferrari walkover European race organizers had feared, so Formula 1 simply lay down and died.

The governing body promptly allowed organizers to apply World Championship status to F2 GP races and thus the unblown 2 litre cars assumed premier status. This would also apply throughout 1953, but an all-new 2.5 litre unblown/750 cc supercharged Formula 1 was then to take effect from 1 January, 1954.

When World Championship status devolved upon Formula 2 for 1952-53, Ferrari, with typical perspicacity, had just the very cars available – 2 litre 4-cylinder F2s whose power and torque left the rival Maserati, Gordini, German BMW and British Bristol-engined opposition simply panting. This was the '500' which took its serial number in the usual Ferrari manner, from the size in cc of one engine cylinder – 500 cc x 4 cylinders = 2,000 cc, ie 2 litres, hence Ferrari 500. The car was uncomplicated – in some ways rather undistinguished – but more than good enough in its day to beat all contemporary opposition, and especially with Ascari behind the wheel, it usually did.

The 500 was a triumph of practicality, sound engineering design, outstanding preparation and the kind of organisation which built the Ferrari name. Significantly, it was also driven by some of the best in the business.

It was yet another Lampredi design. While developing his 'long-block' large-capacity unsupercharged V12 engines, he had also taken his search for simplicity to a new extreme, by abandoning Ferrari's original unblown 2 litre V12 F2 engine – the 166 – and developing instead a simple in-line 4 cylinder twin-cam unit. It had a five main bearing crankshaft and introduced a new type of Ferrari valve-gear; with dual concentric valve-springs around the stem in addition to twin hairpin springs out one side. The thin coil-springs loaded the cam-follower assembly against the camshaft while the hairpins closed the valves into their seats. Inverted cup-type followers contacted the camshaft lobes via rollers. The two valves per cylinder were disposed at the narrow included angle of 58° within a twin-plug cylinder head, and the liners were screwed home into it to obviate head-seal problems.

With this creation, Lampredi was flying in the face of Colombo's design tenets for the Ferrari V12. It had been short-stroke to foster high rpm, and 12-cylinders to create the largest possible piston area for efficient power creation. The 4-cylinders inevitably had a longer stroke, restricting its rev range, and with one third the number of cylinders its piston area was much reduced.

But Lampredi was brutally more practician than theoretician. He appreciated that the simple block would save weight – in fact as much as 92 lb (42 kg). The *Tipo 500* 4-cylinder weighed 348 lb against the *Tipo* 166 V12 at 440 lb. Furthermore, the 65 per cent reduction in the number of moving parts from V12 to in-line 'four' slashed power loss, and also expense of both manufacture and maintenance. Crucially, it also promised greatly enhanced reliability. The 4-cylinder would also develop more usable mid-range torque than the V12, another crucial feature on many of the medium-speed road circuits then in use.

The prototype 4-cylinder first ran on test in the spring of 1951, instantly registering a claimed 170 bhp against the 166 V12's 155 – 85 bhp per litre against only 77.5, and 0.488 bhp per lb versus a mere 0.352. These figures represented a 27.9 per cent gain in power-to-weight ratio, 9.4 per cent better specific power.

A putative 2.5 litre *Tipo* 625 'Formula 1' 4-cylinder unit then raced first, at Bari on 2 September 1951, before the F2 *Tipo* 500's début at Modena two weeks later. Right from its début the *Tipo* 500 was an unqualified success, and through 1952-53 the cars simply won every race they entered, save for two non-Championship events in 1952 and the final Grand Prix of 1953 . . . no fewer than 30 wins in 33 races entered, a stunning

90 per cent victory rate. They achieved 81 finishes from 109 starts with only 18 retirements . . . an astounding record, but the opposition was not really fierce for much of this period.

The 500's torquey 4-cylinder engine was installed in a typically crude Ferrari welded-tube ladder frame chassis carrying a very neat and attractive aluminium-sheet bodyshell on a superstructure arrangement of small-gauge tube members. Front suspension was by double wishbones and transverse leafspring, rear by de Dion axle system with twin radius rods each side.

In their Modena 1951 début the new chipper-grilled 500s were driven by Ascari and his great friend and mentor Villoresi. They left the field for dead until Villoresi retired while Ascari won by a lap from Gonzalez's old Ferrari 166. Through that winter into 1952, *Tipo* 500 modifications included four single-choke Weber carburettors raising power slightly, and minor bodywork changes, made in part to improve cooling and partly to reduce cockpit buffeting. The 1952 season commenced at Syracuse where Ascari, Taruffi and Dr Farina finished 1-2-3, with the delayed Villoresi seventh.

At Pau the works 500s appeared with stub exhausts and the first private owner cars made their début. Ascari won again, and at Marseilles made it a hat-trick. The Championship season opened at Berne. Ascari was away at Indianapolis but Taruffi won for Ferrari from the Swiss Rudi Fischer's private sister 500. Ascari returned for the remainder of the Championship season, and won the Belgian GP from Farina, the French from Farina and Taruffi, the British GP from Taruffi, the German GP from Farina, Fischer and Taruffi (500s 1-2-3-4!), the Dutch GP from Farina and Villoresi, and the Italian GP, a sterner battle in which Gonzalez's Maserati bundled Villoresi out of second place. Not only did Ascari emerge as Ferrari's first World Champion, but he was followed in the table by his team-mates Farina and Taruffi, and by Rudi Fischer, fourth . . . a great achievement for a private owner-driver.

In addition, Ascari (Ferrari) shared victory with André Simon in the Comminges GP, and had won at La Baule. Farina won at Naples and Monza, Fischer in the Eifelrennen and at AVUS, Taruffi at Montlhéry, Villoresi at Les Sables d'Olonne and Modena, and Louis Rosier's private car at Cadours. The Ferrari 500s' only

18 July, 1953 — British GP, Silverstone — The 2 litre Formula 2 Ferrari 500s were handsome, practical and simple but in a sophisticatedly competitive manner. Here the fast-fading Dr Farina (6) scowls his way towards third place behind his team-mate Alberto Ascari and Juan Fangio's rival Maserati, while Mike Hawthorn (8) is fresh from his French GP victory but will finish a tardy fifth, lapped three times after delays.

15 May, 1954 — BRDC International Trophy, Silverstone — Froilan Gonzalez won the final in this Ferrari 625 — the 2.5 litre 4-cylinder development of the basic 2 litre *Tipo* 500 adopted for the new Formula 1 at the beginning of that season. Externally these early 625s were very little different from the neat and functional 500s, although more sophisticated and to my mind less handsome 'Argentine'-style bodies would follow.

defeat that season was at Reims-Gueux where Jean Behra's little Gordini prevailed.

Englishman Mike Hawthorn replaced Taruffi in the team for '53, when the Championship series saw the Ferrari 500s win seven of the eight road-racing rounds; Ascari winning in Argentina, Holland, Belgium, Britain and Switzerland, while Hawthorn sensationally beat Fangio's Maserati to win the French GP, and Farina the German after Ascari's 500 lost a wheel.

But all season the 6-cylinder Maseratis had been improving – being reworked by Colombo! – and Fangio finally beat Ferrari in nothing less than the Italian GP at Monza, after Ascari and Farina spun in the final corner. Perhaps this was *Ing* Gioachino's home-soil revenge upon young *Ing* Aurelio for having outshone him at Maranello . . .

Ascari was again World Champion, and although Fangio placed second in the table for Maserati, *Ferraristi* Farina, Hawthorn and Villoresi filled the next three places.

Meanwhile, in minor races, all four works 500s had retired at Syracuse, but inevitably Ascari won at Pau and Bordeaux, Hawthorn won at Silverstone and Dundrod, Farina won again at Naples, and the private cars – known as '*Starlets*' in Italy – won at AVUS, driven by the Belgian Ferrari concessionaire Jacques Swaters, and Les Sables d'Olonne (Rosier).

For 1954 Formula 2 was replaced by unsupercharged 2.5 litre Formula 1. All but one of the existing Ferrari 500s – there were at least six, possibly seven works cars plus five '*Starlet*' customer versions – were uprated to 2.5 litres to suit, and accordingly reclassified as *Tipo 625s*. As such they soldiered on into 1955, when Maurice Trintignant actually won the Monaco GP in one, but that is another story.

In many ways the 500s secured Ferrari's special standing within the motor racing world, but their record stands as an awful warning to those designers who still don't understand that an ounce of simplicity and practicality can be worth a ton of theory when it comes to Grand Prix racing in the real world . . .

Aurelio Lampredi understood this perfectly, and Ferrari's back-to-back World Championship titles were the reward.

The Mercedes-Benz W196s

★ ★ ★ ★

When Daimler-Benz AG took the momentous decision to return to Grand Prix racing upon introduction of the new 2.5 litre Formula 1 in 1954, every other interested team simply shuddered in its shoes. It was abundantly evident that the Unterturkheim *Rennabteilung* and the sports department still under the formidable figure of *Rennleiter* Alfred Neubauer would pull no punches in a blitzkrieg assault upon the World Championship titles. The forthcoming new

Mercedes-Benz F1 cars were awaited with bated breath and of course they certainly fulfilled almost all expectations when they did finally appear, in time for the French GP in June 1954.

D-B were returning to Grand Prix racing for the first time since 1939. They were willing and able to commit more money and more manpower than any other team in Formula 1, and the best their rivals could hope for was to be the first non-

17 July, 1954 — British GP, Silverstone — Battered beauty; after their crushing début success at Reims-Gueux the Mercedes team's aspirations suffered a rude set-back this slippery day at Silverstone. Even Fangio found the front extremities of his *stromlinienwagen* — chassis '0003/54' — difficult to sight and the car tricky to aim on its under-developed Continental tyres. Here its thin-gauge shell panelling shows signs of impact with those marker tubs on both left and right-hand corners.

16 July, 1955 — British GP, Aintree — What a difference a year makes; Mercedes-Benz filled the first four places in this their penultimate Formula 1 race. Stirling Moss won in the short-wheelbase outboard-braked car '0012/55' shown here, carrying that one-piece hinge-forward bonnet for the first time.

Mercedes home. Their drivers, particularly in 1955, were the best that money and national interest could buy, teaming reigning World Champion Juan Fangio with Stirling Moss, and the two Germans Karl Kling and Hans Herrmann. They developed enormous confidence in the engineering effort and forethought and the tactical and strategic race-planning which backed their cars. Whenever they sat on the starting grid they could be confident that the few rival cars they might not out-run, they would surely out-last. It really did become a case of who would finish first, behind the Mercedes?

Yet, even accepting that state of affairs, the popular legend of Mercedes-Benz's Grand Prix racing invincibility is too often over stated and over-blown.

In reality they never succeeded in establishing total dominance in any of their Grand Prix seasons as a unified marque post-1926. Their fine World Championship-winning comeback in the new 2.5 litre Grand Prix Formula of 1954-55 set new standards, but even then their all-powerful new W196 straight-eight cars stumbled occasionally on performance – as at Silverstone '54 – and on reliability – as at Barcelona '54 and Monaco '55 – so enabling lesser cars to salvage victory.

Thus the Formula 1 Mercedes W196 series won only nine of its twelve World Championship-qualifying GPs in 1954-55, so achieving only 75 per cent success. That palled against what was then recent history, since just two or three years previously in 1952 the Ferrari 500s had won seven out of seven GPs for 100 per cent success, and in 1953 they won another seven out of eight – 87.5 per cent that season, or 93.3 per cent through the two years combined. So why no great Ferrari legend of invincibility? Perhaps because they continued racing – and losing – in later years . . .

But of course, success percentages are mere statistics which cannot reflect popular conceptions – or misconceptions – of the time. More significant during that period was Mercedes's *manner* of winning, because that is what really gave substance if not justification to their legend.

More than mere results, it was the way Mercedes went racing which really rocked the racing world. None could match the Daimler-Benz company's vast commitment to racing in men, money and material. In truth their *Rennabteilung* – racing department's – budget was not open-ended . . . but by the standards of any contemporary rival manufacturer it just seemed that way.

Daimler-Benz had long-since established peerless standards of painstaking background

16 July, 1955 — British GP, Aintree — Superstar — Much of the Mercedes-Benz legend was justifiably built upon engineering forethought, skill, care and excellence; but it was certainly enhanced by buying the outstanding driving skill of the time — the genius of Juan Manuel Fangio. His car here is '0013/55', but I doubt the 'Old Man' would have noticed, and in any case unlike Moss he was hardly superstitious.

Box of tricks; a Mercedes-Benz W196 reveals its jam-packed mechanical make-up. The radiator cores are for water (left) and oil (right), massive finned front drum brakes retard the road wheels via CV-jointed coupling shafts, and the reclining straight-eight engine is topped by the Bosch fuel injection equipment and that long ram-air induction pipe. The chassis itself is a finely-drawn lightweight spaceframe. The Dunlop racing tyres give '0008/54' here away as a D-B museum car; in their racing days Continental supplied the rubber.

research, intricate detail design, precision manufacture and dedicated high-pressure development which no other manufacturer was either willing or able to match. Nothing was too much trouble for D-B's engineers, no conceivable path towards success would remain unexplored. The object was to win, and the commitment therefore was to attempt whatever was necessary to do so. It was simple Germanic logic. In effect, the bill would be picked up later . . .

Even so, the hard F1 truth remains that Daimler-Benz's W196 cars lost one out of every four of their races through 1954-55, so *don't* swallow the legend of unbeatability; not whole anyway . . .

The W196 story began in 1952 when D-B won the Le Mans 24-Hours race and other events with their original production-based 300SL competition Coupes. Racing manager Alfred Neubauer told his technical people then that similar cars with more power, a five-speed gearbox, better brakes and a higher top speed would be necessary should D-B's board require the experimental department to contemplate racing 'seriously'.

In fact the board took its time through 1952, analysing the potential cost of a full return to competition against any promotional and technical pay-off. The new 2.5 litre GP Formula had been announced, to take effect on 1 January 1954, and eventually the board approved an effectively unfettered racing programme to include both a new GP car to this Formula and a sports-racer based upon it to tackle the parallel World Championship.

The company's central design office in Stuttgart-Unterturkheim pitched into the project under Director Hans Scherenberg, with Ludwig

The Mercedes-Benz W196 *Typ Nürburgring* Formula 1 car, 1954-55.

The Mercedes-Benz W196 low-pivot rear suspension with its massive inboard drum brakes.

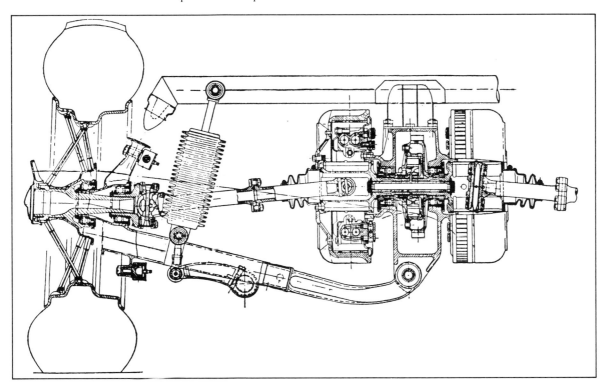

Kraus heading the chasis group, Hans Gass-mann engine design. Rudolf Ühlenhaut's experimental department set up a new *Rennab-teilung* under Walter Kostelezky to build, prepare and race the cars. At its height, this department would be staffed by some 200 designers, engineers and mechanics, with first-priority call upon 300 of D-B's most skilled toolmakers and their machine shop facilities.

Initially the Formula 1 W196 was set down as a front-engined multi-tubular spaceframe car powered by a desmodromic-valved* straight-eight cylinder roller-bearing engine using Bosch

*Mechanically-closed valve-gear, using positive mechanical cam action to shut the valves rather than merely relying on return springs, as conventional. This eliminated valve-float and permitted higher reliable rpm to release more power.

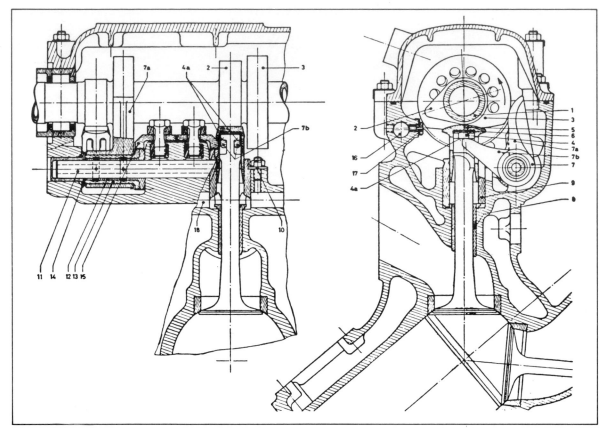

Desmodromic valve gear — Mercedes-Benz W196.

fuel-injection, with drive taken from its crankshaft amidships between numbers 4 and 5 cylinders. This power unit was laid far over to one side to keep its centre of gravity as low as possible, while also offsetting its prop-shaft to enable the driver to sit beside it rather than above it and so further minimize overall height. A purpose-designed five-speed transaxle was mounted at the rear, and a sophisticated low-pivot swing-axle rear suspension was adopted.

Daimler-Benz's original plan was for the F1 W196 ('W' for *Wagen* – car – as always) and a sports racing W196S sister to emerge simultaneously in 1954. But in fact six months or more split these parallel projects. The practical limit of the original M196 engine ('M' for *Motoren*) was 3 litres, which Scherenberg's team chose for their 300SLR sports car, while the F1 M196 engine emerged as 76 mm x 68.8 mm, 2,490 cc. Its two 4-cylinder blocks used welded-up sheet water jackets, and the unit developed 257 bhp at 8,250 rpm – 102.8 bhp per litre. The new cars looked

sensational as prepared for their début in the French GP at Reims-Gueux, featuring centre-seat streamlined bodywork.

Fangio and Kling promptly qualified first and second fastest, and it was immediately clear that Mercedes-Benz's comeback was rewriting the standards at which all other F1 teams would now have to aim. They broke up the opposition and finished first and second, only young Herrmann's engine failing in the third car.

The two W196 streamliners entered for the British GP then proved unsuitable for the ill-defined Silverstone aerodrome circuit, which was slippery and perhaps Continental's new racing tyres were not up to the job. Gonzalez won for Ferrari as Fangio slipped and slithered in his wake, finally finishing fourth in gearbox trouble, his W196's full-width body battered and torn after clipping marker barrels round the course. Kling was totally outclassed and finished a sad seventh.

In time for the German GP at the Nürburgring

two weeks later, three new open-wheeled 'slipper-bodied' W196S were available for Fangio, Kling and pre-war Champion Hermann Lang, while Hans Hermann drove a streamliner. Fangio led most of the way, Lang occupied second place briefly ahead of Kling and although Herrmann dropped out with a fuel leak the German crowds roared with pleasure at the sight of a Mercedes-Benz 1-2-3 parade in their national GP. Unfortunately, Lang spun and stalled, and then Kling was delayed by a torsion bar pick-up failing on his car's chassis, but Fangio came home to win, and Kling rejoined gingerly to finish fourth.

Fangio, Kling and Herrmann drove open-wheelers at Berne in the Swiss GP, respectively winning, retiring and finishing a distant (lapped) third. The same trio reappeared at Monza for the Italian GP, Fangio and Kling in streamliners, and Herrmann winning an open-wheeler drive after he had lapped faster than Lang in practice. But the Italian Maseratis and Ferraris were in close

contention and, although Fangio won, his Mercedes had been at the very least matched for speed by Stirling Moss's Maserati 250F, which broke when leading close to the finish. Kling was blinded by oil spraying on to his goggles and ran out of road, while Herrmann soldiered reliably home fourth. This was by no means imperious domination . . .

A minor Berlin GP was then staged for Mercedes' benefit at AVUS, where Kling the German won narrowly from Fangio and Herrmann – all in streamliners – to please an enormous crowd.

This trio then tackled the Spanish GP on Barcelona's Pedralbes boulevard circuit, and really suffered. Fangio could run no higher than fourth for a long time, eventually inherited second and then retired. Kling, bathed in hot oil, limped home third with his engine about to seize and Herrmann's clutch failed. This was a débâcle. Almost since their début at Reims their fortunes had gradually deteriorated. Even so, they had

14 July, 1955 — British GP practice, Aintree — Piero Taruffi tries his W196 for size — '0015/55', the last complete car built. He was D-B's new number four driver and here is under the experienced eye — and bulk — of the veteran Alfred Neubauer. Even the W196's mirror mounts and farings were the best thought-out in the business.

won five of their seven races, and with his early-season Maserati points, Fangio became World Champion Driver for the second time.

Stirling Moss signed-on to join Fangio, Kling, Herrmann and a handful of guest drivers for 1955, and the *Rennabteilung* now got their act together.

Suspension and handling were improved, weight was saved and a 14 cm (5.5 in) shorter chassis introduced. For the Monaco GP around Monte Carlo an ultra-short wheelbase chassis 6 cm (2.4 in) shorter was developed, with the front drum brakes moving outboard into the wheels. Thus the senior drivers could choose between 1954-style long-chassis or 1955 medium or short-chassis cars. The long and medium lengths used all-inboard brakes as standard, the short-chassis had outboard front brakes. Then a medium-length frame with outboard front brakes alternative emerged at Spa.

In fact the W196 cars built and raced during this one and a half season programme seem to have been as follows:

Chassis '0001/54' – Prototype test hack, presumably that written-off in Hans Herrmann's Hockenheimring testing accident.

Chassis '0002/54' – Race début 4-7-54, 2,350 mm wheelbase, streamliner – Herrmann '54 French and German GPs, and AVUSRennen. Withdrawn from service.

Chassis '0003/54' – Race début, 4-7-54, 2,350 mm, streamliner – Fangio *1st* '54 French GP, British GP, T-car Italian GP. See next entry.

Chassis '0003/55' – Race début 16-1-55, 2,210 mm wheelbase, may have been modification of original 1954 2,350 mm wheelbase chassis of similar serial number, slipper body – Kling '55 Argentine GP, T-car Buenos Aires City GP, André Simon Monaco GP, T-car Dutch and British GPs. Car withdrawn from service.

Chassis '0004/54' – Début presumably 2-7-54, 2,350 mm, streamliner – T-car '54 French GP, Kling British GP, fitted with slipper body as T-car German GP, Herrmann Swiss GP, refitted as streamliner for Fangio *1st* Italian GP, Fangio AVUSRennen, T-car Spanish GP. See next entry.

Chassis '0004/55' – Race début 16-1-55, 2,210 mm wheelbase, may have been modification of original 1954 2,350 mm wheelbase chassis of

similar serial number, slipper body – Fangio *1st* '55 Argentine GP, Herrmann Buenos Aires City GP, crashed by him in Monaco practice – badly damaged, he broke a leg. Car written-off.

Chassis '0005/54' – Race début 1-8-54, 2,350 mm, slipper body – Herrmann Lang '54 German GP, Kling Swiss GP, fitted with streamlined body for Kling *1st* AVUSRennen, refitted with slipper body for Kling Spanish GP; for Moss D-B début '55 Argentine GP, T-car Buenos Aires City GP, Kling Belgian GP. Car withdrawn from service.

Chassis '0006/54' – Race début 1-8-54, 2,350 mm, slipper body – Fangio *1st* '54 German GP, *1st* Swiss GP, Herrmann Italian GP, Herrmann Spanish GP; car retired until hastily prepared as stop-gap for Kling, '55 Italian GP. Car withdrawn from service.

Chassis '0007/54' – Race début 5-9-54, 2,350 mm, streamliner – Kling '54 Italian GP; fitted with 3 litre M196I* 300 SLR sports engine for Moss *Formule Libre* '55 Buenos Aires City GP *1st* in Heat. Car withdrawn from service.

Chassis '0008/54' – Race début 24-10-54, 2,350 mm, slipper body – Fangio '54 Spanish GP; T-car '55 Argentine GP, fitted with 3 litre engine for Kling Buenos Aires City GP, refitted wth 2.5 litre M196 engine for Fangio *1st* Belgian GP. Car withdrawn from service.

Chassis '0009/55' – Race début 30-1-55, 2,350 mm, slipper body – fitted with 3 litre engine for Fangio *1st* Buenos Aires City GP; car retired until hastily prepared with streamlined body for Moss '55 Italian GP. Car withdrawn from service.

Chassis '0010/55' – Race début 16-1-55, 2,350 mm, slipper body – Herrmann/Kling/Moss '55 Argentine GP, T-car Buenos Aires City GP, reputedly rebuilt as 2,210 mm wheelbase for Moss, Belgian and Dutch GPs, retired until fitted with small '55 streamliner body, practice only Italian GP. Car withdrawn from service.

Chassis '0011/55' – No build nor racing record.

Chassis '0012/54' – Race début 22-5-55, 2,150 mm short-chassis, first car with outboard front brakes – all above inboard-brake chassis throughout – slipper body – Moss '55 Monaco GP and *1st*

---

*The M196I sports-racing engine used cast blocks instead of the welded-up F1 type, displaced 3 litres instead of 2.5 and had a different firing order as well as other changes.

British GP, possibly modified to 2,210 mm intermediate wheelbase and fitted with small '55 streamliner body practice only Italian GP. Car withdrawn from service.

Chassis '0013/55' – Race début 2-5-55, 2,150 mm as '12 above, slipper body – Fangio '55 Monaco *1st* Dutch GP, British GP, possibly modified to 2,210 mm as above and fitted with small '55 streamline body, practice only Italian GP. Car withdrawn from service.

Chassis '0014/55' – Début probably 3-6-55, 2,210 mm, outboard front brakes, slipper body – T-car (Fangio) '55 Belgian GP, Kling Dutch and British GPs, T-car Italian GP. Car withdrawn from service.

Chassis '0015/55' – Race début 16-7-55, 2,150 mm, outboard brakes, slipper body – Taruffi '55 British and Italian GPs. Car withdrawn from service.

As can be seen in this list, wheelbase lengths and front brake mountings changed for '55, more nimble SWB cars for Monaco forcing the front drums from their original inboard mounts out into the wheels, while an intermediate WB length became popular. Monaco proved a disaster for D-B, Herrmann breaking his leg in practice and the cars' engines failing in the race. But the team recovered its composure at Spa for the Belgian GP; Fangio and Moss finishing first and second in long and medium-chassis cars respectively, with Kling outclassed and bursting his long-chassis car's engine.

At Zandvoort for the Dutch GP, Fangio drove his Monaco SWB car, Moss a normal '55-spec medium-length and Kling the 'Spa special' '0014' with, I believe, medium-frame plus outboard front brakes. The three cars qualified 1-2-3 to fill the front row of the grid, and Fangio and Moss repeated their Spa 1-2, while Kling spun off. The Fangio-Moss parade had become known as 'The Train'.

The French GP was cancelled following the Le Mans catastrophe, but four W196s ran in the British GP at Aintree; Moss won from Fangio, Kling and Piero Taruffi, a crushing Mercedes-Benz 1-2-3-4 demonstration. All the cars used Monaco-spec outboard front-brake SWB chassis.

The German and Swiss GPs were both cancelled and the Italian GP at Monza became the *Rennabteilung's* last F1 race as D-B decided to

retire from racing and rest on their laurels. Even so, in painstaking pre-race testing, the *Rennabteilung* tried eight cars with all three different chassis-lengths, alternative streamlined and slipper bodies and air-brakes. Streamlined medium-length (2,210 mm wheelbase) seemed superior so two new *stromlinienwagen* bodies, lower and smaller than the 1954 versions, were assembled, it seems, on frames '0010' and '0012'.

For official practice D-B also fielded a long-chassis streamliner, '0009', the SWB Monaco-Spec '0015' and the medium-length outboard front-braked 'Spa special' '0014'. To their dismay, they found that many bumps which had marred the new *Pista de Alta Velocita* speedbowl during their test-sessions had now been eased, rendering the veteran LWB streamliner now the best compromise although its suspension was so soft it was bottoming.

Chief engineer Ühlenhaut called Stuttgart and within 30 hours two extra LWB cars had been prepared and were delivered to Monza on the *Rennabteilung's* amazing 100 mph flat-bed high-speed transporter. Only D-B could have sustained such effort for what was to be their last GP. Fangio and Moss eventually drove LWB cars, with latest-spec streamlined body and the old '54 shell respectively, while Kling drove the LWB slipper-bodied '0006', all this trio using all-inboard brakes. Taruffi used his Aintree SWB '0015', the last W196 frame to be built, with outboard front brakes.

Fangio, Moss and Kling qualified 1-2-3, and on the opening lap they and Taruffi from row four formated into a silver file, Fangio leading Moss, Taruffi and Kling with only one red Italian car maintaining contact. On lap 18 a flying stone smashed Moss's windscreen; he stopped, it was hastily replaced and he rejoined eighth, only to have a piston fail. On lap 33 Kling broke a transmission shaft, but Fangio and Taruffi survived to complete another Mercedes-Benz W196 1-2, the team's fifth of the season and seventh since their come-back began.

Stirling Moss recalls the W196s subjectively as having been '. . . the most dominant Grand Prix cars I ever drove, the best team, the best designers, but not easy cars to drive; I had to concentrate like hell, and they had the most complicated gearchange pattern I ever experienced . . .'.

Irrespective, thus ended an historic 15 months of racing . . . the Daimler-Benz way.

The Lancia D50s

Right at the end of the 1954 season, in the Spanish GP at Barcelona, the Italian Lancia company introduced a startling new 2.5 litre F1 car. It was the latest and potentially the greatest product of the veteran engineer Vittorio Jano's genius – the Lancia D50.

Lancia Corse number one driver Alberto Ascari immediately qualified the car on pole position and led the early stages of the race, only for a manufacturing fault in his car's transmission casing to leak oil on to the clutch and cause his retirement. Even so, the warning was writ large for all Lancia's rivals, even if they might answer to the name of Daimler-Benz . . .

Ever since the vintage period of the 1920s, *Fabbrica Automobili Lancia e Cia* of Turin had been famed for its technically-advanced and highly–sophisticated motor cars. They offered the very best production car performance, handling and roadholding by contemporary standards. After the war, the svelte Aurelia line emerged, and in 1950 when Pinin Farina styled the B20 Coupe with its sloping fastback he set a trend for 2-plus-2 *Gran Turismo* cars which was subsequently taken up by all other GT manufacturers.

However, when Gianni Lancia decreed that works racing team use of the Aurelia Coupes would cease at the end of 1952, he set his heart upon building a true and specialized sports racing car series to project the sophisticated Lancia message to the widest international audience. He was the son of Vincenzo Lancia – company founder and of course Fiat's great driver of the pre-Great War period – and was running the empire in conjunction with his widowed mother, Adele.

His engineering team was headed by Jano, then 62 years old and rightly revered for his glory days with Alfa Romeo between the wars. They now developed a superb series of ultimately 3.8 litre V6-engined sports racing and *Competizione Berlinetta* cars under the D-series programme, D20, D23, D24 and D25. They won the Mexican *Carrera PanAmericana*, the Targa Florio and the mighty Mille Miglia in 1953-54, and although like Jaguar they never won the Sports Car World Championship this was due more to no special interest in it than inability.

Gianni Lancia now turned his attention towards the new 2.5 litre Formula 1 announced for 1954-57. It was the next logical step for his ambitions. He authorized the F1 programme in August 1953, only four months before the new Formula's introduction. Target début was the French GP, on 4 July 1954 – coincidentally the event at which Mercedes-Benz would indeed make their GP racing re-entry.

Gianni Lancia signed-on double-World Champion Alberto Ascari and his inseparable friend and mentor Luigi Villoresi, while his engineers in the Via Caraglia offices knuckled down to their task. When their creation – the Formula 1 Lancia D50 – finally made its début in Spain it was only the second totally-new car to be built to the 2.5 litre Formula, because Ferrari, Maserati, Gordini and Connaught were all using enlarged 2 litre F2 equipment.

Jano and his engine designer Ettore Zaccone Mina decided that whatever approach one adopted to a 2.5 litre unsupercharged engine, its ultimate power was never going to be really spec-

tacular. Therefore, to achieve the optimum performance from such a unit, it made sense to make
it as small, compact and light as possible and
install it in the minimum possible chassis/body
structure. Having minimized size and weight, it
then remained to endow the finished car with the
best-possible handling and traction to make the
most of its good power-to-weight ratio.

To save both space and weight, Jano employed
his preferred V8 engine as a structural chassis
member, its crankcase and heads accepting
chassis loads where otherwise extra engine bay
triangulation tubes would have been necessary.
The front suspension attached direct to the
engine, demanding peerless precision in
manufacture. Therefore the complete D50
chassis was precision surface-finished under a
giant Genevoise GSIP machine, all mating surfaces, engine and suspension pick-ups etc being
accurately machined.

The frame itself was a welded steel multi-
tubular spaceframe derived direct from D-series
sports car experience. The rear-mounted gearbox
and final-drive assembly, detailed by *Ing.* Bertini,
unusually also included the hydraulic clutch
mechanism, as on the Aurelia production car.
Front suspension was independent by coil-and-
wishbone, a de Dion axle on transverse leafspring
appearing at the rear.

Jano minimized the wheelbase by abandoning
the successful inboard-mounted brakes of the
sports cars in favour of an all-outboard drum system. Then to concentrate fuel load well within

Jano's V8 engine design for the Lancia D50 included
carefully stressed cylinder blocks and heads which
formed the high-level triangulation within the multi-
tubular chassis' otherwise unbraced engine bay. Here
the exquisitely-cast top-front engine mount can be
clearly seen behind the right-side suspension pick-up.
Note twin-plug ignition, four Solex carburettors in-vee,
fuel tank outriggers and the engine's *désaxé* alignment
which passed the propshaft through the cockpit's left
side, permitting the driver's seat to be lowered.
Everything about these cars was *beautifully* made.

The side-tanked 1954-55 Lancia D50 V8.

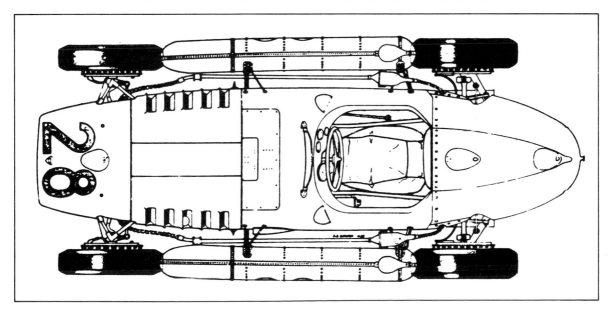

21 October 1954 — Spanish GP meeting, Pedralbes circuit, Barcelona — The sparkling new Lancia D50s await their début, Alberto Ascari about to qualify number 34 on pole position. Number 36 is Luigi Villoresi's. In the background stands one of BRM's transporters, which has brought down their Maserati 250F '2509' for Ken Wharton to drive. Studiously ignoring the Lancias' brilliance — in dark glasses — is BRM designer Peter Berthon . . .

the wheelbase he conceived the D50's most distinctive feature, two long pannier tanks outrigged along either side of the car between its front and rear wheels. They ensured minimal handling change between full and empty tanks, and Jano also considered they would help clean-up aerodynamic turbulence – and therefore drag – between the wheels. Need for a capacious tail tank was thus removed, and so the D50 emerged notably short, squat and light. Its weight concentration within the wheelbase, accompanied by separate forward engine mass and rearward transaxle mass, imparted a low polar moment of inertia, making it the most nimble and 'swervable' of contemporary F1 cars.

The V8 engine was angled within the chassis to pass its propshaft to the left of the driver's seat into an offset transaxle input, thus enabling the driver to drop as low as possible within the high-sided cockpit. The V8 was a chain-driven four-cam design with two valves per cylinder, all plain bearings and four Solex downdraught carburettors instead of the popular Webers. On test it developed 250 bhp at 8,000 rpm. Initially its bore and stroke were 74 mm x 72 mm, 2,480 cc, but

alternatives were tried, including a short-stroke 76 mm x 68.5 mm for 2,486 cc, and an almost 'square' unit of 73.6 mm x 73.1 mm, 2,499 cc.

These raucous engines were started in the cars by team mechanics coupling a portable electric starter to a propshaft extension dog protruding at the rear of the transaxle in the tail. They would pre-heat the oil in its tail-mounted tank with a tailor-made paraffin burner before starting up, and once fired the engines would be revved at a steady 2,000 rpm until thoroughly warmed through. Everything about the cars exuded impeccable toolroom class and quality, and such standards extended throughout the team operating them.

Two cars ran in Spain, Ascari and Villoresi, and although both retired they created a great impression. Through November/December, they and cadet driver Eugenio Castellotti tested extensively at Monza and on the Ospedaletti street circuit at San Remo, assisted by test driver Navone. Fuel tankage was increased from 160 to 200 litres (35 to 44 gallons) to enable the D50s to tackle a 500 km (300 miles) GP non-stop, and five D50s were flown to Argentina for the opening round of the 1955 World Championship series.

There the cars could not be made to handle adequately on the BA Autodrome's geometrical curves. Both Ascari and Villoresi spun off, the former after leading laps 5 to 22, the latter in young Castellotti's car after his own car's fuel pump had failed.

The Turin GP followed on 27 May. An extra 15 bhp had been wrested from the engines – 106 bhp per litre – and Ascari started from pole and won after pressuring Musso into running his leading Maserati off the road. Castellotti and Villoresi placed 3-4. On Easter Monday, the team then contested the Pau GP in southern France, Ascari looking certain to win until a rear brake pipe split. He continued after a stop, with only front brakes operative, and finished fifth. The other D50s placed second and fourth. Ascari then qualified on pole yet again for the Naples GP at Posillipo on 8 May, winning easily while Villoresi ran only third. There was no third car for Castellotti that weekend.

These results were immensely encouraging and two weeks later Lancia entered the Monaco GP in force with four D50s for the usual works trio plus 56-year-old Louis Chiron, the local ace who had won the 1954 Monte Carlo Rally in a Lancia Aurelia. A fifth D50 was present as *muletto*, and Ascari qualified on the front row alongside two

Mercedes W196s. In the race, he could not hold the German cars until all three struck trouble. Just as Ascari was approaching the end of the lap which would have seen him pass the leading Mercedes, by this time stationary in its pit, he slid on spilled oil at the harbourside chicane, and crashed over the quayside into the sea. He was recovered barely injured, save for a broken nose and a soaking. His car was winched out that evening.

Castellotti meanwhile had been delayed, but he salvaged second place for Lancia while Villoresi and Chiron finished 5-6.

The team was concentrating its total effort upon Formula 1 that season, and having abandoned sports car racing Gianni Lancia allowed his contracted drivers to take other sports car rides. Four days after his Monaco ducking, Ascari tried Castellotti's works Ferrari 750 *Monza* sports for size at the Milanese Autodrome, the car crashed and he was killed. The entire Italian racing world was devastated by this disaster. Poor Villoresi could not contemplate racing again for some time, and Lancia Corse's programme simply collapsed.

Gianni and Adele Lancia decided the team would not compete again until a later date, although Jano was permitted to take one car to the Belgian GP for Castellotti as a private entry. The youngster covered himself in glory in prac-

---

May 1955 — Practice for the Monaco GP, Monte Carlo — Alberto Ascari's Lancia D50 is carefully warmed up ready for the great Italian Champion to take it out and equal Fangio's pole position Mercedes' time, one-tenth of a second quicker than Moss whose W196 will complete Mercedes' Lancia sandwich on the starting grid. But Ascari's '0006' will end the race under 12-15 ft of salt water . . . and Scuderia Lancia's last chance of glory will have passed.

24 September, 1955 — Oulton Park Gold Cup, Cheshire — Eugenio Castellotti was a brave and ambitious young driver who put his heart into the job for Lancia, and later Ferrari once the D50s had been transferred to Maranello. Here he is in his second outing — and first race — with a Prancing Horse badge on the D50 in the model's last event of that fateful season.

tice, beating the Mercedes for pole position. But in the race he could not string together such rapid laps, and after running third his car's gearbox seized.

But behind the scenes, *Lancia e Cia* was in dreadful trouble. For five wild years Gianni Lancia had permitted his engineers' creativity to run riot almost regardless of cost. The company's finances now collapsed, with the Italian press avidly stoking the fire. Beset by anxious creditors and labour unions, the Lancias, mother and son, decided to sell out to cement and finance millionaire Carlo Pesenti. So the family lost control of their creation. But the Lancia Corse hardware was too valuable to go to waste, and after further protracted negotiations involving Lancia, Fiat and Ferrari, Gianni's friend Agnelli of Fiat undertook to donate some £30,000 annual sponsorship to Ferrari if they would continue to race the D50s against Mercedes for *La Patria*. This was a great coup for Mr Ferrari whose own outdated cars had become obsolescent and uncompetitive. Now he had fallen heir to the world's finest outside Stuttgart.

On 26 July 1955, a formal ceremony saw six of the eight D50s then extant handed over and transported to Maranello, accompanied by spares, drawings, tools, transport and an almost complete streamliner body intended for the Italian GP at Monza. *Ing* Jano was obliged to leave Via Caraglia in a new-broom operation by Pesenti, and he too followed his D50s to Ferrari.

Initially, it was rumoured the V8 engine would appear in a Ferrari chassis, but in practice for the Italian GP at Monza four D50s emerged completely standard save for fresh Ferrari 'prancing horse' badges. All of them encountered terrible Englebert tyre problems on the new banked speedbowl section, and rather than risk an accident all were wisely withdrawn before the GP. This was a bitter blow for all Italy, as they were the only Italian cars with a hope of keeping the Mercedes fleet in sight.

To the joy of British enthusiasts, however, two cars then ran in the Oulton Park Gold Cup, driven by Hawthorn and Castellotti, but neither handled well on the parkland circuit and Mike merely inherited second place.

This was the 1955 swansong of the Lancia D50, as into 1956 Ferrari would progressively modify the cars' original Jano concept with crude practicality, roughly-welding on brackets where required, dispensing with the engine as a structural member and instead fitting extra engine-bay braces. Fuel load was concentrated back in the tail, and the resultant Lancia-Ferrari D50A – for 'Ameliorato' – cars were ill-handling but powerful vehicles in which Fangio was able to win his third World Championship. Compensation, perhaps, for the failed Lancia dream.

Two original-style true D50s survive, both built-up from parts, one in recent times by Lancia, the other being in Turin's wonderful Biscaretti Museum. The other six were all much modified by Ferrari, and then scrapped in the late '50s, as were the subsequent Ferrari-built Lancia-Ferrari hybrids.

Which was sad – all that promise unfulfilled – for the Lancia D50 looked like the only serious challenge to Daimler-Benz had both continued racing through 1955-56.

1954-58
The Maserati 250Fs
★ ★ ★ ★

Very few rear-engined racing cars have ever approached the sheer aesthetic beauty presented by the best of this classical front-engined family of 2.5 litre F1 cars. One must view the Maserati 250F legend with rather more care, however. Other cars were faster, and more successful – take the Mercedes-Benz W196 as a good example – but few came within a country mile of matching the lovely Maserati's good looks, nor its eminently 'friendly' handling characteristics, and especially not its remarkable production run, for Omer Orsi's Viale Ciro Menotti factory in Modena did indeed put this Grand Prix car into series production. The 250F family of cars consequently provided the mainstay of Grand Prix racing until Cooper inherited that position in 1959-60.

During their four seasons of frontline racing, the 250Fs won only eight World Championship-qualifying GPs, and four of those fell to Fangio in his brilliant fifth-Championship season of 1957, but the cars raced everywhere and anywhere as both works team and private entries. Officine Maserati were 'nice people', talented engineers, gifted artisan craftsmen and above all highly accommodating wheeler-dealers. All of which set the scene for some extremely complex chassis-shuffling to keep all their *clienti* happy, which in turn makes any considered study of the cars' individual histories a real jungle.

There was no one 250F design. Originally the concept was delineated by our old friend Gioachino Colombo, ex-Ferrari, ex-Alfa Corse, assisted by Luigi Bellentani until he moved to Ferrari. Colombo also moved on, and at the end of 1954 30-year-old *Dott Ing* Giulio Alfieri became chief engineer and presided over all subsequent development of the '*due cento cinquante effè*' line.

The 250F 6-cylinder engine was developed from the preceding 2 litre A6GCM/53 Formula 2 unit. It had a detachable two-valve per cylinder head carrying gear-driven twin overhead camshafts, an alloy block with steel liners, dry-sump lubrication, twin-magneto ignition and three twin-choke Weber carburettors. Bore and stroke were 84 mm x 75 mm, 2,493 cc, and 1954-spec power output was around 240 bhp at 7,200 rpm, rising to a peak of 270 bhp at 8,000 rpm in 1957.

Alfieri's immense and continuous experimentation during this period included fuel injection and even, according to Alfieri '43 or 44 different fuel mixtures'. For 1957, he designed a new 68.5 mm x 66 mm, 60° V12 engine of 2,476 cc, with twin ohc on each bank, 24 motor cycle-type ignition coils firing twin plugs per cylinder, and developing nearly 320 bhp at an ear-splitting 9,500 rpm. Early 6-cylinder 250Fs used a four-speed gearbox in unit with the final-drive at the rear of the car, later replaced by five-speed. The cars used coil-and-wishbone IFS and a de Dion rear end with transverse leafspring.

In effect there were six broad groups of Maserati 250F body designs:

1954, 'large' body heavily louvred with elbow-level cockpit sides, brief wrap-round windscreen, oil tank in engine bay quickly removed to tip of tail.

1955-56, 'small' largely unlouvred shell, pro-

15 May, 1954 — BRDC International Trophy, Silverstone — Stirling Moss beginning to show his class on the Formula 1 stage in his newly-acquired Maserati 250F '2508'. It is typical of the early-series louvred-body cars; note the starter orifice in the radiator, the near vertical front suspension coilspring and the 'ultra-modern' partially wrapround moulded perspex windscreen.

gressively higher cockpit sides.

1955-56, one special wide-bodied 'streamliner'.

1956, two-off 'long-nosed' offset transmission cars with lowered seating position and shoulder-level cockpit enclosure.

1957, definitive 'long-nosed Lightweight', high cockpit sides, and slightly more bulky V12.

1958, more compact *Piccolo* model.

These bodies were carried by five broad groups of Maserati 250F chassis, as follows:

Group One – The 1953 A6GCM-based ex-F2 chassis with new 2.5 litre 250F 6-cylinder engines installed as an early-1954 stop-gap expedient to keep customers happy until their true 250Fs could be completed, renumbered '2501' to '2504'.

Group Two – The big-tube 'standard' chassis 250Fs in production from '2505' to '2524', plus '2501' – '2502' and '2504' replacing the A6GCM-based cars which had appeared under those serials.

Group Three – The two offset transmission lowline cars specially built for the 1956 Italian GP, which Moss won, serials '2525' and '2526'.

Group Four – The 'Lightweight' series of 6-cylinder and 12-cylinder cars built for the 1957 season, serial numbers '2527' to '2529' (true Lightweight) and '2530' to '2531' 12-cylinder plus '2532' experimental 6-cylinder.

Group Five – The *Piccolo* short-wheelbase, ultra-lightweight cars '2533' and '2534' built in 1958 after the formal factory team's disbanding on financial grounds at the end of 1957.

Between these groups, the true 250F chassis frames '2501' to '2524' inclusive were of *Tipo 1* design; the offset or *Fuoricentro* cars may be considered as an offshoot on their own; the 1957 factory team lightweight cars driven by Juan Fangio, Jean Behra and Harry Schell were *Tipo 2s*, and the two 1958 *Piccolo* cars were *Tipo 3s*.

But, in the best traditions of Formula 1 the family just continuously evolved and one year's cars would in most cases be updated with a new year's modifications. There were differences between cars supposedly of the same type – for example the later cars offered two wheelbase lengths – Alfieri quoting me 2200 mm and 2280 mm – and chief mechanic 'Guerrino' Bertocchi recalling how Fangio liked the longer more stable chassis and Behra the shorter, more nervous one . . .

Obviously the rigours of racing meant continuous replacement of mechanical and suspension parts as much as money allowed and necessity demanded. So how many Maserati 250Fs *were* built? Maserati issued numbers from '2501' to '2534' missing out '2517' because Italian superstition regards '17' as unlucky. Neither chassis numbers '2503' nor '2510' ever applied to true 250Fs but instead to interim A6GCM-based cars re-engined as above. Their gearboxes were mounted on the rear of the engine, not in unit with the transaxle as in the better-balanced true 250Fs, and they never could use the new engine's power satisfactorily.

These chassis numbers suggest 34 250F-series cars overall, less the two 'GCM variants and the unbuilt '2517', leaving 31 true 250Fs. Right? Wrong ... the works hack '2501' for three arduous seasons was almost totally reconstructed at least twice, so how many cars does it constitute? And numbers '2501' and '2504' appeared originally on ex-F2 chassised cars subsequently replaced by true 250Fs as production gained pace. Chassis '2523' began life with a straightened chassis frame removed originally from and replaced by new in chassis '2507', and was then rebuilt around a later-completed new frame of its own. The old 'ex-2507 ex-2523' frame was then used for another car under the number '2523' ... so there were two '2523's in existence simultaneously. Are you confused? You're not alone ...

Handling and brakes, plus competitive power, made the 250F successful. Alfieri explains: 'Our car handled well due to contributory reasons; one – front suspension geometry, not special, but good – unequal-length wishbones and coil-springs; two – de Dion rear suspension, very soft with transverse leaf-spring; three – our Pirelli tyres very good; four – this first spaceframe chassis was very poor in torsional stiffness, in the wet lateral force was low, tyre friction poor and this made our car perfect for the rain, very pleasant, very special, very lucky ...'

Weak de Dion tubes and transmission bevel-gears posed early problems, but Fangio won in Argentina and Belgium before commencing his new contract mid-season with Mercedes. His young compatriot Onofre Marimon and Villoresi soldiered on, while Moss drove his private car so brilliantly he was invited to run it as a works' entry. They suffered the early problems, because as Alfieri recalled, 'Fangio you see was always very soft, very gentle on the car. In a race he would consume 10-15 litres of fuel less than the others, wear his brakes less, and all other parts of the car too. After he had gone the others were all very hard, rugged on the cars, and we had to make them stronger – but we wanted them lighter and more powerful as well ...'

---

21 October 1954 — Before first practice for the Spanish GP, Pedralbes circuit, Barcelona — Four factory Maserati 250Fs queue in a side street, number 8 being the brand new unlouvred-body spare car, fresh from the Paris Salon stand. Stirling Moss will crash it when he hits the centre throttle instead of the brake. Number 12 is Sergio Mantovani's '2511', 10 Roberto Mieres' '2514', and 14 (last in the line-up) Luigi Musso's '2512'. That's the team's big Fiat transporter in the background.

30 June, 1956 — Practice for the French GP, Reims-Gueux — The famous Maserati 250F 'streamliner' which had made its début on the fast Syracuse circuit at the end of the 1955 season was wheeled out again for the high-speed straights at Reims. Here it carries Piero Taruffi's number — mid-series 250F smooth-bodied number '2' in the background is team experimental hack chassis '2501' for Moss.

---

1 September, 1956 — Practice for the Italian GP, Monza — Officine Maserati's works team line-up is headed by the new *Fuoricentro* offset-transmission car '2525' (number 36) which will win, driven by Moss, then the conventional '2524' also numbered for Moss who is looking into its cockpit, and '2501' for Villoresi.

When Alfieri took technical charge from May 1955, he '... made a smaller body, better streamlined and we did a great study of the engine characteristics to improve its mid-range and 245 bhp maximum. We reduced weights from 620 kg dry, 640 sometimes, down eventually to maybe 610 ... Through 1955-56 we made many experiments. We did a completely new design tubular frame to improve the problems of low chassis stiffness, using more, smaller tubes, changed brake drums, big work on streamlining the exhausts, sometimes one pipe, sometimes two. We ran our streamlined 250F ... I did small model tests in the Milan University wind tunnel. The full-size car was not very good, but was the best of the type I think, better than Ferrari's ...'.

The streamliner was hastily replaced with the *Fuoricentro* offset cars which won the Italian GP. 'At Reims I saw our cars were too slow, and I came back home as passenger in a Fiat 1100 driven by Bertocchi and thought what can I do? And when we arrived back in Modena I said we shall do a new chassis, a new gearbox with a new offset driveline beside the driver so we could sit him lower and a new lower body, and it was all ready for Monza where Moss won ...'

Now for 1957: 'Each year we had done new cars, the 1956 *Fuoricentro* showed good speed but not very good handling but we could not understand why. The technological language of the time was inadequate for our drivers to explain what was happening to us and so we started again with the new lightweight design for 1957, still-smaller

4 August, 1957 — German GP, Nürburgring — Barely believable genius; the Old Man, Juan Manuel Fangio, during his shattering fight-back drive to win this race on the most difficult circuit in the calendar and to clinch his fifth and final Drivers' World Championship title. The car is the factory *Tipo* 2 Lightweight '2529'. Back in Modena after the race Maserati's mechanics discovered its front suspension was completely seized. Despite the handicap, Fangio had been unbeatable.

tubes, more of them, 40 per cent stiffer for the complete chassis and with increased weight bias to the rear, maybe 48:52 weight distribution dry.

'Mr Botasso, engineer of Pirelli, was very nice man, great friend of mine and they decided to stop racing at the end of 1956 but made many, many tyres for us to have in 1957 so not to hurt Maserati. The problem in racing tyres then was not compounds and grip – was only *safety*, to last 500 km Grand Prix distance carrying a heavy car without exploding. We used 17 in wheels purely to reduce tyre stress and add safety – at Monza Ferrari used 16 in and their tyres exploded!

'The V12 offered another solution to the 2.5 litre formula. It was a very good engine and we obtained 300 bhp. We destroyed many in early tests, running late at night and keeping all Modena wake! We had valve-spring and con-rod problems, the rods were too light, but small modification and it became reliable. 10,500 rpm was a lot for 1957 ... we had a good 6-cylinder which we ran in three cars and won races while we ran one 12-cylinder and only learned ...'

Meanwhile Fangio brought Maserati their great emotional World Championship victory in 1957 with his lightweight 250F.

Undoubtedly the greatest classic of all the 250Fs' great races was that year's fantastic German GP at the Nürburgring, where Fangio set out on half tanks to build a lead over the Ferrari team running non-stop. Maserati planned to refuel and change tyres without Fangio being caught by the best of the Ferraris, driven by Hawthorn and Collins. But Fangio's pit stop was slow, 52 sec, because a hub nut spun beneath the car and could not be found. The two English boys had long gone into the lead when Fangio erupted out of the pit lane and began what he rated as perhaps the greatest drive of his whole career; he not only caught and passed them, he simply ate them alive, repeatedly shattering the lap record along the way. After the race he admitted, 'I did things I have never done before and I don't ever want to drive like that again ...'

The individual Maserati 250Fs built during this period were discussed in depth in *Autosport* magazine, Sept/Oct 1981, but briefly were as follows:

Chassis '2501' – 1954, number first applied to a 2.5 litre-engined A6GCM for Roberto Mieres, destroyed in transporter accident on the public road. New true 250F '2515' then delivered to Mieres, and true '2501' début October 1954 Paris Salon wearing Alfieri's prototype 'small' 1955 body;

27 October, 1957 — Moroccan GP, Ain-Diab, Casablanca — Third-string works driver Harry Schell trying hard in his factory Lightweight 250F, chassis '2527', heading towards a fifth place finish in this non-Championship event, the full Officine Maserati works team's official Formula 1 farewell. No other F1 design better exemplifies the front-engined F1 car at its most handsome . . .

works car 1954-57, continuously modified as team's experimental *muletto*. Rebuilt under number '2526' for Keith Campbell (Geoff Duke's motor cycle racing brother-in-law) 1958. After his death in Cadours 500 cc race to Ken Kavanagh, to UK. Won 1956 Australian GP (Moss).

Chassis '2502' – 1954, number first applied to A6GCM as above for Jorge Daponte, to Argentina for national racing. True 250F under this number in model's début, Argentina 1954; became Sergio Mantovani's works car, probably broken-up and cannibalized.

Chassis '2503' – 1954, number applied to A6GCM as above for Harry Schell, 1954, sold to Reg Hunt, Australia, to Kevin Neal etc. Serial never applied to true 250F.

Chassis '2504' — 1954, number first applied to A6GCM as above for 'B.Bira', then engine into new 250F '2504' chassis while A6GCM-type frame sold to Argentina. True 250F '2504' then crashed by BRM driver Flockhart when 'Bira' gave him drive to gain experience. BRM swopped their original '2509' frame with 'Bira' for this damaged frame, which became '2509' thereafter. What had become '2504' later re-chassised by factory, then ex-'Bira' to Bruce Halford, Horace Gould, to New Zealand. Won 1954 GP des Frontières, 1955 New Zealand GP ('Bira'). See '2511' for fate of ex-'2509' frame.

Chassis '2505' – 1954, first serial to be applied immediately to true 250F, works car, to André Simon, 1957 Joakim Bonnier, smartened-up by factory and presented to Biscaretti Museum, Turin, as '2500'. Won 1954 Argentine and Belgian GPs (Fangio), Pescara GP (Musso), 1955 Albi GP (Simon).

Chassis '2506' – Completed June 1954, works car for Onofre Marimon, to Louis Rosier until 1956, Schlumpf Collection, Mulhouse, France. Won 1954 Rome GP (Marimon), Oulton Park Gold Cup (Moss).

Chassis '2507' – Completed April 1954, for Syd Greene's Gilby Engineering Co, GB, driver Roy Salvadori, rebuilt around new chassis after Oulton Park crash, original frame became '2523', to Portuguese collection, now (1988) with Robin Lodge, UK, one of the most original of all surviving 250Fs. Won 1954 Goodwood and Aintree (Salvadori).

Chassis '2508' – Completed May 1954, for Stirling Moss, works-supported from German GP, driven for Moss by Hawthorn, Macklin, Fitch, Gerard etc 1955, to New Zealand supposedly as '2513'; then American collection. Won 1954 Aintree '200', Goodwood, Aintree again (Moss), 1955 Crystal Palace (Hawthorn), Charterhall (Gerard), 1956 New Zealand GP, Aintree '200' and Crystal Palace (Moss).

Chassis '2509' - Completed July 1954, for Owen Racing Organization (BRM), original frame swopped with 'Bira's' '2504', extensively modified for Wharton, Collins, Hawthorn, to Jack Brabham 1955, to New Zealand, now in NZ collection. Won 1955 BRDC International Trophy (Collins).

Chassis '2510' - Interim A6GCM car with 250F engine for Baron de Graffenried, 1954. Used in filming *Such Men are Dangerous*, to Volonterio, to Swiss collection. Serial never applied (so far as known) to true 250F.

Chassis '2511' - Completed August 1954 for Sergio Mantovani, to Scuderia Centro-Sud, distributed to the winds, replica built around recent facsimile frame with original mechanical components, to Japanese collector. Schlumpf Museum car '2511' uses '2509' original chassis. Won 1956 Caen GP (Schell).

Chassis '2512' - Completed August 1954, works car for Marimon in which he was killed during practice for German GP, rebuilt as 1955 team car for Mieres, apparently removed from service mid-'55, possibly later sold as '2518' – see later.

Chassis '2513' - Sold as rolling chassis to Vandervell products for Vanwall R&D. Many years later acquired and completed by David Sankey, UK, began racing in VSCC events.

Chassis '2514' - Completed August 1954 for Luigi Musso, retained as works car 1955, to Gould, to H.C. Spero 1963-64 became first 'historic racing' 250F, to Japanese collection. Won 1956 Aintree '100';

Chassis '2515' - New 1955 team car for Mieres, to Scuderia Guastalla 1956 for Gerino Gerini, updated 1957 to Volonterio, sold later to Tom Wheatcroft for what became his Donington Collection, Derby, England.

Chassis '2516' - New 1955 team car for Behra, to Reg Hunt in Australia, Cameron Millar UK 1963,

---

26 October 1954 — Spanish GP, Pedralbes circuit, Barcelona — The promising Sergio Mantovani cornering his works Maserati 250F '2511' before its brakes gave trouble late in the race and he crashed without injury. The unfortunate young Italian would crash heavily during practice for the Turin GP the following March, striking a bridge abutment head on. He injured one leg so severely it could not be saved, and his racing career was over . . .

to Anthony Mayman collection. Won 1955 Pau GP (Behra), Oulton Park Gold Cup (Moss).

Chassis '2517' – Number not used for superstitious reasons.

Chassis '2518' – Completed September 1955, works streamliner, damaged in factory fire 1956 – retained by factory into 1980s – paperwork possibly sold with '2512'.

Chassis '2519' – Completed April 1956 for Luigi Piotti, driven by him and Villoresi, to Gerini 1958 with high-tailed bodywork.

Chassis '2520' – Works car 1956, to Stan Jones in Australia – father of World Champion Alan Jones – into UK historic racing, to Italian collection.

Chassis '2521' – Completed May 1956, works car, to John du Puy 1957, crashed at Casablanca by Jean Lucas, French collector Serge Pozzoli bought wreck, had it restored at Modena, retained.

Chassis '2522' – Completed March 1956, works car, to Scuderia Centro-Sud 1957, heavily cannibalized, bits to Cameron Millar UK assembled into facsimile frame, to Dutch collection.

Chassis '2523' – *TWO CARS*, first completed April 1956 using straightened ex-Gilby '2507' frame, rebuilt around brand-new frame August '56, raced in Australia, became basis of rebuilt '2504'. Original ex-'2507' frame became V12 hack into 1957, then 6-cylinder reinstalled for Maria Theresa de Filippis, 1958. Ex-Australia to Millar and into UK collectors' hands. Ex-de Filippis ex-V12 hack to South America to UK trade.

Chassis '2524' – Completed September 1956 for Francesco Godia-Sales, to Jo Bonnier 1958, to USA 1961, badly damaged in serious accident injuring driver Phil Cade who retained the car.

Chassis '2525' – Completed September 1956, first *Fuoricentro* ('offset') car for Italian GP, to Tony Parravano USA, to UK, to US collection. Won 1956 Italian GP (Moss).

Chassis '2526' – Completed September 1956, second *Fuoricentro* car for Italian GP, unused until 1958, to Antonio Creus as '2530', to Schlumpf brothers.

Chassis '2527' – Completed December 1956. First of the three famous 1957 *Tipo 2* or 'Lightweight' works cars, to Ken Kavanagh 1958, later to UK, Hon Patrick Lindsay in historic racing, severely damaged at Thruxton, rebuilt around virtually new chassis, to US collection. Won 1957 Argentine GP, Buenos Aires City GP (Fangio).

Chassis '2528' – Completed December 1956. Second *Tipo 2* Lightweight works car, to Francesco Godia-Sales 1958, to Charles Lucas UK, then Neil Corner, retained as Corner family's cherished 'Red Racer'. One of the most original of all surviving 250Fs and one of the most successful. Won 1957 Monaco GP (Fangio), Pau, Modena and Moroccan GPs (Behra).

Chassis '2529' – Last of the *Tipo 2* Lightweight works cars, immortalized by Fangio's heroic victory in the 1957 German GP, to Giorgio Scarlatti 1958, to Bonnier, to Deubel USA to German collection. Won 1957 French and German GPs, 1958 Buenos Aires City GP (Fangio).

Chassis '2530' – Completed June 1957, *Tipo 2* Lightweight chassis, first V12 works car built from scratch, used only in practice for French GP. Used for experimental 6-cylinder car early in 1958, to Argentina, a few remnants taken to UK recently, majority surely remaining in South America. Chassis number used for '2526' when sold to Creus.

Chassis '2531' – Completed June 1957, offset-transmission V12 works car, raced by Behra in Italian GP, to Argentina – less engine.

Chassis '2532' – This serial appeared on the chassis plate of the new *Tipo 3 Piccolo* car which Fangio drove in his last race, the 1958 French GP at Reims-Gueux.

Chassis '2533' – The true first *Tipo 3 Piccolo* super-lightweight smaller car, with shorter wheelbase achieved by angling the driveshafts forward. Built for American Temple Buell's private team, did New Zealand race tour as Scuderia El Salvador, returned to Modena, sold to Joe Lubin, USA, retained unused in original condition, recently sold to an American collector.

Chassis '2534' – The second of Buell's *Piccolo* cars, to the UK 1972, retained in private collection.

Tec-Mec Maserati – A 1959 F1 project commenced at the Maserati factory but inherited by chassis and transmission designer Valerio Colotti when the factory ceased racing. Colotti set-up his own Studio Tecnica Meccanica and had this all-independently suspended 250F 6-cylinder powered lightweight built-up by moonlighting friendly mechanics. Driven by Fritz d'Orey in the 1959 US GP at Sebring, to Tom Wheatcroft for the Donington Collection, UK, and retained.

The Vanwalls

★ ★ ★ ★ ⁄

Guy Anthony Vandervell was born on 8 September 1896, in Westbourne Park, London. His father, Charles Anthony Vandervell, was an electrical engineer who had launched his own business under the name CAV in Willesden Green four years before. CAV became one of the biggest names in the British electrical industry, installing electric lighting in the Houses of Parliament in 1904, developing the first variable-speed dynamo that year and the dynamo-charged battery system. They eventually occupied an extensive factory site in Warple Way, Acton, to the west of London, and C.A. Vandervell raised his son Tony in considerable luxury and gave him a Harrow education, but instilled in him a sense of engineering perfection matched with business acumen which would establish another considerable business.

G.A. Vandervell served as a despatch rider in the Great War and through the early 1920s rode motor cycles in competition, and hill-climbed, sprinted and raced a Clement-Talbot car. In 1922 he had a one-off drive at Brooklands in a single-seat Model T Ford special entered by Royden Albert Rothermel. Meantime he was working in his father's CAV business but not enjoying it greatly, and after C.A. Vandervell sold out to Lucas in 1926 Tony Vandervell told the new management their fortune and walked out. Father set him up in a radio goods retail business in London's West End, but it went under in the 1929 Depression.

R.A. Rothermel, who had entered Vandervell in the Model T special at Brooklands seven years earlier, had been director of the London branch of an American company named the O&S Oilless Bearing Co, which supplied self-lubricating bushes to CAV. Rothermel now resigned, and C.A. Vandervell bought the London company, largely to give his 'difficult' son something to direct.

At last Tony Vandervell had found something to sink his rugged teeth into, and in 1930 he learned of the new American bearing system in which very shallow layers of bearing material were deposited upon thin steel flexible 'shells' to provide easily interchangeable shell bearings. The invention had enormous potential, as conventional engine bearings at that time were usually hefty steel, brass or bronze shells carrying a thick bearing surface of white metal or the tin/antimony/copper alloy known as 'Babbitt'. An alternative common bearing system involved locally casting such materials direct into housings machined in the engine bottom-end. In either case, replacing a run bearing could be a tedious and costly job. Furthermore these primitive bearings provided such a heat-trap that they failed quite often.

Tony Vandervell rushed to America to meet the inventors of the new shell-bearings, John V.O. Palm and Benjamin F. Hopkins of the Cleveland Graphite Bronze Company. Sailing over on RMS *Aquitania* he coincidentally met Delmar Roos, experimental director of Studebaker, and heard first-hand of their recent experience with these 'Clevite' bearings. Roos's name gave Vandervell his introduction to meet Ben Hopkins, the company president, and when he explained his father *was* the CAV electrical giant capable of backing

March 1956 — Private testing at Goodwood sees Tony Vandervell himself trying out his team's brand new prototype 'VW1' teardrop car. Note the beautiful panel finish even before primer, filler and top-coat paintwork was applied. Colin Chapman designed the multi-tubular spaceframe chassis, Frank Costin the aerodynamic bodyshell and Vandervell Products' experimental section provided the powerful 4-cylinder engine. The Old Man had raced cars at Brooklands in the 1920s, and postwar, in his fifties, he liked to drive his GP cars whenever the chance arose. His team and drivers liked to make that as seldom as possible . . .

UK manufacture of the new invention, he successfully badgered Hopkins into granting him the UK manufacturing licence. UK Patent No 409,289 was filed in 1932 and granted on 23 April 1934, by which time a new bearing company – Vandervell Products Ltd – had been formed.

A massive new tailor-made factory was built in Western Avenue, Acton, and the Clevite-based 'Thin Wall' bearings manufactured there under-pinned the British motor industry.

The Second World War brought enormous expansion, and after the war 'GAV' or simply 'The Old Man' or 'the Guv'nor' as Tony Vandervell became known to his staff was approached by Raymond Mays to co-sponsor the BRM V16 project in money and kind. The gruff, tough industrialist had never lost his enthusiasm for motor racing, and above all simply for any challenge, and he became one of the BRM project's main pillars before very quickly discovering that their committee approach stood no chance of success.

After buying them a Ferrari 125 on which to gain experience, and running it as the *'ThinWall Special'* he cut his ties with BRM and became their major rival in British F1 and *Libre* racing. His series of three *ThinWall Special* Ferraris were continuously developed by VP Ltd's racing department-cum-toolroom at the Acton factory.

Their engineering and machining skills were amongst the very best in the world, the 'Guv'nor' was very much an internationalist and he would adopt anything he thought worthwhile, wherever in the automotive world it had originated. Such a pragmatic outlook was unusual amongst the Imperial-minded 'British is best' industrial thinking of the time. Thus VP experimented early on with Goodyear disc brakes on the *ThinWall Special*.

'The Guv'nor' was also a director of Norton motor cycles who were still dominating the racing world with their 500 cc single-cylinder engines delivering a solid 50-horsepower – 100 bhp per litre – a magic figure for any racing engine of that time. He reasoned that four such cylinders on a common crankcase would produce a competitive 2 litre F2 power unit. That class took World Championship status in 1952-53 so he backed development of such an engine and asked Cooper to produce a Ferrari-like state of the art chassis for him.

Norton's Leo Kuzmicki and ex-BRM designer Eric Richter worked with Fred Fox's Acton engineers to produce a basic 2 litre 4-cylinder VP engine. In effect it comprised four Norton pistons, valves camshafts and combustion chambers mounted in-line *en bloc* and now water-cooled. Leyland Motors provided the necessary patterns and cores for casting a Rolls-Royce B40 military 4-cylinder crankcase which VP modified to allow casting in aluminium instead of iron.

Unfortunately, this 2 litre F2 project dragged until the Formula was about to superceded by 2.5 litre Formula 1 for 1954.

Eventually the 2 litre Cooper-based *Vanwall Special* – a combination of 'Vandervell Products' and 'ThinWall bearings' – made its début in that year's Silverstone International Trophy, too late for the formula for which it had been made, but the 56-year old 'Guv'nor' had an enlarged 2.3 litre engine already in hand, and it was followed by a full Bosch fuel-injected 2.5 litre. The *Special* tag was dropped for 1955 and as 'Vanwall' pure and simple the team had some minor success, but essentially got nowhere in their 15 Formula 1 races of 1954-55, despite using drivers of the calibre of Peter Collins and Mike Hawthorn.

After the prototype car had been run through 1954, four of these still basically Cooper-designed but Vandervell Products-manufactured 4-cylinder cars were campaigned as a proper factory team in 1955, driven by Hawthorn, Ken Wharton, Harry Schell and Desmond Titterington.

Although outpaced and out-handled in the four major GPs attended, Schell won four minor British events.

By the end of this second season, the Guv'nor realized something far more sophisticated was required, and that the uncomplicated Cooper people – whom he respected and liked very much – were not equipped to supply it. Consequently he commissioned Colin Chapman and his Lotus collaborator Frank Costin on a consultancy basis to design a completely new chassis and aerodynamic bodyshell for a new 1956 model F1 Vanwall.

They evolved the peerless aerodynamic teardrop design which has become so famous, based around a very sophisticated, lightweight multi-tubular spaceframe chassis.

Stirling Moss was engaged for a one-off début drive at Silverstone, where he promptly won the International Trophy first time out in 'VW2/56'. He then returned to Maserati, while the four new teardrop Vanwalls proved very fast but very unreliable in GP racing that season, and Harry Schell's fourth at Spa provided their only other finish.

---

1 July, 1956 — French GP, Reims-Gueux — Even the tall Mike Hawthorn was well cowled by Vanwall 'VW2', seen here at Thillois Corner. Note the long Costin beak, the NACA duct induction intake sunk into the bonnet panel, mirror farings doubling as driver-cooling cockpit air intakes and wire-spoked Borrani wheels, the fronts enclosing Vanwall-Goodyear disc brakes, the rear discs being mounted inboard on the final-drive cheeks. Those white on black-disc numbers were most unusual.

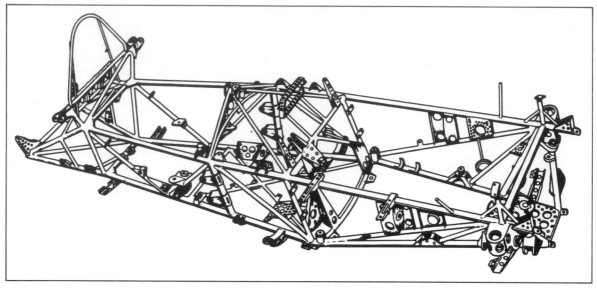

Colin Chapman's spaceframe chassis designed for the 1957 Vanwall.

However, at Reims in the French GP 'Arry got in amongst the leading Lancia-Ferraris after an early delay and gave them a terrible scare. Fangio, Collins and Castellotti had to resort to strong-arm team tactics to hold him off until the tall Van-wall's throttle linkage came apart, and this convinced the Guv'nor that he should invest in better drivers for 1957 so that they could return the compliment and muscle-out 'those bloody red cars' if need be. He hired Moss and Tony Brooks full-time, with young Stuart Lewis-Evans joining them as No 3 from mid-season.

By this time the uncannily quiet teardrop Van-walls were amongst the most powerful cars in Formula 1, producing up to 275 bhp at 7,250 rpm on alcohol fuel that year, while on 120-octane AvGas for '58 they would lose only some 20 hp on that. At Monza the Guv'nor had kicked the tyres of the noisy Ferrari and told their manufacturer, his bearing customer, 'That's where your power should go to, not out there . . .', pointing at its exhausts.

The four original 1956 teardrop Vanwalls were reworked to 1957 trim, with 'Chapman strut' coil-spring rear suspension replacing the earlier transverse leaf. In this form the cars proved faster than ever, and once reliability had been achieved chassis 'VW4' made the breakthrough in the British GP at Aintree, where it had been taken over by Moss after Brooks, battered by a recent Le Mans crash, had kept it in contention during the early stages. Stirling boomed home to clinch Van-wall's maiden GP victory on their home ground, the first all-British major-league GP win since Segrave (Sunbeam) at Tours way back in 1923.

Five new cars were also built that season –

20 July, 1957 — British GP, Aintree — Unusual aspect of the great day when Moss scored Vanwall's maiden *Grande Epreuve* victory after taking over Tony Brooks' car. Here Stuart Lewis-Evans has just brought his sister car into the pits after its throttle linkage parted, disrupting a Vanwall 1-2 display. Tony Brooks offers a Coca-Cola. These two, Vanwall's less-publicized drivers, were both of the highest calibre. Poor Lewis-Evans would suffer fatal burns in the team's last serious GP outing.

25 May, 1958 — Dutch GP, Zandvoort — Stirling Moss on his winning way in Vanwall 'VW10'. Here the car is in its definitive form with Borrani wire-spoked front wheels and Vanwall's own specially cast 'wobbly-web' alloy rears. These wheels were light, stiff and strong, but when fitted at the front the drivers complained that their rigidity diminished steering 'feel'. The tall Chapman-strut style rear suspension coil-damper unit is just visible above the rear tyre.

'VW5' to 'VW10', 'VW9' not being completed – to add to the original quartet, and Moss used '5 to win the Pescara and Italian GPs, really showing 'those bloody red cars' on their home ground.

For 1958 the Vanwalls were further modified, with a better-fared exhaust system and 'wave-web' cast magnesium disc rear wheels though Borrani wires were retained at the front, plus numerous other detail changes to suspension and bodywork. Chassis 'VW1' to 'VW3' and 'VW8' were not assembled during the season, serving as spares, and Moss won the Dutch and Portuguese GPs in 'VW10', and the Moroccan GP in 'VW5', while Brooks won the Belgian and Italian GPs in 'VW5' and the German race in 'VW4'. Unfortunately, neither driver could add sufficient Drivers' Championship points from minor placings to prevent Ferrari driver Mike Hawthorn becoming the first Briton ever to win the World title. Stirling ended the season only one point adrift in second place, and Vandervell achieved his avowed ambition of winning the Formula 1 Constructors' Championship outright.

Tragically, Lewis-Evans's engine 'V5' in chassis 'VW4' – the '57 British and '58 German GP-winning car – blew-up at Casablanca in the Championship-decider, its rear wheels locked

and he crashed heavily, sustaining fatal burns.

Tony Vandervell was in his sixtieth year, worn down by the strain of running his empire in general and by racing in particular. His cars had never before harmed a driver and he was devastated by Lewis-Evans' death, and he withdrew Vanwall from serious competition at that point.

The 1956-58 definitive-series Vanwalls were as follows:

Chassis 'VW1/56' – Race début 5-5-56, transverse leafspring rear suspension – Schell '56 International Trophy, Monaco, Belgian (4th) and French GPs, Froilan Gonzalez '56 British GP, Piero Taruffi '56 Italian GP. Car modified to form 1957 coil-spring rear suspension model 'VW1' – debut 7-4-57 – Moss '57 Syracuse and British GPs (his initial car, taken over by Brooks, Rtd), Salvadori '57 French GP, Brooks '57 German GP, Lewis-Evans '57 Pescara and Moroccan GPs. Car dismantled and cannibalized for spares, 1958 season.

Chassis 'VW2/56' – Race début 5-5-56, transverse leafspring rear suspension – Moss *1st* '56 International Trophy, Trintignant Monaco and Belgian GPs, Hawthorn '56 French GP, '56 British and Italian GPs. Car never completed in

Vanwall 'VW10' shows off its beautifully-made front suspension, and its Norton-derived 4-cylinder fuel-injected engine. The braided pipes carry oil from the nose cooler matrix, the large-diameter rubber hose from the radiator carries cooling water — the hoses running into the riveted oil tank are breathers.

1957 coil-spring rear suspension form. Dismantled and cannibalized for spares.

Chassis 'VW3/56' – Début 29-6-56, transverse leafspring rear suspension – Colin Chapman (practice collision) '56 French GP. Car modified to form 1957 coil-spring rear suspension model 'VW3' – début 7-4-57 – Brooks '57 Syracuse GP. Car dismantled and cannibalized for spares.

Chassis 'VW4/56' – Race début 14-7-56, transverse leafspring rear suspension – Trintignant '56 British and Italian GPs. Car modified to form 1957 coil-spring rear suspension model 'VW4' – début 7-7-57 – Lewis–Evans '57 French and German GPs (crashed), Brooks/Moss *1st* '57 British GP – updated to form 1958 model 'VW4' – début 15-6-58 – Lewis-Evans '58 Belgian and Moroccan GPs (burned out), Brooks *1st* '58 German GP. Car totally destroyed in Lewis-Evans's fatal fire at Casablanca, 19-10-58.

Chassis 'VW5' – Race début 20-7-57, first all-new 1957 coil-spring car – Lewis-Evans '57 British GP,

Moss '57 German GP, *1st* Pescara GP, *1st* Italian GP – updated to form 1958 model 'VW5' – début 18-5-58 – Lewis-Evans '58 Monaco and Dutch GPs, Brooks *1st* '58 Belgian GP, French, British and Portuguese GPs, *1st* Italian GP, Moss *1st* Moroccan GP – extensively rebuilt as 1959 model 'VW5' for Brooks '59 British GP, rebuilt with IRS for 1960, unraced. Car broken-up and cannibalized for 1960 model 'VW11'.

Chassis 'VW6' –Début 12-7-57, 1957 coil-spring car, initially with streamlined body for Reims GP, later converted to standard slipper body – Brooks *1st* '57 Italian GP – updated to form 1958 model 'VW6' — début 19-7-58 – Lewis-Evans '58 British, Portuguese and Italian GPs. Car broken-up.

Chassis 'VW7' – Race début 22-4-57, 1957 coil-spring car – Brooks '57 Goodwood, Monaco and Pescara GPs, Salvadori '57 Reims GP, Lewis-Evans '57 Italian GP – updated to form 1958 model 'VW7' – début 18-5-58 – Moss '58 Monaco GP, Brooks '58 Dutch GP. Car broken-up.

Chassis 'VW8' – Race début 14-7-57, lightweight chassis coil-spring car – Lewis-Evans '57 Reims GP. Car dismantled and cannibalized for spares.

Chassis 'VW9' – Lightweight chassis frame never completed.

Chassis 'VW10' – Race début 27-10-57, 1957 coil-spring car – Brooks '57 Moroccan GP – updated to form 1958 model 'VW10' – début 18-5-58 – Brooks '58 Monaco and Moroccan GPs. Car retained for testing 1959, rebuilt as demonstration car in 1960, retained by VP/GKN into 1986 when sold by auction to Tom Wheatcroft's Donington Collection as a runner – has been driven by the author.

This completes the 1956-58 team car list, four 1956 transverse leafspring cars having been completed, then converted for 1957 into first four of the eight coil-spring rear suspension cars completed that year. All were retained for 1958, though four –serial '1, '2, '3 and '8 – served merely as 'hangar queen' sources of spares. No more than four Vanwalls were fully assembled and running at any one time.

One subsequent front-engined F1 Vanwall appeared:

Chassis 'VW11' – Race début 3-7-60, 'Lowline' car with Colotti-designed gearbox and IRS – Brooks '60 French GP. Car dismantled and retained by VP, to Donington Collection, Derby, England, 1986.

The Guv'nor could not totally resist dabbling in racing occasionally but Vanwall's subsequent appearances in a rapidly changing racing world were pathetic in comparison to the glory which had gone before, retiring from the British GP in 1959, only seventh at Goodwood and retiring from the French GP in 1960, and then finishing fifth in an oversized and overweight experimental rear-engined car in an InterContinental Formula race at Silverstone in 1961.

But all these cars' superb finish and beautiful workmanship bore testimony to the peerless standards set by Vanwall's rugged Guv'nor. In the seven seasons from 1954-60 his cars contested only 29 Championship GPs, and 17 of those were concentrated into Vanwall's two busiest seasons of 1957-58, when they won all but eight.

Through their 'teardrop' period, 1956-58, Vanwall made 63 starts in 25 races, of which they won ten, and in the two major seasons of 1957-58 their tally was actually 48 starts in only 19 races, of which they won nine.

With great style, they achieved Tony Vandervell's aim of 'beating those bloody red cars', and a British marque won the first official Formula 1 Constructors' Championship. They had shown how a green car could win again at top level, and all who followed remembered Vanwall with pride...

---

18 July 1957 — British GP practice, Aintree — Prelude to the great day when Stirling Moss, Tony Brooks and the Vanwall team would become the first British combination to win a *Grande Epreuve* since Major Segrave and Sunbeam at Tours in 1923. The cars here are 'VW4' (as yet un-numbered, foreground) which will start the race driven by Brooks and eventually win in Moss's hands, 'VW1' (18) Moss's original car, and 'VW5' (22) for Stuart Lewis-Evans.

The Ferrari Dino 246

★ ★ ★

In 1958, Mike Hawthorn became the first Englishman to win the Drivers' World Championship crown. He beat Stirling Moss by the narrowest of margins, but it was Moss's Vanwall which carried off the inaugural Formula 1 Constructors' Cup title. To do that, the Acton marque had beaten the Ferrari Dino 246s driven by Hawthorn and his team-mates Peter Collins, Luigi Musso, Wolfgang von Trips, Phil Hill and Olivier Gendebien.

Nevertheless, despite their defeat by Vanwall, these blood-red V6 Ferraris were amongst the most powerful and exciting Grand Prix cars of their period and they enjoyed not inconsiderable success from their inception at the end of 1957 to the close of the 2.5 litre Formula at the end of 1960. They evolved from a design first developed in response to the governing CSI's decision to establish a new 1.5 litre International Formula 2 class in 1957, intended as an adequate stepping stone between 500 cc Formula 3 and full–house 2.5 litre Formula 1 racing.

At the end of 1955, eighteen months before F2's reintroduction, Mr Ferrari briefed his ailing engineer son Alfredo – 'Alfredino' hence 'Dino' Ferrari – and his senior designers to set-down a new F2 engine design under the direction of the veteran Vittorio Jano.

In his agonized memoirs – *Le Mie Gioie Terribili* ('My Terrible Joys') – Ferrari relates how he and Jano spent long hours at Dino's bedside during the long cold winter of 1955-56 discussing the pros and cons of using an in-line 4-cylinder or a six, a V6 or V8. The grieving father in Mr Ferrari recalls, '. . . for reasons of mechanical efficiency,

he (Dino) came to the conclusion that the engine should be a V6, and we accepted this decision . . .' In view of Jano's pedigree and immense experience, this is a little hard to believe. But poor Dino Ferrari was losing his battle against muscular dystrophy, and that winter he developed nephritis, entered renal failure and died on 30 June 1956. In one small way, the long line of Ferrari V6 engines which subsequently carried a representation of his signature cast into their cam-covers, became his epitaph.

Jano's unusual 1,500 cc four-cam V6 design featured a 65° vee angle between its cylinder banks. Five months after Dino's death the first unit ran at Maranello. The British Cooper and Lotus F2 cars then under development used Coventry Climax 4-cylinder engines of about 140 bhp. On the dyno the new Ferrari Dino V6 gave nearly 180 bhp at 9,000 rpm – 120 bhp per litre against the British best of 93.

Ferrari's philosophy had always been that the engine is all-important, chassis, suspension and brakes virtually incidental. His cars seldom handled well or were pleasant to drive, but they were always powerful and usually extremely reliable. As one of his drivers later told me, '. . . you could just climb into a Ferrari and drive your head off, and nine times out of ten it would still be running at the finish. It wasn't until I moved to other teams that I realized just how fragile most Grand Prix cars could be. The Ferraris were phenomenally strong, and always powerful . . .'

The new F2 Ferrari V6 was effectively a scaled-down version of the contemporary Lancia-Ferrari 801 V8, based on a tubular chassis with two large-diameter lower longerons reinforced by a superstructure of smaller tube. Suspension was by coil-and-wishbone up front, de Dion rear. Maranello christened their pretty little car the Ferrari Dino 156 – indicating simply 1.5 litres, 6-cylinders.

This prototype's chassis number was '0011' in the contemporary GP series and it made its racing début on 28 April 1957, in the Naples GP. Luigi Musso flogged it mercilessly to finish third behind his team-mates Collins and Hawthorn in 2.5 litre V8 F1 cars, and it survived happily. In July, the major Reims *Coupe de Vitesse* F2 race allowed '0011' to unleash its power, and Maurice Trintignant scored a fine Ferrari victory over Cooper, Lotus and Porsche.

Meanwhile, alcohol-bearing F1 fuels were about to be banned for 1958 and GP duration slashed from 500 km to 300. Formula 2 was already a pump petrol class, so in the new Dino V6 engine Maranello had a ready-made 'gasoline burner' ripe for enlargement to 1958 Formula 1.

At the end of that 1957 season, the two extant V6 chassis – '0011' and '0012' – were remodelled with more sleek long-nosed bodywork, and V6 engines allegedly enlarged to 1,877 cc. In fact Ferrari engine records quote dimensions of 77 mm x 71 mm for these engines, which is actually 1,983.72 cc. Output was raised to around 220 bhp at 8,500 rpm, and when '0011' was tested against a 2.5 litre F1 V8 at Monza, it proved both slightly faster and easier to drive.

Musso drove '0011' into second place and Collins finished fourth in '0012' in the non-Championship Modena GP on 22 September and a month later at Casablanca Hawthorn drove '0011' with an 81 mm x 71 mm, 2,195 cc engine and Collins '0012' with an 85 mm x 71 mm, 2,417 cc version which was to become the definitive F1 Dino 246 size. These engines, respectively, developed around 240 bhp at 8,500 rpm and 270 bhp at 8.300 rpm on '58 regulation maximum 130-octane AvGas aviation spirit. Despite Asian 'flu, Collins led the non-Championship Moroccan GP briefly before spinning twice, but Hawthorn – also ill – pulled out.

Through the following winter, what were now the F1 Ferrari Dino chassis were redesigned to provide a multi-tubular lattice structure much closer to being a true spaceframe, with more nearly same-size tubing in both the bottom ladder frame and the upper superstructure framing. This so-called 'small-tube' Ferrari frame saved some 25 lb (11 kg) weight against the original 'big-tube' design.

To start the 1958 season in Buenos Aires a third big-tube frame matching '0011' and '0012' was prepared for Hawthorn carrying new short-nose bodywork by Ferrari's usual racing body builder, Scaglietti. The prototype small-tube frame was shipped out for von Trips but seems to have disappointed. It was insufficently rigid, and of the seven cars which works records mention during 1958, only two – possibly three – used this small-tube design. A typical Ferrari mystery is that the records I have been provided with give the same serials to cars which are known to have appeared with big-tube frames at one meeting, and small-tube at the next . . .

Meanwhile, however, the engines had been standardized around the Collins 2,417 cc Casablanca '57 size. Hawthorn's preferred four-spoke steering wheel always featured in the cars he drove, and in Argentina his new car also ran experimental turbo-finned brake drums for the first time. Despite Vanwall and BRM having proved the efficacy of disc brakes, Ferrari felt themselves far removed from Dunlop and Lockheed's latest technology, and remained faithful to the drum brake. Despite being generally powerful and effective, the drum brake systems would fade and burn out, and could not match the reliable consistency of discs, giving their drivers extra headaches.

The 1957-58 family of Dino V6 cars were as follows, a new chassis serial batch starting again at '0001' being introduced for the start of the definitive F1 series:

Chassis '0011' – Race début 28-4-57, 1,500 cc F2, transverse leafspring rear suspension – Musso '57 Naples GP, Trintignant *1st* '57 Reims F2 – fitted with 1,893 cc V6 for F1 – Musso '57 Modena GP – fitted with 2,195 cc V6 – Hawthorn '57 Moroccan GP. Either extensively modified or replaced by new car under same serial with 2,417 cc V6 for 1958 – début 19-1-58 – Musso '58 Argentine and Buenos Aires City GPs, von Trips '58 Monaco GP, Gendebien '58 Belgian GP – refitted with 1,500 cc F2 engine – Hill '58 German GP F2 class. Either extensively modified or replaced by new car under same serial for 1959 to Fantuzzi-bodied all coil-sprung form. Car subsequently broken-up.

Chassis '0012' – Race début 22-9-57, 1,893 cc 'F1', transverse leafspring rear suspension. Collins '57 Modena GP – fitted with 2,417 cc V6. Collins '57 Moroccan GP. Either extensively modified or replaced by new car under same serial for 1958 – début 19-1-58 – Collins '58 Argentine and Buenos Aires City GPs. Either extensively modified or replaced by new car under same serial as 1959 F2. Car eventually broken-up.

Chassis '0001' – Race début 19-1-58, first definitive Dino 246 F1, transverse leafspring – Hawthorn '58 Argentine GP, *1st* Buenos Aires City GP Heat One, Musso *1st* Syracuse GP – Musso Monaco and Dutch GPs, Collins French GP, von Trips British GP. Car broken-up.

Chassis '0002' – Race début 2-2-58, Dino 246 transverse leafspring – von Trips '58 Buenos Aires City and French GPs, Collins *1st* International Trophy Silverstone, Collins Monaco, Dutch and Belgian GPs, *1st* British GP – Collins crashed fatally in this car in German GP. Either extensively modified or replaced by new car under same serial for 1959, eventually broken-up.

Chassis '0003' – Race début 7-4-58, Dino 246 transverse leafspring – Hawthorn *1st* '58 Easter Goodwood – Hawthorn Monaco, Dutch, Belgian GPs, *1st* French GP, British, German, Portuguese GPs – fitted with disc brakes possibly renumbered '0005' – Hawthorn Italian and Moroccan GPs. Either extensively modified or replaced by new car under same serial for 1959, eventually broken-up.

Chassis '0004' – Race début 15-6-58, Dino 246 transverse leafspring – Musso '58 Belgian GP (crashed) and French GP (crashed fatally) – according to records rebuilt or replaced by new car under same serial for von Trips German GP, Hill Italian and Moroccan GPs. Either extensively modified or replaced by new car under same serial for 1959, eventually broken-up.

Chassis '0005' – First reference in records is to Hawthorn's '58 Italian GP disc-braked car which according to Hawthorn was his regular chassis '0003' merely modified – see above – no '0005' reappeared in F1 form until very different 1960 car. Perhaps intended '0005' became '0004' replacing car(s) lost in Musso accidents?

Chassis '0006' – Race début 7-9-58, Dino 256 transverse leafspring – von Trips '58 Italian GP. Another candidate for true '0005', records having become muddled, serial did not reappear until very different 1960 car.

---

17 May, 1958 — Practice for the Monaco GP, Monte Carlo — Mike Hawthorn in his regular Ferrari Dino 246 — chassis '0003' — rounding the *Tabac* corner on the harbour front. Note how the car is rigged with rear-opening clear perspex cowl over the engine's carburettor inlet trumpets, splash-cum-stone guards projecting just behind the front wheels, obsolescent-fashion aero-screen and rakishly upswept exhaust pipes.

19 July 1958 — British Grand Prix, Silverstone — Hard-charging in the sun, but destined for the dark, Peter Collins *en route* to victory in his penultimate *Grande Epreuve*, at the wheel of Ferrari Dino 246 '0002'. Two weeks later he would crash fatally in this car during the German GP at Nürburgring.

Chassis '0007' — Race début 29-6-58, Dino 296 with 2,962 cc 316 bhp engine for 'Monzanapolis' track race, coil-spring rear suspension, fitted with Dino 246 for F1 – début 1-8-58 – T-car '58 German GP, von Trips Portuguese GP, Gendebien Italian and Moroccan GPs (crashed). Either extensively modified or replaced by new car under same serial for 1959, eventually broken-up.

At Easter Goodwood 1958, Hawthorn won in '0003', his only complaint excessive understeer. Mr Ferrari had a long-standing contract with Belgian Englebert tyres and their technology was now outdated by the latest Dunlop Racing covers. On Dunlops the 1958 Ferraris might *really* have performed. Six days after Goodwood, Musso won the Syracuse GP in '0001', and on 4 May Collins won the International Trophy at Silverstone in small-tube '0002'. Three in a row for Dino's memory, but the wailing Italian V6s had not yet faced Vanwall.

Their first confrontation came at Monaco, the Dinos' reliability collapsed and they were beaten – by Cooper-Climax! Zandvoort for the Dutch GP accentuated the Ferraris' handling deficiencies through the high-speed swerving back-stretch. Spa for the Belgian GP then offered the Dinos exactly what they wanted, long straights and open curves, somewhere to unleash their power. Hawthorn started from pole, set fastest lap and finished second, having been fazed by the sight of Musso's sister car wrecked by the road-side. Having seen his friend Collins' Dino overheat badly on the startline he was convinced his engine had broken at top speed and that the wrecked Ferrari was his. Only later was he signalled that all was well, and he began racing again with a will. Still Brooks's Vanwall won.

Reims for the French GP was another power circuit, and there Hawthorn touched 180 mph (300 km/h) on the straights and won handsomely, but poor Musso crashed his sister car and was killed.

At Silverstone for the British GP Ferrari presented three big-tube cars, all badly-handling. Fortunately for Ferrari, Vanwall reliability collapsed, Collins and Hawthorn finishing 1-2. Two weeks later Brooks's Vanwall triumphed again at the Nürburgring. Hawthorn retired, but Collins had

19 July, 1958 — British GP, Silverstone — Mike Hawthorn on his way to yet another second place in his factory Ferrari Dino 246 chassis '0003'. These V6-engined cars were relatively small, light and compact compared to previous V8-engined Lancia-Ferraris. Note Hawthorn's favoured four-spoke steering wheel. The rear-suspension transverse leafspring is just visible below the race number, the obsolescent Houdaille lever-arm damper can be seen down below, and the car is understeering — as usual — a characteristic which the drivers compensated for by inducing often vicious oversteer.

crashed fatally just yards ahead of him while attempting to overtake Brooks.

Three men had now died in the Ferrari Dinos – former chief engineer *Ing* Andrea Fraschetti on test at Modena, Musso and Peter Collins. Only two cars were sent to Portugal where Hawthorn finished second and set fastest lap – worth an extra Championship point in those days – but Moss's Vanwall won. Von Trips was fifth in an ex-Monza 500-Miles 'MI' special car with coil-spring rear suspension.

Now Hawthorn was adamant he must have disc brakes. A set was cannibalized from Collins's 250GT road car at Maranello, and an enlarged Dino 256 engine – 71 mm x 86 mm, 2,474 cc, 290 bhp at 8,800 rpm – was fitted to his regular car for the Italian GP. He lost the lead with clutch slip, but finished second thanks to new team-mate Phil Hill easing back into third. Oliver Gendebien bent the MI car's suspension in a collision.

The Drivers' Championship lay between Hawthorn and Moss, the Constructors' between Ferrari and Vanwall, and five weeks elapsed before the deciding race, the last of the season, at Casablanca. There, Moss won the Moroccan GP for Vanwall, but Hawthorn was second in his disc-braked Ferrari Dino to steal the Drivers' crown by just one point. Immediately after that race, Mike Hawthorn retired from racing, only to die in a tragic road accident in January the following year.

The Dino 246 line of F1 cars screamed on through 1959-60, initially being updated with more capacious Fantuzzi-made bodyshells clothing big-tube frames, coil-spring rear ends and Dunlop disc brakes and tyres. Tony Brooks won the French and German GPs and challenged for the 1959 World Championship right into the final race. For 1960 much lighter Dino 246s were produced with their engines angled across the frame the opposite way to the '59 cars and with side-mounted pannier fuel tanks and coil-and-wishbone independent suspensions front and rear. But by that time the rear-engined revolution was well under way, and Ferrari could only salvage an F2 win at Syracuse and muted F1 success in the last 2.5 litre Formula Italian GP, which the other major teams all boycotted.

The BRM P25s

The original BRM Project 25, 2.5 litre, F1 design was a joint exercise between Peter Berthon and the BRM consultant, Stewart Tresilian. 'Tres' as this popular and talented engineer was known to the Bourne team, had drawn a 4-cylinder 16-valve unblown 2.5 litre engine for the new Formula 1 announced originally for the seasons 1954-57 and later extended for three more seasons to 1960.

Tresillian had previously offered his big-bore, four-valve per cylinder engine to Connaught but they could not raise the money to build it. At Bourne, meanwhile, the BRM top-brass had virtually convinced themselves that the best way to approach the new Formula was to develop one-half of the existing 1.5 litre V16, as a 750 cc blown V8! Fortunately, wiser counsel prevailed, as it became clear that new oxygen-bearing fuels could reliably produce very high power from unblown engines. 'Tres's' 4-cylinder was therefore adopted, but would not be ready until far into the new Formula's second season, 1955. Berthon meanwhile side-stepped potential problems with the original four-valve per cylinder concept by proposing instead just two exceptionally large valves – the inlet being some 2.25 in (5.7 cm) in diameter. By this time 'Tres' had left BRM to join Bristol-Siddeley Engines, and with the P25 well-advanced but by no means raceworthy early in 1955 'PB' (as Berthon was known in BRM-ese) suffered a terrible road accident which sidelined him for months. Tony Rudd took over P25 testing and development in his place.

The new car's chassis used a simple multi-tubular frame braced by rivetted-on stressed sheet panelling to form a rugged semi-monocoque structure. To maintain rigidity, holes to admit driver and engine were kept as tiny as possible, and a letter-box on the side gave access to the master cylinders. The tail cowl was removable. Wheelbase was only 7 ft 3 ins (2.21 m) and the whole car was as compact and light as possible.

Its 4-cylinder engine had four main bearings and the cam-drive gears at the back allowed a low sloping bonnet line up front. 'PB' with Alec Stokes had designed a compact five-speed gearbox projecting behind the rear axle line, while a de Dion tube curved in front of it. Wishbone IFS was used with Lockheed air struts front and rear from the hefty V16s. Since this exceptionally small F1 car's weight distribution was about 50/50 front/rear, heavy braking would distribute loads around 70 per cent front/30 per cent rear. Therefore it made sense to use outboard disc brakes in each Dunlop disc wheel at the front, but just a single disc at the rear, acting on the gearbox. These three brakes would thus share 35 per cent of the braking load on each front disc, 30 per cent at the rear, and so the famous BRM 'cheese-cutter' rear disc brake was born.

While the first two cars – chassis '251' and '252' – were completed and the engine showed 260 bhp – 104 bhp per litre – on the dyno at BRM's Folkingham Aerodrome, the team kept active by racing their V16 Mark IIs and bought-in Maserati 250F.

The new P25 then made its début at Aintree in September 1955, Peter Collins driving '252' but unfortunately a breather pumped oil on to a rear tyre and he crashed. This was caused by an engine scavenge problem, fixed by fitting an extra pump. At Oulton Park, Collins then showed staggering speed to run third until the oil pressure gauge zeroed. He retired, only for the team to find nothing wrong with the engine, the gauge needle had simply been vibrated off its spindle.

Stirling Moss tested the cars, but opted to return to Maserati for 1956, while BRM signed Mike Hawthorn and Tony Brooks instead. But theirs was a disastrous season, for although the cars were very fast indeed, they proved dangerously unreliable and their preparation was too often careless, as at Silverstone where an unfastened engine cover detached at speed and nearly decapitated Hawthorn. Since he had recently been upside-down in another car at Goodwood after a drive-shaft joint seizure, and at Aintree had suffered total brake failure due to a clevis pin falling out, he wasn't at all happy . . .

The rear cheese-cutter disc revolved perhaps twice as fast as those on the front wheels and its high rubbing speed simply ate brake pads. A reduction gear was therefore inserted to slow the disc, which was then ventilated in imitation of brakes used on the Berlin *metro* which Rudd had seen illustrated in a technical publication.

The P25s' acceleration was stupendous, demonstrably the most ferocious in Formula 1, but now the air-struts which had worked so well on the heavy V16s showed 'stiction' in these lightweight 4-cylinder cars. When the struts were cold the cars would sit on their bump-rubbers, and it would take three or four laps before the struts achieved working temperature and the cars would rise Citroën-like to assume a sensible ride-height.

Then at Monte Carlo, in practice for their first Championship GP, valves stretched on the over-run, the large-diameter heads snapped off and demolished the engines, so both cars had to be withdrawn from the race. Then at Silverstone in the British GP, Hawthorn saw signs of an incipient Goodwood-style pot-joint seizure and retired before it happened. Brooks was not so lucky, struggling on after a throttle rod parted only for it to jam wide open at Abbey Curve and trigger an horrendous somersault in which '252' was completely destroyed by fire. The third car '253' broke its timing gears as the crankshaft was rather long and ill-supported by its four main bearings. As it writhed about, it sent the timing gears in and out of accurate mesh

until they failed.

Alfred Owen thereupon established an engineering control committee at Bourne under his Director of Research, Peter Spear, and ordered no more racing until the cars had completed 300 miles (500 km) non-stop on test at competitive speeds. After many problems reminiscent of the V16 era, this target was finally achieved late that year at Monza, with Ron Flockhart driving '254' under close pit control and ordered not to exceed 7,200 rpm. He completed the necessary 80 laps in good order, then 'PB' proved over-confident, waved him on and after only three more laps No 2 inlet valve dropped and wrecked another engine . . . From their début in 1955 to the end of 1956 the BRM P25s had made only eight starts in just five races, and finished only once, Brooks taking second in the Aintree '200'.

Suspension specialists Alec Issigonis and Alex Moulton recommended a zero roll-stiffness transverse leafspring system at the rear, and then Colin Chapman was called in to consult and offered a better idea, fitting at the rear tall co-axial coil-spring/dampers and locating the de Dion tube on a Watts linkage. This transformed the cars, but their now supple suspension moved so freely the half-shaft pot-joints gave renewed trouble. BRM looked hard at Ferrari's ball-splined half-shafts and adopted extremely costly components of similar type.

The American journeyman driver Herbert Mackay Fraser then cheered the team immensely with a charge through the field in the 1957 French GP at Rouen. Quite incredibly this was only the team's fourth-ever Championship GP in their *eighth* active season – but there Flockhart spun '254' on oil, rolled into a ditch and wrote it off. Poor Fraser died in a Lotus Eleven sports car at Reims, Flockhart was still in hospital so Les Leston and Jack Fairman took over for the British GP at Aintree, where Maserati driver Jean Behra was impressed by the little cars' speed through the corners. He had an entry for the following weekend's minor Caen GP in France and asked Raymond Mays of BRM to loan him a P25. The start money for the French Champion was of course excellent, and so he drove '253' fitted with BRM's first ball-spline half-shafts, and promptly scored the team's maiden 2.5 litre F1 victory. Harry Schell drove the sister car at the last moment. He would become BRM's most consistently successful P25 driver.

14 September, 1957 — BRDC International trophy, Silverstone — what should have been the traditional Silverstone 'May meeting' F1 race was moved to the tail end of the season by the disruption of the Suez Crisis. Here Jean Behra — who headed BRM's 1-2-3 finish in the final — corners his victorious '251'. Note its very full cockpit enclosure, the divided-radiator nose, ram-air induction intake, 'Chapman-strut' coil/damper rear suspension and the bunch of bananas exhaust manifolding just visible on the far side of the bonnet.

At the end of the season, against meagre opposition, the three surviving P25s, '251', '253' and '254' finished 1-2-3 in the Silverstone International Trophy, driven by Behra, Schell and Flockhart.

Behra and Schell joined full-time for 1958 but to cure their timing gear problems 'PB' fitted a fifth main bearing to the new '258-series' 4-cylinder crankshafts and unwittingly induced massive friction loss which robbed much horsepower. Meanwhile the old methanol fuel brews had been banned for that season and maximum 130-octane AvGas petroleum spirit made mandatory instead. The old semi-monocoque chassis were also abandoned, and replaced by lighter new true spaceframes, with detachable body panelling, apart from a spoon-shaped undertray which was permanently attached to add rigidity.

Before the new spaceframe cars were fully adopted, Behra drove old '253' modified with a tubular in place of semi-monocoque front frame at Goodwood on Easter Monday. His brake servo failed 'off' and he rammed the brick chicane, writing-off '253'. In the same race, Schell's brake servo failed 'on', and he retired with his brakes smouldering. Before the shunt Behra had said the handling difference between the monocoque cars and the new spaceframe-spec was simply 'jour et nuit'.

In the 1958 Dutch GP the P25s notched BRM's best Championship-round finish yet, Schell second and Behra third but the fiery Jeannot's irritation at being beaten by 'Arry added to his disgust with the five-main bearing engines' power loss and later that year he would just give up and walk away. Where the methanol-burning four main bearing engines gave over 280 bhp in 1957 – over 112 bhp per litre – and a 1957 four-bearing on AvGas showed 260 bhp – 104 per litre – the 'improved' five-main bearing on AvGas developed just 240 – 96 bhp per litre . . . Behra drove hard at Monza and Casablanca but joined Ferrari for '59 . . .

Meanwhile, Harry Weslake, the gas-flow expert from Rye in Sussex, had advised on improved head design and with the 258-series fifth main bearing machined-out for 1959, BRM adopted new timing gears for reliability, with large, coarse teeth not critical to fine backlash tuning.

The Swedish driver Joakim Bonnier joined Schell and 'JoBo' actually won the 1959 Dutch GP to score BRM's first-ever World Championship race victory after ten seasons' racing. Further brake modifications and the adoption of a simplified and lighter chassis in the last two cars built – frames '2510' and '2511' – made the BRM P25s simply the fastest front-engined cars of that year, with fantastic braking ability. Stirling Moss drove '2510' under the BRP team's pale-green colours in the French and British GPs, finishing second at Aintree but the car was then destroyed in the German GP at AVUS when guest driver Hans Herrmann suffered brake failure.

Graham Hill, Dan Gurney and Bonnier then drove the P25s in their last active season, 1960, whereupon all the survivors except '258' – understood to be the Zandvoort-winning car of 1959 – were cannibalized to provide components for the new rear-engined 2.5 litre P48 cars being hastily built to follow Cooper's rear-engined lead.

During their long career, these 4-cylinder BRMs competed in surprisingly few front-line GPs, from 1956 to 1960 actually starting in only 21. They also contested 26 assorted non-Championship F1 and Tasman races 1955-60, and amongst their total 47-race programme they won just that solitary Dutch GP plus seven minor events, including the two preliminary heats of the 1957 International Trophy and the 1959 New Zealand GP Heat at Ardmore.

The P25 cars built were as follows:

Chassis '251' – Stressed-skin car, 7 ft 3 in (2.2 m) wheelbase – first ran 25-6-55, during third rebuild March/June 1956 wheelbase extended to 7 ft 6 in (2.28 m) to accommodate Mike Hawthorn for British GP. Written-off 3 May 1958, International Trophy, Silverstone, driver Ron Flockhart. Won 1957 International Trophy Heat One and Final (Behra).

Chassis '252' – Stressed-skin car, shown to press at Folkingham 23-8-55, first ran 30-8-55, 7 ft 3 in (2.2 m) wheelbase. Written-off 1956 British GP, Silverstone, due to sticking throttle, driver Tony Brooks.

Chassis '253' – Second-series stressed-skin car, completed Easter 1956, crashed at Goodwood, driver Mike Hawthorn; 1957 Caen GP winner, driver Jean Behra, in third rebuild winter 1957-58 fitted with long-wishbone front suspension and new tubular frame forward of cockpit bulkhead. Written-off against Goodwood chicane, 7 April 1958, driver Jean Behra. Won 1957 Caen GP (Behra), Heat Two 1957 International Trophy (Schell).

Chassis '254' – Stressed-skin car, completed September 1956, 7 ft 6 in (2.28 m) wheelbase. Written-off 7 July, 1957, French GP at Rouen after sliding on spilled oil, driver Ron Flockhart.

19 July, 1958 — British GP, Silverstone — Harry Schell at speed in BRM P25 '258', one of the new generation of truly spaceframe-chassised cars, all with detachable bodies (except the undertray). It shows off its neater exhaust system, Dunlop alloy wheels and tiny overall build *en route* to fifth place.

5 July, 1959 — French GP — Stirling Moss cornering the British Racing Partnership's loaned BRM P25 — '2510' — at Thillois, handicapped by an inoperative clutch. In 100°-plus heat he eventually spun here on melting tar and was unable to push-start the BRM's stalled engine. He eventually collapsed from the effort, overcome by the heat. This car was pale green with white wheels and was subsequently written-off after brake failure in the German GP at AVUS, driven by Hans Herrmann.

Chassis '255' – Last stressed-skin car, completed September 1957 using parts salvaged from '254', coil-spring suspension and ball-splined half-shafts from new – used as T-car throughout 1958 – nicknamed 'The Vanguard' by the drivers after the modestly-performing, somewhat aldermanic saloon car of the same name built by Standard! Car dismantled, components into spares stock.

Chassis '256' – First true spaceframe-chassis car. Completed May 1958, eventually rebuilt before being broken-up to free components for rear-engined P48 production. Serviceable parts had already gone into the prototype rear-engined car '481', August 1959.

Chassis '257' – Spaceframe car. Completed May 1958, broken-up winter 1959-60, serviceable parts into rear-engined car '482'.

Chassis '258' – Spaceframe car – surviving chassis carries correct stamp '273'. Completed June 1958, the 1959 Dutch GP winner, retained as display car, auctioned in BRM Collection sale, Earls Court, London, October 1981, and now (1988) owned by Amschel Rothschild in UK.

Chassis '259' – Spaceframe car. Completed October 1958 – raced by Ron Flockhart in New Zealand Jan/Feb 1959 – reduced to spares by February 1960, broken-up. Won 1959 Lady Wigram Trophy and New Zealand GP Heat Two (Flockhart).

Chassis '2510' – Spaceframe car. Completed March 1959, used by BRP team for Stirling Moss and Hans Herrmann. Written-off 2 August 1959 in German GP at AVUS, Berlin, driver Herrmann.

Chassis '2511' – Spaceframe car. Completed June 1959, raced in Argentina and at Goodwood 1960, last P25 to be raced by works team, broken-up sometime after February 1960. Won 1959 Silver City Trophy, Snetterton (Flockhart).

As a postscript; this quote from Tony Rudd BRM chassis state report. 9 February 1960: *'Bonnier says '258' is the best but would have '2511' if '258' wasn't available. Schell said that if he could not have '257' he would like '2511'; Flockhart thinks '2511' is as good as '259' ...'*

Let Stirling Moss have the last word. In 1987 he told me, 'I have to say it, the BRM P25 really was a *bloody* good car ... perhaps the finest front-engined Formula 1 car ever built ...'

That's praise indeed, from a man who really did know.

The Cooper-Climax Type 51s

★ ★ ★ ★

When the Cooper-Climax cars driven by wily Australian Jack Brabham won the World Championship titles in 1959 and 1960, they set the seal on Grand Prix racing's so-called rear-engined revolution.

As we have seen, there was nothing new about mounting the racing car's engine behind the driver, see pages 83-93. But even though Auto Union eventually got it right with the de Dion rear suspended D-Type cars in 1938-39, they never really managed to dispel the popular myth that mounting the engine behind the driver was inseparable from daunting handling characteristics. In fact this configuration would effectively remain tainted where high-powered cars were concerned until 1958-59 when Cooper showed how it could be done, won those back-to-back World Championship titles in 1959-60 and persuaded the rest of the racing world to follow suit.

So what kind of animal was the rear-engined Cooper-Climax which wrought the revolution?

Charles Cooper was an inter-war racing mechanic and small-time garage proprietor from Surbiton, Surrey. In 1946, his infectiously enthusiastic son John plotted with boyhood friend Eric Brandon to build a chain-driven, motor cycle-engined, single-seater special for 500 cc 'poor man's Formula' racing. They used the Coopers' Garage workshop and plant in Hollyfield Road, Surbiton, to cut-and-shut two Fiat Topolino baby saloon car chassis. They then welded the transverse leafspring independent front ends back-to-back and put their engine behind the cockpit to simplify direct chain-drive

to the rear axle. They named the finished slim-bodied little car 'the Cooper Mark I'. It was a great success, rivals clamoured to buy replicas, and eventually on 19 December 1947, Charles and John set-up The Cooper Car Company Ltd to build a pilot batch of 12 improved 500 cc cars.

From this small beginning, Cooper became the world's biggest manufacturer of production racing cars through the 1950s. Their cars virtually dominated that class of racing throughout its life, and meanwhile John Cooper persuaded his always ultra-conservative and cautious father to diversify . . .

They built small conventional sports cars with water-cooled engines up front, and from them stemmed their famous front-engined Cooper-Bristol Formula 2 single-seaters in which Mike Hawthorn leapt to fame during the 1952-53 Grand Prix Formula. John was commissioned by millionaire industrialist Tony Vandervell to produce his first 'Vanwall' Formula 1 chassis and then Cooper Cars discovered the ultra-lightweight single overhead camshaft Coventry Climax FWA proprietary fire-pump engine. This little 4-cylinder power unit had all the prerequisites of a good racing engine, since it produced excellent power for its minimal all-aluminium weight.

The FWA became the mainstay of the 1,100 cc sports car class, used by many specialist manufacturers, Cooper included. John mounted his FWAs in the rear of neat little multi-tubular chassis derived from the proven 500 cc series. But obviously chain-drive was out of the question, so he adopted the Citroën *Traction Avant* front-drive transaxle instead, simply turned about face and modified to drive the rear wheels of the new Cooper sports car.

Hollyfield Road's bearded jazz-bandsman chief designer Owen Maddock drew the new Cooper-Climax Type 39 around this drive-train, and clothed it in the briefest of streamlined bodies with the driving seat exactly on the centreline, a vestigial rules-fulfilling passenger seat cramped alongside. These little 'Bob-tailed' Coopers with their sharply cut-off Kamm-effect transom tails were a roaring success.

They dominated their class in 1955-56, and during that latter season enlarged 1,500 cc FWB versions of the basic Climax engine became available. Meanwhile, the CSI governing, body had already announced a 1,500 cc pump-petrol Formula 2 single-seater racing class for 1957, and to encourage interest in this new division, a number of 'dress-rehearsal' F2 races were run in the UK late in '56. Lotus entered their Type 11 sports racing cars with road-lighting gear removed, but Cooper did the job properly and prepared an open-wheeled racing design based on the Bobtail sports minus outboard body hoops. This was known as the Type 41 and these little cars, still with their Citroën *Traction Avant* transaxles, won everything in sight. Many orders flooded in for 1957.

Early that year, while testing both Rob Walker's front-engined Connaught and his little Cooper-Climax T41 F2 prototype at Goodwood, works driver Roy Salvadori was greatly impressed by the rear-engined car's incredibly nimble handling and forgiving nature. Its light weight compensated for the Climax engine's lack of power, and Roy declared that if they put a 2 litre engine in a chassis like that it could shine in GP company on a tight course like Monaco. Rob Walker was fascinated by the idea and offered to finance development of such a car. John Cooper believed that a long-throw crankshaft, new liners and pistons could enlarge the FWB towards 2 litres – 1,960 cc in fact – and it was clear that around 180 bhp in an 800 lb (364 kg) car – 0.22 bhp per lb – could work.

Rob's famous chief mechanic Alf Francis developed the engine to breathe through 42 mm choke Weber carburettors, and while Salvadori was contracted to drive for BRM at Monaco, Cooper's Australian second works driver Jack Brabham agreed to drive the new bitsa there.

Unfortunately he wrecked the car in practice, but Rob's mechanics hastily fitted the special engine into a second-string standard F2 chassis, and Jack ran *third* late in the race until vibration broke the car's fuel pump mounting. The pump dropped down, its drive parted and the engine starved into silence. Jack pushed the car across the finish to be classified sixth.

The Cooper works and Rob Walker teams continued to run basically F2 cars in Formula 1 for the rest of that year, ostensibly using 1,960 cc

---

19 January, 1958 — Argentine GP, Buenos Aires — The historic moment as Stirling Moss took the chequered flag to become the first driver to win a post–war *Grande Epreuve* in a rear-engined car. The little 1.96 litre Rob Walker-owned Cooper had humbled the might of a full-strength Ferrari Dino team.

30 March, 1959 — Glover Trophy, Goodwood — Stirling Moss demonstrating the spirit of the heyday of the rear-engined Cooper-Climax; note the neat little car's simple, well-fared lines, eight-spoke cast magnesium wheels, large-sized rear Dunlop Racing tyres, pannier fuel tanks alongside the cockpit (note the filler cap) and rear-mounted Coventry-Climax FPF 4-cylinder engine. That's a breather pipe from the nose-mounted dry-sump oil tank flapping in the breeze beneath the nose.

engines but sometimes with mere 1,500s which should not really have been allowed in the premier class. Salvadori finished fifth in the British GP and second at Caen, and Brabham second in the International Trophy F1 race at Silverstone.

Then early in 1958 Walker entered his 1.96 Cooper-Climax for Stirling Moss in the Argentine GP at Buenos Aires, and Stirling *won!*

A further-enlarged 2,014 cc Climax engine was then developed, approaching closer to the 2.5 litre F1 limit, and with this installed in his Walker Cooper – while Moss was driving for Vanwall – Maurice Trintignant won the Monaco GP. For the rest of that season Leonard Lee of Coventry Climax authorized manufacture of 2.2 litre versions of the 4-cylinder engine, but faster circuits now packed the calendar and the rear-engined Coopers were simply overwhelmed.

However, Moss won the Aintree '200' in Walker's 2 litre, Salvadori qualified on pole and was second at Silverstone, then third in the British GP, Moss won in Walker's 2.2 at Caen, and Roy was *second* in the German GP at the Nürburgring.

Obviously if the now twin-cam Climax FPF engine could be enlarged to a full 2.5 litres, it had great potential in the light and nimble Cooper chassis. Lee's chief engineer Walter Hassan made this move for 1959. A modestly revised block was

cast to accommodate bore and stroke of 94 mm x 89.9 mm, 2,495 cc. The existing twin-cam head was modified to suit but at first was intentionally under-valved in case the new crankcase should prove weak. In fact once this full-size FPF was running it became obvious there was strength to spare, so larger ports were quickly adopted with bigger valves. Within four months of detail design commencing on 1 December 1958, the first Climax 'two and a halves' made their début in works and Walker Coopers.

Meanwhile, Charlie Cooper had insisted that transverse-leaf independent suspensions be retained front and rear, but at John's and Jack Brabham's insistence the 1958 Mark III or Type 45 (essentially F2) cars adopted coil-and-wishbone IFS while still retaining the leafspring rear. This was a major advance, and the 1959 Mark IV or Type 51 single-seaters followed suit in both F1 and F2 forms.

Their Achilles' heel had always been their Citroën transaxles, and early in 1958 Brabham had gone to the ERSA works in Paris where the basically three-speed 'boxes were converted to four-speed as a 'go-faster mod'. Jack '. . . can remember trying to explain to them what we needed in the way of a stronger case . . . I finished up with all the patterns spread out on a bench, putting Plasticene on them and scraping the cores

and so on. We made about six gearboxes, all cast with extra strengthening ribs . . .' and these were just about man enough to handle the extra horse-power, first of the 2.2 litre engines, and then of the full-sized 2.5s.

Jack left no stone unturned in his search for extra performance. He had obtained ZF limited-slip diffs from Germany, while John covered his tracks so that old Charles wouldn't hear of the extra expense: 'We wouldn't have won a race without 'em . . .'

Jack also corresponded at great length with an Australian engineer friend named Ron Tauranac, later to design and build the Brabham and Ralt production racing cars in Britain. Ron advised on many chassis mods, including added top rear wishbones to relieve the leafspring of wheel loca-tion duties, and final-drive drop-gears to ease ratio changing so the cars could be matched bet-ter to varying circuits.

At the time, Salvadori was considered the bet-ter driver, but he signed with Aston Martin for 1959 while Jack's greasy-fingered technical dedication made him a kindred spirit to John; a valuable engineer as well as being a determined and very fast driver of intense will and application.

Since Vanwall had retired from racing, Stirling Moss joined Walker's private Cooper team alongside Trintignant, while John also signed American Masten Gregory and a 20-year-old New Zealand boy named Bruce McLaren to join Brabham.

Of 13 F1 races entered in 1959, Coopers won eight, Moss signalling the new 2.5 car's potential

10 May, 1959 — Monaco GP, Monte Carlo — First *Grande Epreuve* victory for the Cooper works team as Jack Brabham hustles his Type 51 2.5 litre car around the Monegasque street circuit. Here the bottle-green car's nose is lifting, its tail squatting and the rear wheels beginning to slide as he applies the 4-cylinder engine's meaty mid-range torque.

---

26 September, 1959 — Oulton Park Gold Cup — Jack Brabham displaying a typical Cooper cornering charac-teristic as his second-placed works Type 51 lifts its inside front wheel through one of the Cheshire circuit's tighter corners. Losing front-end adhesion in this way helped balance the rear-engined car's inherent ten-dency to oversteer and enhanced their nimble yet sta-ble handling. Whether this was achieved intentionally or otherwise seems debatable . . .

19 June, 1960 — Belgian GP, Spa-Francorchamps —Jack Brabham during his extraordinary run of five consecutive *Grande Epreuve* victories in the new Type 53 'Lowline' Cooper-Climax during his second consecutive Drivers' World Championship season. The broader, flatter form of these 'Lowline' cars is very evident here as 'Black Jack' brakes hard for *La Source* hairpin. On the Masta Straight he was exceeding 175 mph (292 km/h).

with victory first time out at Goodwood on Easter Monday, Jack second in his wheel-tracks. Jack then scored the factory's maiden win in the International Trophy at Silverstone, followed by World Championship level success at Monaco one week later. He won again in the British GP at Aintree, Moss won in Portugal and Italy, then in the non-Championship event at Oulton Park.

While Cooper had gladly supplied Walker with his chassis, they could not help him with transmissions and instead of the factory Citroën-ERSA system Rob commissioned new transaxles from former Maserati designer Valerio Colotti. This enabled Moss to race very competitively, but manufacturing tolerances were poor and the transmission failed repeatedly to wreck Stirling's chances. When the Walker car survived for imperious victory in Portugal and Italy, with Jack finishing third at Monza, The Cooper Car Company clinched the Formula 1 Constructors' World Championship title.

The Drivers' Championship then depended upon the inaugural United States GP, run on 12 December at Sebring, Florida. Moss's Walker Cooper was modified with coil-spring strut rear suspension but its transmission failed again. Jack led, only to run out of fuel in the closing stages, leaving his young team-mate Bruce McLaren to win. But Jack was able to push his car across the finish line for fourth place, clinching the Drivers' title.

In 1960, the Cooper T51s scored one final success in the season-opening Argentine GP – McLaren again – and then new works-team T53 or 'Lowline' Coopers got into their reliable stride, Jack winning five consecutive GPs to secure an historic Championship double which would not be repeated until 1985-86 by Alain Prost of McLaren … Cooper's dumpy little, wheel-waving Type 51 cars had undoubtedly changed the course of motor racing at its highest level, and from 1960 every serious class of single-seat competition car would follow their lead, with the engine behind the driver.

1960
The Lotus-Climax Type 18s

★ ★ ★ ★

Back in 1960 the starkly practical 'coffin-on-wheels' shape of the rear-engined Lotus 18 set new performance standards in Formula 1. Without question, it was the most potent chassis/engine combination *per se* produced in the seven seasons of the 2.5 litre Grand Prix Formula.

In 1959 and 1960 the so-called 'Rear-engined Revolution' was sweeping through Formula 1. Cooper rubbed-in the message. In 1959 it was a close-run thing against the heavier, less nimble, front-engined traditional cars, but by the end of that season other teams, led by BRM, were already following Cooper; engines were going behind the drivers for 1960, and Colin Chapman's Lotus 18 became Cooper's most dangerous rival.

But while the Lotus 18 was faster than the Coopers, it was crucially less reliable. Jack Brabham won five consecutive GPs in the lastest 'Lowline' Cooper-Climax, and led two works Cooper team 1-2s. In comparison, Stirling Moss's Rob Walker-entered Lotus 18s won two GPs and two minor F1 races, while Innes Ireland's works Team Lotus 18 won three non-Championship F1 events. On balance honours were roughly even by year's end, but significantly Lotus fortunes were on the way up. . . while Cooper's were entering rapid decline.

When Colin Chapman had sat down to design his Type 18 he had 18 months' racing with his front-engined 'Vanwall'-shaped Lotus 16s behind him. They had understeered 'like pigs' and were also structurally inadequate.

Old Charlie Cooper had thoroughly enjoyed 'Chunky' Chapman's discomfort with the 16s.

When Cooper designer Owen Maddock asked if he should do stress-calculations for their chassis, the old man roared with laughter. 'No boy,' he guffawed, 'Chapman does that and 'e's up all night weldin' 'em when they break.' He was too . . .

In 1978 – no doubt with benefit of hindsight – Colin told me emphatically – 'In 1958-59 we were playing around with Formula 1. The front-engined cars were Formula 2 designs and nothing more. As far as I'm concerned the first Formula 1 car *I* ever designed and built was the Type 18 . . .'

When he followed Cooper's lead with that car, he made its chassis more beefy than the 'thick 22-gauge' cigarette-paper tubing used in the old 16s, yet the 18 was still very light because it was so simple. It had aluminium fuel tanks within the wheelbase, 22-gal (100 l) over the driver's legs alone, 44/56 front/rear weight distribution and suspension in which fixed-length half-shafts provided top lateral location for the rear wheels.

Transmission was by the positive-stop Lotus five-speed 'queerbox' in its latest form with gears behind the diff unit. Its great advantage was speedy ratio-changing to match new circuits. The basic 18 frame doubled as F1 or F2 with either 2.5 or 1.5 litre Climax FPF 4-cylinder engines installed, while there was also a simplified, cheaper and less butch version for Formula Junior.

The aluminium-bodied prototype made a sensational début in the Argentine GP on 7 February 1960, driven by Innes Ireland who finally finished sixth with a shattered front brake disc and only

1 August, 1960 — Silver City Trophy, Brands Hatch — The inaugural event run on the extended 2.65 mile GP circuit at the Kentish venue was won by Jack Brabham's 'Lowline' Cooper, but the lion's share of non-Championship F1 race glory that season went to the Lotus 18s. Here John Surtees corners Team Lotus's '372' very hard, at the dawn of his four-wheeled career. Note the flimsy-looking coil-and-wishbone front suspension, twin radius rod rear end and the large-diameter tubular half-shaft which doubled as upper lateral location for the rear wheels.

one front wheel steering properly after having led easily. Then back home, in shorter races, Innes simply shone. He began with Team Lotus's first outright single-seater win at F2 at Oulton Park, slashing 5.2 sec off the lap record. Sixteen days later he beat Moss's Walker Cooper twice in the day at Easter Goodwood, winning both F2 and F1 races in works 18s, to give Team their first Formula 1 victory.

Innes later told me, 'There was no comparison between the old 16s and the new 18. It was like night and day. Beating Stirling was really something, suddenly being a celebrity . . .'

Certainly his car had impressed Moss, who recalled how 'for 37 laps at Goodwood I had a view of the Lotus tail-end . . . there was no doubt the car had superior traction and it was faster through the corners, even faster than I was when I was really trying . . . I was being beaten, and the same thing happened two or three weeks later at Silverstone. The same car, same driver, same situation and same result – except that at Silverstone Innes broke the lap record and I broke one of the Cooper's suspension members, a thing I had never done before . . .'

Any good racing driver has a shrewd idea which drivers he can handle and which he can't. Stirling was the best in the world, no question. He was confident he could handle Ireland any time on equal terms, so now he had to achieve equality in equipment.

Immediately after Goodwood, Rob Walker had ordered a customer 18. There were no concessions, no assistance, just a straightforward customer sale. Walker's dark-blue 18 was delivered just a week before Monaco, and with a Lotus 'queerbox' installed it promptly carried Moss to victory there.

Twenty-six years later, Stirling recalled the 18; 'a fantastic racing car by the standards of its day in 1960, but it was never as nice a car to drive as the old Coopers, it was quicker but you had to balance it between fairly narrowly-defined limits and you certainly couldn't take the liberties with it that the Cooper always allowed – in fact seemed to enjoy!

'On first acquaintance I found it was staggeringly fast and responsive . . . so responsive that it was simply an extension of the driver and if it wasn't doing just what you wanted it to do, then there were a host of adjustments which could be made. Perhaps too many . . .

'And in some ways it was curiously insensitive. For example you could change the camber on the rear wheels, or their toe-in, without noticing very much difference on the road. It was all too easy to make a change and find an improvement and so do something else which made it worse, and so on and on, until time ran out and you had merely worn-out the engine trying different things.

'I tended to limit work on the Lotus so that starting with the same tyre pressures front and rear I could get a little more oversteer or understeer by changing pressures and refined this by altering the damper settings. I didn't often change the anti-roll bars ...'

In the Dutch GP at Zandvoort he had a puncture and finished fourth, then at Spa a wheel came off when a half-shaft broke and put him in hospital with broken legs and crushed vertebrae. He returned in time for the Portuguese GP in August, won the Oulton Park Gold Cup and dominated the US GP at Riverside, the last race to the dying 2.5 litre Formula, by which time Walker had a choice of two 18s for him.

Meanwhile at Spa, almost at the same moment as Moss crashed, private owner Mike Taylor was badly hurt on the opposite side of the circuit in the ex-Argentine prototype F1 18 when a steering column weld broke and the wheel broke free in his hands. In the race Team Lotus driver Alan Stacey was killed in his 18 after apparently being struck in the face at speed by a bird. It was a tragic meeting ...

Chapman was berated by some – notably by Taylor's rugged mechanic Brit Pearce – for building too light and putting his drivers at risk, beefing-up parts only after something broke. In all, Lotus at Cheshunt officially built 26 Formula 1 Type 18s, numbers '369' to '376' and '900' to '917', but many were repaired and rebuilt around

14 August, 1960 — Portuguese GP, Oporto — Stirling Moss managed to get himself disqualified from this event which provided Jack Brabham with his fifth consecutive GP victory of the season. Here the Walker Lotus 18 shows off its severely utilitarian 'biscuit-box' lines. Note there was still no requirement under 2.5 litre F1 regulations for any roll-over protection behind the driver's head.

6 August, 1961 — German GP, Nürburgring — With the revamped Walker Lotus 18 fitted with more sleek Type 21-like body panelling Stirling Moss spoiled the more powerful Ferrari team's day by winning the shower-swept German GP on Dunlop high-hysteresis wet-weather tyres. Note the roll-over bar behind Stirling's head, as required by the new season's 1.5 litre F1 regulations.

6 August, 1961 — German GP, Nürburgring — The last victory — Moss the Maestro acknowledges the chequered flag at a *Grand Epreuve* for the last time as the Walker Lotus 18/21 splashes across the finish line while umbrellas are raised in the packed Sporthotel grandstand. This was also the last Championship-qualifying race win for the first successful series of Lotus F1 cars — the Type 18s.

new frames, and a number of 'unofficial' cars undoubtedly escaped the record-keeping process.

Walker replaced the 'queerbox' in his cars with now-reliable Colotti gearboxes while Team retained the 'queerbox' and experimented with both inboard and outboard rear disc brakes. At Oporto, Ireland's 18 actually carried both, their calipers being piped-up to choice.

The youthful Jimmy Clark had his second GP drive in a Team 18 at fateful Spa, finishing fifth for his first point-score; while World Champion motor cyclist John Surtees was another Lotus 18 F1 débutant, hitting the headlines with second place in the British GP, and then started from pole, led the race and set fastest lap before retiring in Portugal. There Clark bent his 18 in practice and Team mechanics used all their welding rod repairing it, finally using fencing wire as filler.

At Championship level, Ireland was out of luck. At Spa he'd been very competitive. He felt 'I had the measure of the Coopers and Phil Hill's Ferrari early on at Spa but I got delayed when the bloody clutch began slipping and then I had one of my enormous spins when I tried to make up time...'. Despite winning three non-Championship races perhaps his best drive was at Oulton Park where he led both Moss and Brabham and was drawing away until once again his luck ran out.

For 1961, 1.5 litre Formula 1 began, with a new minimum weight limit. Chapman produced the much-refined Lotus 21 with streamlined body and ZF gearbox but a sale to Walker and Moss was vetoed by the Team's Esso fuel company sponsor, because they were contracted to BP. Walker's private 18, like many others, was instead updated with 21-style ideas, replacing the halfshaft by upper links as lateral location in the rear suspension, and adopting more slippery, lower frontal area bodies.

How Moss drove his obsolete car to beat the much more powerful, but less wieldy Ferraris at Monaco, and again at the Nürburgring (one win with each body style), is all now part of racing legend. The Maestro also won two minor F1 races in the Walker Lotus and three more in his father's UDT-Laystall team's 18/21s. At Monza for the Italian GP, his car was very tired so Ireland offered his works 21 instead with Chapman's approval. Innes had grown in racing as a Lotus man and the marque's success was genuinely important to him. If Stirling could beat the Ferraris at Monza the Manufacturers' Championship could be Lotus's, but it didn't happen, both Moss and Ireland retiring their swopped cars.

By this time one Walker chassis had been cobbled up with a new Climax V8 engine, and in UDT's pale-green colours early in 1962 it was this car which ended Stirling's supreme career, against the St Mary's ess bank at Goodwood on Easter Monday – two years after the rear-engined Lotus had first made its name there. Nonetheless, Colin Chapman's Type 18 had pointed the way ahead, and founded Team Lotus's pre-eminence in Formula 1 design.

1961
The Ferguson-Climax Project 99

★ ★ ★

The tractive advantages of four-wheel drive have long attracted racing car designers, but such systems have always suffered from the apparently inseparable problems of extra complication, and extra weight. There has also been a problem of driver adaptation and acceptance of such a system, because a four-wheel drive racing car behaves in a manner totally foreign to most drivers weaned on rear-drive racing cars in which they can balance rear-wheel power and adhesion against front-tyre slip angles and steering response. Not only traditionally but also in terms of physical perception when on the ultimate limits of cornering power, putting drive through the

steerable front wheels upsets the sensory inputs a driver receives through the steering wheel in his hands and this had always tended to disturb and confuse the mere human at the controls. An answer was finally involved in the 1970s and came close to being put into effect by Williams in 1982 – a six-wheeled car with the non-steerable rear-four powered, and the unpowered front pair steered.

Irish inventor and industrialist Harry Ferguson made his name and fortune with a patented safety tractor plough-draw principle, and he manufactured thousands of Ferguson and Fordson tractors featuring this system. He was

15 July, 1961 — British GP, Aintree — Jack Fairman learning to use the revolutionary Ferguson-Climax Project 99's four-wheel driven traction in the heavy rain which fell for much of the race. This was the last front-engined Formula 1 car to appear, and the first to use four-wheel drive successfully. Note the centre-lock Dunlop alloy wheels and the frail but legal roll-over bar.

also fascinated by four-wheel drive and the possibilities of applying it to an advanced passenger car design, and in 1960 Claude Birch of Harry Ferguson Research master-minded design of their Project 99 experimental racing car to prove the Ferguson four-wheel drive concept before a wider audience.

He based his design upon a long, slender and simple yet robust multi-tubular spaceframe chassis, and at a time when most F1 manufacturers were going over to rear-engined configuration, he chose the traditional front-engined layout. Even then, although his car was to be brutally functional, it still emerged as quite the lowest and leanest front-engined Formula 1 car ever built.

It used a Coventry-Climax 4-cylinder engine canted to keep it low and offset at the front to send its propshaft spearing to the left of the driver's seat and controls which were offset to the right. The drive passed via a five-speed constant-mesh Ferguson gearbox through a central differential unit to prop-shafts leading fore and aft to Ferguson differential final-drive units, which then drove via short constant-velocity jointed half-shafts to the road wheels.

This Ferguson-patented, three-differential layout offered permanently-engaged four-wheel drive, but the mechanism enabled torque-split front-to-rear to be altered between each run. Dunlop disc brakes were used and an aviation-style Dunlop 'Maxaret' anti-lock braking system was tested in which brake-line pressure was automatically relieved if wheel sensors should detect locking, as in a skid. This was therefore a sophisticated forerunner of the highly successful ABS systems now offered as standard in many higher-performance production cars – many of which, of course, also now feature four-wheel drive as standard.

The organizational brain behind Harry Ferguson Research was the retired racing driver and former Le Mans winner Major A.P.R. 'Tony' Rolt, and he arranged for the new experimental car to be loaned to his friend Rob Walker's racing team for an experimental race-proving programme in 1961. This was in fact rather too late for the car, which had originally been intended as a 2.5 litre machine, but now the new 1.5 litre Formula 1 had taken effect. This served to emphasize the problems facing the P99 as it was inevitably rather heavy and complex as well as having all the

---

23 September, 1961 — Oulton Park Gold Cup — Stirling Moss taught himself how to drive a four-wheel drive racing car to such good effect that here in Cheshire he actually won the only Formula 1 race ever to fall to such a system. Photographer Geoff Goddard's low-level angle here shows off the Project 99's unusual suspension systems, with the lower wishbones at hub (and half-shaft) height.

unavoidable power-loss associated with its all-driven transmission system. Its horsepower drain was a fair percentage of the 2.5 litre Climax engine's 240 bhp output, but it was proportionally that much greater where the 150 bhp 1.5 litre engine was concerned.

However, British InterContinental Formula racing was at that time seeking to perpetuate old 2.5 litre F1 racing – the capacity ceiling in fact being 3 litres – and the P99 in R.R.C. Walker Racing's dark Scots-blue and white colours, made its racing début in this class, at the British Empire Trophy race, Silverstone in June 1961. It was driven by the reliable and steady Jack Fairman, and one week later reappeared in the British GP at Aintree, now powered by the requisite 1.5 litre engine. There in pouring rain it really showed outstanding acceleration and adhesion in conditions where essentially there was none. After team-mate Stirling Moss had retired his Lotus 18, he took over the Ferguson from Fairman, and before he was black-flagged for a push-start he really was immensely impressed with its potential.

Stirling always has been a sucker for new-fangled gadgetry, and the P99 and its handling foibles simply fascinated him. He regarded it as a challenge to both his natural driving abilities and perhaps to his intelligence, and in extensive testing he simply taught himself how to drive a four-wheel drive car quickly and invented the technique from instinct, perception, inspiration and not a little perspiration ...

That September, the Maestro raced the car again in the Oulton Park Gold Cup. Rain showers damped the circuit, which made the most of the 4WD system's traction and cornering power and with his new-found driving skills he enjoyed a runaway victory – scoring the only Formula 1 race win *ever* for a four-wheel drive car.

After this outing, Ferguson Research continued to use the vehicle for its original purpose, not as a public promotional racing car but as an experimental mobile laboratory. It amassed a vast amount of research data for the company, and did not race at all during 1962. It was then, however, returned to Rob Walker's team and entered for Jo Bonnier in the Swiss mountain climb at Ollon Villars. The Swede used its terrific traction to set FTD and smash the course record. The following winter the car went off for a Tasman racing tour of New Zealand and Australia,

The office — Ferguson's P99 cockpit was well offset to the right of the car by the left-side propeller-shaft tunnel and transmission housing. Here at the Donington Collection in 1973 its offset pedal well is clearly visible, together with the interlock-guarded left-hand gear-change gate and the perforated sheet stiffening panel welded to the left-hand — transmission-side — of the spaceframe where it helped resist torque loads.

where it was driven with minor success by Innes Ireland and Graham Hill. It vividly demonstrated its dragster-like acceleration but was outperformed around a full lap of the tight antipodean circuits by lighter conventional F1-based cars.

In 1964 the 'Fergie' as it was affectionately known – just like its tractor ancestors – really found its true motor sporting *métier*, on the short, steep, twisty venues used to decide the RAC British Hill-Climb Championship. Former Champion Peter Westbury drove the car on loan and utterly dominated the series, clinching another title and proving conclusively that 4WD was the system of the future where this highly-specialized form of motor sport was concerned.

Thereafter, the old car – still in Walker's hallowed livery – was preserved by its creators, and after their absorption into the GKN industrial group it eventually found a sympathetic and comfortable home on permanent loan to Tom Wheatcroft's magnificent Donington Collection of single-seater racing cars, at the Donington Park racing circuit near Derby.

The 'Sharknose' Ferrari Tipo 156s

★ ★ ★

Some racing cars become truly historic because of their rarity, others because of their immense success. Some assume almost mystic significance within the enthusiast's mind because of their total extinction—like the so-called 'Sharknose' Ferraris.

These cars dominated the first year of 1.5 litre Formula 1 racing in 1961, but Mr Ferrari always had a singularly unsentimental attitude to his team's cars. Initially, once they became obsolescent but were saleable, he would sell them. Later, after some drivers had hurt themselves in Ferraris and the company was roundly vilified by the Italian media – and occasionally even by the Vatican – he refused to sell any open-wheelers, and they were scrapped instead at Maranello. This is what happened to the 1961 World Championship winners after their poor second season of 1962, and today despite rumours of an engine surviving here or a gearbox there so far as I know nothing proven to be from those cars survives.

Ferrari had dabbled in 1,500 cc Formula 2 racing even since its introduction in 1957. Their Vittorio Jano-designed 65° 4-cam 'Dino' V6 engine developed for that class grew to 2,417 cc for Formula 1 – as described on page 154 – but through 1959 the crude front-engined chassis which they powered were overshadowed by Cooper's rear-engined revolution. Major change had to come, but it was only against strong in-house opposition that the team's Tuscan ex-Alfa Romeo chief engineer *Ing* Carlo Chiti succeeded in forcing through a prototype rear-engined F1 Ferrari in 1960.

Team drivers Phil Hill, Wolfgang 'Taffy' von

Trips and tester Richie Ginther all reported favourably on this new car's behaviour – relative to the front-engined 246/256 cars – and Ginther raced it in the Monaco GP. It was subsequently fitted with a 1.5 litre F2 Dino V6 engine and driven by von Trips it demolished British and Porsche opposition to win the Solituderennen outside Stuttgart. It was third behind Porsches after being delayed in the Modena GP, then won the F2 class in the Italian GP at Monza. It was obvious that Ferrari's F2-based rear-engined weaponry for the new 1961 1.5 litre Formula 1 would take some beating.

Meanwhile, British interests had bitterly opposed the governing CSI's changes to Formula 1. But while they fussed and fumed, Ferrari had quietly got on with the job, and the British 1.5 litre V8 engine projects were so late starting that Cooper, Lotus and even BRM had to make do with F2 4-cylinder Climax engines for most of 1961, leaving Maranello's V6s well placed to slaughter them.

Ing Chiti finalized his definitive 1,500 cc F1 design in the autumn of 1960, developing an all-new V6 engine for it plus more aerodynamic bodywork for a chassis similar to the 1960 F1/F2 prototype's – chassis '0008' in the contemporary front-engined F1 car sequence.

Chiti widened the included angle between cylinder blocks from Jano's original 65° to 120°. He was able to do this because the engine was now going behind the cockpit, and it provided a lower centre of gravity while also simplifying a lighter crankshaft design. More weight was saved by reducing con-rod length and big-end diameters. Each cylinder head was retained by only eight studs instead of the 65° unit's twelve, though the twin overhead camshafts per bank were chain-driven as before, from two half-speed gears on the short four-main-bearing crankshaft's nose. Chiti adopted the 73 mm bore and 58.8 mm stroke of the Solitude 65° F2 engine to produce a displacement of only 1,476.6 cc.

One major difference between the new 24-valve, 24-plug engine and the Jano 65° V6s was that its cylinder bank offset was transposed. Jano had followed his own Lancia V8 lead in setting the 65° units' left-side bank ahead of the right. Now Chiti reverted to Ferrari tradition, right-bank ahead of left.

All major castings were in Silumin light alloy, and 'the 120' was claimed to weigh 225 lb (102 kg), 30 less than the Coventry Climax FPF 4-cylinder. Initially Ferrari claimed 190 bhp at 9,500 rpm although initial tests yielded only a genuine 177, and even that was still 30 more than the FPF. This represented 118 bhp per litre (0.78 bhp per lb). Meanwhile the old '65s' were mildly modified as second-string units, pending completion of sufficient '120s' for a regular three-car team.

The multi-tubular chassis was crude and hefty, possibly better than a Cooper's – at least all its tube runs were straight – but not a patch on Lotus, BRM or even Porsche lightweight practice. The 120° engine was accommodated between bulged-apart top chassis rails, while the frames for the 65s used straight rails. A 65 would easily fit into a 120 frame, but not vice versa. The bodywork was much improved from 1960 standard, introducing the famous twin-nostril allegedly low-drag nose from which the model won its nickname.

Drivers were to be the Americans Phil Hill and Richie Ginther, and 'Taffy' von Trips. Meanwhile an Italian consortium of racing teams named the *Federazione Italiana Scuderie Automobilistiche*, FISA, (not to be confused with motor racing's future renamed CSI-replacement governing body using the same initials) was pledged to develop new Italian driver talent. Ferrari provided one car for their chosen candidate, 25-year-old Milanese Giancarlo Baghetti. He actually gave the new Ferrari its début at Syracuse on 25

19 May 1962 — Dutch GP meeting, Zandvoort — Phil Hill's 'Sharknose' Ferrari 156 screaming through the partly-wooded back-section of the Dutch seaside circuit, but unable to repeat his 1961 pole position. His time then had been 1:35.7; now he improved to 1:35.0 but John Surtees's Lola-Climax made pole fully 2.5 sec faster still. British F1 developments had left Ferrari floundering...

24 April, 1961 – Syracuse GP, Sicily – Young Giancarlo Baghetti polishes his goggles in the pits before taking out his FISA-entered Sharknose to qualify second fastest. Next day he will win on the new Ferrari's race début. The car is the prototype '0008', its engine a 65° V6.

April 1961, driving the old rebodied 1960 prototype '0008' with 65° engine. He was only narrowly beaten for pole position by Dan Gurney of Porsche, and then sensationally *won* easily!

The World Championship began at Monaco on 14 May, Ferrari entrusting the still experimental 120° V6 chassis '0001' to works tester Ginther, while Hill and von Trips had 65° engined cars, '0003' and '0002'. Stirling Moss narrowly beat them in his obsolete Walker-team Lotus 18. Ginther was second and set fastest lap, Hill third while von Trips was classified fourth after his car failed late on. Phil has described the race as 'similar to seeing which is quickest round a living room, a race horse or a dog . . .', meaning that Lotus handling had outdone Ferrari horsepower, thanks to the tight street circuit.

That same day, Baghetti won the minor Naples GP in FISA's 65° car. The Dutch GP at Zandvoort eight days after Monaco saw Ferrari go to town and for the rest of that season the Sharknose cars' record looks like this:

DUTCH GP – von Trips *1st* '0004'; Hill 2nd '0003/2*'; Ginther 5th '0001'.

BELGIAN GP – Hill *1st* '0003'; von Trips 2nd '0004'; Ginther 3rd '0001'; Gendebien 4th '0002'.

*New 120° chassis bearing the Monaco 65° car's chassis number apparently for customs carnet reasons.

FRENCH GP – Baghetti *1st* '0008'; Hill 9th '0003'; Ginther '15th' '0001'; von Trips rtd '0004'.

BRITISH GP – von Trips *1st* '0004'; Hill 2nd '0003'; Ginther 3rd '0001'; Baghetti crashed '0008'.

GERMAN GP – von Trips 2nd '0004'; Hill 3rd '0003'; Ginther 8th '0001'; Mairesse crashed '0002'.

ITALIAN GP – Hill *1st* '0002'; von Trips crashed fatally '0004'; Baghetti rtd '0003'; Ricardo Rodriguez rtd '0006'; Ginther rtd '0001'.

Thus the Sharknoses won five of the seven GPs contested, only ever being beaten by Moss in Walker's pestiferously obsolescent Lotus, at Monaco and again at the Nürburgring – the two most demanding 'driver's circuits' on the calendar.

But the Ferraris qualified on pole everywhere but Monaco, Hill taking five pole positions to von Trip's one at Monza, and they set five fastest race laps, Ginther at Monaco and Spa, Hill at Reims —where the factory Ferraris led and failed in the heat, leaving young Baghetti to score a sensational maiden victory by inches from Gurney's Porsche – and the Nürburgring, and Baghetti at the fated Monza race.

There the Drivers' World Championship was to be decided between Hill and von Trips, Ferrari

15 July, 1961 — British GP, Aintree — Late in the race as the rain has cleared and the sun breaks through, 'Taffy' von Trips heads his Ferrari 156 — chassis '0004' — towards victory. The screen-foot louvres feeding cooling air into the cockpit had been taped before the start to exclude rain. Now air — and water? — pressure had popped both seals; the car's Sharknose has also been mildly tagged at some stage.

already being assured of the Constructors' title, but on the second lap of the Italian GP von Trips collided with Jimmy Clark's Lotus 21 which had made an exceptionally fast start and '0004' careered into a spectator fence, killing 14 spectators before somersaulting back on to the road and killing its hapless driver . . .

Phil Hill won and became the first American World Champion Driver, but it was a cheerless victory after such tragedy. Ferrari withdrew from

9 September, 1961 — Practice for the Italian GP, Monza — Bird's eye view of 'Taffy' von Trips' Ferrari 156 '0004' in which he qualified on pole position for the morrow's race, and in which he would collide fatally with Jim Clark's Lotus 21. This shot emphasizes the fishlike form of these exceptionally long-tailed cars; note the separated intake grilles denoting installation of a 120° V6 engine. The earlier 65° engined cars had a single central intake grille. The perspex-cowled orifices ducted cool air on to the inboard rear brakes.

racing again that season, missing the US GP.

Amongst turmoil at Maranello that winter eight top Ferrari executives including Chiti walked out. Mr Ferrari had always cultivated strength in depth, and with Chiti gone, he promoted engine development colleagues Franco Rocchi and Walter Salvarani, veteran consultants Luigi Bazzi and Vittorio Jano remained available and two young design office engineers were also briefed for Formula 1, Mauro Forghieri and Angelo Bellei.

Before leaving, Chiti had been working on 120° V6 developments including a two-valve head with twin-plug ignition, a two-valver with three plugs, a three-valver with two plugs and a four-valver with one plug. A prototype 24-valve V6, claimed to develop 210 bhp at 10,000 rpm, appeared in the Sharknose displayed at the New Year's press conference.

Mr Ferrari had negotiated with Stirling Moss for a private blue-painted 'Sharknose' to be run by Rob Walker's team, but the Maestro's near fatal Lotus accident at Easter Monday Goodwood put paid to that.

After a competitive start to the new season, as at Monaco where Hill and newcomer Lorenzo Bandini finished 2-3 and Phil nearly won, the Sharknoses hardly featured. The new 6-speed gearbox was favoured in 'overhung-behind-the-rear-axle' form despite a new inboard type having been announced. It appeared in practice at Monaco but at Spa all gearboxes were outboard. Thereafter the new British V8s demolished Ferrari hopes. Forghieri's wide-track experiments added to the drivers' frustrations by making their cars slower still along the straights. The team missed the French GP ostensibly due to strikes in Italy, re-emerged with a single entry for Hill at Aintree with the inboard gearbox and 120° 12-valve headed engine but the car proved hopeless. A new interim car, with improved frame and a conventional nose intake instead of the nostril nose, appeared with the team back to full strength at the Nürburgring, but in the rain they were badly beaten again . . . not only by the British V8s but also by Porsche's latest flat-8.

Their full 1962 record looks like this:

PAU GP – Ricardo Rodriguez 2nd '0003'; Bandini 5th '0006'.

AINTREE '200' – Hill 3rd '0007'; Baghetti 4th '0001'.

BRDC INTERNATIONAL TROPHY – Innes Ireland* 4th '0001'.

NAPLES GP – Willy Mairesse *1st* '0001'; Bandini 2nd '0006'.

MONACO GP – Hill 2nd '0007'; Bandini 3rd '0001'; '7th' Mairesse '0004'.

BELGIAN GP – Hill 3rd '0009'; Ricardo Rodriguez 4th '0003'; Baghetti rtd '0001'; Mairesse rtd '0004'.

BRITISH GP – Hill rtd '0007'.

GERMAN GP – Ricardo Rodriguez 6th '0006'; Hill rtd '0002'; Bandini rtd '0008'; Baghetti 10th '0007'.

MEDITERRANEAN GP – Bandini *1st* '0009'; Baghetti 2nd '0003'.

ITALIAN GP – Mairesse 4th '0008'; Baghetti 5th '0003'; Bandini 8th '0006'; Hill 11th '0002'; Ricardo Rodriguez '14th' '0007'.

Eight Sharknoses had been built during 1961, the original modified prototype rear-engined car '0008' run by FISA and wrecked by Baghetti at Aintree after its historic win at Reims-Gueux and minor successes at both Syracuse and Naples – then being followed by '61 frames '0001'–'0006' with two appearing under '0003's, number as revealed by Ferrari factory records.

In 1962 it appears that three more were built, chassis '0007-0008-0009', that bearing the prototype number '8' being the interim lighter-framed conventional-nosed car developing the design towards 1963 which emerged at the Nürburgring and did quite well at Monza.

Thereafter Mr Ferrari again bowed out of racing and the Sharknose Ferraris – their reputation much dimmed – had run their final race, and were without exception, it appears, put to the torch.

But although discredited in 1962, and scrapped at the end of that season, their 1-2-3-4 finish in the '61 Belgian GP and the 1-2-3 result at Aintree cannot be forgotten. Beating outclassed opposition is not necessarily difficult, but in 1961 Ferrari certainly showed how to do it in great style . . .

*Car loaned to UDT-Laystall team for Ireland's one-off drive.

1962-63
The BRM P578s
★ ★ ★

After 12 years of trying, the BRM team of Bourne in Lincolnshire had only succeeded in winning one Championship Grand Prix – the Dutch event of 1959 – and four non-Championship F1 races of doubtful significance when the concern's owner, industrialist Sir Alfred Owen, issued an ultimatum for the 1962 season. It was in essence brutally frank and simple: 'Secure major success this season, or be shut down.'

Ever since it had become obvious that the governing CSI was going ahead with its policy of slashing Formula 1 from 2.5 litres to just 1.5 litres capacity for 1961, the pressure had been on for BRM to complete design and development not only of a suitable new F1 engine but also of a lightweight and well-handling chassis to accommodate it.

After the Dutch GP of 1960 there was something of a palace revolution at Bourne, in which the long-serving technical director Peter Berthon was effectively relieved of everyday racing team responsibility, and was instead seconded to the Harry Weslake Research consultancy down at Rye on the Kent coast where he was to work on future BRM projects, leaving his former assistant Tony Rudd in technical charge at Bourne.

One of Berthon's immediate tasks was to complete design and detailing of the new Project 56 1.5 litre BRM V8 engine intended for the new Formula, not only as a works team power unit but also as one which could be put into small-quantity production for customer sale. This was to be done on much the same basis as Coventry Climax had developed with great success for their 4-cylinder 2.5 and 1.5 litre racing engines, and

were now intending to continue with their own V8 ideas.

Tony Rudd's men at Bourne were to pursue detail development of the new V8 conceived and laid out under Berthon's direction, and they did this working in close conjunction with the Shell Oil Company's research boffins, pursuing what was at that time highly sophisticated frontier research into efficient combustion at exceptionally high rpm, for that was to be the key to the new engine's potency.

The P56 emerged as a 90° V8, with twin gear-driven overhead camshafts per bank actuating two valves per cylinder disposed at an included angle of 80°. The crankshaft was a Nitralloy forging carried in five main bearings with side-by-side big-ends, fully counterbalanced. Bore and stroke were 68.5 mm x 50.8 mm, 1,497.7 cc, and with Lucas fuel injection the handsome little power unit was soon producing 184 bhp at 10,000 rpm, with a peak 100.15 ft/lb torque at 8-9,000 rpm – 122.6 bhp per litre unblown.

Meanwhile the team's original 2.5 litre P48 rear-engined cars of 1960 had been much-improved by Rudd who developed a new wishbone IRS system to replace their hefty 'Chapman struts' which was introduced in September that year on chassis '487', the first so-called 'rear-engined Mark II' model.

In common with Coventry-Climax, BRM were late buckling down to work on their new V8 and no way was it going to become available until very late in the first season of 1.5 litre racing, 1961. Therefore, Coventry Climax FPF 4-cylinder engines were acquired by the team for the greater

23 April, 1962 — Glover Trophy, Goodwood — Graham Hill in what would become his 'Old Faithful' BRM chassis '5781' rounding Madgwick Corner at high speed on his way to the new 1.5 litre P56 V8's maiden outright race win. The Tony Rudd-designed spaceframe car was exquisitely made and brilliantly well-packaged. Note BRM's retention of Dunlop alloy wheels, the distinctive 'stack-pipe' early exhaust system and the flexibly-thin elektron sheet body panelling, retained by carefully spaced Dzus fasteners.

part of that Championship season, and new Mark II-derived P57 lightweight chassis were built to receive them. These BRM-Climaxes were campaigned through the 1961 season, with mediocre results, and the prototype Mark III or P578 V8-engined car then made its bow during practice for the Italian GP at Monza. This chassis '5781' was not raced there, but stayed on for quite extensive testing. It was an extremely neat, very handsome little car and the Italian press raved about it, never mind the English . . .

It was successful, and became number one driver Graham Hill's regular car for 1962. Further works team cars were built during that winter, only for the programme to be set back when '5782' being tested at Witham Aerodrome by Bourne's new ex-Ferrari driver Richie Ginther caught fire. The brand-new car was burned out, but its valuable V8 engine and gearbox were salvaged.

Another new car, '5783' was soon completed, but after appearing at Goodwood and Aintree this car was written-off by Ginther in a race accident at the Silverstone May meeting. Because of this, BRM were back to '5781' for the Dutch and Monaco GPs, where Richie drove an old P57 Mark II instead, albeit updated with a V8 engine. Initially the V8 engine used separate vertical stack-pipes to each of its eight cylinders, but they progressively dropped off when racing, and were replaced by Spa with a low-level system. Nonetheless, the cars had won the nickname 'The

Stackpipe' BRMs, and it has stuck with them ever since.

A new P578, actually No 4 in the series but numbered '5783', became available for Ginther at Spa and he drove it thereafter, while Hill had a new '5785' available from the British GP in July.

During that 1962 season, these works BRM P578 cars made no fewer than 40 starts in 22 races, including heats, and won eight of them, seven falling to Hill and one to Ginther. They occurred in the order Brussels GP Heat One, International '100' at Goodwood, International Trophy at Silverstone, the Dutch GP at Zandvoort – BRM's second–ever World Championship-qualifying race win – the German GP at the Nürburgring, Italian GP at Monza, Natal GP Heat One at Westmead in South Africa (Ginther's only victory) and the South African GP at East London in which Graham actually clinched both the Drivers' and Formula 1 Constructors' Championship titles after Jimmy Clark's Coventry Climax engine in the leading Lotus 25 lost a plug-bolt and pumped away its oil. Sir Alfred Owen had ordered results, and with both World titles in their grasp by the end of the season, Berthon's basic engine design and Tony Rudd's team's development and application of it had certainly delivered!

These P578 cars continued in modestly updated form into 1963, when the works team used them to make 28 starts in 15 races, reigning champion Graham Hill also making two starts in the experimental prototype P61 monocoque car. From those 28 P578 starts, Hill and Ginther achieved four more victories – in the Lombank Trophy at Snetterton, Aintree '200', Monaco and United States GPs and four second places, Richie Ginther significantly finishing second to his team leader at both Monaco and Watkins Glen, NY.

In the summer of 1963 one P578 was loaned through BP to the Italian Mimo Dei's Scuderia Centro-Sud for whom it was driven very aggressively by Lorenzo Bandini ... out of the Ferrari works team for that season but about to force his way right back in with his bold performances in the Italian-red BRM. He made his début in the car, actually Graham's regular early-1962 'Old Faithful' chassis '5781', in the Silverstone International Trophy in May, and then returned to it in the French GP on 30 June. Hill, Ginther and Bandini finished 3-4-5 in the British GP at Silverstone behind Clark's victorious Lotus 25 and John Surtees's works Ferrari 156. Bandini was then fourth in the Solitude GP and blistered his way into third place on the front row of the German GP grid at the Nürburgring, only to be sidelined by a collision on the first lap of the race. He was third in the Mediterranean GP at Enna, Sicily, and had a works Ferrari ride in the Italian GP at Monza. There Centro-Sud ran veteran Maurice Trintig-

nant in '5781' and he subsequently bought it for his own F1 swansong in 1964, the car then being resprayed French blue.

For 1964 BRM produced their definitive 1.5 litre monocoque cars, the improved P61 Mark 2s – better known as P261s, see page 195 – and Centro-Sud took over the spaceframe V8 cars '5785' and '5784' normally driven that season by Giancarlo Baghetti and Tony Maggs. The final works team entry of the P578 was that of cadet driver Richard Attwood in '5781' resprayed BRM dark green with a Dayglo orange nose-band for the occasion, at Easter Monday Goodwood, where he finished fourth.

Meanwhile, customer-standard V8 engines, initially on Weber carburetors instead of fuel injection, were sold in 1962 to privateers Tony Marsh and Jack Lewis, for use in their newly-acquired ex-works P57 1961 chassis, '573' and '572' respectively. Unfortunately these engines were under-powered, under-prepared and as far as the privateers were concerned over-described and over-priced, and the venture ended rapidly amidst great acrimony.

However, many later BRM P56 V8 engines were provided to other private entrants for use mainly in Lotus and Brabham chassis although Gilby and Scirocco also made use of them, and they generally performed very well and were

---

5 August, 1962 — German GP, Nürburgring — In a rain and mist-swathed epic, Graham Hill proved himself and his car by beating off the race-long attentions of John Surtees in a Lola-Climax V8 and Dan Gurney in a Porsche flat-eight. Graham and BRM were well on their way to winning the season's World Championship titles. By this time '5781's V8 engine had a low-level exhaust system replacing the stack-pipe expedient.

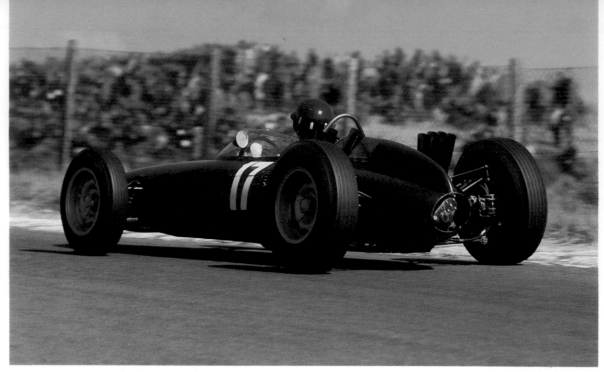

20 May 1962 — Dutch GP, Zandvoort — Graham Hill has his BRM P578's seven surviving organ pipes singing out loud and clear as he tears through the dunes towards his maiden *Grande Epreuve* victory; only the second in BRM's history, but the first of their World Championship season. The 'stackpipe' exhausts were an easy but fragile expedient, the V8's shrill note progressively changing as more pipes fell off . . .

highly regarded through the period 1962-65, on a par with the relatively few private Coventry Climax FWMV V8s, but of course well behind the works engines of both types.

Those years of 1.5 litre racing were a happy hunting ground for private teams in Formula 1, and with BRM V8 power UDT-Laystall Team Lotus 24s won at Crystal Palace (Innes Ireland) and Karlskoga, Sweden (Masten Gregory) in 1962, and at Easter Goodwood (Ireland) in 1963. That second season also saw the tough Swiss ex-motor cyclist Jo Siffert win the Syracuse GP in his private Lotus-BRM 24, and when he bought a Brabham chassis for 1964 he retained the BRM V8 engine and won the Mediterranean GP at Enna, beating Clark's Lotus by 0.1 sec and Ireland's new BRP-BRM by 1.1 sec. What's more, Siffert would do the trick there again the following year, again BRM powered and this time beating Clark to the finish by 0.3 sec. Ireland, incidentally, had previously won the '64 season-opening *Daily Mirror* Trophy race at Snetterton in the monocoque BRP-BRM. Graham Hill drove the Willment Team's Brabham-BRM in the Rand GP at Kyalami, South Africa in December '64, and enjoyed another easy win.

By 1965 the old ex-works P578 cars were decidedly long in the tooth, but 'Mimo Dei's Scuderia Centro-Sud soldiered on, having taken back Trintignant's 'Old Faithful' '5781' alongside '5784' and '5785' for drivers like Gregory, Ludovico Scarfiotti, Roberto Bussinello, Chris Amon on one occasion (International Trophy), Giampiero Biscaldi, Giorgio Bassi and Baghetti. These three rather battered, tatty and tired red-painted cars made the type's swansong appearance on 12 September 1965, in the last 1.5 litre formula Italian GP at Monza, Bassi's '5781' engine failing after nine laps, Gregory's '5784' gearbox after 23 laps and Bussinello's '5758' V8 losing its oil pressure after 58 laps – he was classified thirteenth.

That was four days less than three years after Graham Hill's 'Old Faithful' had actually won that race on that circuit, with Richie Ginther second in '5785', a performance which erased the memory of the V16 BRMs' terrible disgrace there in 1951, and really rammed home the fact that BRM had arrived as a front-line team, with not a weak link in the chain. After winning the World Championship titles in 1962, they and Graham Hill were runners-up in every other 1.5 litre formula season, 1963, '64 and '65, and it was their P56 V8 engine-series which made it possible, and these P578 spaceframe cars which made the Bourne team accustomed to winning through 1962-63.

The Lotus-Climax Type 25s

★ ★ ★ ★ ★

The twenty-fifth Lotus model had a more profound and far-reaching effect upon the development of Grand Prix car chassis design than any other single model in history. It dispensed with the tubular-steel members which had previously provided the basic structural members for most GP cars since the mid-1930s, and popularized instead aeronautical-style stressed-skin 'monocoque' construction.

There had been monocoque-chassised racing cars before the Lotus 25, and there were some which were more truly 'monocoque' – ie 'single-shell' – but none of them achieved such immense success nor revolutionized Grand Prix car design in the manner achieved by Colin Chapman's prettiest brainchild.

Even in 1962, so-called monocoque construction had already been the most significant structural element of aeronautical engineering for over 50 years, beginning with Frederick Handley Page in 1911 and achieved brilliantly by Louis Béchereau's first streamlined fuselage using its skin as its main load-bearing structure in his 1912 Deperdussin racer.

Amongst racing cars, Howard Blood's Cornelian Indy car of 1915 most probably had the first true monocoque chassis. It set no trends. Neither did pioneer aviator Gabriel Voisin's monocoque-chassised streamlined GP cars of 1923, nor the British sprint specials of Alec Issigonis and Laurie Bond, 'Spike' Rhiando's Trimax 500 cc F3 design or Tom Killeen's sports cars. But Jaguar's monocoque centre-section D-Types won Le Mans in 1955-57, and as we have seen the BRM P25 F1 car began life with a semi-

monocoque fuselage. Still throughout this post-war period, the multi-tubular F1 spaceframe held sway until Colin Chapman and Team Lotus changed all that in 1962.

Arguably the greatest engineer/driver combination the Grand Prix racing world has ever seen — Colin Chapman who created the Formula 1 Lotus cars, and Jim Clark who drove them with such skill, elegance and gentlemanly grace.

James Allington's lovely drawing of the 1962 Lotus-Climax 25.

Colin was above all a talented and daring stress man, continually developing ever-lighter, ever-stiffer chassis designs. Tests with the prototype Lotus Elan sports car proved its fabricated sheet backbone chassis immensely rigid for its weight. In 1961, during the lunch-hour at a local restaurant near Lotus's Cheshunt factory in Hertfordshire, he sketched a scheme on a table napkin to apply a backbone chassis to a single-seat racing car.

He later told me how he thought, 'Why not space the sides of the backbone far enough apart for a driver to sit between them?' He went on, 'At the same time we'd had years of trouble with wrapping aluminium fuel tanks around tubular spaceframes and trying to stop them chafing through. So if we made the sides of the backbone as box-sections we could carry fuel inside them in rubber bags . . .' He outlined a design along these lines which was drawn up for him largely by draughtsman Alan Styman, to accept the new Coventry Climax V8 engine and a ZF gearbox.

The early months of 1962 saw Team Lotus mechanics Dick Scammell and Ted Woodley working closely with Lotus engineering director Mike Costin, Chapman himself and the Cheshunt panel-beaters in a partitioned-off corner of the Team Lotus workshop. They were putting together the prototype Lotus 25 which Colin suspected might not work out, but was worth a try anyway.

Its structure comprised two parallel D-section monocoque booms which formed the fuel tank housings each side of the driver's reclining seat, linked laterally by a stressed-skin undertray panel, a bulkhead between cockpit and engine bay, a dash-panel frame and a forward bulkhead providing front suspension mounts and including a hefty crossbeam to tie the bottom wishbone pick-ups across the car. The height of the D-section side pontoons diminished aft of the cockpit and continued rearwards to pick-up each side of the engine, then terminated in a fabricated steel loop diaphragm which picked-up rear suspension and gearbox mountings. The top of the entire structure was left open to form what would become known as a 'bath-tub' monocoque, closure being by detachable moulded GRP body panelling.

The main objective was enhanced torsional rigidity for less weight. The rigidity of the chassis is the ultimate arbiter of consistent cornering performance. In olden days with beam axles the beam itself governed the angular relationship of one wheel to another, but independent suspensions removed that beam, whereupon the car's chassis became the link. If wheel angles and suspension geometries were to be governed accurately then rigidity of the chassis became crucial.

Tests revealed that the 1961 Lotus 21 space-frame's torsional stiffness was only 700 lb/ft per degree deflection, and bare weight 82 lb (37.3 kg). Weight rose to 130 lb (59 kg) with all brackets and aluminium fuel tanks attached.

Now the new alternative Type 24 spaceframe chassis also prepared for the V8 engines had a bare weight of 72 lb (32.7 kg) for little better rigidity, while the new Type 25 monocoque finally weighed-in at just 65 lb (29.5 kg) bare, yet offered 1,000 lb/ft per degree rigidity rising to what was at that time a staggering 2,400 lb/ft per degree when the new Coventry Climax V8 was bolted into its rear bay. This quantum leap was to show itself not so much on faster corners against rivals with a spaceframe only half as stiff, but allowed Lotus to use more supple suspension which, combined with their monocoque rigidity, paid off in slower turns.

Colin recalled the finished prototype – chassis 'R1' – as '. . . quite the cleanest and nicest-looking car we'd ever made. There were no holes in the bodywork, the engine and gearbox were beautifully cowled-in and it all worked very well . . .'.

It was unveiled in the Zandvoort paddock for the Dutch GP opening the 1962 World Championship season, and Jimmy Clark led the race handsomely before clutch failure. Thereafter, the Lotus 25 established itself as *the* car to beat, the standard-setter of its time. It repeatedly led all opposition and either won or broke. Five Type 25s were built that season. 'R1' was eventually handed to Jimmy's number two Trevor Taylor, but through no fault of his own it was destroyed in a *finish*-line collision in the French GP at Rouen.

Car 'R2' was to be destroyed in another blameless Taylor accident at Enna, Sicily, in 1963 when he was sprayed with flying stones by Bandini's sliding Centro-Sud team BRM and was stunned by a pebble.

Car 'R3' would become the earliest Lotus 25 to survive into collectable old age, but like 'R4' was much cut about by its new owners from 1964, the private Parnell Racing Team. 'R4' was then severely damaged in Dick Attwood's 1965 Belgian GP shunt at Spa. A virtually new car – more replacement Type 33 than 25 – was in theory built up around its remains by Parnell's

20 May, 1962 — Dutch GP, Zandvoort — Unrivalled beauty; first time out for the brand-new monocoque-chassised Lotus 25. Here Jim Clark looks rather uncomfortably reclined within 'R1' as he rounds the *Hunzerug* corner behind the Zandvoort pits. Note how tiny the Grand Prix car had become, its front suspension coil/dampers and Climax FWMV V8 engine fared-away within the moulded glass-fibre bodywork. The only mod from 'straight out of the box' condition seems to be the three tiny deflector tabs added to the windscreen moulding to give Jim a more peaceful ride.

5 August, 1962 — German GP, Nürburgring — The race in which Jimmy's startline omission in 'R2' probably cost him and Team Lotus the year's World Championship titles. Here after his delayed start he is streaking around the majestic 14 mile *Nordschleife* to salvage fourth place from the ruins. He is wearing Dunlop khaki rain-proof overalls. What an exquisite little car.

boys and eventually emerged under the putative chassis serial 'R13' though it was apparently better known to all involved simply as *'Percy'* . . .

The last of the 1962 25s, 'R5' was another victim of Trev Taylor's legendary bad luck, this one being destroyed in a crash during practice for the 1963 Belgian GP when he apparently set off after the lunch-break, quite unsuspecting that a vital rear suspension bolt had been removed and the link allegedly retained only by a chubby screwdriver plopped into the vacant hole! This 'retaining pin' dropped out in the high-speed right-hander at Stavelot and the Lotus ran wild, torpedoing the wooden observer's hut there and blasting a huge hole clean through it. Despite the devastation nobody was hurt, but 'R5' was history . . . at least until 1988 when ex-Team mechanic Cedric Selzer completed a handsome replica 'rebuild' of the car.

And what of the 25's successes? Well, Clark won the Belgian GP, only the 25's third Championship race and set fastest lap in 'R1'; the British GP at Aintree from pole, setting fastest lap in 'R2'; was fourth after a brilliant recovery drive – having stalled on the line – at the Nürburgring, won the US GP from pole plus fastest lap in 'R3' and took over Trev Taylor's 'R2' to win the non-Championship Mexican GP to add to his Oulton Park Gold Cup victory in that same car. In 'R3' he won the Rand GP at Kyalami, with Taylor second in 'R2', then this Team Lotus 1-2 was reversed in the Natal race at Westmead.

The 1962 Championships reached their climax in the last race of the year, the South African GP at East London. After starting from pole, leading easily and setting fastest lap, Jimmy was robbed of the title by an engine oil-leak in 'R5', the World Championships passing to Graham Hill and BRM instead. The combination of Clark and the Lotus 25 then took the World Championship by storm in 1963 with the car changed only in detail from its developed-1962 form, plus use of Coventry Climax's now fuel injected instead of Weber carburetted V8 engine.

·Later-series Type 25 tubs were skinned in thinner 18-gauge Alclad aluminium-alloy sheet. Thickness was not constant throughout, but essentially a saving of 2swg was made which trimmed even more weight. Many detail refinements, some beefing-up for reliability and considerable weight-saving applied by engineer Len Terry was largely responsible for making the 25 *the car* of 1963.

Team Lotus began the new season fully equipped with 1962 cars 'R2-'3-'4-'5' but as already described would lose chassis '2 and '5 during the season. New car 'R6' emerged for the non-Championship Austrian GP at Zeltweg aerodrome that September, equipped with the latest flat-plane crankshaft Climax V8, with low-level instead of over-the-gearbox exhaust system, and the gearbox itself was no longer the faithful but hefty and complex German ZF, but a British-made Hewland five-speed instead.

All this work made the 25 reliable and when Dunlop R6 racing tyres were introduced, their grip combined with Jimmy Clark's consummate driving skill made the 1963 Lotus 25s near-unbeatable. Just look at their record that year; five non-Championship race wins and *seven*

Championship-qualifying GPs, a record within one season, all to Jimmy Clark. Nobody could touch him, or his car.

For 1964, a new Type 33 monocoque was on the way, designed by Terry under Chapman supervision around new 13 in diameter wheels carrying the latest wide-tread Dunlops which heralded the 'doughnut' design racing tyre. Chapman sold 'R3' and 'R7' – which had been new for Team Lotus in South Africa – to the Parnell Team to acept BRM V8 engines for the new season, and 'R4' would follow them later in the year. Old 'R6' was retained and updated to approach 33-spec and Pete Arundell joined Clark as his new number two.

At Monaco Clark ran 'R6' and Arundell 'R4', the Champion's car using the latest wheels, tyres, uprights, gearbox, driveshafts and rear suspension with the top radius rod relocated on the hub-carrier at the same height as the lateral link, whereas formerly it had been at hub-height. This system distributed braking torques and traction more evenly between the two rods and provided better control.

Arundell's 'R4' retained the earlier geometry though also on the new fat tyres and journalists dubbed these variants the 25D and 25C though to Team Lotus both were simply 25Bs. 'R4' was first loaned to the Parnell Team for the Austrian GP –a Championship round for the first time that

season – by which time poor Arundell had been grievously injured in an F2 race at Reims and Mike Spence had replaced him.

Meanwhile the first Type 33 'R8' had been completed. Where the Type 25s' inner cockpit panelling ran parallel from seat-back to dash panel, then kinked inwards to converge into the pedal-box, the 33s' were straight, converging all the way from seat-back to pedal-box, making a stiffer tub overall. The first Type 33 'R8' was badly-damaged in its début race at Aintree and was never the same again and Jimmy was always happier with his 'Old Faithful' 25 'R6' until the later 33s emerged, first 'R9' new in Germany '64, then 'R10' in South Africa on New Year's Day 1965.

For 1965 Team Lotus concentrated upon their Type 33s, but Clark used 'R6' to win at Goodwood and in the French GP, *en route* to his second Championship title in three season's racing. It was a wonderful record, and the Lotus 25s overall won 14 Championship GPs, and 11 non-Championship F1 races in their overall four-season life at the top.

I must confess that merely the memory of those elegant, tiny, apple-green cars at speed with Clark's dark-blue helmet just above the coaming, the master so relaxed and capable, and such a gentleman, still makes the eyes mist over. Famous cars indeed, and so very, very pretty...

---

8 September, 1963 — Italian GP, Monza — Jim Clark on his winning way in 25 'R4' and on the brink of clinching his and Team Lotus's first-ever World Championship titles. The central yellow stripe had been introduced for the British GP at Silverstone in July — now on his way to seven Championship-qualifying GP victories within the season Clark was to immortalize the cars bearing this livery.

1963
The Indianapolis Lotus-Ford Type 29s
★ ★ ★ ★

In May 1962, when he first saw the brand-new monocoque Lotus 25 at Zandvoort, the American driver Dan Gurney exclaimed 'My God, if someone took a car like this to Indianapolis they could win with it!'. He invited Colin Chapman to attend that year's Indy 500 at his – Gurney's – expense, to size-up the objective. The previous year John Cooper and Jack Brabham had rocked the Indy establishment to the core by tackling the Speedway classic with an F1-derived 2.7 litre 4-cylinder Cooper-Climax. Not only was it totally 'the wrong shape' with its engine 'in the wrong end' but 'Goddammit it's *green*, even the colour being anathema to Indy superstition. In fact USAC design had stagnated badly since the early 1950s, and Brabham finished ninth amongst the traditional 4.2 litre Offenhauser front-engined roadsters, displaying terrific speed through the turns, and only losing out along the straightaways. That year's Indy purse totalled $400,000, the winner taking $117,975, a very worthwhile target. Now in the 1962 race Dan was driving a rear-engined Buick Special for Californian hot-rodder Mickey Thompson. Rear-engined chassis clearly had a future in such antiquated company, but Dan found Thompson's design was not the car to prove it.

Colin Chapman was simply stunned by his first sight of Indy racing, 'I thought I'd gone back 15 years . . .', he told me, '. . . I could imagine this was what it must have been like to watch the Mercedes and Auto Unions pre-war at Tripoli. I thought, well – all you've got to do is to get an engine with about half the power of those great lumps of junk, build a decent chassis and you've won the race . . .'

Coincidentally, Ford Detroit were also eyeing Indy. Engineers Don Frey and Dave Evans were in the crowd that day, and while Colin and Dan – who had finished twentieth – returned to Europe, Frey proposed a Ford engine for the 500 based on experimental alloy blocks intended for the Falcon sedan. Evans approached leading Indy chassis men. In Cheshunt, Hertfordshire, Chapman was framing an Indy Lotus proposal to Ford.

On 23 July, he and Gurney met Frey and Bill Innes, head of Ford's foundry and engine division, and Colin expounded his concept for a relatively low-powered but economical Indy car capable of completing the 500-Miles with only one refuelling stop against the Offys' usual two or more. Each stop cost some 30 sec, but the greatest margin of victory in the previous five '500s' had been only 27.6 sec, and in 1961 was barely eight. The elimination of just one refuelling stop could therefore win the race. Colin won approval to pursue the project further, but Ford naturally hedged their bets, by talking further with Indy chassis specialist A.J. Watson, constructor of the last four Indy winners.

Indy posed a psychology problem for Ford. Their last dabble in 1935 had been the US motor industry's PR disaster of the century — until they went one better with the Edsel. They now arranged a survey of the Speedway, and acquired a 4-cylinder Offy engine for comparative testing. It yielded 407 bhp at 6,000 rpm on alcohol, and when their V8 put out 351 bhp on petrol and 400 on methanol they knew they had the power whichever route they chose — Chapman, or Watson.

Then Team Lotus and Jimmy Clark nudged Ford's elbow by winning the 1962 United States GP with the Lotus 25. The winning car 'R3' was trailed down to Indianapolis after the Watkins Glen race, and there Jimmy rocked all the spectators with the tiny 1.5 litre car's fantastic cornering speeds. Ford wanted to buy a 25 to test, but no available US driver had the experience to drive it. Instead, they dropped an engine into Nelson Stacey's Galaxie stock car for Daytona tests that November. He lapped at 154.8 mph (258 km/h) on methanol and 146.7 mph (244.5 km/h) on gasoline, respective fuel consumption being 2.2 and 6.41 mpg (1051/100 km to 361 l/100 km). A computer run then predicted Indy lap speeds of 150 mph (250 km/h) for a rear-engined Lotus-powered by-Ford and the decision was taken to 'go gasoline'.

Senior engineer Bill Gay flew to Europe to finalize designs with Colin Chapman, and to order special 58 mm Weber carburettors which Colin recommended for simplicity and economy, despite fuel-injection being universal amongst the Indy Offies.

Len Terry detailed the new Type 29 design from Colin's brief. Its bathtub monocoque mirrored Type 25 configuration, though now with the minimum Indy wheelbase of 96 in (2.4 m), 5 in (25 cm) greater than the F1 Type 25s. Its tub was wider and deeper than the 25 to improve tank space and rigidity, and was further stiffened by the engine, rigidly installed at eight points. A special dispensation was obtained from USAC to allow the use of rubber fuel bags when fibre-sheathed metal tanks were strictly mandatory. Six cells were used, two in each side pontoon, a fifth behind the seat bulkhead and the sixth a fibre-sheathed aluminium scuttle tank above the driver's legs. Suspension was similar to the 25's, but for larger diameters or heavier gauges throughout. The track was identical to the 25's but alternative suspension pick-ups allowed the hull to be slung either symmetrically between the wheels or asymmetrically with a 2.875 in (7.3 cm) offset to the left to compensate for the left-turn only rectangular layout of the Speedway.

Ford's new pushrod ohv Indy V8 was founded on the 4,260 cc Fairlane pushrod unit, but with alloy crankcase, block and head castings. Bore was slightly narrowed and mechanically-operated valves replaced hydraulic tappets. The unit weighed 70 lb (32 kg) bare in alloy against 150 lb (68 kg) stock, and fully-assembled with all accessories it scaled 360 lb (164 kg) and was

March 1963 — Snetterton testing of the protype Lotus-Ford 29 'mule' complete with unpainted aluminium body panelling and the Ford V8 stock-block engine on stack-pipe individual exhausts. Here Jimmy Clark is at the wheel and the car is as yet on symmetrical suspension, without the shorter left-side bias which would be adopted at The Brickyard.

March 1963, with a finish coat of Team Lotus racing green the finished '29/1' is shown to the press in the Lotus works at Cheshunt prior to being shipped to Indianapolis where it will stand the USAC Speedway racing establishment on its ear . . .

Indy stack-pipe — the 1963 Lotus-Ford 29 in cutaway.

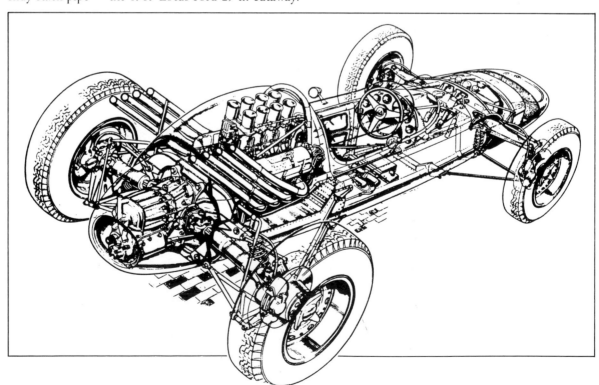

expected to produce 370 bhp at 7,000 rpm – 88 bhp per litre (1.02 bhp per lb). A four-speed Colotti Type 37A gearbox was adopted, although most of the time only two speeds would be used.

The prototype of the three Type 29s to be built was first tested by Jimmy Clark, its aluminium bodywork unpainted, with symmetrical suspension and separate stack exhausts, at Snetterton in March 1963. It was then flown to the USA for further evaluation at Ford's Kingman test track in Arizona, which it promptly lapped at 165 mph (275 km/h). The engine was unreliable so a final shakedown was fixed for Indy, but the intended special engine snapped a camshaft on the dyno. A replacement was hastily built-up and flown to Indianapolis where it was cobbled into a runner using wiring looms and parts cannibalized from a hapless pair of Fairlane hire cars! Few realized how makeshift the programme had become, especially as the car then performed to order.

Clark first drove the 29 around 'The Brickyard' on 24 March. Next day he was lapping happily at 146 mph (243 km/h) against Parnelli Jones' existing 1962 roadster lap record of 150.729 mph (243 km/h). Using Dunlop in place of Firestone tyres and a lower final-drive ratio next day, Gurney lapped at 150.501 mph (251 km/h) the second-fastest ever Indy lap and exactly as the computer predicted. The Lotus-Ford people were delighted. Their car covered 457 miles (762 km) trouble-free and two weeks later the gasoline engine design was frozen as Ford's 'Project AX230-2'.

Indy qualifying occupies the whole of May. When the Lotus 29s of Clark and Gurney ran very fast on Firestone's new 15 in tyres, the roadster establishment screamed. They claimed they were being 'forced' to run obsolescent 16 in wheels and tyres, and that Firestone should withdraw the 15s or make them available to all. Strangely, there was no protest about Mickey Thompson's special 12 inch Sears Allstate tyres, but then they were not quick. . .

Firestone made the 15s generally available, sparking a stampede for a hastily-cast batch of Ted Halibrand's alloy Indy wheels. Lotus's perforated disc Dunlop wheels then began to crack, and only one set of cast Halibrands could be obtained, on loan from Smokey Yunick whose car had just been wrecked by Curtis Turner. Lotus planned to share that single set between their two race cars for qualifying, but on 18 May Gurney hit the wall in turn one, ruining his 29's right-side and two of those precious wheels. Jimmy had to qualify on the best available Dunlop wheels, while Lotus crew chief David Lazenby and his men prepared the 'Mule' prototype car for Dan to race. Jimmy's four-lap average of 149.75 mph (250 km/h) placed him fifth on the grid, and next day Dan qualified the 'Mule' on row four at 149.019 mph (248 km/h).

Final pre-race panic was then to find an experienced pit crew, Bill Stroppe's Mercury stock-car team being called in from Atlanta, while Pete Weismann – later a celebrated transmission designer – handled the hoses. Meanwhile, the first Saturday in May had seen an excellent omen as Texan Lloyd Ruby shook USAC by setting a 106 mph (177 km/h) lap record and leading all the roadsters for 40 laps at Trenton NJ, in an ex-F1 Lotus 18.

On 30 May, the 500-Miles began with Parnelli Jones setting out to build a time cushion from the Lotus-Fords to permit his extra pit stop(s). He lapped at 151 mph (252 km/h) and stopped on schedule at 62 laps. As the other roadsters pitted, the tiny Lotus 29s – Team Lotus green for Clark, American racing white with dark-blue stripe for Gurney – moved forward. On lap 67 they lay first and second, with Jones 17 secs behind in third. At 70 laps Clark's average was a record 141.793 mph, (236.3 km/h), and at 80 laps – 200 miles (333 km) – it was 142.566 mph (237.6 km/h). On lap 92 Gurney lost 42.2 sec changing three wheels and refuelling, allowing Jones into second place.

On lap 95 Clark rushed in for 32 sec, rejoining third while Jones led. At 100 laps – 250 miles (417 km) – Jimmy lay second 40 sec behind Jones. At 116 laps the yellow caution lights blinked on signifying that the field must maintain station at reduced pace, and Jones made his second stop to retain the lead.

At 130 laps Jones's record average was 142.495 mph (237.5 km/h); Jimmy lay second and Dan sixth. While the 29s could not close on Jones, he was unable to draw away from them, and an inevitable third pit-stop faced him. Gurney climbed to fourth, then under another yellow light Jones made that final stop, rejoining after 21 secs, 11 sec ahead of Clark with Gurney now third. It was Jones versus The Revolution; the enormous Speedway crowd were going wild!

Lap 172 saw Jimmy only 10 sec behind Jones;

lap 173, 7 sec. By lap 177 only 5 sec split the Lotus from the lead. But now as Jones backed-off, his Offy was blowing smoke. Oil was reported on the roadster's left side and simultaneously Jimmy's 29 began to slide in the turns and he fell back. Dan lost third place in another stop for fuel and tyres, did two more laps, then returned for his rear wheels to be tightened. Jones's car was clearly dropping oil. Chief Steward Harlan Fengler had warned at his pre-race briefing that any car dropping oil would be black-flagged, so Clark sat back and waited.

Johnny Poulsen, Jones's Agajanian team crew chief, was in animated conversation with Fengler. Glasses were trained on the roadster. Fengler thought the spray looked like water. On lap 189 Eddie Sachs spun on the 'fluid' and clipped a wall, next lap he lost a wheel and crashed properly. The yellow light came on, Jimmy was slowed by roadsters ahead, and could just see Jones's tail drawing further into the distance. After several laps of this he passed the baulking cars, but the stewards did not react.

With seven laps to run the green flashed on, Jimmy now 22 sec behind Jones. On the slick Speedway he could do no better than recover 3 sec of that deficit, and then Jones had won from Clark's Lotus 29 by 19 sec, the delayed Dan Gurney finishing seventh. Jimmy's second-place money was $55,000, Colin's Ford deal yielded another $20,000 bonus for qualifying both cars, and $25,000 more for second place, plus all expenses paid. The writing was on the wall; the Indy roadsters' days were numbered.

Later that year the 29s ran in the Milwaukee '200', Jimmy leading from start to finish, lapping all but A.J. Foyt's second-placed roadster, Dan third. In September the Trenton '200' saw Jimmy and Dan qualifying with 32-33 sec laps, the quickest roadsters failing to improve on 35s!

At the end of 1963, the 29 which Dan had crashed in Indy qualifying was sold to Lindsey Hopkins and at Indy '64 as the *'Pure Oil Firebird Spl'* Bobby Marshman lapped at a record 158 mph (263 km/h) in it, using the latest four-cam Ford V8 racing engine. Clark's new Lotus-Ford 34 qualified on pole, but Marshman was second quickest and his 29 led until a transmission oil leak retired him after 33 laps. Jerry Alderman then bought the car for Al Miller to drive in the 1965 and '66 500s, the old car finishing fourth and then being demolished in the famous 1966 start-line pile-up.

By 1965 Len Terry had perfected the Lotus-Ford Type 38 in which Clark finally won this great American track classic, and that finally buried the front-engined roadster racing cars. But it was the neat, sensational Lotus 29 which had set the ball rolling in 1963 and which taught American racing, once so infinitely superior to European practice, how much their technology had stagnated; a famous achievement, and a triumph for the road racing fraternity.

31 May, 1963 — Indianapolis 500-Miles — Jimmy Clark in the Lotus-Ford 29 picking his way between the oil smears to finish second behind Parnelli Jones's stricken Offy roadster and come within an ace of winning the USAC track classic at his first attempt. Note the enormous Firestone track tyres.

The BRM P261s

In 1962, the technical lead represented by the Lotus 25 was quickly recognized by several rival teams. One of the quickest to respond, as they had been to follow Cooper's rear-engined lead in 1959, was British Racing Motors at Bourne.

Chief engineer Tony Rudd supervized design of an exploratory semi-monocoque exercise, combining a full stressed-skin forward fuselage with a tubular-framed rear engine bay to carry the latest development P56 V8 engines. This car's forward monocoque differed from the Lotus 25 'bathtub' type in having its stressed skin extended into a complete 360° tubular section encircling both the driver's legs and the fuel tank section behind his shoulders. Immediately aft of that, the tub terminated and tubular trusses then supported engine and rear suspension. This new car took Project number 61 in the BRM design register, but although it taught Rudd and his team a great deal about monocoque construction its hybrid configuration was not a success.

It was tested initially by Graham Hill over 49 miles (82 km) at Snetterton on 13 June 1963, and was then taken to Zandvoort where Graham tried it in practice for the Dutch GP but preferred his regular spaceframe P578 for the race. He covered another 91 miles (152 km) in the new car, 'P61/1' (or simply '611') at Zandvoort on 24 June, the Monday following the GP, and the team then loaded-up and headed south to Reims-Gueux where the French GP was to take place the following weekend. Graham then drove '611' there for the first time on 26 June.

The new BRM looked neat, if rather gawky, certainly lacking the cultured elegance of the shapely spaceframe P578s. But it was exceptionally slender, and proved very quick along the Reims-Gueux straights. Although Graham had distinct reservations about its handling, he qualified second fastest. Unfortunately just before the race began '611' had to be push-started, which cost a one minute penalty, but he salvaged third at the finish behind Jim Clark's Lotus and Tony Maggs's Cooper.

The semi-monocoque was then consigned to further testing, at Silverstone and Snetterton in July and August, before reappearing for another high-speed GP, the Italian at Monza. There Graham again performed well in practice, qualifying second, and he featured prominently in the race, actually taking the lead eight times past the pits until '611's' clutch failed after 59 exciting laps.

Obviously the additional chassis stiffness afforded by the semi-monocoque car, its small cross-section and minimal frontal area had potential, and Rudd decided to drop the tubular rear bay, which testing had shown weakened the chassis torsionally, and laid down a revised 'P61 Mark 2' all-monocoque design for 1964. It featured rearward extending monocoque horns projecting behind the cockpit, running low along either side of the V8 engine to pick-up a suspension-mounting diaphragm bulkhead around the clutch-face/gearbox joint. Initially, Tony intended this chassis to carry modified V8 engines, in which the head porting was reversed to give outside inlets and an in-vee exhaust system on top of the engine. Development of the necessary new heads took longer than expected, and a modest

12 September 1965 — Italian GP, Monza — 1.5 litre Formula 1 at its best; World Champion Jimmy Clark's Lotus 25-derived Type 33 'R11' leading the pack into the *Parabolica*, harried by Dan Gurney's Brabham BT11, ultimate winner Jackie Stewart's BRM P261 '2617', Graham Hill's sister '2616', Lorenzo Bandini's new Ferrari 1512 '0008' and Mike Spence's Lotus 33 'R9'. Trailing them are John Surtees' Ferrari 1512 '0007' and Jo Siffert's Brabham BT 11.

redesign had to be made to cut broad slots through the horns, to enable existing-style low-level exhaust manifolding to pass through.

Someone decided that 'P61 Mark 2' was too cumbersome a moniker for the new BRM, and juggled the numbers around to coin plain, simple P261. It stuck, and the first all-monocoque chassised BRM emerged as chassis '2612', first turning a wheel at Silverstone on 7 February 1964. Initially Graham Hill could not fit into its confined cockpit, so Tony Rudd's painstakingly-calculated chassis stressings and the inner cockpit skins took a pounding as Graham made space for himself with a hammer!

This cigar-shaped BRM was easily the most handsomely purposeful rear-engined car Bourne had yet built. It was on 15 in wheels and tyres, shortly to be superceded by Dunlop's latest 13 in wide-tread 'doughnut' tyres and wheels to match. But Graham raved about '2612's' handling. They qualified second-fastest for its race début at Snetterton on 14 March 1964, and led in torrential rain until the car aquaplaned off the main straight into an unyielding bank and was written off.

This was a serious blow, but the second car '2613' was almost complete in the Bourne 'shop and '2614' would emerge the following month. In all, including the mourned prototype '2612', BRM built five P261s that season, serials '2612' to '2616'. Number one driver Hill used chassis '4 and '5 most of the season, changing to '6 for the United States and Mexican GPs ending the series. Number two driver Richie Ginther drove '3 for the first time in practice for the Aintree '200' on 18 April, but crashed luridly during practice, ploughing across a muddy lawn inverted with his crash helmet and the car's thankfully strong roll-over bar gouging up the turf. Once repaired, chassis '3 became the diminutive Californian's regular car.

Hill and BRM retained a chance of winning both World titles into the final race at Mexico City, only to be nudged into a spin by Bandini's Ferrari, crumpling '2616's' V8 exhaust pipes against a steel barrier. Graham finished out of the points, Clark's Lotus expired on the very last lap and Graham had to drop his worst score, because he had scored so often that season. Thus John Surtees and Ferrari became Champions with a lower points aggregate than that of Hill and BRM!

In fact Graham's P261 results sequence in the 10 1964 World Championship rounds reads 1-4-5-2-2-2-Rtd-Rtd-1-11, his victories coming at Monaco and Watkins Glen (both for the second consecutive time), his only two retirements at the rugged Zeltweg aerodrome circuit in the inaugural Austrian GP and at Monza. There '2615' was powered by the first centre-exhaust BRM V8, but its clutch failed at the start and Graham was out in the first few yards. Every time he finished – save for Mexico – he had been in the points.

Meanwhile Ginther's record had been 2-11-4-5-8-7-2-4-4-8 – scoring seven times with not a single GP retirement but not achieving as much as BRM's now realistic management felt he should with such good equipment. At least his first second place had been behind Graham at Monaco – another BRM 1-2 in mechanically the toughest race of the year.

Jackie Stewart was signed in Ginther's place for 1965, and a new car '2617' was built for him. As is familiar history, the wee Scot took to Formula 1 like a duck to water, started excellently and improved until Graham Hill was having to watch him warily. While Graham's 1965 Championship GP record reads 3-1-5-5-2-4-2-2-1-Rtd, Jackie's almost matched it, save for poorer reliability; 6-3-2-5-2-Rtd-1-Rtd-Rtd. Graham scored his sensational third consecutive win at Monaco after a mid-race excursion up the chicane escape road, and also completed a second BRM hat-trick in the lucrative US GP at Watkins Glen. Stewart finished ahead of him at Spa, Clermont, Zandvoort and at Monza where the determined Clydesider won narrowly in a near dead-heat BRM 1-2 finish. For the third successive season, Graham Hill and BRM were runners-up in both the Drivers' and Constructors' World Championships.

BRM owner Sir Alfred Owen then ordered Rudd and the Bourne racing shop, at short notice, to prepare a team of suitably enlarged P261s to tackle the Tasman Championship in New Zealand and Australia, where the Owen Organization had important industrial interests. While the new 3 litre Formula 1 regulations were

about to take effect from 1 January 1966, the 1.5 litre V8 engine was by no means dead. Many were now in circulation and with the new H16-cylinder F1 works team engine not due until later in '66, there would meanwhile be an interim F1 home for enlarged P261s.

For the Tasman tour, the existing P56 1.5 litre V8 engine design was enlarged to P60 1,970 cc form, and installed in chassis '6 and '4 they were campaigned down-under by Hill, Stewart and Dickie Attwood. In face of heavier and less nimble 2.5 litre, 4-cylinder Tasman cars from Brabham and Lotus they won both the New Zealand and Australian GPs, plus the Lady Wigram Trophy at Christchurch, NZ, and other rounds at Levin, Teretonga, Sandown Park and Longford, Tasmania. Stewart was 1966 Tasman Champion, in the works P261s.

Back in Europe, BRM sold '2615' to private entrant Bernard White's 'Team Chamaco Collect', and on May Day Max Wilson drove it into fourth place in the Syracuse GP in Sicily.

Incredibly, Stewart notched BRM's fourth consecutive victory in the Monaco GP, driving '2617' with Tasman V8 engine, and Hill was third in '2616'. But in the next race, at Spa, Stewart was caught out badly by a flash rain shower on the opening lap. His '2617' crashed into a roadside garden in the hamlet of Masta, its monocoque was crushed and the Scot trapped inside until released by Hill and Bob Bondurant whose own two BRM P261s had also crashed in the same area. Stewart recovered, but for '2617' the accident was fatal.

Jackie missed only the French GP where BRM's new P83 H16 ran well for the first time in practice, and he returned to the fray in '2614' for the British, Dutch and German GPs.

Hill's F1 results in these first six Championship rounds of '66 with the Tasman BRM read 3-Rtd-Rtd-3-2-4, while Stewart's record was 1-Rtd-absent-Rtd-4-5. The big P83s were then raced in Italy, the US and Mexican GPs and failed every time. Bondurant's Italian GP in White's '2615' was his last drive for the somewhat eccentric owner, Innes Ireland taking over thereafter for the minor Oulton Park race, where he was fourth, then the US and Mexican GPs where he retired both times.

Still Bourne had not finished with their P261s, Stewart, Attwood, Piers Courage and Chris Irwin sharing chassis '4 and '6 in the 1967 Tasman

Championship, this time with V8 engines taken out to their maximum 2,070 cc.

Stewart won his second New Zealand GP and Lady Wigram Trophy, and emulated Hill's Australian GP win of the previous season. But the BRMs were bettered by Jim Clark's works Lotus 33 with its 2 litre Coventry Climax V8 engine, and failed in defence of their Tasman title.

The BRM Tasman tours were managed by Tim Parnell, whose own private F1 team had long campaigned elderly Lotus chassis powered by BRM V8 customer engines. Now the Parnell team became an effective BRM second-string for 1967, intended to keep ex-Team Lotus number two Mike Spence in F1 and to provide experience to cadet drivers like Courage and Irwin. Spence's Parnell P261 finished sixth in the International Trophy at Silverstone.

The 1967 French GP was run on the tight Bugatti Circuit at Le Mans on 2 July, and there after practice Stewart opted for BRM's spare old

'2614' V8 instead of his intended 3 litre H16. He drove it home in third place, beaten only by the two works Repco Brabham BT24s. This was the Bourne team's last race with the long-lived P261, three and a half years after the model's introduction. Parnell then entered Irwin in their quasi-works Tasman V8 in the British GP, finishing seventh ahead of David Hobbs in the White car, and in the Canadian GP on 27 August 1967, Hobbs drove '2615' in the type's final Championship GP start, finishing ninth after a stop for clean goggles.

New 2.5-litre V12 P126 cars – note the transposition – armed Bourne's 1968 Tasman Championship assault, driven by Bruce McLaren and Pedro Rodriguez, but they had an elderly P261 V8 as spare and Pedro raced it in the Warwick Farm '100' at Sydney on 18 February and finished sixth. In Europe the model was dead but refused to lie down, for Bernard White's '2615' had been converted to accept a 3 litre BRM V12

---

12 September, 1965 — Italian GP, Monza — Jackie Stewart about to score the first of his record-breaking 27 World Championship-qualifying Grand Prix race wins in BRM P261 chassis '2617', seen here from the gantry on the entry to Monza's 180° *Curva Parabolica*. Note the car's low-cross-section, cigar-shaped, full-monocoque hull, and its outside inlet/in-vee exhaust, V8 engine.

24 July, 1966 — Dutch GP, Zandvoort — Graham Hill doing his best against 3-litre Repco-Brabham opposition in the 2,070 cc 'Tasman BRM' P261 chassis '2616'. These cars were pressed into World Championship use pending satisfactory development of the intended replacement 3 litre H16-cylinder P83 cars. Note the prominent 'Owen Racing Organisation' lettering applied in '66. Here Graham would finish second behind Jack Brabham's 3 litre V8.

engine. Hobbs used it in the Race of Champions and International Trophy early in the year, then it reappeared in the August Oulton Park Gold Cup, accompanied by a Motor Racing Stables Tasman V8 entry for Tony Lanfranchi. There Lanfranchi finished fifth, Hobbs sixth behind the only four quality entries.

Still the irrepressible White wasn't finished. His V12-engined '2615' was taken to Monza for the Italian GP where Frank Gardner found it in poor order and wrongly geared and failed to qualify. The ancient car was then sold to Tony Dean, who drove it into second place behind a Formula 5000 Lola-Chevrolet in the very minor 1969 Spanish GP at Jarama, Madrid. Ben Moore entered the car yet again for the Oulton Park Gold Cup, on 16 August 1969, with this time it was driven by Charles Lucas who retired after only six laps with ignition failure.

That, finally, really was the end of the five-year international F1 career of arguably the finest series of 'green' Grand Prix cars ever to be built at Bourne. They had won only six Championship GPs, but significantly finished second or third no fewer than 16 times. They also won one non-Championship F1 race – Stewart's 1965 International Trophy – and no less than 17 Tasman events, including heats and preliminaries, and in all these minor events combined they also totalled 24 second and third place finishes.

During the 1.5 litre P261 period 1964-65, BRM really was an exemplary team, running well–engineered cars efficiently and successfully, and redressing the marque's once-sullied reputation accumulated through an initial decade of mismanagement and misfortune.

The Eagle-Weslake V12s

★ ★ ★

American driver Dan Gurney and his fellow for-mer Le Mans winner Carroll Shelby, creator of the early-'60s Cobra sports car project, formed All-American Racers Inc for 1965, essentially to win the Indianapolis 500-Miles on Goodyear tyres. They initially entered a Lotus and two Halibrand Shrikes in the 1965 500, while Gurney was spending his last season as a Formula 1 Brabham works driver and AAR's new purpose-built factory was being completed at Santa Ana, California. Gurney wanted to fly his all-American flag in F1 with the start of the new 3 litre Formula in 1966. To design new cars for both Indy and GP racing, he hired Lotus engineer Len Terry, whose Type 38 had just won at Indy driven by Clark.

Len designed a Lotus 38-like full-monocoque Indy car for AAR, christened the Eagle after the national emblem and bearing a delightful beak-like nose treatment in celebration. He then adap-ted this design to Formula 1 road racing, reducing the fuel capacity. In fact the Indy design was com-promised slightly to facilitate this conversion to road racing, low roll centre heights featuring in its suspension geometry, in spite of Terry believing that a higher roll axis would suit Indy better. Furthermore, despite offset asymmetrical sus-pension being common at Indy at that time, Len adopted symmetrical suspension for the track car to generate development experience for the road racer.

Four Eagle Type T1G F1 monocoques were completed in 1966, skinned in 18-gauge aluminium unlike the 16-gauge-skinned track cars. This alone saved 50 lb (22.7 kg) weight. The full monocoque tubs had 360° stressed skin scut-tle and seatback sections either end of the cockpit opening. In his suspension and other tube-com-ponent design, Len enlarged the diameter and reduced wall thickness compared to his Lotus 38 to gain strength without weight penalty. He also planned to fit a second brake disc and caliper on the inboard end of each live front stub axle to add braking power at the front, but this idea was shelved.

AAR adopted the 'Anglo-American Racers' title for Formula 1 and commissioned an all-new 3 litre V12 engine, designed and built by Aubrey Woods and Weslake & Co of Rye, Sussex. Woods was an ex-BRM engineer who had worked alongside Dan Gurney when he had driven for the team in 1960. A Weslake 3 litre V12 design with four-valve per cylinder heads had been rejec-ted by BRM for the new Formula in favour of their own H16, yet by the summer of 1965 a twin-cylinder test engine to this design was giving good results, which had attracted Gurney.

The engine contract was signed in October 1965 for six Eagle-Weslake V12s, and space for AAR's British base was provided beside Weslake's premises. The new engine would miss the start of the new season so AAR bought four stop-gap 2.75 litre Coventry Climax FPF 4-cylinder engines to put race-development miles on at least one chassis. Outputs ranged from 190 to 235 bhp, and the best of these 'old nails' was fitted in chassis 'AAR-101' and tested at Goodwood on 8 May 1966, when Gurney was simply stunned by the 4-cylinder's frantic vibration.

Its maiden race came in the Belgian GP at Spa, where Dan qualified last and finished seventh

after a mid-race stop to relieve himself in the roadside ditch! He just wedged a rock under the Eagle's wheel and left its engine ticking over. At Reims, in a more continent performance, he finished fifth in the French GP to score AAR Eagle's first Championship points.

The need for better steering lock had led to the rear lower wishbone legs being kinked to give space, and anti-dive was taken out of the front geometry. At Brands Hatch Dan qualified third and held second place until broken piston ring lands retired '101'. Engine problems grounded the Eagle again at Zandvoort where he both qualified and ran fourth.

AAR engine specialist John Miller rebuilt and developed at least one of the Climax units at Santa Ana to find 255 bhp. Dan ran fourth at the Nürburgring with this engine but a broken condenser bracket dropped him to seventh at the finish.

At Monza he qualified with the Climax engine but raced the first Weslake V12 Type 58-powered car instead. A week after first dyno test this engine gave a claimed 364 bhp, with Monza only one week away, so it had been rushed out there and installed in chassis 'AAR-102'. Phil Hill practised Eagle-Climax '101' while Dan found problems with the V12's fuel system. When oil temperature soared in the race he retired after 17 laps.

Both Climax and V12 cars ran in the US and Mexican GPs. The V12 overheated and threw out its oil at Watkins Glen, then was driven by Bondurant in Mexico where fuel feed problems retired it. Bondurant's '101' had been disqualified for receiving outside assistance in the US, while

7 August, 1966 — German GP, Nürburgring — Dan Gurney in his Climax FPF 4-cylinder powered Eagle prototype '101' entering the *Sudkehre* on his way to finishing seventh on the damp *Nordschleife* circuit. Here the Len Terry-designed full-monocoque car shows off its handsome lines. Note that the front suspension coil/damper units are tucked inboard, well out of the airstream, and the characteristically square-shouldered Goodyear racing tyres.

4 September, 1966 — Italian GP, Monza — Dan gave his new 3 litre Gurney-Weslake V12-engined Eagle '102' its début in the Italian World Championship round but found his troubles were only just beginning. Still the Anglo-American Racing team's metallic dark blue and white cars were the most handsome F1 machines around.

Dan finished fifth with it in Mexico. Car '101' reappeared in Gurney's hands in the 1967 South African GP, retiring again before being sold to Castrol for A1 Pease to drive in Canada.

Castrol support for 1967 replaced AAR's original sponsor Mobil, whose departure left the F1 team grossly under-financed.

Oil blow-by in the V12 had been traced to excessive clearance in cylinder liner fit. Gurney had a new '413 bhp' engine in '102' for the Race of Champions at Brands Hatch, accompanied by new team-mate Richie Ginther in chassis '103', with its prototype V12 giving a claimed 409 bhp. They ran 1-2 in the final before trouble with experimental brake pads retired Ginther, but Dan won narrowly from Bandini's Ferrari. This was most encouraging.

Though undeniably beautiful, the Eagle was a heavy car at around 180 lb (82 kg) over the minimum limit. California's Harvey Aluminum company advised replacing the aluminium skins with magnesium, and steel components with titanium. Ginther failed to qualify at Monaco and Indy, at Zandvoort he felt unable to compete in modern racing and abruptly retired. Dan ran third briefly at Monaco only for '103's' Lucas fuel metering unit drive-belt to break.

Chassis 'AAR-104' then emerged, the 'mag-ti

Eagle' using Harvey Aluminum's magnesium and titanium, visibly different from its sisters with close-spaced magnesium skin rivetting. All suspension links were titanium, the top front wishbone alone saving nearly 1.5 lb (0.7 kg) weight. Titanium exhaust manifolds saved 20 lb (9 kg); '104' scaling 1,192 lb (541.8 kg) overall, 88 lb (40 kg) lighter than its nearest sister. Chassis '103' was subsequently fitted with a titanium suspension set and some of Weslake's V12 castings were changed from aluminium to magnesium to trim some more weight.

In '104' Gurney was fast at Zandvoort until the metering unit failed again. But at Spa he set a new lap record despite low fuel pressure causing a top-end misfire and he won the Belgian GP in grand style, just one week after winning Le Mans for Ford. It was the zenith of Dan's fine career.

Bruce McLaren then became second driver for the French GP in '102' with Dan in '104' qualifying on the front row, but both retired. In the British GP meeting, three Weslake V12s broke expensively. In Germany Gurney nearly won, but with three laps to go and a 45 second lead and a new lap record to his name, a UJ cross sheared. Bruce McLaren had already retired with another broken V12.

In Canada Dan finished third in '103', and at

---

12 March, 1967 — Race of Champions, Brands Hatch ↽ Dan waiting to start the race which would provide his first Formula 1 victory in a car of his own company's design and manufacture. To his left is his always-reticent late, great Australian racing mechanic Tim Wall — who had cared for Moss's Walker Cooper in Buenos Aires '58 — to the right Rouem Haffenden. At the rear of the Eagle-Weslake, team-mate Richie Ginther is fiddling . . .

Flawed power-house — while the AAR Eagle cars were so good-looking, their 3 litre Gurney-Weslake V12 engine was also arguably the most handsome in Formula 1 1966-67 but its power and reliability were suspect.

Monza three Weslake V12s failed again, one in practice, one in Gurney's '104' while leading and one in guest driver Scarfiotti's '103', within the opening six laps. Gurney ran '104' as a lone entry in the US, where its suspension failed, and Mexico, where he holed its radiator at the start.

By this time Dan was highly dubious of Weslake's ability to sustain manufacturing and assembly quality under the pressures of Formula 1. When in South Africa in 1968 he retired with oil leaks and overheating, and a spare engine installed for a post-race Goodyear tyre test then proved in poorer shape than the race unit, Dan severed his Weslake tie and set up a new shop in Ashford, Kent, to build and test the engines. From 1 May 1968, the team's entire UK operation, engine and race shop were concentrated there. One V12 was tested on the BRM dyno at Folkingham where it gave no more than 390 bhp – another rude shock after Weslake's claims, for the BRM dyno was hardly considered pessimistic.

An improved Eagle Mark 1A V12 was being developed, the team missed Spain and reappeared at Monaco where Gurney started from the back of the grid and retired early. More races were missed before reappearance at the British GP, but although running quicker Dan again retired. He was ninth at the Nürburgring, after running third

early on before a tyre was damaged. Monza was hot and fast, and the V12 wilted under the strain of climbing from thirteenth to seventh – its oil pressure disappeared.

There Dan tried one of Bruce McLaren's new McLaren M7A cars with Cosworth DFV engine, and next day he arranged to drive it for the rest of the season, setting his partly-developed Eagle-Weslake aside.

At Santa Ana, new ex-Lola designer Tony Southgate was drawing the 1969 F1 Eagle. It was to be a neat slim car with all-magnesium skins and outboard front suspension aiming at minimum weight, and a Cosworth DFV engine was considered in view of the V12's continuing fragility, and insufficient budget for further serious development.

But money was so short, and Dan so unhappy at the fire risk in a magnesium car – mindful of Schlesser's awful death in the air-cooled magnesium Honda at Rouen – that in November 1968 AAR abandoned further F1 plans. All-American Racers would concentrate upon US racing henceforth, Anglo-American Racers as such being wound-up. A buyer was sought for the V12, Honda expressing brief but unfulfilled interest, and the most gorgeous of all 3 litre Formula 1 cars would be raced in earnest no more.

The Lotus-Cosworth Type 49s

★ ★ ★ ★

When the CSI introduced 3 litre Formula 1 on 1 January 1966, Colin Chapman's Team Lotus were caught between engines. Short-term they had to run cars using stretched 1.5s from the old Formula, while BRM slowly developed the full 3 litre H16-cylinder unit which Colin had ordered. But behind the scenes he had a longer-term option, the Cosworth-Ford DFV V8 which he had commissioned from Keith Duckworth, with Ford of Dagenham paying the bill. Design began of a new car to carry it.

Like the BRM H16 this engine was designed to be suspended from the rear bulkhead of a three-quarter length forward monocoque, acting as the rear part of the chassis by accepting transmission and suspension loads. Already the Lotus 39 designed by Chapman's right-hand man Maurice Phillippe for the still-born 1.5 litre Climax flat-16 engine in 1965 would have have used a similar mounting, although that unit would have been steadied by aviation-style perforated angle-beams on either side.

Colin had specified '... a simple car which wouldn't give us any problems, so we could sort-out the engine...' and in May 1967 the first Lotus 49 emerged. Its monocoque fuselage was a twin-boom affair totally enclosing the driver's legs and feet up front, with an enclosed 'midship tank behind his shoulders, its forward skin forming his seat back. The tub was skinned in 18-gauge L72 Alcad aluminium-alloy sheet rivetted and shaped over internal mild-steel bulkheads. Suspension followed familiar Lotus practice, with robust fabricated top rocker arms actuating inboard coil-spring/damper units tucked well out of the airstream on the footbox flanks. At the rear, triangulated tubular frames attached to engine block and heads provided inboard suspension pick-ups, with a cross-beam offering lower mounts bolted beneath a tailor-made, very light but uprated ZF 5DS12 five-speed and reverse transaxle. Some connected with Team Lotus considered the German 'box under-engineered for the job it had to do. They proved to be right.

As always with a Chapman F1 car concept, there was only just enough car to do the job everywhere in this design. There was nothing staggeringly innovative about any part of it; the 49 was never another 25, nor a later 72, nor 78/79, but Colin merely wanted a simple car sufficient to race the brand-new unknown quantity engine, and this was it.

The first of the five Cosworth-Ford V8s planned for Team Lotus that season was handed over on 25 April 1967, two days after completion and five months after commencement of manufacture. The original race-début target date of 7 May, the Monaco GP, was postponed, and the two Type 49s then extant made their classical début at Zandvoort, as had the epochal Type 25 before them. It was a fairytale début. Graham Hill's pole position practice time was fully 4.2 per cent faster than the existing record, an astonishing margin. He led but retired after setting fastest lap, leaving team-mate Jim Clark to win as he pleased.

In performance terms, the three 49-DFVs built that season simply set new standards. They took pole position in the next 11 consecutive GPs, and while Graham often led races it was always

Clark's sister car which would survive to win three more times, in the British, US and Mexican races. The ZF gearbox proved a weak point, and early in 1968 the easily-gutted, omni-adjustable quick-change Hewland gearbox would replace it.

At the end of 1967 a money crisis arose. At the London Motor Show, Esso – who had been Team Lotus main backers for many years – confirmed their withdrawal from racing sponsorship. Chapman's men hunted a replacement, and found John Player tobacco. Gold Leaf Team Lotus was born and national-colour racing teams would – apart from Ferrari – become a mere memory from the past.

Pre-GLTL new Lotus 49 'R4' appeared for the South African GP opening 1968 and Clark promptly won to overtake Fangio's career record of 24 *Grande Epreuve* victories, setting the new mark at 25. This GP also saw the DFV engine's début in another customer's hands, Ken Tyrrell's Equipe Matra International running Jackie Stewart in a Matra-DFV special, which led briefly. Team Lotus had lost exclusive use of the new engine.

Special 2.5 litre DFVs, known as DFWs, were then used in Team's Tasman Championship 49s racing in New Zealand and Australia from January to March '68. Original 49 chassis 'R1' and 'R2' excelled, GLTL cigarette-packet livery replac-ing Team's traditional BRG-and-yellow on that tour.

Back in Europe, the incomparable Jimmy Clark was killed in an insignificant F2 race at Hoc-kenheim, but Graham Hill brought GLTL bounc-ing back from this shattering catastrophe, winning the Spanish and Monaco GPs consecutively.

Team Lotus's experience with new-generation, ever wider-tread Firestone tyres had indicated that more rearward weight bias would be advan-tageous. Consequently, they ran 'R5' brand-new at the Race of Champions with a huge oil tank over its gearbox instead of in the nose. Wider deep-cone wheels carried the latest Firestone tyres, but 'R5' was then reworked more com-prehensively to become the first Lotus 49B.

Here Chapman and Phillippe lengthened its wheelbase by raking the front suspension arms 3 in (7.6 cm) forward to put more load on the car's rear end. To limit rear-wheel toe-steer, tunnels were sunk into the lower rear quarters of the monocoque tub, and the lower radius-rod pick-ups resited well-forward in them. The engine still mounted in its classical manner, while on the back of it more substantial subframes carried the rear suspension, oil tank and Hewland's latest 'bunch of old mangle-gears', the FG400 gearbox.

James Allington unveils the 1967 Lotus-Cosworth Ford 49.

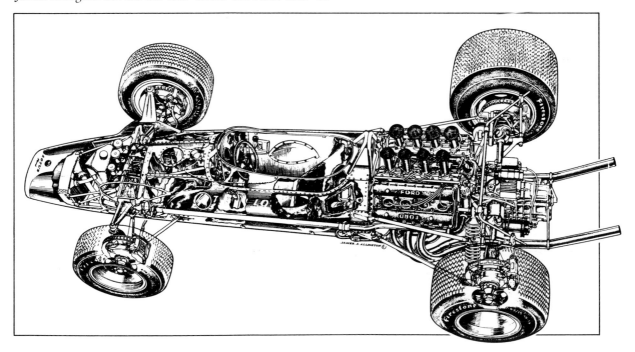

17 June, 1967 — Practice for the Belgian GP, Spa-Francorchamps — Jim Clark showing off the new Cosworth-Ford DFV V8 engine's vicious power characteristics under hard acceleration as the torque chimes in and squats Lotus 49 'R2' tail down/nose high. Note the twin-braced roll-over hoop, even in 1967 standing lower than the top of the driver's head which it was meant to protect, air-deflector windscreen, broad Firestone racing tyres and aerodynamic drag-inducive naked engine installation. They would learn — quickly.

---

26 May, 1968 — Monaco GP, Monte Carlo — Graham Hill heads towards the maiden victory upon its début of the Lotus 49B 'R5', pictured here entering the *Tabac* corner on the harbourside. The car's nose fins were intended to balance the aerodynamic download effect of that duck-tail shaped engine cowl. Note the air-deflector windscreen and Team Lotus's garish new Gold Leaf tobacco sponsorship livery. The hallowed green-and-yellow had long gone.

Now the DFV's heads carried no suspension loads direct. An upswept engine and gearbox cowl was now adopted, and whatever aerodynamic downforce this imparted was trimmed-out by a pair of wide-span nose fins, so total download now acted more or less about the car's centre of gravity.

Hill had won the Spanish GP in ex-1967 season/ex-Tasman chassis 'R1', and now at Monaco in 'R5's' début as a true 49B he won another race of attrition, while new team-mate Jack Oliver destroyed 'R1', the remains being rebuilt subsequently as new 49B 'R9'. This 'salvage and restore' policy became standard, and accounts for the nine Type 49 entities actually using 12 individual chassis numbers. There were never 12 Lotus 49s extant simultaneously.

The semi-wedge 49Bs ran two more races only, as more ambitious aerofoil aids were on the way. At Spa, where Oliver débuted 'R6', strutted chassis-mounted rear aerofoil aids were introduced by Ferrari and Brabham, their effect balanced by trim vanes on the nosecones. Chapman was to become in effect the high priest of this new strutted aerofoil technology, his 49Bs progressively adopting taller, wider and more powerful wings. His drivers became test pilots penetrating the unknown . . .

For the 1968 French GP at Rouen, Team rigged its 49Bs with strutted 'foils acting direct upon the rear suspension uprights to convert maximum download into pure traction. Colin estimated 400 lb (182 kg) download at 150 mph (250 km/h), but in practice Oliver edged 'R6' into another's slipstream and it just slithered away from under him and crashed into a brick gate-post. Oliver survived his car breaking in two, but 'R6' would only reappear around a totally rebuilt tub.

New 49B 'R7' emerged for customer Rob Walker at Brands Hatch, where driver Jo Siffert promptly won the British GP! Team had loaned Rob 'R4' starting the season but it was destroyed in his Dorking garage fire, 'R2' standing-in until 49B 'R7' was finished.

High wings dramatically increased drive-line loadings. Firestone's sticky new YB11 tyres aggravated the problem, removing cushioning wheelspin to condemn many a half-shaft or UJ to failure.

Heavier shafts and joints were adopted, and in March 1969 strutted airfoil aids doubled-up, fore and aft, acting on both front and rear suspensions. Passive mounts, with the wing incidence pre-set were normal, but in Mexico City for the 1968 Championship-deciding GP - which Hill and Lotus won – a feathering rear wing was employed.

At Barcelona, for the Spanish GP on 4 May 1969, the two works 49Bs for Hill and Rindt wore the largest, tallest, widest wings yet, skinned in aluminium over too-few section formers which left their mid-span surfaces unbraced. The wings collapsed, and both cars crashed spectacularly. Graham's already once-rebuilt 'R6' would be rebuilt again, but Jochen's horribly mangled 'R9' had to be scrapped. It had only made its début in South Africa, where another new 49B, 'R11', had been raced by Mario Andretti, before being sold to American privateer Pete Lovely, who still owns it today. After the Barcelona incidents, the CSI banned strutted wings in the middle of practice for the next GP, at Monaco. Team Lotus cobbled together semi-wedge gearbox covers instead from their transporter's interior panelling.

4 August, 1968 — German GP, Nürburgring — Graham Hill blinding his way round in the murk in brave but fruitless pursuit of the genius of Jackie Stewart, long gone in his Cosworth-engined Tyrrell Matra MS10. Graham would finish second in 'R5' here sporting one of the strutted rear aerofoils of which Colin Chapman became almost literally the high priest until they were banned after collapses during the following season's Spanish GP at Montjuich Park, Barcelona.

19 July, 1969 — British GP, Silverstone — Jochen Rindt's Lotus 49B 'R6' here shows off its new post-Barcelona regulation-size wings, once again in pursuit of Jackie Stewart, in this instance driving what would become his World Championship-winning Matra-Cosworth MS80. Note the late-series 49B's top-ducted nose radiator configuration, and the broadest Firestone racing tyres yet. The deflector-screen is still in favour, but note how roll-over protection has grown thus far in the 49 family's two-year life.

There was a new 49B 'R10' present for Hill, while Richard Attwood deputized for the injured Rindt in a 49T with right-angle front suspension, chassis 'R8' built specifically for Hill's Tasman tour the preceding winter. It had just returned from Australia under tons of rotting fruit in a delayed freighter, and the Team Lotus lads hastily burrowed down to it upon their return from Barcelona and prepared it just in time to leave for Monte Carlo.

Despite all this, incredibly Hill still won his fifth Monaco GP, his second in a row in a Lotus 49B; Siffert was third in Walker's 'R7' and Attwood fourth, having set fastest lap, in his 'old nail'. Who said Lotus F1 cars were fragile? First, third and fourth in what was mechanically the toughest GP on the calendar indicated otherwise.

Using new regulation low wings Hill and the recovered Rindt battled each other at Zandvoort, and the abrasive Austrian established himself as the faster, subsequently having a series of terrific battles with Jackie Stewart's World Championship-winning Matra MS80, which the ageing Lotus 49B was not quite man enough to win, until Jochen eventually notched his long-awaited first Grand Prix victory, at Watkins Glen in 'R6'. Hill crashed 'R10' there when a tyre deflated, and caused him serious injury.

So Team Lotus's third season with the 49s ended with two more GP victories to their credit, but their World titles had been lost to Matra-DFV and Jackie Stewart.

Now the Type 49s had run *far* beyond their expected life due to the failure of the intended replacement four-wheel drive Type 63s. The 49s had become notorious for their fuel-system doggedly refusing to scavenge the last few gallons from their now multiple bag tanks, and for roasting their drivers with hot air from the nose-

2 June 1967 — Dutch GP meeting, Zandvoort — Jimmy Clark tries his Cosworth-Ford V8-powered Lotus 49/2 for the first time watched by Colin Chapman (left) and mechanics Eddie Dennis and Alan McCall (right). The great Scot would win this maiden race to usher in a whole new era of Formula 1.

26 May 1968 — Monaco GP, Monte Carlo — Graham Hill hustles the prototype Lotus 49B — chassis 'R5' — into the Tabac corner on the way to his fourth Monegasque victory, and his second consecutive GP win of that season. Team Lotus were fighting to recover from the loss of Jimmy Clark.

mounted radiator. To improve cooling and aerodynamic performance, top-ducted radiators had been adopted in time for the 1968 Italian GP, venting hot air upwards over the driver's head. Add the fierce, often instrument-wrecking natural vibration of the DFV, plus the 49s' proneness to savage pitch and tail-light wandering under braking – which Siffert ('Last of the Late-Brakers') exploited to the full in close company – and you can understand the Lotus 49 family's imperfections; but the old cars had yet another season left in them.

Early in 1970, as development of the replacement Type 72 lagged, four old 49Bs – works team chassis 'R6', 'R8' and the freshly reincarnated 'R10', plus Walker's veteran 'R7' – were reworked to carry new 13 in front wheels and Firestone tyres as the Type 49C. Meanwhile a final 49B had been built-up as a display car for Ford of Britain, finished in GLTL livery and numbered 'R12'. It would not be used in anger.

Hill was replaced by John Miles as No 2 to Rindt, while the barely-recovered twice-World Champion took over Siffert's drive for Walker. The old cars proved remarkably competitive until the startling new Type 72 made its début, and when that required an early partial redesign the works 49Cs were dusted down for a final front-line World Championship outing at Monaco. There Rindt triumphed, pressuring race leader Jack Brabham into a dreadful mistake at the very last corner, and diving by to win. This was the Lotus 49 family's twelfth and last GP victory, its thirteenth in representative Formula 1 and its twenty-first overall, including Tasman races.

Through 1970 Miles, Hill and Lovely raced 49s most often, Emerson Fittipaldi made his GP début in 'R10' at Brands Hatch, and finally as late as April 1971, Tony Trimmer drove Rindt's Monaco-winning car, faithful old 'R6', which had had such a long and sometimes violent history, in the Good Friday Oulton Park International. He finished a distant sixth, four laps behind Rodriguez's winning BRM, after a pit stop, and so this classic Grand Prix design's representative International career ended. What had begun as a simple stop-gap design merely to prove an engine had served brilliantly far beyond its normal life expectation.

The Ferrari Tipo 312Bs

★ ★ ★ ★

During the life of the 3 litre Formula, commencing in 1966, Ferrari's four-cam 3 litre V12 engines and the slimline chassis carrying them were progressively developed until in 1968 their drivers Chris Amon and Jacky Ickx were able to qualify on the front row nine times, eight to Amon, and take four pole positions, three of them his. They made 30 F1 starts, but were often unfortunate, finally winning just one Grand Prix and adding one second place and three thirds. Three of the six 312/68 cars used were effectively written-off, and poor reliability robbed Ferrari of what could easily have been three more GP wins and the World Championship titles.

The company then ran into industrial and financial crises in 1969 but still returned to endurance racing, if low-key, after a year's lay-off. Mr Ferrari also took the long-term strategic decision for chief engineer Mauro Forghieri's men to develop a 3 litre flat-12 F1 engine for 1970 while *Ing* Stefano Jacoponi took F1 team responsibility to do his best with the increasingly obsolescent V12. It was unable to match the combination of high power, muscular torque, light unit weight and modest fuel consumption – permitting the cars it powered a lower startline weight – then being demonstrated by the rival Cosworth-Ford V8. Only three F1 Ferrari V12s were built that season, and despite protestations that the further-revised 48-valve engines now delivered 435 bhp, Amon doubted they even matched 1968 power. Efforts to cut internal friction by reducing main bearing area also proved catastrophic.

Against this background, Forghieri was detailing his new flat-12 engine which had begun life as a potential client project for a low-drag aero engine. Its horizontally opposed 'Boxer' layout made it capable of installation within a thin wing section. But Forghieri knew this concept could be moulded into the best-integrated F1 car ever to emerge from Maranello, and development work of a suitable *Aero*-type, internally-framed, monocoque fuselage to carry the unit to war quickly progressed. The horizontal 'Boxer' layout, some people calling it a 180° vee, provided a very low centre of gravity. Shallow height also cleared airflow beneath the rear wing and saved a little weight compared to the V12. Dimensions were 78.5 mm x 51.5 mm, displacing 2,991.01 cc.

Four-valve per cylinder heads borrowed from late-series V12 experience. In the initial form piston and crankshaft problems caused a string of testing failures, not least involving lubrication, solved on the tilting dyno bed at Maranello, devized earlier to investigate cornering surge conditions in the V12s. The new Boxer motor was a very high-revving unit and to minimize friction losses its crankshaft revolved in just four main bearings, two plain shell bearings amidships and ball-bearing races at nose and tail. This left the crankshaft with rather dubious support and after initial breakages crankshaft torsionals were controlled by the addition of a Pirelli cushion-coupling between crankshaft and flywheel, achieving reliability to match 460 bhp at between 11,500 and 11,700 rpm. By 1974, 312B-series power would rise to 495 bhp, and by the end of the engine's useful life in 1979-80 it was delivering nearer 510 bhp at 12,000 rpm, which few doubted.

The light-alloy block-cum-crankcase was cast in two parts, united on a crankshaft centreline bolted flange. The heads were cast in crisp aluminium alloy disposing four valves per cylinder actuated by double overhead camshafts.

Light-alloy cylinder liners were used, cooled by water circulation at their upper ends, by oil circulation down below. The crankshaft was machined from a steel forging, each of its six crankpins carrying two con-rods. Its nose take-off gear drove alternator, ignition distributor and fuel metering unit via gears and pinions. The crankshaft tail drove the valve-gear train. A tiny flywheel incorporated the rubber vibration damper. Forged titanium con-rods were used, with plain big-end bearings, although rollers were used experimentally on occasion. Mahle forged aluminium pistons were used, pocketed for valve clearance and 'squish'.

A single oil pressure pump driven off the rear of the right-hand cylinder head timing gear fed the oil filter mounted behind the fuel metering unit, then on into the front of the block. The scavenge pump resided in the same housing as the pressure pump, returning oil to the tank which chased around the car in the various 312B, 'B2, 'B3, 'B4, 312T and 'T2-3-4-5 models in which the numerous variations of this wonderful workhorse power unit featured.

I had two cars, the 1973 *Spazzaneve* 'B3 prototype and a 1977-spec 312T2 briefly in my care, and precious little seemed to be interchangeable at all between their two engines.

Internal dimensions of the 312B series flat-12s certainly varied enormously, as did the precise design of their castings and internals, and layout of their ancillaries. Only overall configuration and external dimensions, within an inch or so, remained constant through their 11 long seasons of competition. Ferrari listed late-series dimensions as 80 mm x 49.6 mm, giving a unit cylinder capacity of 249.31 cc, or 2,999 cc overall. The 1979-80 engine was 650 mm long, 680 mm wide and 300 mm tall and weighed 180 kg (396 lb) with accessories attached.

Back at the start of this long flat-12 programme,

Heart of the matter — *Ingegnere* Mauro Forghieri's Ferrari 312B flat-12 racing engine was originally developed in this peerlessly shallow configuration to fit within the smooth wing line of a Franklin aeroplane project. Slung beneath the high-level rear boom of a 1970-71 Formula 1 Ferrari chassis it proved remarkably effective as a Cosworth-Ford V8-eater . . .

16 August, 1970 — Austrian GP, Österreichring — Ferrari performing in force as Jacky Ickx in chassis '001' tears round the picturesque and high-speed Styrian circuit towards victory, with team-mate Clay Regazzoni's sister car— chassis '003' — following in his wheel tracks. These Forghieri-masterminded Ferraris were for many years the most exquisitely packaged cars ever produced at Maranello.

as the prototype car and engines approached completion into the autumn of 1969, Ferrari's V12 cars' fortunes slumped from bad to even worse. Eventually Mr Ferrari ordered that they miss the German GP altogether to prepare the new 312B for a début in the Italian GP at Monza. But the new engine failed repeatedly in testing, and this continuing sequence of mechanical mayhem was the final straw for Chris Amon, who left in disgust. Pedro Rodriguez drove for the remainder of the season, sixth at Monza, then driving V12 car '017 within its capabilities in Canada, the US and Mexico, finishing latterly fifth and seventh. Ferrari had made only thirteen F1 starts, and achieved just six finishes that season of 1969, so in effect they could only improve. . .

When the new 312B made its delayed début in 1970 it looked simply sensational. Its round-oval *Aero* style chassis suspending the engine beneath a rearward-projecting beam was by far the neatest, most attractive and best-integrated pack-

16 August, 1970 — Austrian GP, Österreichring — Superstars both — Jacky Ickx and the Ferrari 312B chassis '001' howling around the Österreichring's hills *en route* to victory.

18 April 1971 — Spanish GP, Montjuich Park, Barcelona — Clay Regazzoni was destined to retire this Ferrari 312B —chassis '004' — with fuel pump failure, but his team-mate Jacky Ickx finished second in the wake of Jackie Stewart's new Tyrrell; a podgy ugly duckling of a car in contrast to the wonderfully well-integrated lines of these Italian flat 12s.

age yet created under 3-litre F1 rules. Even today it remains a monument to surpassing elegance and taste of design. It remained arguably the best packaged of all Ferraris until the Postlethwaite 156 turbos appeared in 1985.

Five 312Bs were built that first season; including two chassis serial '002', the original being destroyed by fire in a first-lap collision upon its début, in the Spanish GP at Jarama, then being replaced by a completely new car taking the same serial number.

Ickx returned from a year with Brabham as number one driver, and 312B development may be judged by its results; achieving its first finishes in its fourth race – fourth and eighth in the Belgian GP – then able to qualify on the front row and set fastest lap in its fifth race, in Holland, able to take pole position for its sixth race, in France, then qualifying on pole for four of their next seven races while placing on the front row in *all* seven.

The cars set fastest lap in six races, including five of the season's last six, and from a total twenty-five 1970 starts they achieved seventeen finishes, won four of the last five races of the season and were first and second in three of them, actually 1-2-7 with their three-car entry in Austria

driven by Jacky Ickx, Clay Regazzoni and Ignazio Giunti. This rocked the Cosworth brigade to their very foundations, but the new cars had come on song just too late that season to win the World Championship titles. Ickx, who won the Austrian, Canadian and Mexican GPs in '001' had a chance of the Drivers' title until a fuel pipe broke at Watkins Glen, where Rindt's posthumous crown in the Lotuses was assured. Regazzoni won the Italian GP in '004'.

The Ferrari 312B – or retrospectively the so-called 'B1' – cars which were built were as follows:

Chassis '001' – Race début 7-3-70 – Ickx '70 South African, Monaco and Dutch GPs, *1st* Austrian and Canadian GPs, also United States and Mexican GPs – Ickx '71 South African and Questor (Ontario, California) GPs. Car retired from service, preserved for many years in Ickx's private collection.

Chassis '002' – Race début 19-4-70 – Ickx '70 Spanish GP. Car destroyed in fire after collision on opening lap.

Replacement chassis '002' – Race début 7-6-70 – Giunti '70 Belgian, French, Austrian and Italian GPs, Regazzoni British GP – Andretti *1st* '71

18 April, 1971 — Spanish GP, Montjuich Park, Barcelona — Jacky Ickx drove 312B '003' home into second place, beaten yet again by Jackie Stewart by this time in a Tyrrell-built Cosworth car. Here in 1971 trim the Ferrari shows off the latest generation of ultra-low profile Firestone racing tyres intended to maximise sidewall rigidity between tread and wheel rim. Note the neat wing forms, low-level exhausts and shaped oil cooler ducts above the gearbox at rear. The author found this car 'drove like a Rolls-Royce' in later years at the Donington Collection.

South African and Questor GPs, Andretti Spanish GP. Sold to Schlumpf brothers, now *Musée National de l'Automobile,* Mulhouse, France.

Chassis '003' – Début (as Monaco GP T-car) 8-5-70 – Ickx '70 Belgian, French, British and German GPs, Regazzoni Austrian GP – Ickx '71 Spanish GP, Ickx *1st* Rindt Memorial (Hockenheim), Andretti Dutch GP. Sold to Tom Wheatcroft for his Donington Collection, Derby, England.

Chassis '004' – Race début 6-9-70, last 312B (or pure 'B1') to be built – Regazzoni *1st* '70 Italian GP, Regazzoni Canadian, United States and Mexican GPs – Regazzoni '71 South African and Spanish GPs, Rindt Memorial (Hockenheim), Ickx '71 Italian and United States GPs. Sold to Luigi Chinetti, North American importer.

For 1971, three revised new 312B2 models were built, serialled '005-6-7', while existing 'B1s' '001-2-3-4' would appear in 1970 form before at least one was modified to 'B2 trim, if we believe the chassis numbering. But since such a conversion if achieved in totality would entail one of the new squarer-section 'B2 monocoques, to replace the round-oval near cylindrical section of the original 312B tub, we can take the numbers with a pinch of salt – perhaps there was a little 'never mind the history, let's make the customs carnets fit . . .'? However, the cars did in any case have to be re-skinned where necessary in 16-gauge aluminium to meet new fuel tank sheathing requirements.

The definitive 'B2 tub had a reduced frontal area and adopted a more wedge-shaped flat-topped, vertical-sided form. The inboard front suspension of 1970 was retained, but at the rear Forghieri mounted the coil/dampers above the gearbox, actuated by bell-crank extensions of the upper suspension links. Engine modifications were made to improve combustion.

Ickx, Regazzoni and Andretti drove, and Ferrari won consecutively the first three races of the new season; Andretti the South African and non-Championship Questor GPs (at Ontario Motor Speedway, California) in '002' and Regazzoni at Brands Hatch in the new 312B2 '005'. Later, Ickx won a minor Hockenheim race in '003', but the new 'B2's only win other than at Brands Hatch would be Ickx's masterly wet-race performance in the Dutch GP. Overall, the flat-12 Ferraris made 31 starts in 1971, finishing 16 times and notching five wins but only two at Championship level, one each for 'B1' and 'B2', while their three non-Championship wins split two each; 'B1 and 'B2.

Yet in that first half-season of '71 the Ferraris had won five of the seven races held, qualifying on the front row every time, on pole three times and setting four fastest race laps. In the second half they then made 17 starts in seven races, and finished only five times, though placing 3-4 in the German GP. They were four times on the front row, took one pole position, at Silverstone, but set only one fastest lap, driven by Ickx in the US GP.

So a season which had started so well simply fell apart in ill-handling and unreliability. Had Ferrari's success run been concentrated in one calendar season, instead of being split across the back-end of 1970 and early part of '71, the cars would have made history indeed . . .

The Lotus-Cosworth Type 72s

★ ★ ★ ★ ⭒

During the Lotus 49's three seasons of front-line service, 1967-69, Colin Chapman became increasingly irritated by this essentially simple design's inevitable deficiencies. In particular, Graham Hill's habit of covering countless practice miles trying to find what he considered proper bump-stop suspension settings drove Colin 'round the twist'! He once told me, between laughter at the memories, 'My big dream for a car for Graham was one with rising-rate suspension so he could never get on a bump stop! Then he couldn't play around with it, and that alone would have made my season ...'

In the autumn of 1969, as soon as the four-wheel drive Type 63 cars proved that approach a complete blind alley, Colin and Maurice Phillippe argued out a new concept and drew-up a specification. While the 49 had been merely 'a bracket' to unite the first Cosworth DFV engines with wheels, fuel and driver, what became the new Type 72 concept developed around two major factors – integration with a new Firestone racing tyre development, and optimizing aerodynamic form to generate maximum possible download under the CSI's new wing restrictions.

In order to race with tyres of such soft compound that they had formerly only been usable as 'qualifiers', minimum unsprung weight, and the isolation of brake heat from the hub/wheel/tyre

---

April 1970 — Hethel Aerodrome, near Wymondham, Norfolk — Jochen Rindt demonstrating the Lotus 72 prototype before the press upon its public unveiling at Group Lotus's factory. It looked sensational, its wedge-form, hip radiators, all-inboard brakes and triplane rear wing apparently far in advance of any other Formula 1 car yet seen. However, its original concept would soon prove flawed ...

assemblies, became vital. Minimum overall weight and smooth, pitch-free ride characteristics were also sought. Chapman and Phillippe decided to use rising-rate suspension to provide very soft springing without the constant-rate lack of control which allowed dangerous bottoming under full tanks. Torsion bar springs were chosen as the neatest progressive-rate system, while 'compound' torsion bars – an inner solid bar splined into one end of an outer sleeve to halve overall length – placed the least demand on space.

Indianapolis experience with the 1968 Type 56 turbine cars had shown their wedge-shaped aerodyamic profile to be very effective in generating negative lift or 'download'. To employ that shape on the 72, the nose radiator was replaced by a radiator on each hip amidships. This removed one heat source which had roasted drivers so often in the 49s, and siting the oil tank in the tail further minimized cockpit temperatures, and added rearward weight bias. This extended the rear-tyre loading philosophy already explored in the 49B.

Mounting the disc brakes inboard, front and rear, slashed unsprung weight and isolated a major source of heat from the wheels where experience had shown how much it could distress an already hard-worked racing tyre. The new monocoque chassis was wedge-shaped in profile, and much was made of its external flush-rivetting – aerospace style – to minimize aerodynamic sur-

Tony Matthews' cutaway view of Emerson Fittipaldi's 1971 Lotus 72.

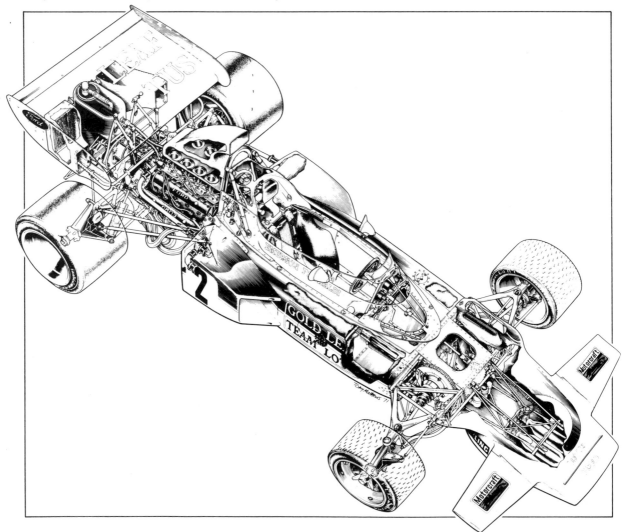

face drag. The shape's aerodyamic download was to be enhanced and trimmed by a new-design three-tier tail wing and large nose 'planes.

Neat little linkages with rising-rate geometry operated the torsion bars front and rear, and the front wishbones' forward pick-ups were lower than their rearward ones to provide anti-dive. At the rear the forward pick-ups were higher than the rearward ones to give pronounced anti-squat, preventing the car burying its tail under power. In this way Chapman and Phillippe planned to promote a level ride, and thereby achieve more constant aerodynamic performance.

At the rear the DFV engine was attached by four bolts, and suspension loads were carried on sandwich plates assembled into the Hewland FG transaxle casing. The wing package was another new development, using a three-tier rear 'foil which enabled the entire assembly to run at a greater combined incidence angle than was feasible with a one-piece wing, which would have stalled. But when introduced, the new cars suffered terrible teething troubles, mainly with the brakes and handling. The cars seemed to roll excessively and lift their inside rear wheels in cornering, but wet practice for the minor Silverstone race saw them finding adhesion where essentially there was none, something which would remain characteristic of the 72s throughout their long front-line life.

After another poor showing in the Silverstone race, Chapman headed a major rethink. Only '72/1' was taken to Monaco, as spare car, but astonishingly Rindt won in his elderly 49C.

Meanwhile, both the anti-dive and anti-squat angularity was being removed from Jochen's '72/2', which involved totally remaking and reskinning the tub, and chassis '1' was to lose its anti-squat, which merely entailed changing the rear suspension frames bolted to the engine. This car was entrusted to Rindt's new team-mate John Miles, who was still finding his feet in Formula 1. A new parallel suspension, '72/3', finally became available for him in August, for the German GP at Hockenheim. His old prototype '72/1' was then reduced and rebuilt as new with parallel suspension to become the late-delivered replacement for Rob Walker's wonderful old warhorse Lotus 49C 'R7', driven by Graham Hill. The rebuilt blue-liveried 72 took the serial '72/4' but its active life was to be brief.

The 72 had come of age after these extensive

modifications. In his parallel-suspension '72/2', Rindt won the Dutch GP on merit and the French GP with luck. At the British GP at Brands Hatch the car introduced the engine air-box to modern Formula 1, gulping air into its injection trumpets from ducts situated either side of the roll-over bar. This at least would set new trends. Again Rindt scored a lucky win. At Hockenheim his Lotus could match Ickx's speed in the ever-improving flat-12 Ferrari and again won on merit, by 0.7 sec.

In Austria, Rindt then lost fourth place after a spin when his car's engine tightened, while Miles brought his car to a safe halt after a front brake-shaft snapped. For the next race, the minor Gold Cup at Oulton Park, stop-gap solid brake shafts were fitted to Rindt's '72/2'. The dark-blue Walker '72/4' made a muted début with Graham Hill installed. Rindt won the second heat there, then came the Italian GP at Monza. . .

Rindt and Miles drove their usual cars while new team member Emerson Fittipaldi had a new works car '72/5'. On the Saturday morning, Rindt took out '72/2' running experimentally without wings, with standard brake ratios and on unscrubbed new tyres. Under braking from maximum speed into the right-handed *Curva Parabolica*, the car's right-front brake shaft probably snapped, and the reaction of having the left-front wheel fully-braked and the right-front completely free dragged Rindt crashing into the left-side Armco barrier which parted, enabling the car to demolish itself against a hefty stanchion. Rindt was killed. Miles left the team.

At Watkins Glen, new Team Lotus drivers Fittipaldi and Reine Wisell finished 1-3 to clinch the posthumous Drivers' title for Rindt and confirm Team Lotus's fourth Formula 1 Constructors' Championship.

For 1971, many changes were then made to the cars, including a new lubrication system. Firestone were to introduce a new low-profile tyre to find more consistent contact patch control, and this involved suspension modifications to accommodate the new lower wheel/tyre centre-lines. For the Good Friday Oulton Park meeting '72/5' used a new one-piece rear wing and an in-line oil tank replaced the old saddle type to clean-up the car's unruly slipstream.

For the chassis number pedant, the Lotus 72 progression had been first to '72B' with the

2 July, 1972 — French GP, Charade circuit, Clermont-Ferrand — The young Brazilian driver Emerson Fittipaldi on his way to second place in the now so-called 'black-and-gold' liveried John Player Special Lotus 72, '72/7'. The 'gold' was actually a flat almost beige shade which merely looked gold on film and TV.

removal of anti-squat, then '72C' with the removal of anti-dive and consequent restructuring of the tub. At Monaco '71, the '72D-spec' emerged in Fittipaldi's regular '72/5' with rear suspension geometry revised to match the new low-profile Firestone tyres more efficiently. This new system introduced twin radius rods each side with parallel lower links, replacing single radius rods and reversed lower wishbones. These changes helped tame a violent transition from understeer to oversteer, troublesome earlier that season.

At Silverstone for the British GP, the original lop-eared style airbox was replaced by a tall single-scoop design. Maurice Phillippe left Lotus that autumn, and prior to the US GP the 72s were further modified to delete their rising-rate rear suspension geometry; no longer advantageous since it seemed to exacerbate chronic vibration problems with the new low profile tyres.

But 1971 was Team Lotus's worst F1 season since 1959, as they failed to win a single race. They had been handicapped by the impact upon morale of Rindt's death, but more so by the relative inexperience of their two new drivers. Additionally, Fittipaldi had hurt himself in a mid-season road accident perhaps more than he cared to admit, and he seemed to have lost momentum.

New 1972 regulations then demanded fuel tank protection in 16-gauge sheet, so existing active 72s were reskinned. A new sponsorship policy also introduced the black and gold 'John Player Special' livery in place of the garish old red, gold and white Gold Leaf design. Fittipaldi was now fully fit. He proved his real worth as his 72s won the Spanish, Belgian, British, Austrian and Italian GPs, plus minor F1 events at Brands Hatch, Silverstone and Vallelunga and a one-off 312-mile *Libre* race at Brands Hatch. Team secured their fifth Formula 1 Constructors' Championship title on the strength of Emerson's successes.

For 1973, Ronnie Peterson joined Emerson in further developed Type 72s. Firestone's top management had dithered about whether or not to stay in racing, so Lotus changed to Goodyear, which meant considerable suspension retuning to match the different tyres. Regardless, Fittipaldi still won the first two GPs of the season untroubled in South America. In Brazilian GP practice, the elderly cars were more than a second faster than the opposition, an advantage so great they were faster even on full tanks, demonstrating an awesome combination of chassis, tyre and driver power.

New deformable structure tank protection regulations were to take effect from the European season-opening Spanish GP. Martin Waide drew the 72s' conversion, the ageing tubs being unstitched and rejigged, reappearing for the Race of Champions with double-skinned crush pads formed into integral radiator pods which replaced the earlier separate mouldings. A series of alternative airboxes and extended wing-mounts appeared, while Peterson's cars were progressively reinforced to withstand his awesome driving style. He set the performance standards of the season but lost several races through car failure until in July at the French GP he finished and won at last.

There was inevitable rivalry between Peterson and Fittipaldi, but the reigning Champion's cause suffered at Zandvoort when a wheel collapsed during practice, effectively destroyed his faithful '72/5'. A virtually new car slowly had to be built up to replace it.

The 72s' fiercest opposition came from the new ultra short-wheelbase Tyrrells and the hip-radiatored McLaren M23s. Both these designs had more even weight distribution than the rear-biased Lotuses, to place greater load on their front tyres, also produced by Goodyear.

Although Lotus won the lion's share of the races to clinch their sixth Constructors' Championship title, and their second in consecutive seasons, their successes were split between Peterson and Fittipaldi, which allowed Jackie Stewart to steal the Drivers' Championship in his Tyrrell.

Into 1974 an intended Lotus 72 replacement – the Type 76 – was on its way. Fittipaldi had left for McLaren, and Peterson was joined in Team Lotus by Jacky Ickx who won the minor Brands Hatch race in pouring rain against the odds. But the new Type 76 cars then failed dismally, and so the faithful if now positively geriatric 72s raced on.

Ronnie Peterson's amazing skills reaped victories at Monaco, Dijon and Monza, and three more different circuits it's hard to imagine. So effective did his '72/8' prove that a final all-new Type 72 was built, chassis '72/9'. But its completion was delayed as parts were cannibalized to repair '72/8' after a heavy accident during practice

1 July, 1973 — French GP, Ricard-Castellet — Ronnie Peterson on the way to his maiden *Grande Epreuve* victory in Lotus '72/6', here showing off its impeccable cuneiform lines, hip radiators, the far outrigged rear wing still legal at that time, almost Baroque-styled engine airbox and its subsequently controversial Melmag disc wheels.

7 July 1974 — For the French GP on the tight little Dijon-Prenois circuit, the brilliant Swedish driver Ronnie Peterson proved unbeatable in what should by that time have been his obsolescent Lotus 72 — chassis '8'. Here he is, leaning hard — as always — upon those outside wheels, and showing Mike Hailwood a thing or to in McLaren 'M23/1' behind . . .

at the Nürburgring.

Ending that season at Watkins Glen, the 72s ran into a massive understeer problem on the latest generation of Goodyear tyres, which were better tailored to the front-end demands of Ferrari, McLaren and Tyrrell.

Lotus's 1975 season was catastrophically bad for several reasons. Group Lotus was in trouble, and Chapman's personal attention was often distracted. Money was short, insufficient to invest in serious development of that long-overdue replacement car. Of more vital and obvious effect, Goodyear's tyre development now catered for the needs of Ferrari and McLaren, and tyres matching the eccentric demands of the Lotus 72 were unavailable. The so-called 'lightweight' '72/9' was still not ready for Ronnie's use as the season began. Things went from bad to worse, and the 72s raced their last at the end of that year.

These cars came to have charisma, and enormous success by F1 standards, plus an almost unbelievably long life at the top, but to me they still seem to fall just short of that elusive top drawer which contains the all-time great Grand Prix cars.

In the final reckoning, the Lotus 72s competed in a staggering 96 F1-inclusive races between 1970 and 1975, of which they won 25, including 20 Championship GPs. Until 1986 their victory record made them the most successful Grand Prix cars of all time, but the McLaren-TAG Turbo MP4/2 family eventually overtook them with 22 wins from 48 races, 1984-86.

The Lotus 72s' 20 Championship-status victories were spread over five seasons from a total of 76 GPs contested, whereas the preceding Lotus 49s' 12 GP victories were accumulated from only 41 GPs in just three-and-a-bit seasons. Similarly, the Lotus 25s' 14 GP victories came from only 34 contested in four seasons. So whereas the Lotus 25s won 41 per cent of their Grand Prix races, the Lotus 49s won only 29 per cent and the 72s just 26 per cent. At the risk of upsetting those readers whose interest stops short of 1980s cars I will emphasize the McLaren-TAG Turbo MP4/2 family's great success rate – no less than 48 per cent . . .

You see? By such standards, the Lotus 72 clearly rates less than top-drawer status, despite being so indisputably high-rated. Neither was it a neat design; it was cluttered, rather fussy, Team Lotus's mechanics recall it as 'a swine to work on', so perhaps it was over-complicated. But here we are applying the most merciless criteria – the Lotus 72s were truly classic racing cars by any normal standard.

1970-73
The Tyrrell-Cosworths, 001-006/3

★ ★ ★

In 1970 a new Formula 1 regulation took effect which made rubberized bag-type fuel tanks mandatory. This was bad news for the reigning World Champion team, Ken Tyrrell's Equipe Matra International, for their 1969 Matra-Cosworth MS80 driven by Jackie Stewart had carried its fuel direct in a closely subdivided monocoque chassis, which could not be converted to house bag tanks.

So Tyrrell needed new chassis for 1970. Matra had been taken over by Chrysler (whose French satellite was Simca) which precluded any further association with the Cosworth-Ford DFV engine. But Tyrrell and Stewart preferred it to the alternative V12 unit Matra-Simca were now offering. Matra refused to sell special chassis to the British team, so Tyrrell looked elsewhere. Short-term he ordered three new March 701s, but clearly the only way ahead was to build his own cars, and that required a designer to match Stewart's proven class.

Derek Gardner was the man. Formerly with Ferguson, he had looked after the four-wheel drive system used in Tyrrell's experimental Matra MS84 car the previous year. He was a deep thinker, very capable and well-qualified. Perhaps just as important, he was not widely-known in the racing world. He could keep his mouth shut. Nothing should be allowed to compromise the working relationship between Team Tyrrell and March Engineering. Tyrrell commissioned Gardner to create a simple car, requiring minimal development to achieve competitiveness. The mechanism of racing sponsorship demanded that it be ready for the Oulton Park Gold Cup on 22

August. Any later '. . . and you might as well chuck it in the Thames . . .'

Derek started work on what would be his first ground-up car design in February 1970, working in a converted bedroom at his home in Parklands Avenue, Leamington Spa, Warwickshire. He analysed all contemporary designs and decided upon an all-round aerodynamic form, minimum legal weight, and a central low polar moment mass concentration to promote the most favourable front:rear weight distribution. He commissioned construction secretly, ordering castings and having the first monocoque tub built by Mo Gomm's specialist sheet-metal 'shop in Old Woking, Surrey, not far from Tyrrell's Ockham base.

The new monocoque was an open-topped 'bath-tub' type, matching the Matra MS80's coke-bottle shape to house four bag tanks around the centre of gravity well within the wheelbase. It was formed over fabricated steel bulkheads, with 18-gauge NS4 malleable aluminium alloy skins. Suspension and outboard brakes were 'sophisticated conventional' and the DFV engine drove via a Hewland FG400 transaxle. After tenth-scale model tests in the University of Surrey wind tunnel at Guildford, Derek devised an unusual nose cowl with a wide blade-like 'foil above an underslung 'shark's-mouth' radiator intake.

The car was around 100 lb (45.5 kg) lighter than the team's March 701s, just 32 lb (14.5 kg) over the minimum weight limit. It cost Ken Tyrrell £22,500, less engine and gearbox, compared to the purchase price of £9,000 each for the 701s. Now it had to prove its worth.

4 October, 1970 — United States GP, Watkins Glen — Jackie Stewart trailing in to retire the prototype Tyrrell '001' after a scintillating display, leading at record pace until a plastic oil pipe had come unclipped, flopped down against a hot exhaust manifold, melted and pumped away the engine's lifeblood. Note the blade-foil sharkmouth nose treatment, well-inboard flapped rear wing, bulbous fuel-filled monocoque centre-section and *genuine* roll-over protection.

It had an unreliable début at Oulton Park but Stewart broke the lap record twice before engine failure. He then elected to drive it in the last three GPs of the year, in Canada, the USA and Mexico. Tyrrell '001' promptly started in pole position in Canada and on the front row at Watkins Glen and Mexico City. Stewart led both the Canadian and US GPs, and ran second in Mexico. Gardner had done his job well.

For 1971, Elf-Team Tyrrell was formed, backed by ELF fuel and Goodyear tyres. They tested interminably pre-season at Kyalami, South Africa. Stewart ran one engine there for 986 miles (1,643 km)! With a new engine '001' then passed 1,400 miles (2,333 km) before a pebble jammed between the throttle pedal and its bracket, and Stewart crashed. The car's left-front corner was crushed back some 4-5 in (10-12 cm), so it was rushed home and hastily repaired.

A second car '002', the first entirely Tyrrell-built Tyrrell, was almost finished, its body lengthened 4 in (10 cm) to accommodate tall number two driver François Cevert.

Back at Kyalami for the South African GP, Cevert mangled both ends of the new car while

Stewart qualified '001' on pole, but was handicapped by indifferent tyre and engine performance during the race and finished a poor second. Three minor races followed with Stewart's '001' the lone Tyrrell entry, beaten each time. The team was just beginning to wonder how good their car was, when Stewart's uprated new '003' was introduced at the Spanish GP in Barcelona.

With luck, Stewart won, and then asserted massive dominance, adding victory in the Monaco, French, British, German and Canadian GPs by season's end, while Cevert won the US GP in his regular '002' and finished second behind Stewart in France and Germany, and third in Italy. Stewart thus simply walked away with the Drivers' Championship, and Tyrrell easily won the Constructors' Cup competition at their first attempt.

After the Spanish win, a new wedge-shaped nose cowl resembling the contemporary Matra MS120's was tested. It cancelled more lift than the blade nose, with less drag, but required more than the existing rear wing to balance its effect. Gardner returned to the University of Surrey for further wind tunnel model research.

Stewart damaged '003' badly at the minor Silverstone meeting prior to Monaco. It was hastily repaired and the Matra-like nose was tried in Monaco practice before Stewart raced with the blade-type, starting from pole fully 1.2 sec faster than his closest challenger. Despite running with virtually no rear braking, he led throughout to win brilliantly and set fastest lap.

For the Dutch GP at Zandvoort both Tyrrells used squat ram air-boxes scooping into the induction trumpets. The Lotus 72s had been using small intakes to feed clean air since the previous year's British GP, and Matra used a rough snorkel-type airstream guide, not properly sealed. Now Gardner's properly sealed airboxes really confirmed an F1 fashion. They worked well if kept clear of hot-air issuing from the radiator ducts.

Also new in Holland, although only shown on '003' in scrutineering, was a bluff nose cone, reminiscent of that on a Porsche 908/3 sports racing car. It extended to the legal maximum width ahead of the front wheels, faring airflow over them, killing the tendency to induce

aerodynamic lift which they, as effectively rotating cylinders interposed in a moving airstream, inevitably generated. Interrupting this phenomenon reduced that lift together with its inevitable companion, drag. It yielded immense dividends.

The bluff nose made its racing début in the French GP at Ricard-Castellet where Stewart and Cevert finished imperiously first and second. At Silverstone for the British GP, both Tyrrells wore bluff noses and Stewart's win was so convincing that '003's' engine was sealed and its capacity checked. The spare car, '001' received a bluff nose in time for the German GP, another Tyrrell 1-2. They then won both North American races. A third long-wheelbase car '004' was completed right at the end of the season as a spare for Stewart.

Early in 1972, Team Tyrrell used their familiar '003' and '002' cars. Stewart blooded the spare '004' at Monaco, but immediately after the Belgian GP at Nivelles the prototype 'series two' Tyrrell, a square-cut and stumpy ultra-short wheelbase chassis, '005', was completed.

Gardner explained how he '. . . wanted to build

The 1971 Tyrrell-Cosworth 003 by Tony Matthews.

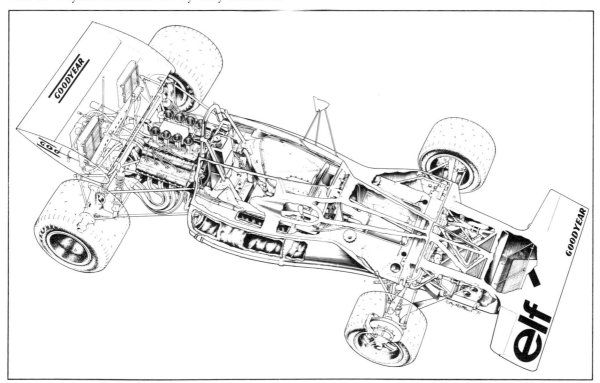

May Day, 1972 — Spanish GP, Jarama — Jackie Stewart lining up his 1971 World Championship-dominating Tyrrell '003' for a right-hander, but in this case heading towards retirement. This unusual angle demonstrates the famous and highly successful car's fuel-bloated 'Coke-bottle' centre section.

14 July, 1973 — British GP, Silverstone — Yes, well, nobody's perfect. Jackie Stewart spinning away his chances at Stowe Corner in the new deformable-structure regulation Tyrrell '006/2'. Derek Gardner's extremely low monocoque chassis relied largely upon the detachable moulded cockpit surround to fare-in the driver. Note the 'Trident' airliner airbox, blade-like nose with oil-cooler intake, front deck-top chimneys to cool inboard front brakes, hip water radiators — carrying the race number '5' — and far outrigged rear wing.

16 June 1973 — practice for the Swedish GP, Anderstorp — Jackie Stewart cornering hard in the historic Tyrrell-Cosworth 006/2 in which he ended his glittering career as three-times World Champion Driver and winner of a record 27 Championship-qualifying Grand Prix races.

a small car, a light, manoeuvrable, well-handling car. The type of car Jackie could make the most of . . .'.

It was as wide as its predecessors, but lower and shorter, aiming at a much lower polar moment of inertia, and with all inboard brakes to reduce unsprung weight. Cevert bent the new car in practice at Clermont-Ferrand, after setting fastest time. Stewart was quick in it in practice at Brands Hatch before another minor shunt. It was not raced. There Cevert's '002' was severely damaged, but was repaired for the Nürburgring, only to be

crashed again. In Austria '005' reappeared with outboard front brakes and a tall airbox resembling a Trident airliner's centre engine pod. Stewart raced it and led.

For the North American races another 'series two' car, '006' was completed for Cevert. Before the era of that historic first-series of Tyrrell F1 cars had passed Stewart won both races in Canada and the USA, and Cevert completed a fine Tyrrell 1-2 at Watkins Glen.

Through 1973 Stewart would go on to win the South African GP in '006' and then took over a

14 July 1973 — British GP, Silverstone — François Cevert in his sister third-generation deformable-pad Tyrrell '006'. He finished fifth. This car was written off on 23 September in the unfortunate Frenchman's collision with Scheckter during the Canadian GP at Mosport Park.

new deformable structure-chassised 'series three' Tyrrell '006/2' – back on all-inboard brakes as standard – in which he would win at Silverstone in its minor-race début, then the Belgian and Monaco GPs to equal Jim Clark's best-career record of 25 *Grande Epreuve* victories. He raised that record to 26 in the Dutch GP, and finally to 27 in the German race at the Nürburgring. Cevert was second to the Scot in Belgium, Holland and Germany, but Team Lotus accumulated more Constructors' Championship points with both their drivers, Fittipaldi and Peterson winning races. Even so, Stewart clinched his third and final Drivers' Championship title, but Cevert's regular

car '006' was written-off in a Canadian GP collision and then he was killed during practice at Watkins Glen in a hastily completed replacement car, '006/3', which was utterly destroyed.

After that accident, towards the end of the afternoon practice session, Stewart and guest Tyrrell driver Chris Amon lapped briefly in their cars, and then Ken Tyrrell cancelled their entries for the US GP and the team began the sad journey home. Stewart was now retired, one of the very best racing drivers the world had ever seen; and the era of Tyrrell's greatness departed with him, and with the tragic death of his great French team-mate. . .

The Ferrari Tipo 312Ts

★ ★ ★ ★

Through the 1974 season Ferrari re-established itself as a serious force in Formula 1 following two indifferent Grand Prix seasons. Their time and money-consuming sports-racing car programme had for the first time been abandoned, and Maranello's racing department concentrated its efforts totally upon Formula 1.

During 1974 their model 312B3 flat-12 had been developed into a very successful design which failed only narrowly to win Ferrari's first Constructors' Championship title for 12 years. This failure was caused partly by the relative inexperience of number one driver Niki Lauda, until the team failed him in the crucial deciding races at the end of the year.

Lauda's team-mate was the hugely experienced and capable – if not quite so quick – Clay Regazzoni. Ferrari's concentration upon F1 and the completion of their own private Fiorano test track, just across the main Formigine Road from the Maranello factory, enabled them to test interminably, and Lauda was always available. Under the direction of chief engineer Mauro Forghieri, they could literally throw everything at it in their extensive tyre testing for Goodyear.

For the following three years, 1975 to 1977, Ferrari really were on top of their game. They still had their failures, and their inevitable internal politics, but without that they would not have been Ferrari. As it was, they became the first F1 team in history to put together a hat-trick of consecutive Constructors' Championship titles.

At the end of their promising 1974 season, the racing department had taken stock. Major failures at Österreichring and Monza had damaged their cause. The 312B3-74 chassis had survived without major modification other than detail aerodynamic changes, but *Ing* Forghieri felt that the basic concept still offered as yet untapped potential. It was actually on 27 September 1975, before the team left home for the Championship-deciding US GP at Watkins Glen, that the new year's prototype 312T model was unveiled to the press at Fiorano.

Forghieri followed the path trodden previously by Derek Gardner of Tyrrell and Robin Herd of March in 1972, seeking to concentrate mass within the wheelbase to minimize polar moment of inertia and so produce a highly manoeuvrable, nimble car. To the average F1 driver it might be too nervous, but to a Ronnie Peterson, Jackie Stewart or in this case Niki Lauda it could be formidably quick.

Whereas the preceding 312B3's front suspension coil-spring/dampers had nestled each side of the foot box, and a spidery forward tube subframe picked-up the leading elements of the lower wishbones, now the redesigned 312T tub carried all its major front suspension components on the forward face of its monocoque's front bulkhead.

The design used rising-rate coil springs. The front of the tub was considerably narrower than 'B3's. Disc brakes were outboard at the front, inboard on the cheeks of the new lateral (or *trasversale*, hence '312T') gearbox at the rear.

The tub itself used Ferrari's familiar hybrid construction in which the stressed-skin monocoque structure was reinforced internally with steel strip and angle framing. Water radiators were just

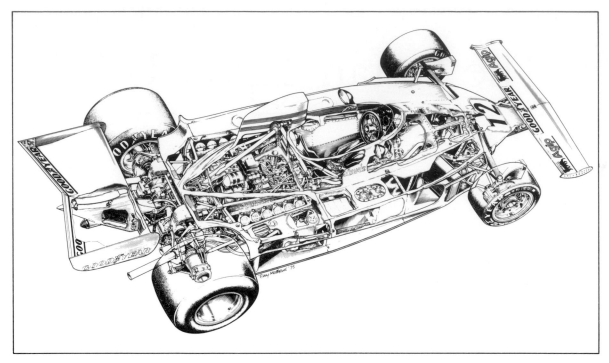

Tony Matthews' superb drawing of a 1975 Ferrari 312T.

25 May, 1975 — Belgian GP, Zolder — Clay Regazzoni's Ferrari 312T '022' locked in combat with Ronnie Peterson's now obsolescent Lotus 72 'R9'. Formula 1 by this time was all about good tyre-to-road contact, good aerodynamic download performance, and good horsepower assisted by the most imposing airboxes in the business . . . Ferrari scored high in all departments.

8 June 1975 — Swedish GP, Anderstorp — Niki Lauda could only qualify his Ferrari 312T '023' on the third row of the starting grid, but he won the race convincingly in this his first World Championship-winning season.

behind the front wheels, oil coolers just ahead of the rears, all fed by skilfully formed ducting within the moulded body panels. Compared to the 'B3s, the wheelbase was longer, at 2,518 mm (99.1 in) and the track narrower, front and rear.

Obviously the most significant technical innovation was the lateral gearbox, which mounted on the rear of the flat-12 engine but with most of its mass now ahead of the axle line, within the wheelbase, adding to that central mass concentration. The gearbox input was turned through 90° by bevel gears to enable the gearbox shafts to be arranged laterally, final drive being by spur gears. Franco Rocchi's engine development team, meanwhile, had worked hard on the 3 litre flat-12 engine, and in its latest form they claimed 500 bhp at 12,200 rpm. In Fiorano testing, Lauda instantly found the new car more demanding to drive than the 'B3, but its ultimate limits certainly seemed higher, and with practice he was able to drive closer to those limits for longer than hitherto. He was maturing too. Soon he was soon breaking all 'B3 records in testing at Fiorano, Vallelunga and Ricard-Castellet.

When the team returned from racing the old 'B3s in South America at the start of the 1975 season, two new 312Ts were prepared for the South African GP at Kyalami in March, Lauda taking the prototype car '018' and Regazzoni '021'. The intervening two chassis numbers '019' and '020' were – according to Ferrari – allocated to the last two 'B3 models, neither of which was raced, '019' being heavily damaged in a testing accident and being broken-up while '020' just became a potential display chassis before collector sale. Thus '018' remains rather isolated as the 312T prototype, with '021' commencing the transverse-gearbox flat-12 series proper. The series would extend to include the further types 'T2 to 'T5, comprising no fewer than 26 more F1 chassis built in the six seasons 1975-1980.

Lauda opened the 312T's account by winning the minor Silverstone International, and then added victories in the 1975 Monaco, Belgian, Swedish, French and US GPs, while team-mate Regazzoni won the minor 'Swiss GP' at Dijon in France and the major German GP at the Nürburgring, to bring Ferrari their first Constructors' Championship title since 1964 and Lauda his first Drivers' Championship crown.

23 May, 1976 — Monaco GP, Monte Carlo — Starting from pole, leading all the way and winning outright seemed natural to Niki Lauda in Ferrari's second Constructors' Championship season until James Hunt's McLaren M23s came on song and then at Nürburgring Lauda crashed so badly. This is Ferrari 312T2 chassis '026'.

Between them these two drivers made 30 starts that season, including the early 'B3 outings in South America and South Africa – where only Regazzoni raced one of the older cars. They recorded 24 finishes, eight firsts; one second, four thirds, two fourths, three fifths, two sixths, a seventh, eighth and ninth and one lowly thirteenth. Between them, Lauda and Regazzoni took no fewer than nine pole positions and set six fastest laps.

Ferrari had undoubtedly clambered right back on to the top of the Formula 1 pile, and for Mauro Forghieri, as he told me '. . . the 312T design marked the maximum of my entire career in 28 years with Ferrari.' Crucially, these exceptionally potent cars had also been immensely reliable, in the finest Ferrari traditions so vital to promotion of their high-performance production road cars. Lauda only failed to finish one race – the Spanish GP at Barcelona, in which he and his team-mate managed to ram each other on the opening lap.

Ferrari's first *trasversale* season had been very much the more competitive 1970s equivalent of Mercedes-Benz domination in the 1950s. Initially, however, the new car's début at Kyalami had been indifferent, Lauda crashing '021' during practice when another car's engine blew-up ahead of him and he slithered off on its spilled oil. His engine then lacked power during the race, because its fuel metering unit drive-belt had stripped some teeth and slipped, which restricted output to around 440 bhp, less than the rival Cosworth brigade.

Lauda's Silverstone win then marked the début of the third 312T to be built, chassis '022'. Another new chassis '023' was ready for his use at Monaco and he won in it. Regazzoni crashed '018'

heavily at the chicane, both drivers had already crashed in practice so the mechanics had a hectic time that weekend. Lauda owed them the joy of victory.

For Zolder new exhaust systems were fitted in search of improved low-speed pick-up. Lauda raced the older system and had a manifold split on lap 58, losing 300 rpm for the remaining dozen, but he still won by a margin of 19 seconds. Anderstorp saw a very lucky Ferrari win, Lauda first inheriting second place and then the lead from two ailing Brabhams.

The fifth 312T, '024' made its début at Ricard-Castellet for the French GP but its engine failed on lap 7, sidelining Regazzoni. In contrast Lauda proved utterly uncatchable in '022' and won decisively. Ferrari flopped in the British GP and then at the Nürburgring, Lauda led handsomely until a tyre punctured. The Austrian GP was another rain-stopped farce, then for the Italian GP at Monza, Lauda's '023' was fitted with a standard engine for the race, while Regazzoni used a revised 'high-torque' unit. They started 1-2 on the grid and finished 1-3, Regazzoni deliriously victorious while Lauda, handicapped by a damper problem, fell behind Fittipaldi's second-placed McLaren after holding the lead for 45 of the 52 laps. Even so, this clinched the world titles for Ferrari and Lauda, on Italian soil. The *tifosi* in the stands went mad.

Monza-headed engines were then used for the final race of the season at Watkins Glen.

Eleven days after that event, on 26 October, 1975, Ferrari's new 1977 contender, the 312T2, was unveiled at Fiorano, but its career is another – if slightly less successful – story . . .

1973-76

The McLaren-Cosworth M23s

★ ★ ★ ★

During the summer of 1972 all Formula 1 teams were planning cars with fuel-tank-protecting deformable structure pads as would be mandatory from the Spanish GP, opening the 1973 European season. Team McLaren, based at Colnbrook, west of London, thought more deeply than any other. They decided to build a properly-integrated, tailor-made monocoque to optimize their long-held tenets of strength, practicality, simplicity and quality workmanship.

Engineer Gordon Coppuck had been mainly responsible for McLaren's highly–successful and innovative CanAm and Indianapolis cars since 1968, but when F1 designer Ralph Bellamy decided to return to Brabham at the end of 1971, Gordon assumed charge of Formula 1 as well. He laid out the new 1973 F1 car, drawing deeply upon his experience with the wedge-shaped Indianapolis McLaren M16. McLaren's design had always pivoted around a workshop discussion including team principals, drivers and mechanics in addition to the nominal designer. It worked well for the team for many years.

Gordon's basic M16 shape had followed the Lotus 56 and 72 wedges' lead of 1968-70. This took full advantage of the constant high-speed regime prevailing at Indy. Now, during 1972, Gordon recalled how '. . . we had taken an M16 tub and a Cosworth rear end from the M19, sat them down on the workshop floor, looked at them; thought about them, and weighed them, and all the answers told us the right thing. Do it. So we did, and the M23 came into being . . .'.

The existing M19C F1 car handled well but was slow on the straight, and overweight. Its good handling was attributed to its big wings and rising-rate front end, its poor straightline speed to induced drag from those big wings and high profile drag from the bulbous, heavily-riveted tub. The new M23 was Gordon's first F1 design. Its tub was formed in 16-gauge aluminium sheet, shaped over a massive fabricated steel bulkhead at the front and a capacious tank section at the back. The Cosworth DFV engine and Hewland gearbox bolted on in the conventional manner.

The new tub tapered in planform, and at the front in both section and profile. Unlike the detachable radiator sidepods of the Lotus 72 and the M16 Indy cars, the new M23s were formed as an integral delta-form extension of the monocoque structure, doubling up as two-stage deformable protection under impact. Fuel was concentrated amidships to promote Matra/ Tyrrell/March-like low polar moment. All previous McLaren F1 tubs had contained fuel full-length.

The M23's cockpit was as confined as possible to narrow the tub and ease airflow into the hip radiator ducts, which housed both water radiators and oil coolers. There was rising-rate front suspension, and at the rear some vital unsprung weight was saved by dispensing with conventional sliding spline drive-shaft joints, fixed-length shafts with floating axles plunging through needle roller bearings in the upright instead. At the time of its release in February 1973, the M23 was unusual in being so fully bodied, following Gardner's lead with Tyrrell '005' the preceding summer.

In the next four seasons, 13 McLaren M23s

would be built, chassis number '13' being skipped for superstitious reasons and the final car taking the number 'M23/14' instead. They would bring their drivers two World Championship titles and their manufacturer one Formula 1 Constructors' Cup victory, and they would win no fewer than 16 Championship-qualifying Grands Prix, and arguably 17 if another on-the-road victory is counted from which car and driver were subsequently disqualified. Overall they won 21 Formula 1 races. The series was incredibly long-lived, like the equally-successful Lotus 72, being in front-line use through four full seasons 1973-1976.

In 1973, four M23s were built, followed by four more in 1974, and two in 1975. No new M23s were produced in their second Drivers' Championship season of 1976, but two new works cars and the final private-entry car for American Brett Lunger followed in 1977 before the type was finally replaced by the slow-to-develop M26. Of all these cars, chassis 'M23/4', 'M23/7', 'M23/8' and 'M23/9' were effectively written-off in racing accidents. Only 'M23/7' would not be rebuilt, while number '4 was resurrected as a non-running promotional show car for Marlboro who were the team's sponsors from 1974. Number '8 was rebuilt as another show car, taking the chassis tag number '10, and number '9 was rebuilt as a running museum piece in later years.

Meanwhile, the M23s had developed more or less through B, C, D, E and F-specifications, although the borderlines from one to another were rather foggy, and specs were sometimes reversed as well as further developed. The official McLaren list of alternative M23 specs looks like this:

M23B – 1974 chassis change around the front bulkhead to accept alternative progressive-rate or rocker-arm front suspension – longer wheelbase – parallel-link rear suspension.

M23C – 1975, further revised suspension – different airbox – driver-adjustable front anti-roll bar – short nose and side panel extension aerodynamics.

M23D – 1976, from 1 May, low regulation airbox – short lived, driver–adjustable, rear anti-roll bar – air starter introduced – six-speed McLaren-Hewland gearbox – longer cockpit surround extending onto nose cone to accommodate James Hunt.

M23E – 1977 detail changes headed by redesigned front uprights to cater for new-diameter Goodyear tyres.

M23F – Category for McLaren–made parts intended for private-customer sale.

In the M23's début at Kyalami, 1973, Denny Hulme took his first-ever GP pole position in it, then led the race, but punctured a tyre and finished only fifth. Through the rest of the season the works M23s would qualify regularly within the first three or four on the GP grids. 'M23/2' appeared for Peter Revson in the minor Silverstone race on 8 April, finishing fourth while Hulme retired the prototype. Three M23s were available in time for the first 'deformable structure' GP in Spain on 29 April, and at Zolder on 20 May Hulme's car introduced the Graviner life-support system to Formula 1, supplying the driver with breathable air in event of fire.

Denny won the Swedish GP luckily, though he also set fastest race lap. All three M23s then ran for the first time in the British GP on 14 July, an event notorious for 'Scheckter's shunt'. New recruit Jody Scheckter lost control ending lap one between the pits and main grandstand and spun ahead of the pack, causing a multiple accident which eliminated nine cars and stopped the race. Revson won the restarted race in 'M23/2' while Denny finished third. Scheckter's 'M23/3' was still under repair one week later when the new 'M23/4' emerged as team spare at Zandvoort for the Dutch GP.

The Canadian GP was another shambles due to bad weather, but Revson won again, this time in 'M23/4', while Scheckter collided with Cevert's Tyrrell and mangled 'M23/2's' left-front corner and side pod. In the US GP at Watkins Glen, Hulme and Revson finished 4-5 and Scheckter retired when a rear wishbone broke, fortunately this time without hitting anything hard.

In 1974, the Texaco-Marlboro McLaren team was born, with Hulme being joined by Emerson Fittipaldi. McLaren's previous Yardley cosmetics sponsorship continued into the new year with a one-car operation running an allegedly identical M23 for Mike Hailwood.

During the winter at Colnbrook, two brand-new M23s had been built up, chassis '5 and '6. The rear wing mandatorily had to come forward some 10 in (25 cm) from its 1973 position, but since this was measured relative to the rear wheels

17 June, 1973 — Swedish GP, Anderstorp — Denny Hulme acknowledging victory in McLaren-Cosworth 'M23/1' — a lucky win in some respects, in fact the first of several fortunate successes for the wedge-shaped McLarens in their long front-line life.

the answer was obviously to move the rear wheels further back. This left the wing in relatively clean air, well aft of the airbox. Airflow was also improved by widening the rear track to minimize wing interference from tyre turbulence. The front bulkhead was modified to accept either constant-rate geometry rocker-arm front suspension or the old progressive system. Wheelbase was stretched 3 in (7.6 cm), rear track 2 in (5 cm) and geometry changes were made to improve low-speed traction.

Hailwood's Yardley–liveried prototype 'M23/1' was modified to similar spec, and chassis '4 in Marlboro livery became team spare. Fittipaldi took to both team and car like a duck to water, but at Buenos Aires inadvertently knocked-off the electrical 'kill-switch' on his steering wheel. By the time he realized his mistake he had lost much ground. Hulme in his LWB M23 inherited the lead on the penultimate lap and won.

Fittipaldi started from pole and won in his native Brazil, and then added the minor Brasilia race to the M23s' tally, the cars having thus won

the season's first three F1 races. Now McLaren began experimenting in earnest, just as Derek Gardner had with the Tyrrells in 1971.

The seventh M23 emerged for Hailwood's use in Yardley colours at Silverstone on 7 April, then in the Belgian GP Fittipaldi became the first driver to have won two GPs that season. Hulme set fastest lap. The new slimline airboxes appeared at Dijon-Prenois and vestigial plastic skirts were adopted round the bottom of the car. While they survived they seemed to add a down-load effect, but once they touched the road surface at speed, they vapourized.

A further modified M23 – chassis '8 – emerged at Brands Hatch, but at the Nürburgring poor Mike Hailwood shunted chassis '1 in practice and then destroyed chassis '7 in a race accident which ended his career. The Yardley operation ended the season with David Hobbs and later Jochen Mass as driver, in the Marlboro team's spare chassis '4.

Fittipaldi had been accumulating points with high placings all season. He was second by just 0.8

19 July, 1975 — British GP, Silverstone — In the sunlit calm before the storm, Emerson Fittipaldi hares out of Woodcote Corner past the pits in 'M23/9'. Subsequently a series of savage rain squalls drenched the circuit and 14 cars crashed with varying degrees of severity, the Brazilian inheriting victory.

sec at Monza, won the Canadian GP and secured the World titles for himself and McLaren at Watkins Glen.

Through 1975 Mass became Fittipaldi's regular number two, and wrote-off two team cars, both ironically on his home soil at the Nürburgring. He was also awarded victory in the Spanish GP when it was abandoned after a terrible accident, and Emerson won the Argentine and British GPs, but lost his Championship title. New chassis '9 had appeared with Brabham-crib pullrod front suspension and while many experiments went on with wheelbase lengths Gordon Coppuck's intended replacement M26 design made only slow progress back home. After Mass destroyed 'M23/8' at the Nürburgring, a replacement which should have been 'M23/10' was hastily completed in time for Monza, but due to paperwork problems it was actually number 'M23/8-2' and took over the old car's documentation. In the final race at Watkins Glen, Fittipaldi regained the fire which had seemed to desert him that season, and he finished a close and fighting second.

That winter, he abruptly joined his brother Wilson's Copersucar F1 team, and James Hunt took his place at McLaren. Their M23s were lightened by some 30 lb (13.6 kg) in time for the Brazilian GP opening the 1976 season. Chief mechanic Alastair Caldwell had developed his own pet theories in a new six-speed gearbox, which plugged some gaps around many courses.

At Interlagos Hunt immediately qualified in pole position ahead of Lauda's Ferrari.

Another Caldwell development then appeared at Kyalami. The normal electrical starter motor was a heavy affair ill-suited to any racing car. Now he introduced a compressed-air starter instead, using an onboard reservoir chargeable from any airline and activated by a small solenoid. An onboard battery sufficient to turn over the normal electric starter was now redundant, saving more vital weight and complication. This invention would be taken up by every F1 team.

Both cars practised at Kyalami wearing plastic aerodynamic underskirts, but they were removed after protest during a dispute over legal wing heights and what now constituted the 'underside' of the car.

Again Hunt started on pole and he was beaten by Lauda's Ferrari by only 1.3 sec after a hard race. Hunt and the wedgy McLaren then scored their first joint victory at Brands Hatch one week later. At Silverstone Hunt won again, dominating totally in what was becoming his regular car 'M23/8-2'.

In Spain new lowered-airbox regulations took effect, McLaren adopting an eared model in the M23D-spec. The two McLarens seemed set for a 1-2 victory in this race until the luckless Mass's engine blew, leaving Hunt a winning margin of nearly 31 sec over Lauda. But at post-race scrutineering Hunt's McLaren proved to be 1.8 cm too wide across the rear wheel rims, and it was disqualified. McLaren protested and had the penalty reduced to a $3,000 fine. But this took time. In the interim Lauda's Ferrari was declared winner, then demoted after appeal. This created an atmosphere of gross controversy which intensified as the season – and the Lauda-Hunt battle – progressed.

Meanwhile for the Belgian GP at Zolder the M23s' rear track had been narrowed by machining the inside wheel faces and adjusting the wishbone mounting points to match. Oil coolers had returned from the tail to the sidepods, but not precisely to the Spanish GP position. This robbed the wing underside of air and diminished download, and the M23s proved uncompetitive for three GPs until the error was recognized and corrected in time for the French GP. As if by magic the old balance had returned. At that point in the season, halfway through the Championship, Hunt was a massive 47 points behind his main rival, Lauda of Ferrari.

How he and McLaren fought back to win the French, British, German, Dutch, Canadian and US GPs and were then disqualified from the British victory in Lauda's favour, and how Lauda then crashed near-fatally at the Nürburgring is all part of racing legend.

In Austria the prototype replacement M26 at last emerged but was not raced. In the Dutch GP Mass raced the M26, unhappily ...

Spot fuel checks at Monza during Italian GP practice saw McLaren adjudged guilty of using illegally high-octane Texaco mix, and although this interpretation was subsequently overthrown, in the short-term it still destroyed the team's chances there.

This dramatic season then reached its climax in the last three rounds, Canada, the USA (East) and

---

22 May, 1976 — Practice for the Monaco GP, Monte Carlo — 'M23/9' again, this time as number two driver Jochen Mass's regular mount. This shot demonstrates the M23's multiple cuneiform lines, its combined water and oil hip-radiator ducts doubling as deformable-structure monocoque protection. Note the large-eared engine airbox and experimental use of an extra low-level rear wing which if properly end-skirted would have captured greater ground-effect download a year ahead of Lotus ...

31 July 1976 — practice for the German GP, Nürburgring — James Hunt hurtles round the *Karrussel* banking in his McLaren M23, heading towards a shattering 7 min 6.5 sec pole position lap and ultimate victory next day, in the last of the classical Grand Prix races ever to be held on the majestic 14.2 mile North Circuit of the Nürburgring. Times were changing . . .

Japan, and Hunt won the first two events in ever-faithful 'M23/8-2' and finished third at Mt Fuji after a dramatic tyre change to steal the Drivers' Championship by one point from Lauda –though McLaren could not catch Ferrari in the Constructors' Championship. On the road Hunt had matched Jim Clark's record of seven GP wins within one season, only to be disqualified from two of them, then reinstated in one!

In 1977, the team played safe for the South American season-openers by fielding their trusty M23s although intensive winter development had improved the M26. Two new M23s were built, chassis '11' for Hunt and '12' for Mass. Hunt put his new car on pole at Kyalami then won in old '8-2'. which was the twenty-first and last win for a works-entered McLaren M23, if we count the subsequently disallowed Brands Hatch victory. Hunt then raced the M26s from the Spanish GP, leaving Mass to tail-off the M23s' front-line career. Gilles Villeneuve made his F1 début in '8-2' at the British GP, and it was then driven by F2 star Bruno Giacomelli in the Italian GP on 11 September 1977. This was the works' last M23 entry, almost exactly four-and-a-half years after the type's début at Kyalami in March '73.

Brett Lunger subsequently ran his specially-built private chassis '14 on into 1978, and other M23s became the backbone of virtual club-level Formula 1 based in the UK. Eventually a young F3 newcomer named Nelson Piquet gained early F1 experience in Lunger's older 'M23/11', and again at Monza, on 10 September 1978, he finished ninth to mark the last World Championship appearance for a most remarkable McLaren design.

The Lotus-Cosworth Type 79s

★ ★ ★ ★ ✦

Ferrari were just hitting new heights with their model 312T and McLaren were defending their World Championship titles with the M23s through the summer of 1975, when Team Lotus found themselves in really deep trouble. Their Type 72 cars had at last run out of competitive development. The specialized tyres they required were no longer being made.

Colin Chapman pondered the future. In August 1975 he compiled a 27-page concept document specifying ideas and asking his engineers questions to prompt detail development of a new concept in Grand Prix design. He presented it to his engineering director, Tony Rudd – former technical head of BRM – who was to establish a new research and development unit within Group Lotus. As Tony tells the story, that brief was far more than just an outline for a new car design – indeed a whole new car concept. It was a measure of Chapman's greatness.

'He realized that in racing we were down and out, and that we'd got it all wrong by the latest standards. And he made the right long-range strategic decisions while still involved in racing day-to-day. Not only did he suggest the way to go, but he also listed all the things he didn't know, and then he left it to an old has-been like me and to a bunch of new boys to tell him all the answers . . .'

Rudd was anything but a has-been – he wouldn't have been holding down his post with Lotus if that was so – but he had not been closely involved with their racing cars until research and development began under his direction at Ketteringham Hall, a rambling old country house not far from the main Lotus plant at Hethel. Lotus had acquired it virtually derelict, and had undertaken extensive restoration work. Former Brabham and McLaren designer Ralph Bellamy became one of its first inmates with a project to develop a new racing gearbox. Rudd's Esprit production car group arrived soon after, and with that project's conclusion Chapman put Rudd in charge of long-range F1 research. This new unit was to operate quite independently of Team and its everyday race commitments and pressures. It was to give Chapman the answers he wanted and to test the feasibility of the type of car he had outlined.

Another early member of the Ketteringham research and development group was Peter Wright who had worked with Tony Rudd at BRM in 1969, when he (Wright) conceived advance plans for a wing car . . . Peter had followed Tony to Lotus after a spell running Specialized Mouldings' wind tunnel, for he held a degree in aerodynamics. After they had left BRM, their putative wing car programme had been discarded by the new regime. Wright had eventually joined Lotus to run their plastics research, and when that programme had been completed successfully his brilliant mind was harnessed to the new F1 development programme.

In his BRM wing-car concept, tapering stub wing sections had been formed each side of the central chassis tub to clean up aerodynamic turbulence between front and rear wheels. At Peter's recommendation, Robin Herd has introduced a similar layout in his 1970 March 701, but did not follow the idea through.

Through the autumn of 1975, Wright, Rudd and Bellamy discussed Chapman's questions of principle. What Colin wanted them to do in essence was simple – to use the whole car form to generate advantageous aerodynamic effect, instead of merely loading an aerodynamically redundant hull with relatively tiny wings. Everybody tried to harness airflow over the cars. Few had yet tackled the potential of airflow underneath them.

The 'Fawlty Towers' group at Ketteringham now began extensive wind tunnel model tests. During the war, Rudd had managed Rolls-Royce Merlin aero engine fault investigation. He recalled the inner wing section radiator mounting of the de Havilland Mosquito aircraft, using ducts sunk into the inner wings' leading edges, air passing through the core and then exhausting from conveniently-sited ducts further back on the wing.

A model mimic section was tested inverted in the wind tunnel to provide negative lift. Lift: drag ratio was the vital criterion – the best possible lift for the least possible drag – and that Christmas Tony received a simple message from the tunnel testers at London's Imperial College, '*The Mosquito flies . . .*'

A scheme was hatched to mount ducted radiators of this type in convenient pods each side of a slender central monocoque chassis. Airflow beneath the pod underfloors – or underwings – would be protected from aerodynamic infilling each side by a skirt system extending from the car's side panels down to the road.

Bellamy drew the car, Wright refined its aerodynamics, Mike Cooke ran a load-simulating test-rig to check every component as it was made. Unacceptable deflection brought immediate redesign until stiffness proved adequate. Once Bellamy had finalized his layouts, Martin Ogilvie detailed the new Lotus Type 78 car's suspensions and other 'bits that moved', while Ralph completed the chassis and both combined to design the body.

The prototype Lotus 78 'wing car', '78/1' to enthusiasts or more properly 'JPS/15' according to its sponsor-orientated chassis plate, was first driven at Lotus's Hethel Aerodrome by Ketteringham shop foreman Eddie Dennis. Nigel Bennett, a former Firestone tyre engineer, conducted onboard instrumentation testing with borrowed Goodyear equipment, while Team

22 May, 1977 — Monaco GP, Monte Carlo — Mario Andretti locks his Lotus 78 — chassis '78/3' — into the street circuit's former Station Hairpin, the 'wing-car' showing off its very wide front track, nose-mounted oil cooler and sidepod-mounted radiators, the top ducts just beyond exhausting hot air upwards. The underwing-section tanks were formed beneath the area topped by the two circular non-drip fuel fillers, around the car's centre of gravity.

drivers Mario Andretti and Gunnar Nilsson drove. By the time Chapman decided to race the 78 his research and development group had amassed 2.2 miles (3.6 km) of test-recording tape, completed over 150 individual investigations, 54 rig tests and 400 hours of wind-tunnel time at Imperial College. The statistics were impressive, but did the car work?

Although aerodynamic values realized full-size were only some 75 per cent of those predicted in the tunnel, yes it did. Known as the 'John Player Special Mark III' the Lotus 78 made its public bow at London's Royal Garden Hotel.

Its part-aluminium honeycomb monocoque nacelle was very slim, with broad panniers each side between front and rear wheels, containing the 'Mosquito' radiator ducts, air exiting over shaped wing fuel tanks whose underside swept up at the rear to form an expanding-section chamber against the road surface.

As air flowed through the venturi section provided by the entry to this chamber – the 'throat' between the lowest section of tank and the road – it accelerated. As air is accelerated through a venturi like this so its pressure drops. The new Lotus harnessed this pressure drop to suck itself down against the roadway, load up its tyres and so gain cornering and tractive grip. To prevent this low-pressure area being infilled by air rushing in at either side, deep 'Cellite' side plates extended close to the road, initially with bristle skirts and later sliding but rigid skirt-panels providing the final seal. Conventional wings and fins provided trim and balance, but still there was more.

A neat innovation on the 78 shown – actually the second 4 in (10 cm) longer chassis 'JPS/16' – was the oil tank integrated into the bell-housing spacer between engine and gearbox. This was to be copied by all, like most other features of this latest Lotus design.

The car's configuration gave a forward weight bias, further enhanced by the oil cooler in its nose duct ahead of the front axle. Three fuel cells sat in line abreast behind the driver's seat-back, one in the tub, one in each sidepod. This concentrated fuel load around the car's notional centre of gravity and achieved Chapman's requirement for *'minimum change in handling and response as the fuel load lightens'*.

The front track was wide, close to the maximum limit, so it could literally 'stick out a paw' on the turn-in to a corner to improve 'bite'. Its front end grip was in fact the greatest the drivers had ever known. It could always overwhelm rear-end grip if the drivers pressed too hard, but this characteristic also enabled near zero-slip differentials to limit wheelspin. In a more conventional design such differentials would have merely washed out front-end grip to induce uncontrollable understeer. At Andretti's request, a USAC-style driver-adjustable rear anti-roll bar was adopted, plus a preferential fuel drainage system, also familiar in USAC racing, to allow him to choose the order in which his three fuel cells were emptied – thus further adjusting weight bias within the car during a race.

Andretti and Chapman had a superb working relationship and Mario's Lotus 78s led more World Championship race laps than anyone else through 1977. He won GPs at Long Beach, in Spain, France and Italy, and his team-mate Nilsson won a fifth, in Belgium, in the rain. Only five engine failures and three other mechanical faults denied Andretti and Lotus the World Championship titles.

Although the 78 undoubtedly showed the way ahead, it needed refinement, and this produced the Type 79 true 'ground-effects' car of 1978. Ronnie Peterson joined Andretti as poor Nilsson

5 June, 1977 — Belgian GP, Zolder — The popular Gunnar Nilsson in '78/2' heading towards his unique World Championship Grand Prix victory on the Limburg circuit, after team leader Andretti had crashed. Almost Colin Chapman's only criticism of the rugged Italo-American was that 'He will try to win the race on the first corner . . .'. Here one can see the flexible aerodynamic skirts along the lower edge of the 'wing-car's' sidepanel, which minimized lateral aerodynamic infill of the low-pressure area created beneath the car's underwings.

had developed a fatal cancer. Type 78s '2 (Peterson) and '3 (Andretti) raced-on into the new year while the new 79 was being finalized.

Mario won at Buenos Aires, Peterson in South Africa, before the new 'JPS Mark IV', or Lotus 79, emerged. Its pannier underwings formed a more sophisticated venturi section against the road surface, and Team Lotus now hoped to find the missing 25 per cent of aerodynamic download lost between wind tunnel and actual car in the Type 78. One major objective was to improve airflow through the side panniers, and to achieve this the outboard fuel tanks and rear suspension spring/dampers of the 78 were deleted, fuel being concentrated in a large single 'midships cell behind the driver with suspension elements tucking well inboard.

Unfortunately the prototype '79/1' – or 'JPS/19' – proved structurally inadequate in testing and was set aside. 'JPS/20' then emerged around a stiffened monocoque with more cockpit room for Peterson's lanky frame. This car was severely damaged when Andretti drove it in the wet minor meeting at Silverstone, and it was rebuilt in

much-refined form – matched later by '79/3' ('JPS/21') – before its second race and first GP in Belgium, which Mario won and in which Ronnie was second in a 78. Ronnie took over '2 thereafter, and Andretti adopted '3. Chassis '79/1' was also rebuilt to latest spec as a late-season spare, and when Mario wrecked '79/3' in Austria, its salvage went on to a new chassis as '79/4'. At Monza Ronnie shunted '2 in practice, had to use '78/3' in the race and crashed fatally. Jean-Pierre Jarier took the drive for the US and Canadian GPs, and shone, proving the cars' quality and – some believed – 'blowing the whistle' on Andretti's performances . . .

The 'Black Beauty' Lotus 79s made 20 starts in 11 GPs that year, won six, and took four second places, a third, a sixth, one tenth and a fifteenth, with six retirements. They took 10 pole positions – eight to Andretti, one to Peterson and one to Jean-Pierre Jarier – the last seven in consecutive races. They added five fastest laps – two each to Andretti and Peterson, one to Jarier. When they were beaten for fastest lap they still set second and third fastest times – behind only the

---

December 1977 — Initial testing of 'JPS/19' or Lotus '79/1' in progress at Ricard-Castellet, Andretti driving the car rigged with tall pitot-head air-pressure recording. The underwing sidepods 'sucked' beautifully but their immense download pinpointed grievous deficiencies in this first chassis' rigidity.

16 July 1978 — British GP, Brands Hatch — The great Ronnie Peterson aims Colin Chapman's wonderful 'Black Beauty' Lotus 79 — chassis '2' — round Paddock Hill Bend, this time destined for early retirement, and Team Lotus for a rare 1978 defeat. During this ultimately clouded season, their Type 79 proved ground-effects aerodynamic theory in Formula 1.

Brabham Fan-Car – in Sweden; third and fourth at Ricard; second and third at Zandvoort – by 0.01 sec behind Lauda's Brabham-Alfa Romeo – and fourth fastest (by Jaricr) in Canada.

So this remarkable if marred season saw Team Lotus take the Constructors' title by 86 points to Ferrari's 58, and Mario Andretti became World Champion from the late Ronnie Peterson.

The 79s ran into 1979 while the intended replacement Type 80 was being developed. Today this Lotus season tends to be recalled glibly as a total disaster. In truth it started pretty well, although it was immediately clear that the opposition were not only following where Lotus had led into ground-effects aerodynamics, but were immediately threatening to do a better job . . .

The 1979 Lotus 79s wore green Martini livery. They made 15 starts in the first seven races, and finished in the points – ie in the first six – 11 times. In contrast, the final eight races yielded only four finishes from 16 starts, just once in the points –

Andretti's fifth at Monza, with new team-mate Carlos Reutemann seventh.

Peter Wright considered, 'In its day the 79 had been very effective, but then it had been the only proper ground-effect car around, and a lot had been compromised to make it effective . . . Now in 1979 it was up against second generation ground-effect cars which showed-up its deficiencies in cooling, brakes and also in structural stiffness I am afraid. While we tried to find out what was wrong with the new Type 80's aerodynamic behaviour we had to go back to the 79 and with the pressures of the calendar preventing proper testing and development it was no longer adequate into the second half of the season . . .'

The one-time epochal Lotus 79s' front-line racing career ended at Watkins Glen on 7 October 1979, where neither finished. But nevertheless the Lotus 79 was a classic beauty whose innovative technology, building upon that of the Lotus 78, totally redirected the course of all racing car design.

The Brabham-Alfa Romeo BT46B 'Fan-Cars'

★ ★

The message of the Lotus 78/79 designs' ground-effect aerodynamics was quickly recognized in 1978 by Brabham's South African-born chief engineer Gordon Murray and his right-hand man David North. Their Brabham-Alfa Romeo BT46 cars were proving very competitive with all but the striking new Lotuses, and they began to address the problem of designing a ground-effects car around the wide, low-level Alfa '115-12' flat-12 engine. Its heads projected obstructively into the very area where ground-effect venturi tunnels should be sited.

They investigated a front engine mounting, and even placing the fuel tank between engine and gearbox. It would have worked that way, but the multiple joints were bound to be heavy and handling changes between full and empty would have been spectacular!

In desperation they re-read the regulations, and spotted a loophole under which an extractor fan could be used to reduce air-pressure beneath the car so long as its 'primary function' was not 'aerodynamic' in the Formula 1 sense, in that rather than being intended to affect the performance of the car generated from its motion through the air, its primary function could be claimed to be drawing air through a radiator to cool the engine. They had already used a small fan in a panic attempt to cool the old BT45C model's horizontal oil matrices above the engine in South America, though there was no real link between the two ploys.

The Fan-Car device became a most celebrated case of rule-bending, for drawing air through a radiator is still literally an 'aerodynamic' function, unless my grasp of the English language is at fault, but even today its creator insists it was utterly legal, and indeed it was declared so by the racing authorities, after its further use had been effectively banned by a change in their regulation wording . . .

So the famous Brabham BT46B Fan-Car came about. The initial idea had occurred around Kyalami time, which is very early – hard evidence of Murray's perceptiveness. The team's staff of approximately 40 at Chessington set about building two cars for Monaco. All the bits were made and ready, but skirt and fan development delayed their race début. At last two cars, modified chassis 'BT46/6' and 'BT46/4', appeared in the Swedish GP which Lauda won while Watson also shone.

Their BT46Bs had emerged carrying large horizontal water radiators above the engine, the whole engine bay area being sealed against ambient pressure in-fill underneath by flexible skirts extending down to the road surface with sections even sealing the slots in which the driveshafts and suspension arms rose and fell. Massive effort went into finalising skirt, fan and radiator.

Thermodynamics consultant David Cox calculated the number of fan blades, pitch and optimum rotational speed required. Typically Murray and North agonized over potential problems and sought to design them out right from the start. The fan drive was taken from the gearbox lower shaft, but this would have created an H16 BRM-like problem if direct drive had been employed, since the inertia of the fan making the

17 June, 1978 — Swedish GP, Anderstorp — Reigning World Champion Niki Lauda at speed in Brabham's 'fast one' — the BT46B chassis '6 'Fan-Car'. Here this daring and controversial device shows off its standard pyramid-section BT46 monocoque form, but note the horizontal cooler sunk into the rear-deck just behind the head-rest moulding. It was through this cooler that air was drawn by the gearbox-driven fan spinning around a horizontal axis in the extreme tail, at the end of that cylindrical trunking between the rear wheels. The probe above the nose is a true-airspeed/over-car pressure pitot head.

17 June, 1978 — Swedish GP, Anderstorp — Business end of the Brabham BT46B in its only public outing. Here the careful aerodynamic sealing around the engine compartment is obvious. Note the lateral sealing skirt with its abrade-resistant rubbing edge, the flat-12 Alfa Romeo engine's exhaust megaphones and the vast fan assembly; also the end-plate supported rear wing offering unrivalled flow beneath its working under-surface. The horizontal fin extending laterally from the bottom edge of the sloping monocoque side between the wheels is also visible here.

gearbox input shaft run-on while the driver fought to slow it down sufficiently to find another gear would cause some problems. Therefore a sprag clutch was fitted at the back of the gearbox to uncouple the fan as the driver kicked-out the clutch proper. To avoid a nasty pit accident a cut-out device was also added to enable the mechanics to disengage the fan with the engine ticking over.

A spur-gear drive train was necessary to raise the fan hub sufficiently to accommodate fan blades of reasonable radius. The problem of a racing start shock-loading the fan drive led to another friction-plate clutch going into the hub assembly. Brands Hatch testing then showed surprisingly there was *no* need for either the sprag clutch or pit disengagement devices, as the gearchange seemed unaffected even when the sprag locked solid. But the original plastic replacements disintegrated, and so did glass-fibre-filled fans. Within a week of the Swedish GP magnesium fan blades were cast and new hubs machined from the solid. Only three were ready in time.

Skirt sealing at the sides and rear had caused no problem, but the front lateral skirt ahead of the engine bay caused endless headaches until David North devised a brilliant system involving two stitched–sailcloth sausage-shaped bags with a system of coinciding edged holes; this enabled the bags to be inflated by under-chassis airflow and then remain inflated against pressure and road surface changes which tried to force them clear of the roadway.

The first day's practice at Anderstorp wore away this complex front skirt, but Brabham's men fitted a skid on its leading edge for the second day and thereafer it worked superbly well. Even sitting in the pit-lane the cars would squat down when the throttle was blipped and the fan revved, but five teams protested its legality even before Lauda and Watson qualified 1-2 behind a Lotus 79, and the Austrian won the race, showering dust and grit from the fan efflux in his car's wake.

Before the next race, the fabulous Fan-Car and any and all successors using that system were henceforth banned from competition, although the Swedish result was confirmed and the Fan-Car itself never declared illegal ... a famous sidelight – and some would say highlight – in Grand Prix racing history.

The Williams-Cosworth FW07s

★ ★ ★ ★

As we have seen, in 1977 the epochal Lotus 78 introduced the idea of harnessing airflow beneath the car to enhance its cornering power, and the idea was then developed into the definitive 'ground effects' Lotus 79 in 1978. But in 1979 Team Lotus's intended next stride forward, the Type 80 proved a hopeless flop, and others were to hone the ground-effects principle to its keenest edge. The long line of Patrick Head-designed Williams-Cosworth FW07 cars led the way.

Patrick had become Frank Williams's chief engineer when the long-time team owner was edged out of his original company and started again from scratch as 'Williams Grand Prix Engineering Ltd' in 1977. Patrick – an ex-Lola, Scott F2 and Trojan F1 engineer – had been impressed by the Lotus's lap times in 1977, but only began to believe in the principles it demonstrated during the Lotus 79 season of 1978, when his own Williams FW06 car driven by Alan Jones was amongst the very best of the rest.

For the new year he then attempted to build a better ground-effects car. The resultant Williams FW07 inevitably resembled the Lotus 79 superficially 'but I tried to optimise that layout'. He did not do this alone, aided in WGPE's Didcot, Oxfordshire, factory initially by a quiet, reflective young engineer named Neil Oatley, and then by an ex-Hesketh engineer, Frank Dernie. Dernie joined in January '79, by which time Head and Oatley were well advanced on FW07 design.

At Watkins Glen at the close of the previous season, Jones's FW06 had suffered a structural failure, which mortified Patrick. It was a salutary reminder of the forces he was playing with in Formula One. He and Frank Williams also considered that, after Jones's '06 car had finished second and then ran second in their last two races of '78 that these cars could remain competitive in the early races of '79. They were mistaken, having under-estimated the development pace of the opposition. The non-ground effects '06s were completely outpaced by the new-generation cars as soon as racing recommenced, in Argentina.

For the first time WGPE fielded a full two-car team with drivers Alan Jones and Clay Regazzoni. They scored no points in the new year's first three races. Sponsorship money from the their Middle Eastern backers was slow to appear, delaying the new '07s. The first prototype 'FW07/1' was at last completed in time to go to Long Beach, California, for the fourth GP of the season, but there it lay in the Tech Center, unused beneath a dust sheet.

By the end of April, the money was freed, and two '07s emerged for the Spanish GP at Jarama. Both retired, but it was significant that in race morning warm-up Jones's '07 – even with a full fuel load – had left Andretti's Lotus 80 for dead. Mario simply gasped: '... I couldn't stay with him ...'

In the race, Alan set the second fastest lap, bettered only by a Ferrari using qualifying tyres to regain lost ground after a pit delay. The Williams men quickly began to appreciate FW07's enormous potential ...

Patrick had based his car upon a slender aluminium-honeycomb panelled monocoque chassis, with a single fuel cell behind the driver's

29 April, 1979 — Spanish GP, Jarama — At this event Alan Jones demonstrated the new Williams-Cosworth FW07's potential for the first time. Here the ground-effect car, chassis 'FW07/1', its design prompted by the Lotus 79, shows off its highly efficient sliding skirt system — visible beneath the sidepod — its shallow-section nose 'foils and the deeply end-plated rear wing.

shoulders. The Cosworth DFV V8 engine was bolted rigidly to the back of that tank section to carry transmission and rear suspension in conventional style. Outrigged sidepods housed their ground-effect undersides or wing sections, sealed against outside infilling airflow by skilfully-fashioned, spring-loaded sliding skirts. These devices were actually very light but rigid, and rode against the road surface on extremely hard-wearing ceramic inserts, the only material which would reliably survive high-speed abrasion against the tarmac.

Obviously the suction created as airflow was accelerated beneath the sidepod underwings acted in all directions so not only did the underwings themselves have to be rigid and strong to resist deformation or collapse, but also the skirt guide system had to be friction–free and precise to prevent the skirts binding as they were drawn inwards by the low pressure. If a skirt should jam within its guides it could stick up, clear of the road surface, instantly allowing outside air to rush in and fill that vital low–pressure area. This would abruptly and dramatically reduce download and give the driver the fright of his life as a car which had been cornering happily at perhaps 150 mph (250 km/h) became suddenly 20 mph (33 km/h) beyond safe limits!

At around 180 mph (300 km/h) the initial FW07 underwing forms could generate a stagger-ing 4,000 to 5,000 lb (1,800-2,250 kg) downforce to enhance the car's normal static weight of only 1,300 lb (590 kg). And this was purely a dynamic loading effect, not onboard mass to be braked and accelerated – it was almost a 'something for nothing' effect, and WGPE simply did it best.

At Zolder, Jones qualified third fastest despite having broken a skirt. He then led the potent Ligiers which had started the season so well. This was the first time since 1969 that a Williams-entered car had led a Grand Prix! The spell lasted until lap 40 when Alan retired with electrical failure.

At Monaco, Regazzoni finished second to score Williams's first points of '79. There followed a gap in the calendar before the French GP and Patrick Head used that breathing space to test at Dijon, where Jones's '07 simply destroyed the lap record. Renault's turbocars were to come good in that race, however, and they finished first and third, split by a Ferrari. Jones was fourth – the leading Goodyear runner home – Regazzoni sixth.

Then followed a stunning Silverstone test session pre-British GP. The lap record stood at 1:18, Jones was already down to 1:13.6 when a newly-developed engine under-faring was attached, and he promptly lapped in an unbelievable 1:12.18. Williams's sheer grip foiled Renault's turbo horsepower in the race and the FW07s ran 1-2 before Jones's water pump split and Regazzoni won! This was the first Grand Prix win for Williams, but Jones rubbed it in by winning the next three GPs in a row; Germany, Austria, Holland. In Austria, Clay was second in a wonderful 1-2 WGPE triumph, and then third behind the Ferraris at Monza, where their driver Jody Scheckter clinched the Drivers' Championship.

The FW07s thereafter completed this remarkable début season with another superb 1-2 in Canada. Although Jones was only third in the Drivers' Championship he had won more GPs than any other, Scheckter included. Early disappointments with the '06 cars and late development of the '07s had cost Williams dear ... It came right in 1980.

The engineering team believed they needed a car two seconds a lap quicker to win that year. They developed a stiffened-monocoque FW07B with composite undersides extending the underwing back through the rear suspension to generate even greater downforce. It seemed promising, but in practice for the Argentine GP at Buenos Aires proved unstable due to aerodynamic 'porpoising'*. Consequently the B-spec components were hastily stripped off and Alan notched his sixth GP victory without them – new team-mate Carlos Reutemann cooking his

(*A fore-and-aft pitching caused by the skirts losing seal and killing download whereupon the affected end of the car rises; as the skirts regain seal, download reappears, slamming the car down against its springs. They rebound and the process becomes self-exciting!)

engine on home soil, too eager to do well.

Alan finished third in Brazil, Carlos sixth in South Africa to score his first point for Williams. Both FW07s were sidelined by collisions at Long Beach, while at Didcot an alternative B-spec package had been developed with modified undersides stopping short of the tail and improved cooling systems. These definitive FW07B cars made their début in the Belgian GP at Zolder. Pironi's Ligier beat Jones there, the '07B slowed by a blistered tyre, but Carlos was third and WGPE now led the Constructors' Championship table.

Jones lost the Monaco GP with differential failure, letting Reutemann through for his first Williams victory. The Argentinian's luck then deserted him in Spain as he was rammed by another car and Jones salvaged a lucky win in a very sick car. But FISA then stripped this event of Championship status for political reasons, robbing Jones and WGPE of nine valuable points.

At Ricard for the French GP, the British team was implacably determined to defeat the French on home soil. Jones uttery destroyed both Renault and Ligier to take an historic victory. He also won the British GP with Carlos third. The fast Hockenheim and Osterreichring circuits followed, with the German and Austrian GPs. In Germany the '07Bs were beaten into second and third by a Ligier, and in Austria by a Renault turbo, accumulating more points. At Zandvoort, Jones broke a skirt against a tall kerb. Nelson Piquet's Brabham won, cutting Jones's Cham-

---

14 July, 1979 — British GP, Silverstone — Clay Regazzoni broke Frank Williams's eleven-season Formula 1 duck by giving the new-series FW07 cars their maiden victory here on Williams Grand Prix Engineering Ltd's home soil. The car is chassis 'FW07/2'.

pionship lead to just two points.

At Imola, Piquet beat Jones fair and square to take a one-point lead. Williams then arrived in Canada with four cars, eight Cosworth engines, 5.5 metric tonnes of spares and 26 people. Piquet's engine failed, leaving Jones to win both race and Championship title.

The team were determined to stay up on their toes for the final race of the season, the US GP at Watkins Glen one week later. Jones and Reutemann promptly dominated and finished 1-2 yet again. Williams Grand Prix Engineering Ltd were Formula 1 Constructors' Champions of the World . . .

That November, Alan Jones won the Australian GP at Calder in his '07B – a non-Championship event which his late father Stan had won many years before. Then in Europe the French-dominated FISA governing body suddenly slapped an arbitrary ban upon the use of sliding skirt aerodynamic systems. The Formula 1 constructors fought against this ban and ran the 1981 South African GP without FISA sanction, using sliding-skirt cars. Reutemann won for Williams but of course FISA disallowed Championship points.

WGPE then rushed out an unskirted so-called 'clearance car' – the FW07C – for the offical 1981 World Championship opening round at Long Beach, California, using chassis '11 and '12. They finished 1-2 yet again, Jones and Reutemann, and again at Rio in reverse order. In Argentina, Piquet's new lowering-suspension Brabham proved uncatchable, WGPE having to adopt a similar lowering ploy to regain ground-effect beneath their latest chassis. At Imola Jones unfortunately rammed his team-mate, though Reutemann still finished third.

At Zolder, the Argentinian won after Jones crashed and suddenly Carlos was running away with the Driver's Championship, until at Monaco his car's transmission failed; Jones inherited the lead briefly but suffered fuel starvation. He then threw away a superb lead through driver error in Spain.

The Renault turbos seemed uncatchable until the '07Cs were revised aerodynamically in time for the German GP. But Jones's earlier mysterious fuel starvation fault reappeared and robbed him of yet another probable victory. This starvation problem possibly cost Jones 12 Championship points and perhaps the first back-to-

---

Core of the Williams FW07 design was its nicely-made folded and seamed aluminium-honeycomb monocoque chassis. Note how the double-fold top scuttle sections were rivetted and bonded to the lower panels with robust inserted bulkheads providing suspension pivots and pick-ups. The front coil/dampers are tucked away inside the tub to free airflow entry into the all-important sidepods. As high-sided moulded carbon-composite chassis were adopted in later years, the '07 cars' deeply incised cockpit area would be recognized in retrospect as a weakness of their design — but it caused few problems at the time . . .

April 1982 — United States GP (West), Long Beach, California — Keke Rosberg would emerge as the season's World Champion Driver in Williams cars, beginning the year as here in the ultimate Williams FW07C cars, this one chassis '15' in the long series.

back Drivers' Championship titles since his compatriot Jack Brabham with Cooper in 1959-60.

Reutemann triggered a collision at Zandvoort, which left him and Piquet neck-and-neck for the Drivers' title. They raced on into the final round at Las Vegas, where Reutemann's always suspect psyche seemed to crack under the pressure and Piquet cantered home as Champion: but Jones had won the race, his last before retirement. WGPE had long since secured their second consecutive Constructors' Cup title.

During that season, the D-spec FW07 monocoque had been completed, number '16' in the series, used by Jones in the later races but intended originally more as a test tub to accept a four-wheel drive back end using front-sized small tyres. This ruse would have enabled it to make full use of enormously long aerodynamic underwings. The tyres' low frontal area would have permitted enormous straightline speeds, and wind tunnel tests in the company's own wind tunnel – which they had now installed at Didcot – had already indicated a 75 per cent improvement in lift drag ratio compared to the standard '07C. Unfortunately FISA again juggled the rules to ban six-wheeler cars just as the '07D project in this form was taking off.

By that time Head's design team was also well-advanced on a new shorter, lighter replacement for the whole FW07 series. This FW08 was born as a six-wheeler, but after the ban it appeared in 1982 as a conventional four-wheeler ... which carried Keke Rosberg to the Drivers' Championship.

But both Jones and Reutemann left racing, leaving WGPE with new drivers Keke Rosberg and Derek Daly, before the stubby new '08s replaced the '07s at the Belgian GP. In the '07C's final races, Reutemann finished second in South Africa with Rosberg fifth; in Brazil Keke was second but disqualified after a terrific performance, then he was second again at Long Beach. Reutemann abruptly left racing on the eve of the Falklands War.

During its long run, the Williams-Cosworth FW07 series ran to 17 individual chassis. They won back-to-back Constructors' World Championship titles, and 18 F1 races, 15 of them World Championship GPs. They marked the high-tide of ground-effects F1 technology and proved in Frank Williams's case that nobody should scoff at the perennial 'no-hoper' teams in motor racing. With the right personnel, and the right breaks, they might just come good ...

The Renault RS Turbos

★ ★ ★

In 1977, the naturalized French Régie Renault became by far the largest motor manufacturer to become involved in Formula 1 since the days of Mercedes-Benz over 20 years earlier. The giant French national motor company's President, Bernard Hanon, had boldly authorized a programme to develop and race the first cars to take advantage of the long-fallow 'Three Litre Formula's' 1.5 litre supercharged option.

In modern times Renault had supported competition vigorously at more minor level, their involvement characterized most notably by Amédée Gordini's engine development programmes in conjunction with Jean Redele's specialist Alpine motor company at Dieppe.

Back in 1973 a series of sports car Alpine-Renault *Barquettes* had been introduced for the European 2 Litre Championship, powered by an all-new Renault-Gordini 90° V6 four-cam racing engine known as the *Type* CH1 after Usine A. Gordini's late technical manager, Claude Hard. It was a compact 90° iron-block engine, designed by François Castaing, and after a disappointing début season in 1973, revised A441 *Barquettes* won all seven rounds of the 1974 Championship series.

Contemporary 2 litre Formula 2 was to admit pure-bred racing engines alongside the stock-block units from 1976, so an F2 V6 programme was set-up and during 1975 a new turbocharged version of the Alpine-Renault *Barquettes* – the A442 – was successfully introduced to World Championship of Makes endurance racing. Engineer Bernard Dudot master-minded this Garrett AiResearch turbocharged adaptation of

the V6 engine, Renault's long-term target being the – for them – glittering prize of the Le Mans 24-Hours classic.

Turbochargers are induction air compressors powered by a turbine wheel introduced into the escaping exhaust gas flow, like a water-wheel in a torrent. They save the mechanical power loss of conventional superchargers, but although efficient and capable of extracting very high power were regarded somewhat suspiciously in road racing for their throttle-lag – the interval between the driver opening the throttle to accelerate and exhaust gas flow following suit to spin-up the turbocharger wheels. These problems would be minimized, if not totally eradicated, in the white heat of competition.

Once Hanon gave the go-ahead for Formula 1 research, an experimental Alpine *laboratoire* single-seater was built in the Dieppe racing shop, designed by André de Cortanze. Aerodynamicist Marcel Hubert developed its sleek body with Ferrari-like full-width nose wing, while the sheet aluminium tub itself was a slab-sided 'Coke bottle' in planform, carrying in-line hip radiators either side of its engine bay.

Meanwhile in the Gordini workshops at Viry-Châtillon, one of the sprawling Parisian suburbs south of the capital, technical head François Castaing with Jean-Pierre Boudy and Bernard Dudot developed a turbocharged 1.5 litre version of their already successful iron-block V6.

The Michelin tyre company had achieved considerable competition success with Alpine-Renault, and now decided to support their Formula 1 venture to promote their radial-ply tyre technology internationally and hopefully steal some of Goodyear's monopolistic glory. Consequently, the *laboratoire* Alpine Type A500 turned a wheel for the first time on Michelin's Ladoux test track near Clermont-Ferrand on 21 May 1976.

Works F2 and sports car driver Jean-Pierre Jabouille ran an extensive turbo test programme that summer in the A500, and it looked sufficiently promising for approval to be given to enter F1 racing in 1977.

Meanwhile, in April '76, Alpine had just been absorbed as a Renault subsidiary, and a company named Renault Sport was founded to handle the Régie's wide-ranging competition interests. It was run by ex-driver Gérard Larrousse.

Renault announced their Formula 1 plans in December 1976, but the car itself would not appear until the following May. It emerged as the yellow-liveried Renault RS01, a neatly-packaged car, inevitably reminiscent of recent F2 Alpines, its Hubert body remodelled and developed from the A500 baseline in the St Cyr wind tunnel. The aluminium tub was folded from two large alloy panels, stiffened by internal steel strap-plates. It

was designed as a simple car, minimizing potential chassis problems to enable engine and tyre development to proceed unhindered. The F1-spec engine – financed largely by ELF petroleum – was known as the *Type* EF1.

Turbocharger plumbing was neater than on the jury-rigged A500, including a block-type intercooler nestled between engine and rear of tub to cool the boost-charge – thus increasing its density – between turbo compressor and the induction 'log' on top of the engine. Chausson oil and water radiators were slung in-line just ahead of the rear wheels, and transmission was via a six-speed Hewland FGA400 gearbox. Bodywork was elegantly styled, made by Moch in moulded Kevlar.

The RS01 made its racing début on 16 July 1977, in the British GP at Silverstone, the open aerodrome course promising to be well-suited to turbo engine characteristics. A maiden outing public failure in France would have been hard to justify and in some respects Renault still had more to lose than gain by participation. Certainly they stood to suffer from the 'Man Bites Dog is News' syndrome for initially at least if anyone

Renault's EF1 1.5 litre V6 in definitive twin-turbocharged form; note its twin KKK turbochargers, one to each three-cylinder exhaust branch, the bright-metal cylindrical objects just ahead of the rear suspension top wishbones being the pressure-relieving waste-gate valves (see their separate small-diameter exhaust pipes). The turbocharger compressor sections' charge was piped forward into the intercooler matrices visible in the rear of the sidepods, the induction manifolds from the top of each intercooler then feeding the induction 'logs' atop the engine. The water radiators are visible raked forward through the 'pod top louvres.

8 April, 1979 — United States GP (West), Long Beach, California — a bad day for the Renault Sport team. This is René Arnoux's RS01 — chassis '03' — after breaking its left-side inboard half-shaft UJ on race morning. Note the detached shaft propped against the inboard stump. A similar failure had turned team-mate Jabouille's car sharp left at 170 mph (283 km/h) into the trackside wall the previous day, so Renault wisely scratched from the race. A large single Garrett turbocharger was used in these early-series Renaults.

12 August, 1979 — Austrian GP, Österreichring — Renault's new-series twin-turbocharged ground-effect cars set them winning from the French GP of '79 . . . here René Arnoux is using all 'RS12's turbocharged engine's horsepower to set fastest lap while running third in the opening stages ahead of team-mate Jabouille in the sister car 'RS11'.

beat them it could only be a microscopically smaller specialist concern. Renault ran the danger of being expected to suceed merely by reason of their size.

At Silverstone, Jabouille qualified twenty-first, and retired early after the induction manifold split, venting boost to atmosphere to leave him puttering around as a simple low-compression 1,500 in a 3 litre race. After a break for further development, Jabouille then ran in four more GPs, Holland, Italy, the USA and Canada, never finishing and even failing to qualify in Canada. The main problem with this increasingly premature-looking race programme was that its technical back-up was at best part-time, at worst half-hearted. Renault Sport were still desperately trying to win the Le Mans 24-Hours race with their turbocharged sports prototype cars, and the Viry-Châtillon team simply lacked both the capacity and the man-power to tackle Formula 1 as well.

This state of affairs persisted into 1978, so their F1 programme remained confined to a single car for Jabouille, commencing in South Africa after ignoring the World Championship series's South American overture. Jabouille normally drove chassis 'RS01/2', but instead raced '3 at Long Beach and Zolder. His qualifying record for the year read 6-13-12-10-11-10-11-12-9-3-9-3-9-22 as development progressed – note the late season improvement after Le Mans, significant because Renault had at last won the great 24-Hour classic, whereupon the sports car programme was closed down, and all hands turned to Formula 1...

Renault's first finish came at Monaco, tenth, but in France the engine failed after one lap ... In Sweden, Jabouille was fifth fastest in first qualifying, looking more stable than the Ferraris on the

same Michelin tyres, but his final practice was spoiled by engine problems in one car and a flat battery in the spare. The RS01s were encouragingly less destructive of their tyres than the Ferrari T3s. But in France, Jabouille observed, 'Throttle response, power, everything has to be better before I can challenge for the front row...' It would come.

At Hockenheim the radiators were packed with ice in qualifying to combat hot weather, and in Austria a new water-cooled intercooler was introduced. Jabouille tested his two cars back to back, one with water intercooling, the other without, and the new system was consistently faster, the engine no longer losing power as it got hot; hitherto a major in-race problem.

At Monza many drivers were then shaken by the Renault's straightline speed. Villeneuve reported, 'It's incredible, it passed me on the straight like you can't believe. It must be 10 km/h faster than anything else here'.

Both Renaults there were fitted with improved intercoolers and new pistons and rings. At Watkins Glen, Jabouille then finished fourth to score Renault's first F1 World Championship points. Although in Canada he was only twelfth after rain prevented him setting-up the chassis adequately in qualifying and pick-up problems ruined his chances in the race, reliability was improving. In all the RS01s made 14 starts, and were classified as a finisher five times that season.

Renault Sport still lacked race-wise experience compared to their rivals, most of whom expected to set-up their cars fairly accurately in the factory before revisiting circuits on which they had often raced their F1 cars before. But now the Régie made their serious début in Formula 1 with a proper two-car team for 1979, Rene Arnoux joining the veteran Jabouille who was now by far the world's most experienced turbocharged-engine road racing driver.

Chassis designer Michel Tetu, ex-Ligier, completed a new RS10 ground-effect car in time for the Spanish GP. Both drivers were equipped with RS10 models for Monaco, but Renault changed their system so that while 'RS10' was driven by Arnoux, Jabouille's broadly similar sister car was now 'RS11'. It was slightly lighter with a new front wing and other detail changes. Both cars used twin KKK turbochargers, one per bank instead of replying upon a single large Garrett 'charger feeding both banks. This greatly

improved both throttle response and mid-range punch and at last the Renaults were to prove not only truly competitive, but began to set new standards.

After Monaco there was a month's break before the French GP at Dijon-Prenois. During pre-race testing the Renaults served notice, they were coming on song at last. Last time there in 1977, Andretti's Lotus 78 had taken pole position at 1:12.21; now, two years later, Jabouille took it in 'RS11' at 1:07.19, with Arnoux's new 'RS12' right alongside him to make it a bright-yellow Renault turbo front row. The partisan crowd loved every Gallic moment of it.

In Monaco the new cars' intercoolers had leaked, so at Dijon they were strengthened and team manager Jean Sage and his men merely hoped for a cool race day. They got it, and Jabouille charged round to win handsomely and only Villeneuve's win-or-bust aggression in the Ferrari bundled Arnoux back into third place for a Renault Sports 1-3 finish; their first-ever Formula 1 victory and the first ever for a turbocharged 1.5 litre F1 car – and all on their home soil.

After that terrific performance, the cars were expected to excel on the better suited expanse of Silverstone for the British GP. Jabouille qualified on the front row, but misfortune and mismanagement wrecked his race before a valve spring failed, while Arnoux finished second in 'RS12'. The Renaults were on pole for the next four races in Europe, but fell off the tightrope rather in North America where their only finish was Arnoux's second place at Watkins Glen. In Italy it was an all-Renault front row, which mightily concentrated Ferrari's mind on turbocharger plans for 1980-81 ... But reliability continued to handicap the Régie's team.

A fourth wing car, 'RS14' ran in North America. Water-spray brake cooling was employed at Montreal where the circuit was very hard on brakes and the turbo engine's relative lack of overrun braking accentuated the problem. At Watkins Glen where the weather was cold and wet the Renaults, traditionally light on Michelin's rubber, were unable even to heat the tyres adequately so grip was always lacking.

The French team ended this first-ever successful F1 turbo season with a record of 28 starts in 14 GPs – discounting non-starts due to suspect drive-shaft UJs in Long Beach – and they finished only eight times, the 1-3 result in France backed

25 September, 1983 — European GP, Brands Hatch — Renault's turbo F1 light was fading fast, about to show the way to Ferrari's too, when this shot was taken at Druid's Hairpin, with Eddie Cheever's Renault RE40 '04' on the outside riskily interlocking wheels with Renault Sport's former hard man René Arnoux in his Ferrari 126C3.

by seconds in Britain and the USA, sixth in Austria and one finish each 8-9-10 elsewhere. They did not finish in the Dutch, Italian and Canadian GPs, a fruitless autumn. Reliability was still poor, but it would improve immensely.

In 1980-83 their drivers Jabouille, Arnoux and especially Alain Prost were able to challenge fiercely for the World Championship titles, but without ever winning them, due more to the management and research and development shortcomings inevitable in a huge organization than to serious hardware deficiences. From 1978 to 1983 the French team placed in sequence twelfth, sixth, fourth, third, third and second in the Constructors' Championship, and a fall to fifth in 1984, when they failed to win a single race for the first time was a fall indeed.

Renault Sport had always been forced to fight its war with one arm tied behind its back, for French labour laws and social requirements forced them to observe rigid working hours and tightly control overtime and weekend working. Even with enthusiastic union support, they could never exploit the seven days a week, 24 hours a day commitment of the British teams' people, nor their flexibility and speed of response. The speed at which urgently required modifications can be made can win or lose the next race. Neither did Renault have on hand the myriad small specialist sub-contractors available in the UK, nor on the Emilian plain in Italy.

Nothing is easy in Formula 1, but right from the start it had been harder for the largest manufacturer in the business . . . and Renault's decision to take on the specialists, with a largely untried engine concept, and to pay the price of their pioneering, was a brave one which had changed the face of Grand Prix racing, and would produce the most powerful road racing cars the world has ever seen.

The Ferrari 126C2 Turbos

★ ★ ★

As Renault's turbocharged approach to Formula 1 racing began to pay off in 1979, Ferrari's 312T4 cars secured both World Championship titles – the Drivers' for Jody Scheckter, the Constructors' for Ferrari.

Meanwhile at Maranello, *Ing* Mauro Forghieri's design team began work on a replacement for their excellent 3 litre flat-12 engine series. It was to be a turbocharged 120° V6 – the first forced-induction Ferrari for nearly 30 years. On 9 June 1980, the prototype Ferrari 126C turbo was unveiled at the *Pista di Fiorano*, and the team subsequently blooded the type in competition in 1981.

Ferrari's engine group at Maranello was headed by veteran engineers Franco Rocchi and Walter Salvarani – the gearbox specialist – assisted by Angelino Marchetti, all answerable to chief engineer Forghieri.

Their V6 offered several advantages over alternative V8 and 4-cylinder studies. With each cylinder bank only 'three cylinders long' not only the block but also the crankshaft and camshafts could be shorter and therefore much stiffer. With fewer moving parts than a V8 it offered lower friction loss, while compared to a 4-cylinder it offered greater piston area overall while the reduced surface area of each individual piston minimized thermal problems. The wide 120° vee provided plenty of space between inlet cam covers to accommodate the turbochargers and electronic ignition and fuel injection gear. In addition, the V6's relatively narrow base chamber left plenty of space each side for unobstructed ground-effects under-surface tunnels unlike the old flat-12.

All engine castings were in light alloy and the four valves per cylinder were actuated by twin overhead camshafts per bank, gear-driven from the crankshaft nose. Where the flat 12's bore and stroke dimensions at that time were 80 mm x 49.6 mm, the new V6 had a wider bore and shorter stroke, 81 mm x 48.4 mm, to displace 249.4 cc per cylinder, 1,496.43 cc overall.

To accommodate the boost available from the prototype car's German-made Kühnle, Kopp und Kausch – 'KKK' – exhaust-drive turbochargers, compression ratio was low, at 6.5:1. Ferrari's performance figures on introduction claimed only 540 bhp at 11,000 rpm, compared to the quoted 510 bhp – but probably more – at 12,000 rpm of the contemporary 312T5-tune flat-12. More significantly, at 7,500 rpm the turbocharged 1,500 delivered 100 bhp more than the flat-12 at similar revs.

To provide accurately-metered fuel/air charge throughout the rev and turbo-boost ranges, Ferrari had worked closely with Lucas and Magneti Marelli on their fuel injection and latest 'Digiplex' electronic ignition systems. The KKK turbochargers were preferred for racing, despite long testing of alternative American Garrett turbos and a Swiss-made Brown-Boveri Comprex pressure-wave supercharger. The 126CK V6 KKK version – the Comprex being the 126CX – delivered a claimed 560 bhp at 11,500 rpm into 1981, this figure then rising to 580 bhp at 11,800rpm in 1982, 620 bhp at 11,500 in 1983 and 680 bhp at 11,500 rpm in 1984. It weighed 175 kg (375 lb) – so its 1981 output represented no less than 373.3 bhp per litre or very nearly 1.5 bhp per

Mauro Forghieri's engine group at Maranello tackled 1.5 litre turbocharged Formula 1 with this 120° V6 engine, here displaying the complex exhaust and waste-gate arrangement crammed within its broad vee, and low-level induction system.

lb –and in 1982 tune these levels rose to 386.6 bhp per litre and 1.54 bhp per lb. The flat-12 in its final form had been lighter, only 160 kg (352 lb) – without any turbocharging ancillaries nor having to resist turbo-style internal temperatures and pressures. However, if it delivered as much as 530 bhp, which seems probable, that represents only 176.6 bhp per litre, but 1.5 bhp per lb ...

The new turbo engine developed rapidly, Ferrari evolving a system in which fuel was introduced into the incandescent turbo tract on the over-run to burn and so keep the turbines spun-up and ready to give instant response as the driver re-opened the throttle. With the AGIP fuel company's boffins, an atomized-water injection system was also developed and power went on rising.

During 1981, Ferrari found their feet with the new 126CKs, and from the start of practice at Long Beach it was evident they would be a real threat once sorted-out. But with luck, and Villeneuve's driving, they actually won two GPs, Monaco and Spain. Everyone was impressed with their engine power, few with their notoriously ill-handling and unruly chassis performance.

At this point, in the same way Ferrari had caught up with British state of the art F1 chassis manufacture in 1963 by hiring John Surtees and Michael Parkes, so they did it again by hiring Dr Harvey Postlethwaite ex-March, Hesketh, Wolf

and Fittipaldi, as chassis designer. 'All it needs now,' said their rivals, 'is for Harvey to give them a halfway decent chassis, and we won't see which way they've gone ...' In Constructors' Championship terms, this is what happened in 1982.

With Wolf four years earlier, Harvey Postlethwaite had introduced the folded aluminium-honeycomb sandwich form of F1 chassis construction. The material comprised two thin sheets of aluminium sandwiching foil honeycomb filling, to which the skins were carefully bonded. Harvey's method used honeycomb tub panels folded into two reclining 'U' sections which were then united along a centreline joint to form the finished tub. Now he planned to stiffen these skins with very light, very rigid, moulded carbon-composite bulkheads. Once set up, production of the first 126C2 chassis took about a month. Later, Ferrari could crack-out a new tub in one-and-a-half days.

The tub section was octagonal, like the riveted-sheet 126Cs, but it was lower overall yet with a higher-sided cockpit, the sides merging into an all-enclosed dash panel surround and fore-part which tapered smoothly into an integral foot-box structure in the nose. The bonded tub emerged as a shiny aluminium Ferrari chassis without a rivet line in sight. It was claimed to be 4.8 kg (10.56 lb) lighter than the 126C's.

At the rear the further-developed 126C V6

25 April, 1982 — San Marino GP, Imola — The fateful day on which the Ferrari team ripped itself apart as the chain of events began which led indirectly to Gilles Villeneuve's fatal accident two weeks later in practice at Zolder. Here are Villeneuve who led most of the way and should have won in Ferrari 126C2 '058' (race number 27) and his ambitious team-mate Didier Pironi, 126C2 '056' (race number 28), who nipped by in the closing stages and hung on to what was popularly regarded as a 'stolen' victory . . .

engine was retained as a fully-stressed structural member accepting rear suspension loads. Water radiators and induction-charge intercoolers resided in the rear halves of the sidepods, with shaped underwings moulded into a one-piece undertray beneath replacing the original two-piece design. Hot air exhausting from the various coolers exited through louvred slots cut into the pod sides. The new full-width front wing sat neatly above the nose-cone instead of being split by it as in the 126C.

The 126C2 certainly looked superb, very neat and tidy for a modern Ferrari and beautifully made in every detail. New 'C2s '055' and '056' made their racing début in South Africa. One major early problem was sheer tyre consumption. After four seasons with Michelin, Ferrari had returned to Goodyear. Initially the contemporary American-made tyres and the Italian chassis seemed ill-matched, but as test miles accumulated, the problems were rapidly resolved.

The new cars, driven by Gilles Villeneuve and Didier Pironi excelled at Imola, against meagre opposition – for the San Marino GP was boycotted by ten FOCA teams in dispute with the FISA governing body. Pironi won, but Villeneuve had been leading before Pironi disregarded team convention and pit signals, rushed into the lead and denied Villeneuve what the French-Canadian regarded as his rightful victory. This created a foul atmosphere within the team and 13 days later, during practice for the Belgian GP at Zolder, a tragic outcome. Villeneuve was desperately trying to better Pironi's time on his final qualifying run when he collided with a slow-moving March.

His Ferrari 'C2, chassis '058', planed off the March's right-rear wheel and cartwheeled at high speed, landing nose down in yielding sand which instantly trapped the front of the car, and snapped it in two. The seatback bulkhead ripped out, along with the unfortunate Villeneuve's seat-belt mounts, and he was thrown out with fatal results. What had happened was one of those freak accidents which happen perhaps once in 10 years. It seemed unlikely to recur . . .

After Villeneuve's death, Ferrari did not start in the Belgian race, but reappeared at Monaco with a one-car entry for Pironi who raced '059' and almost scored a fortunate win.

For Detroit, Postlethwaite adopted pull-rod front suspension which provided a massive increase in front-end rigidity and transformed the cars' feel. If Pironi had not stalled and become involved in a massive startline accident at Montreal he would have 'walked the race, no problem'. Thereafter the cars were redesigned around the new suspension.

Patrick Tambay joined fellow-Frenchman Pironi from the Dutch GP at Zandvoort where Didier won handsomely in '060's race début. The cars were consistently competitive now, finishing 2-3 in Britain and 3-4 in France and Pironi looked to have the Drivers' Championship at his mercy, only to sustain ghastly leg injuries in wet practice at Hockenheim, in a near carbon-copy of Villeneuve's accident. His 'C2 '061' was demolished.

Tambay and the team responded brilliantly by winning the race next day, using '060'. He was then fourth in Austria, but at Dijon F1 G-forces pinched a nerve in his neck and he was unable to start the Swiss GP, which ran without Ferrari in consequence. His car there was chassis '062', the first 126C2B to be built pull-rod from the ground up. Pull-rod chassis '063' and '064' followed by year's end.

Mr Ferrari invited Mario Andretti to rejoin his team for the Italian GP at Monza and the former World Champion responded brilliantly by setting '061' on pole and finishing third behind Tambay's second-placed '062'. Tambay was then again unable to start the final race of the season at Las Vegas, where Andretti suffered one of the 'C2's too-prevalent suspension failures and retired '061'.

All development work had been set back by Pironi's Hockenheim accident. Ferrari set about salvaging what they could, and edged their fifth Constructors' Championship title in eight seasons, and the first ever with a turbocharged engine – modest consolation after such bitter adversity.

Overall they had made only 22 starts in the season's 16 GPs, running only a single car in the Monaco, Detroit, Canadian, German, Austrian and Las Vegas GPs and failing to compete at all in the Belgian and 'Swiss' events. Even so, they won three of the 14 GPs which they did start, and added four second places, five thirds, two fourths, three eighths, and one ninth-place finish. The team's four retirements involved three accidents and Andretti's rear suspension failure at Las Vegas, but not one engine failure.

18 July, 1982 — British GP, Brands Hatch — Gentleman driver Patrick Tambay took over Villeneuve's number 27 Ferrari C2s for the completion of the 1982 season — here he is on his way to third place behind Drivers' Championship leader Pironi in 126C2 '061', but he will win the German GP at Hockenheim after his fellow Frenchman's career has been ended by yet another fearful practice accident. Lightning can strike twice ...

Into 1983, at very short notice, the FISA governing body applied new 'flat-bottom' rules to Formula 1. Ground-effects tunnel sections within the wheelbase were out. Ferrari began to rethink their projected moulded carbon-composite 'C3 design for the new year, and in the interim modified existing 'C2B chassis '063' and '064' to flat-bottom spec, alongside new 'C2B/83s '065' and '066' which were built flat-bottomed from new.

Patrick Tambay had been joined in the team by former Renault driver Rene Arnoux. In most early season races Arnoux drive '064', Tambay '065'. They lacked rear-end adhesion and traction at Rio, and seemed too heavy and slow in Brazil. For Long Beach, Ferrari found adhesion by harnessing the download of enormous new rear wings with extra winglets projecting forward on both sides, supported by the full-width main 'foils' end-plates. They had the power to haul these high-drag/high-lift devices very competitively round the street circuit – Tambay qualified on pole and led easily until he was rammed by Rosberg's Williams at a hairpin. Arnoux finished third despite two stops to change tyres. At Brands Hatch's Race of Champions, he led before burning out three sets of tyres and being forced to retire as no more were available.

Pull-rod rear suspension was fitted in time for Imola to '062', '064' and '065'. Arnoux promptly qualified on pole but Tambay won with his teammate third. At Spa, Tambay both qualified and finished second behind Prost's Renault. At Detroit, Arnoux felt at home and qualified '064' on pole, with Tambay third fastest. Things went very wrong in the race, neither 'C2B finishing. In Canada, however, Arnoux was supreme, starting from pole again in his faithful '064' and leading all but four laps around his scheduled refuelling stop. Tambay was third after having to nurse an overheated rear tyre in the closing stages.

I discussed the season with *Ing* Postlethwaite the following week: 'The problem now,' he observed, 'is convincing ourselves that the 'C3 is adequately better than the 'C2. After Canada, to be adequately better it'll have to win by a clear lap ...'

Unusually, there was then a five-week break in the calendar before the British GP at Silverstone in July. The new carbon-composite 126C3s had convinced their creators, and so the Ferrari 126C2s, the first turbocharged cars to win the Formula 1 Constructor's Championship, had run their last race.

The McLaren-TAG Turbo MP4/2s

★ ★ ★ ★ ★

McLaren International – formed in September 1980 – began as a partnership between former Team McLaren directors Teddy Mayer and Tyler Alexander, and the ambitious, less experienced but highly talented former Project 4 team trio of Ron Dennis, Creighton Brown and engineer John Barnard.

He was an ex-Lola and McLaren design engineer who had made his name in the big-time with Vel's Parnelli and Chaparral Indy cars. He had developed a concept for an ultra-rigid but lightweight Formula 1 chassis moulded in aerospace-style carbon-composite, instead of being fabricated as conventional at that time from the usual aluminium honeycomb sheet materials.

One of the great problems facing ground-effects car designers around 1979-1980 was the necessity to enlarge their sidepod underwing surfaces as much as possible, which led them to produce ever-narrower central monocoque chassis. As the chassis structure lost cross-sectional area, so it was in danger of losing torsional rigidity, and without such rigidity along its central spine a ground-effects F1 car could not make proper use of whatever download its underwings might generate.

Carbon-composite materials were extremely rigid for their weight. With skill and care they could be moulded into almost any shape one might require, without that inherent rigidity being compromised. Since the individual carbon fibres – little thicker than a human hair – were arranged in ribbons, then woven as cloth and saturated with resin which was then set and cured

into a solid matrix, the new material did not noticeably fatigue. If properly designed and cured, the kind of cracking found in work-worn aluminium honeycomb chassis would be entirely prevented. Where in aluminium panels a square hole would be asking for serious stress cracks to propagate from the hole's sharp corners, in an adequate carbon-composite structure one could cut holes of any convenient shape – stars if you wanted – and quite confidently expect no trouble.

The only perceived problem with these new materials was that while being exceptionally rigid in torsion, and good in tension, they were suspect in compression, and aluminium honeycomb certainly performed far better in impact absorption, unless a composite structure liable to be impacted was very carefully designed indeed.

With assistance from Arthur Webb, a British Aerospace composites engineer, John Barnard narowly won the race to produce the first carbon-composite moulded F1 monocoque car, in his 1981 McLaren-Cosworth MP4/1. This new model narrowly beat release of the Colin Chapman/Peter Wright created composite Lotus 88, and when driven for the MI team by John Watson it scored an exciting and very emotional maiden victory in that season's British GP. During 1982 the popular 'Wattie' and Niki Lauda – in his come-back season after a two-year retirement – then won four more Championship GPs in MP4/1B cars, updated but still Cosworth-powered.

Early in 1983, the still basically 1980-designed MP4/1Cs with their Cosworth engines carried

Watson to victory at Long Beach, before the turbocharged engines finally stormed the last redoubts of 3 litre naturally-aspirated engine opposition. Through that late summer, in their last four Cosworth-powered races, the McLarens proved themselves the best of the non-turbo rest.

On 28 August 1983, a new Porsche-built TAG Turbo V6 engine was then introduced in an interim MP4/1E chassis at the Dutch GP. It was driven by Niki Lauda, while Watson drove a '1C as if inspired to finish a fine third overall . . . marking the end of a McLaren-Cosworth partnership which had survived nearly 16 years.

Next time out, at Monza, both McLarens were '1Es using the new TAG-Turbo V6 engines, and they completed the season, showing real form in South Africa where Lauda ran second and looked set to challenge Patrese's leading Brabham-BMW only to suffer an electrical failure near the finish.

There followed a winter's development of all-new McLaren MP4/2 cars tailored to their Porsche custom-made turbocharged engine, and this completed the prelude to what would prove to be an historic Formula 1 season.

The TAG Turbo by Porsche programme had been born soon after McLaren International's foundation in 1980-81, when the new board began to discuss possible replacements for the ageing and increasingly outclassed Cosworth V8. John Barnard had a vision of being able to dictate a properly integrated design including both engine and chassis, instead of just buying someone else's engine off the shelf, then cobbling together an afterthought chassis 'which would fit'. He wanted to be a Ferrari – or Mercedes-Benz – not merely what Mr Ferrari himself has so often disparaged as a mere *Assemblatore* or *Garagista* . . .

Teddy Mayer of the McLaren old guard was alarmed by the potential costs of turbocharged Formula 1, but he and his long-time associate Tyler Alexander pressed for a decision on choosing available BMW or Renault turbo engines. Barnard vetoed such haste. He and Dennis asked, 'Who can build us a turbocharged engine?' and at that stage Porsche was suggested. If Ron could raise the money to commission such an engine as a paying customer, Porsche was happy to help. Dennis told them to go ahead to plan an engine around John's detailed requirements, and he then

set about finding the money to pay for it. He found a backer in Williams sponsor Mansour Ojjeh's *Techniques d'Avant Garde* (TAG) concern. TAG Turbo Engines was formed, the production contract was signed with Porsche in December 1982, and by that time the prototype TTE-PO1 V6 unit was already running on the Weissach dynos.

The prototype V6 was displayed at the Geneva Salon in April 1983, a tiny 80° four-cam V6 with twin turbochargers, one on each 3-cylinder exhaust bunch. Its block was cast in crisp aluminium alloy as were the heads, while the

---

McLaren driver Alain Prost and his German engineers responsible for the Porsche-designed TAG V6 engine at the German Grand Prix of 1987, hoping to end Honda's GP domination at that time.

ribbed block itself, using Nikasil liners was as neat and pretty as it was functional, a work of art. Each head, no wider than the average man's hand–span, had two gear-driven camshafts actuating four valves per cylinder disposed at a narrow included angle. It weighed about 330 lb (150 kg). Designer Hans Mezger's preferred bore and stroke dimensions were published as 82 mm x 47.3 mm, displacing 1,499 cc, and Porsche claimed an initial 600 bhp, an immediate 75 bhp gain for McLaren compared to its Cosworth DFY V8s. Output per litre was around 400 bhp, or 1.81 bhp per lb. With development, even though the TAG Turbo would never accept ultra-high boost effectively, this little engine came to develop some 980 bhp – a little matter of 653 bhp per litre, or practically 3 bhp per lb weight. Peak power was produced between 10,000 and 11,500 rpm, though the power band was claimed to be useable from as low as 8,500 rpm.

For 1984, a new regulation ban on mid-race refuelling was accompanied by a car tankage reduction from 250 litres (55 gal) to only 220 (48.4 gal). Consequently fuel economy matched to sheer power became crucial, and the new engines' Bosch management system had to balance performance against economy in the most competitive and efficient ratio. With MI paying, Bosch developed a 100 per cent electronic 'Motronic MS3' engine management system exclusively for TAG Turbo Engines, via Porsche R&D. It had many early problems, but became the class of the field in 1984. It employed sensors and a processing unit to control solenoids which adjusted the fuel metering jets to govern fuel quantity and to time its delivery to each cylinder precisely in line with demand from moment to moment.

The new MP4/2 tailor-made turbocharged cars were built only at the last minute before the first race at Rio de Janeiro opening that season. Barnard's thoughtful approach to design before first cutting metal, or rather carbon cloth, had given remarkable stability to his creations. The original MP4/1 tub made by the Hercules Corporation in Salt Lake City, Utah, USA in 1981 had been so successful only minor modifications were made for the second and subsequent units. The large plan-area ground-effect '4/1s which raced through 1981-82 were hard to tell apart exter-nally, and then the flat-bottom MP4/1C which replaced them with Cosworth power for 1983

retained that unmistakable family likeness.

Barnard's MP4/2 tub redesign was governed by the TAG Turbo V6 being shorter than a Cosworth V8, and by the 220 litre (48.4 gal) fuel limit/refuelling ban preventing use of an undersized tank such as Brabham had used in 1983. The complex tub tooling was retrieved from Hercules and modified, and new small-tank tubs were moulded in Utah, then shipped to MI's spotless Woking workshops for completion as the new MP4/2-series cars. Barnard added a new rear sus-pension and took some of the interim car com-promises out of the chassis, and put them instead into the engine.

As the first new cars were being completed, just in time for the start of the season, so a production engine specification was frozen for the TAG Turbo V6. To save weight over 10 or so develop-ment prototypes used in 1983, it demanded titanium main crankcase studs and a lightweight cast magnesium inlet manifold which replaced the hefty original bolt-together machined-section type used for shape experimentation.

MI's requirement was for a float of some 15-20 complete race engines with some five-ten extra sets of parts available at any time. By June 1984 they would have complete engines Nos 21-35 in use.

MI built only four MP4/2 chassis for 1984, as follows:

Chassis 'MP4/2-1' – New for Niki Lauda, Rio, uni-quely in World Championship history driven by him in every GP that season, *1st* in South African, French, British, Austrian and Italian GPs, 2nd in Canadian, German, Dutch and Portuguese GPs, 4th European GP (at the *ersatz* Nürburgring), Rtd Brazilian, Belgian, San Marino, Monaco, Detroit and Dallas GPs – World Champion 1984.

Chassis 'MP4/2-2' – New for Alain Prost, Rio, *1st* there in Brazilian GP, also thereafter in Monaco, Dutch, European and Portuguese GPs, 3rd Cana-dian GP, 4th Detroit GP, 7th French GP, Rtd Belgian, Dallas, British and Austrian GPs.

Chassis 'MP4/2-3' – Present incomplete at Rio, spare car raced by Prost to *1st* San Marino and German GPs, 2nd South African GP, Rtd Italian GP – also used by team as test chassis until com-pletion of chassis '4.

Chassis 'MP4/2-4' – Completed just too late for mid-season North American races, drafted into

Niki Lauda, World Champion 1984, in the European GP, the race in which he very nearly lost his title chances, at *Ersatz* Nürburgring. The McLaren-TAG Turbo MP4/2 was simply outstanding that year.

test team to replace chassis '3 and logistical timings thereafter prevented it ever joining the race team.

Thus the McLaren MP4/2s actually won 12 of that season's 16 Championship-qualifying GPs (including the rain-shortened half-points Monaco GP). Prost equalled the existing record of seven GP victories in one season but still failed – by just half a point – to prevent his team-mate Lauda winning his third Drivers' Championship title. In fact the McLarens between them led 51.25 per cent of that season's total GP laps. Lauda averaged no fewer than 4.5 Championship points per race, Prost 4.469. The cars won the last seven consecutive GPs.

Prost led over 35 per cent of 1984's GP laps, and Lauda over 16 per cent. It was a remarkable *tour de force* highly reminiscent of the best that Daimler-Benz could ever achieve in their GP seasons. The fact that MI achieved so much with only three race cars and that Lauda should win the Championship using the same car all season was in modern terms quite extraordinary.

But it is worth considering the context in which these remarkable McLaren-TAG Turbo cars shone so brightly. Were they making the best of 'a bad season' which simultaneously afflicted Brabham, Ferrari, Renault and the rest? Was it really the poor performance of others which had made the McLarens look so good? Or was it the clear superiority of the Porsche-produced engine which would have achieved the same success in any other front-line chassis?

While so many rival teams did indeed have an unreliable year I suspect that – apart from Ferrari which suffered other problems – they really had to run so hard just to keep McLaren in sight that they simply came apart at the seams . . .

In qualifying, and occasionally in the race, Brabham-BMW had an obvious performance edge, Nelson Piquet regularly out-qualifying the McLarens and leading races before retiring. Some other cars arguably outhandled the McLarens, notably the Lotus-Renaults, but on the day only Brabham-BMW posed a consistent and serious threat.

On the early occasions when McLaren did not win from strength, they could always win on reliability, fuel efficiency and driver wit, and in the services of Prost and Lauda they had two of the top four drivers of their era . . .

What wins races is possession of the best combination on race day. If any vital ingredient is mis-

Alain Prost in the 1984 European GP at *Ersatz* Nürburgring in his McLaren MP4/2, showing off its neat form, far-forward driving position and complex multi-foil rear wing. The 'vents' along the side are merely black livery marks, substituting for the team's normal cigarette sponsor logo in a nation where such advertising is rightly banned.

sing, the chance is lost. In 1984, MI's superbly-integrated McLaren MP4/2 chassis/engine package proved good enough for its drivers to extract virtually everything their TAG Turbo engines had to offer, and that was plenty – lots not only of competitive horsepower, but also of usable mid-range torque. Bosch's super-expensive tailor-made management system made it the most fuel efficient F1 engine around, and the cars almost always finished with fuel to spare. They ran Michelin tyres at a time when they were the class of the field. At most circuits on raceday this combination proved simply too hot for the opposition to handle.

Some observers, notably in the European press, doubted McLaren's contribution to the equation and put it all down to Porsche know-how. They were deluding themselves. Porsche did a superb job on TAG Turbo's behalf, no question, but McLaren had won the 'Cosworth class' in their last four outings with the DFV/DFY engines through 1983, and now they had simply continued that dominance at a higher level after receiving their turbocharged engines. And they were *their* engines, for MI had commissioned the design in broad detail and uncompromisingly policed the project while Porsche designed and manufactured the power units so brilliantly.

At the end of 1984, the glory of McLaren-TAG Turbo and Porsche was truly indivisible ... and right through to the end of 1987 there was so much more to come.

Into 1985 the MP4/2s' successors, the modified MP4/2Bs, continued the run and Prost became Champion while McLaren International made it two Constructors' Cup titles in succession. With the MP4/2C cars in 1986, Prost again narrowly edged the Drivers' title, to become the first driver since Jack Brabham in 1959-60 to win back-to-back Drivers' Championships and in 1987 Alain broke Jackie Stewart's long-standing career record of 27 GP wins, in the McLaren-TAG Turbo's swansong. For 1988, McLaren adopted Honda power, and progressed from strength to utter domination ...

1986-87
The Williams-Honda FW11s

★ ★ ★ ★

When the Williams Grand Prix Engineering team changed from the naturally-aspirated 3 litre Cosworth V8-series engines to a turbocharged alternative late in 1983, Frank Williams forged a relationship with Honda R&D in Japan.

For much of the 1984 season which followed, Honda were feeling their way into manufacturing a 'driver-friendly' F1 turbo engine combining a decently–restrained torque curve with adequate reliability. Still Williams team leader Keke Rosberg contrived to win the Dallas GP in what had become the notoriously difficult Williams-Honda FW09 car, and then for 1985 Patrick Head, Frank Dernie and their engineering team at Didcot began work on an improved carbon-composite chassised FW10 design which with Honda coming up to scratch eventually enabled drivers Nigel Mansell and Keke Rosberg to win the last three races of the 1985 World Championship series.

Then for 1986 the FISA governing body reduced F1 cars' maximum fuel capacity from 220 litres (48.4 gal) to just 195 (42.9 gal), placing even heavier emphasis upon performance with fuel economy. This element in the regulations made modern turbocharged Formula 1 hugely attractive to such major research-orientated manufacturers as Honda; and installed in the new '195 litre regulation' Williams FW11 chassis, Honda's 1986 F–Type V6 engine consistently demonstrated the best power-cum-fuel economy-cum-reliability factor in World Championship racing.

Patrick Head's FW11 design was very much a state of the art, high-tech car, carrying Honda's twin-turbocharged four-cam 80° V6 engine plus a mass of electronic microprocessing equipment to handle its boost, ignition and injection requirements, plus driver-to-pit radio communications and car-to-pit in-race telemetry, enabling the pit crew to watch the gauges while also monitoring their driver's reaction (or obedience) to radioed instructions and advice. 'The driver . . .', said Patrick, with just a trace of understandable but mischievous relish, 'can no longer tell us lies . . .'

The FW11 was based upon a moulded carbon/Kevlar/aluminium composite chassis, being exquisitely crafted, beautifully made in all respects. Merely the fit between engine cover and mechanicals beneath had to be seen to be believed, clearance being barely measurable in millimetres in some crucial areas. This was evidence of Williams' investment in advanced computer-aided design/computer-aided manufacture (CAD/CAM) technique, an expensive General Electric CALMA system.

The FW11 design itself was very much an evolutionary development of 1985's sometimes troubled, subsequently dominant, FW10-series, which was itself Patrick Head's first attempt at moulded carbon-composite chassis construction. He and WGPE composites specialist Brian O'Rourke worked out the design and methodology between them in the winter of 1984-85, when Patrick had decided he needed a chassis of the greatest possible cross-section. Logically therefore, it should form the outer periphery of the body, and that dictated moulding it in composite.

14 October, 1983 — Practice for the South African GP, Kyalami — Keke Rosberg in the prototype Williams-Honda FW09 preparing for the Anglo-Japanese alliance's maiden race. The 80° V6 twin-turbo engine was an untidy and rather makeshift-looking affair as is obvious here, but it certainly delivered some horsepower — albeit in a rather crudely unrefined manner. The induction path from turbocharger into sidepod-mounted intercooler then up the front of the engine into the 'log' on top may be clearly followed.

The initial FW10 was successful, especially in its 1985 late-season 'FW10B' form, and the 1986 replacement FW11 was superficially very similar, and good enough when driven by Nigel Mansell and new team driver Nelson Piquet to wrest the Formula 1 Constructors' Championship away from McLaren-TAG Turbo . . .

Both FW10 and FW11-series tubs used laminated carbon double-skins sandwiching Kevlar – which is like a stiff brown paper – honeycomb in their upper sections while the lower, less curvaceous cockpit sides were reinforced internally with aluminium honeycomb foil. Where in FW10 two small front suspension bulkheads were machined from aluminium, the FW11 tubs used no aluminium bulkheads at all; everything was carbon-composite.

The '11s were also lower than the '10s, and a little longer, and whereas the '10's roll-over bar was a bolt-on-tubular affair, '11s used a composite base pyramid moulded into the chassis with a steel hoop on top matching each respective driver's height.

The smaller 195 litre 1986 fuel cell enabled Williams, like others, to lay their drivers back into a less-forward driving position, lowering his head fully 4 in (10 cm) and permitting an even lower bodyline. The toluene-based 'funny fuel' which Honda's V6s burned was also accommodated lower. The 1986 tub emerged some 1.5 in (3.8 cm) longer than an FW10's while the new F-spec – 'F for Frugal' – Honda engine was also slightly longer than its E-Type predecessor, so FW11's wheelbase was 112 ins (2.84 m) against FW10's 109.5 in (2.78 m). Suspension was FW10B, but for a 2 in (5 cm) wider rear track and a better-integrated six-speed gearbox casing to support it all.

The cars built and their successes were as follows:

1986 FW11 series:

Chassis 'FW11/1' – Race début 23-3-86 – Piquet *1st* '86 Brazilian GP, Piquet Spanish GP. Spare for Mansell at Monaco. Withdrawn from race team service.

Chassis 'FW11/2' – Race début 23-3-86 – Mansell '86 Brazilian GP, Mansell Spanish, San Marino and Monaco GPs, *1st* Belgian GP, *1st* Canadian GP, Detroit GP, *1st* French GP, British (not raced) and German GPs, Mansell's spare car for Portuguese, Mexican and Australian GPs.

Chassis 'FW11/3' – Début 23-3-86 – New at Rio as regular spare car, raced by Mansell *1st* British GP.

Chassis 'FW11/4' – Race début 27-4-86 – Piquet '86 San Marino, Monaco, Belgian, Canadian and Detroit (crashed) GPs.

Chassis 'FW11/5' – Race début 6-7-86 – Piquet '86 French and British GPs, *1st* German GP, *1st* Hungarian GP, Austrian GP, *1st* Italian GP, Portuguese, Mexican and Australian GPs.

Chassis 'FW11/6' – Race début 10-8-86 – Mansell '86 Hungarian, Austrian and Italian GPs, *1st* Portuguese GP, Mansell Mexican and Australian GPs.

FW11s – all using F-Type engines from the start – were ready in time for the '86 Championship curtain-raiser in Brazil, where Nelson Piquet won for the team after Mansell suffered a first-lap collision.

1986 was very much WGPE's season, with Mansell versus Piquet for the Drivers' title and the Constructors' Championship sewn-up in Italy, well before season's end. Their cars had made a total 32 starts, had retired eight times but from their 24 finishes had finished 21 times in the top three places, scoring no fewer than nine victories, and adding seven second places and five thirds. What's more their cars led all but one of the series' GPs at some stage, and overall led a dominant 53.07 per cent of the total race laps comprising that 16-race season.

Pondering the programme that August, Patrick Head told me that the team's 1-2 domination of the European GP at Brands Hatch had been '... probably our best race, our only 1-2 so far, and a race run at enormous pace, continually setting new lap records and with both cars handling pretty well and neither driver complaining of anything; both in good nick after the finish. We controlled the turbo boost they could run, using the radio from the pits. We instructed them to use the lower race-boost setting and the data we received in the pits told us that they *were* using it ...'

The drivers had a four-position boost selector; position '1' being a fuel conservation mode, '2' and '3' race boosts on higher or lower levels, and '4' providing an extra 50-60 bhp 'banzai' boost *for very limited use only!* It was not available to the drivers at every race ... Of the two alternative race boost positions, '2' burned slightly too little fuel, hence less than optimum power over race distance; '3' slightly too much, so the drivers normally juggled between these two.

The actual telemetry processing and transmitting box on the car, which dumped information into the pits receivers once a lap, was smaller than a cigarette packet and weighed mere grams, far belying its usefulness when combined with the two-way radio link in race strategy. By 1986 For-

By 1986-7, the Williams-Honda engine installation in their FW11 cars was a good deal more tidy.

mula 1 again embodied genuine team effort. The driver was no longer on his own once the start light flashed to green ...

Changes to the FW11s were mostly detail only, mainly to the water and turbocharge cooling systems. Preventative reinforcement was necessary in certain areas, as in UJ design after Mansell suffered failures in the first-start of the British GP – fortunately for him the race was stopped and restarted, enabling him to win in the spare car – and in Austria, probably costing him the World title. Also in Austria, Piquet's air inlet temperature control failed, allowing the induction log temperatures to soar, causing pre-ignition which destroyed a piston. That was the first time in *fourteen* races that Williams-Honda had failed to score points. Eat your heart out Daimler-Benz...!

Mansell still stood a fine chance of the Championship into the final round at Adelaide, only for a spectacular Goodyear tyre failure to dash his hopes.

WGPE then embarked upon what turned out to be the successful defence of their 1986 Constructors' Championship through 1987. Their new FW11B cars were improved in a multitude of fine details. While the outer shell of the monocoque chassis moulding remained much the same shape, both its internal bulkheads and its carbon-composite moulding lay-up had been altered. Major bulkhead redesign had involved the seat back which was raked more steeply to recline the driver and so lower his head – lower head, lower roll-over bar, improved airflow clearance on to the rear wing. In the FW11s Nelson Piquet had already been seated as low as he could go while remaining capable of seeing out, but Nigel Mansell could lie lower. Now he did.

Another major redesign provided the FW11Bs with improved cooling systems using different water radiators, though still side-ducted as before.

Honda R&D's engine development had of course gone roaring ahead through the winter of 1986/87, as always in pursuit of greater power and fuel efficiency, but this time with the added factor of making the most of FISA's new pop-off valves which were applied to restrict boost pressure through both qualifying and the races themselves to no more than 4-bar.

Honda's 1987 V6 emerged as the 'G-type' featuring externally a revised turbocharger installation and revving to a stunning 13,000 rpm. Both Williams and new Honda user Lotus received these G-Type engines, but the FW11Bs' turbochargers were initially angled more outwards than Lotus's, the Ketteringham team subsequently matching Williams practice.

As the season progressed an improved 'GE'-spec Honda engine emerged, back to the 1986 12,000 rpm rev limit 'E' for further-enhanced fuel efficiency, and that was followed by the 'GE2' – 'GE Phase 2' – and then a bewildering series involving type-serials like 'GE2-1' or 'GE2-5'. Late in the season one engine spec seems to have become settled, 'GE2-1'.

Eight FW11B-series chassis were built, each moulded new – none based on the obsolescent FW11 tubs, but only five of them were 'standard' FW11Bs. Frank Dernie directed development of a computer-controlled 'active-ride' suspension system intended to limit pitch-change within the cars by use of microprocessor-controlled hydraulic jacks on each suspension corner in place of conventional dampers. Two late-season active-ride cars were built, using special tubs with the system's hydraulic pipework moulded integrally into them, and there was also a one-off 'FW11C' – chassis '7 – built specifically for a promised Honda V10 3.5 litre naturally-aspirated engine, which went eventually to McLaren for 1989.

The cars built and their records were as follows:

1987 FW11B/C series:

Chassis 'FW11B/1' – Début 10-4-87 (Rio as spare) –Regular spare car, eventually to Mexico City in bare chassis form but built up hastily for Mansell *1st* '87 Mexican GP, the car he crashed during Japanese GP practice at Suzuka. Only mild damage, repaired for race day – which cannot be said of driver.

Chassis 'FW11B/2' – Race début 12-4-87 – Piquet '87 Brazilian GP, crashed by him in practice for the San Marino GP at Imola and written-off.

Chassis 'FW11B/3' – Race début 12-4-87 – Mansell '87 Brazilian GP, *1st* San Marino GP, Mansell Belgian, Monaco and Detroit GPs, *1st* French GP, *1st* British GP, Mansell German and Hungarian GPs, *1st* Austrian GP, Mansell Italian GP, spare at Estoril and Jerez, intended race car crashed by Mansell during Mexican GP practice.

Chassis 'FW11B/4' – Début 10-4-87 (at Rio as bare chassis) – completed at Imola, Piquet '87 Belgian, Monaco, Detroit, French and British GPs, *1st* German, *1st* Hungarian GPs, Piquet Austrian GP, team spare thereafter.

Chassis 'FW11B/5' – Début 29-5-87 – New at Monaco as spare for Mansell, spare at Detroit, as active suspension car for Piquet *1st* '87 Italian, Portuguese and Spanish GPs.

Chassis 'FW11B/6' – Début 3-7-87 – New chassis present as back-up at Ricard, Hungaroring and Österreichring, Piquet '87 Mexican and Japanese GPs, in chassis form at Adelaide.

Chassis 'FW11C/7' – Unraced chassis tailored to never-delivered 3.5 litre Honda V10 cylinder engine. Converted to accept 3.5 litre Judd V8 as 1987-88 development hack.

Chassis 'FW11B/8' – Race début 21-9-87 – New active suspension car, Mansell '87 Portuguese

13 July, 1986 — British GP, Brands Hatch — Nigel Mansell led a memorable Williams-Honda 1-2 victory in this event, driving FW11/2 seen here. He set fastest race lap from his team-mate Nelson Piquet, the Honda-engined pair being alone in breaking the 1 min 10 sec barrier during their race-long duel.

GP. *1st* Spanish GP, in chassis form at Suzuka, for Piquet Australian GP.

Nigel Mansell fought a season-long duel with his team-mate (and formally team-leader) Piquet and staged a late charge for the Drivers' Championship –after WGPE had again cornered the Constructors' Cup - only to crash during practice for the Japanese GP and miss the last two races. Piquet became World Champion by default.

WGPE's cars had made only 29 starts in the 16 races, Piquet missing the San Marino GP at Imola after surviving an awful-looking high speed crash in practice, and Mansell suffering his end-season problem. Again, eight of those starts ended in retirement, but yet again Williams-Honda won in nine of their 21 finishes, and added seven second places and two thirds – thus finishing in the top three in no less than 18 of their 21 finishes. Oh yes, and they led an increased proportion, 56.49 per cent, of the Championship's total race laps.

Once again, for Head, the highlight of the season was a British race, in this case the British GP at Silverstone in which Piquet looked to have the race sewn-up but was reeled-in and beaten into second place by his delayed and therefore infuriated English team-mate. 'As a car manufacturer,' said Head, 'it's always pleasing to see any race won by a car which has been driven *absolutely* flat-out for the entire duration without anything going wrong . . .'

Around August, however, WGPE had suddenly became inconvenient to Honda, and the Japanese walked away from the final year of their existing contract, intending to supply their 1988 engines instead to McLaren and Lotus.

So the Williams-Honda marriage which had lasted over four seasons ended in divorce, but during their Constructors' Championship years of 1986-87, Didcot and Wako, Japan, could reflect upon a joint 61 World Championship F1 race starts, which yielded 45 finishes – 39 of them in the top three places, including 18 victories, 14 second places and seven thirds, no mean achievement by any standards, and one of which the manufacturers of any of our 50 famous racing cars would surely have been immensely proud.

I'm sure Emile Levassor himself would have approved. . .

Index of Personalities